D1101243

State Parties and National Politics

State Parties and National Politics:
North Carolina, 1815–1861

♦

Thomas E. Jeffrey

The University of Georgia Press ♦ *Athens and London*

© 1989 by the University of Georgia Press
Athens, Georgia 30602
All rights reserved
Designed by Mary Mendell   Set in Trump Mediaeval
The paper in this book meets the guidelines for permanence
and durability of the Committee on Production Guidelines for
Book Longevity of the Council on Library Resources.
Printed in the United States of America
93 92 91 90 89   5 4 3 2 1
Library of Congress Cataloging in Publication Data

Jeffrey, Thomas E., date.
State parties and national politics : North Carolina, 1815–1861 /
Thomas E. Jeffrey.
p.   cm.
Bibliography: p.
Includes index.
ISBN 0-8203-1090-5 (alk. paper)
1. North Carolina—Politics and government—1775–1865.
2. Political culture—North Carolina—History—19th century.
3. Political parties—North Carolina—History—19th century.
4. United States—Politics and government—1815–1861.   I. Title.
F258.J44 1989
320.9756—DC19
88-25998   CIP

British Library Cataloging in Publication Data available

To Pamela, for making it all worthwhile

Contents

Tables

Maps and Figures

Acknowledgments

My research into the politics of antebellum North Carolina began more than a decade ago, when I was a graduate student at the Catholic University of America. Over the years I have benefited immensely from the support and encouragement of numerous individuals and institutions. I owe a large debt of gratitude to Jon L. Wakelyn, who guided my work through its earliest stages as a doctoral dissertation, and to Whitman H. Ridgway and Maxwell H. Bloomfield, who served as readers for the dissertation. Through their trenchant criticism and helpful suggestions, I first became aware of the complexities of antebellum party politics. More recently, I have derived great benefit from the stimulating criticism of Jeffrey J. Crow, Michael F. Holt, Richard P. McCormick, and Joel H. Silbey, who were kind enough to take time out from their own work to read an earlier version of this manuscript. I am especially grateful to Professor Silbey, who also read several chapters of the revised manuscript. To James H. Broussard I express my thanks for reading drafts of the first chapter and the appendix and for reacting so graciously to my criticism of his own important work on early southern politics. I have also benefited from several stimulating conversations with Daniel W. Crofts and from his careful reading of my chapter on slavery and secession. I am doubly thankful to Professor Crofts for allowing me to read his unpublished quantitative study of southern unionism and for giving me permission to cite his paper in my book.

Harry L. Watson and Marc W. Kruman have both published important monographs on antebellum North Carolina parties. Professor Watson has always been a friendly critic of my work and, on more than one occasion, has gently prodded me to rethink my conceptions (and misconceptions) about antebellum North Carolina parties. Professor Kruman's interpretation of party politics in the Old North State is in many respects sharply different from my own. Nonetheless, his work has forced me to evaluate my own arguments more carefully and to assess my evidence more critically.

Over the years I have made many research trips to North Carolina and have made extensive use of the collections at the North Carolina Division of Archives and History in Raleigh, the Southern Historical Collection and the North Carolina Collection of the University of North Carolina Library at Chapel Hill, and the manuscript and rare book collections of the Perkins Library at Duke University in Durham. The archivists and librarians at these institutions have been uniformly courteous and helpful.

I owe a special debt to Reese V. Jenkins, director and editor of the Thomas A. Edison Papers, who generously allowed me to take time out from my responsibilities as associate director to complete the research and writing of this book, and who has consistently encouraged me to pursue my interest in antebellum political history. I am also grateful to my other colleagues at the Edison Papers, particularly Robert Rosenberg, who prepared the final versions of the graphs and provided me with valuable technical assistance in preparing the "electronic manuscript" that was sent to the University of Georgia Press. I am indebted also to Malcolm L. Call, Madelaine Cooke, Melinda Conner, and the rest of the staff at the University of Georgia Press for their help in turning my manuscript into a published work. I am thankful as well to Amy Rebar for her excellent cartography, and to my wife, Pamela, for her proofreading of the innumerable versions of my manuscript, for her early work on the graphs, and, most important, for her patience and understanding over the last six years.

Some of my research has appeared previously as articles in the *North Carolina Historical Review,* the *Journal of Southern History,* and *Carolina Comments.* These journals have very kindly given me permission to reproduce parts of these articles. Finally, I wish to acknowledge my thanks to Dan T. Carter, who years ago first called my attention to the fascinating field of North Carolina politics.

State Parties and National Politics

Introduction

During most of the antebellum period, political competition in North Carolina took place within the framework of a national party system. In the Old North State, as throughout the nation, the two parties that vied for popular favor were highly competitive and evenly balanced. Although the Whigs were the majority party from 1836 until 1850 and the Democrats were in the ascendant thereafter, only a few percentage points usually separated winners from losers in state and national elections. In order to ensure party unity and a full turnout of voters, both parties developed an elaborate organizational structure and a popular style of campaigning. A consistently high level of voter participation, far surpassing that of modern political campaigns, attested to the success of these methods.

The party system in antebellum North Carolina thus embodied most of the characteristics that historians have ascribed to the second American party system as a whole—competitiveness, sophisticated party machinery, and high voter turnout. In one important respect, however, North Carolina differed significantly from other states. In most parts of the country the Whig party had collapsed by the middle of the 1850s, but in North Carolina the Whigs remained a viable political force until the Civil War and, to some extent, even thereafter.

Historians of the second party system have disagreed sharply over the relative importance of national, state, and local issues in the political culture of antebellum America. Practitioners of the "new political history" have argued that most antebellum Americans had little interest in the Bank of the United States, the protective tariff, or the other national economic issues that have played a central role in traditional accounts of the party battles of the Jacksonian era. Instead, they claim, party loyalties at the grass roots were conditioned by a variety of state and local issues, often religious and cultural in nature.[1]

This interpretation has not won universal or unqualified acceptance among historians. Indeed, in recent years there has been a reaction against the so-called ethnocultural interpretation and a reaffirmation of the importance of national issues. As one scholar has pointed out, antebellum politicians "did not slight such national questions as the tariff, internal improvements, or public land policy, when they were before the voters. Rather they discussed them almost incessantly; even candidates for state and local office commonly took positions on national issues. . . . National controversies provided an essential rallying standard for state and local party organizers."[2]

This study will not attempt to take sides on the question of whether national issues, on the one hand, or state and local issues, on the other, were more important to the voters. Instead, it will proceed upon the premise that national, state, and local issues all played important roles in the functioning of the party system. Because North Carolina was only one component in a national system of parties, Tarheel politicians found national issues to be indispensable in linking their state organization with the national party in Washington. At the same time, because party leaders depended upon the voters in their constituencies for political success, they could not afford to be oblivious to the local interests of the electorate. The contours of the party system in North Carolina were shaped by the interaction of national issues with local interests, and one of the purposes of this study is to examine the connections and explain the interplay between the two.

Two recent studies provide the backdrop for my own examination of the second party system in North Carolina. Harry L. Watson's *Jacksonian Politics and Community Conflict* is a microscopic analysis of the genesis of political parties in Cumberland County, North Carolina. The strengths of Watson's study lie in his careful examination of the relationship between community conflict and grass-roots party alignments, and in his steady focus on the linkages among political issues at the local, state, and national levels. By demonstrating how party leaders attempted to make their national programs relevant to the fears and aspirations of their local constituency, Watson has contributed significantly to our understanding of the dynamics of the second party system.

The weaknesses in Watson's study are those inherent in any case-study approach. To what extent is the one county under investigation representative of North Carolina as a whole? Watson has not proven convincingly that Cumberland County was a microcosm of North Carolina or even necessarily of the Cape Fear region in which it was located. Indeed, its large concentration of Highland Scots, its earlier Federalist proclivities, its lopsided Democratic majorities, and, most important, its strong urban orientation made it, in many respects, a most untypical North Carolina county.[3]

Whereas Watson's book focuses almost exclusively on the early years of the second party system, Marc W. Kruman's *Parties and Politics in North Carolina, 1836–1865* passes quickly over the formative years to concentrate on the party battles of the post-Jackson period. According to Kruman, the wellspring of party conflict in North Carolina can be found in the intense disagreement between Democrats and Whigs over a variety of state issues such as internal improvements, banking policy, and state aid to schools and asylums. Although Kruman stops short of claiming that party positions on state issues were monolithic, he notes that "given the limited sanctions that parties had over their supporters, it is remarkable how united the parties actually were."[4]

The following study will present a quite different argument about the relationship of the two parties to state issues. It will demonstrate that sectional conflict between the plantation counties of eastern North Carolina and the small-farm counties of the west played a pivotal role in determining how the parties would react to state issues. Both parties were coalitions of eastern and western interests, and important state issues like internal improvements, the apportionment of the public school fund, and the creation of new counties tended to divide the legislators within each party along sectional lines. For this reason party leaders urged a policy of toleration and forbearance on state issues and stubbornly resisted efforts to turn them into tests of party orthodoxy. At the same time strategists in both parties tried to promote harmony within their ranks by rallying their forces behind cohesive national issues and by avoiding the mention of state issues in their platforms and other official pronouncements.

The absence of official positions on state issues did not totally preclude partisan discussion of local concerns. Indeed, the willingness of the parties to tolerate divergent viewpoints on issues like internal improvements allowed local activists the flexibility to assume any position that conviction or political expediency might dictate.

The ability of parties to exploit such issues at the local level does not mean that they were able to offer clear-cut alternatives at the state level. On the contrary, the system could work smoothly only so long as local activists refrained from trying to impose their views on the entire party.

The introduction of the "free suffrage" issue in 1848 inaugurated an important transformation in North Carolina politics, as militant westerners demanded that the parties take official positions on state issues like internal improvements and constitutional reform. The resulting shift in focus from national to state politics weakened the Whigs, who found it increasingly difficult to harmonize the conflicting sectional interests within their party. But once confronted with the responsibility of governing, the Democrats also began experiencing difficulties in reconciling the interests of their two sectional wings.

In one sense the revival of state sectionalism during the 1850s acted as a destabilizing force, because it practically guaranteed that neither party would be able for long to monopolize the reins of power. But, paradoxically, the injection of state issues into the political arena also strengthened the party system by keeping the parties competitive and by forcing their leaders to address the most pressing local concerns of the voters. Even after 1850 North Carolina parties did not present clear-cut alternatives on state issues. But both parties became increasingly adept at developing strategies to direct sectionally divisive issues into safer partisan channels. The intense competition between Whigs and Democrats over state issues, along with the immunity of the two parties to the twin viruses of ethnocultural conflict and slavery agitation account for the remarkable vitality of the second party system in North Carolina on the eve of the Civil War.

Any study of the development and evolution of parties must ultimately address the questions of what those parties stood for and why the voters divided their loyalties among them. Recent studies of the second party system have suggested that Democrats and Whigs differed sharply over the role of government in promoting economic development and social reform. The Whigs favored a policy of active government at both the state and national levels, whereas the Democrats endorsed the doctrine of the negative state.[5] The evidence for North Carolina does not support this dichotomy. As elsewhere throughout the nation, Whigs and Democrats in the Old North State disagreed strongly about national policy issues relating to banking and currency, executive power, and the public lands. At the same time, both parties espoused the principles of strict construction, states' rights, and negative government, and they justified their national policies as embodiments of these principles. At the state level, on the other hand, neither party officially endorsed the doctrine of negative government. Indeed, influential leaders in both parties were willing to use the power of the state to promote internal improvements and public education.

This is not to say that consensus was the dominant theme in the politics of antebellum North Carolina. Party differences were sharp, and these divergent views reflected real disagreement about the direction of economic development in nineteenth-century America. During the first half of the century the number of banks increased phenomenally, and that institution stood as both agent and symbol of the profound changes that were taking place in the nation's economy. In North Carolina the Whigs defended both the national bank and the state's own banking institutions, sometimes at great political risk to themselves, and they justified paper money as a necessary medium of exchange. The Democrats denounced the banks as "manufactories of rogues and swindlers" and generally took a hard-money stance on currency issues.

The parties also disagreed about the role of the corporation in the economic life of the nation. The Whigs viewed corporations as engines of progress and sought to promote their growth through the passage of limited-liability laws. The Democrats regarded corporate institutions as dangerous concentrations of power and consistently tried to restrict their activities by making the personal property of the individual stockholders liable for corporate debts. As nineteenth-century America moved rapidly from a rural agrarian society to an urban industrial one, the Whigs looked toward the future with optimism; the Democrats, with trepidation. As Marvin Meyers succinctly put it: "The Whig party spoke to the explicit hopes of Americans as Jacksonians addressed their diffuse fears and resentments."[6]

The leaders of North Carolina's Democratic party were not, however, agrarian radicals bent on restoring a lost Arcadia. Indeed, these men often had intimate connections with the very institutions they were attacking. Prominent Democrats like Louis D. Henry, Romulus M. Saunders, and Robert Strange owned stock in banks and even served as bank attorneys and directors. Although they controlled the state government for much of the antebellum period, the Democrats failed to enact even one piece of antibanking legislation. Despite the fervor of their rhetoric, the leaders of the Democratic party were too thoroughly enmeshed in the workings of the market economy to offer the voters genuine alternatives on banking and currency issues.

The question of why antebellum Americans supported their respective parties with such intense loyalty is one that has intrigued historians for generations. Some have viewed the behavior of antebellum voters as a manifestation of socioeconomic class divisions within the electorate, whereas others have minimized the importance of economic distinctions and have emphasized the role of religious and ethnic tensions, community conflict, and negative-reference groups.[7] An examination of the social bases of party allegiance in North Carolina offers little support for the argument that party alignments were primarily a product of conflicting economic interests. Neither party was associated exclusively with one economic group or with one section of the state.[8] There is abundant evidence, however, that deeply rooted social conflicts, some of them dating as far back as the Revolutionary War, exerted a profound influence in shaping the pattern of grass-roots alignments during the antebellum era.

Most histories of the second party system in North Carolina begin with the revival of the contest for the presidency in 1824 or with the controversial events of Andrew Jackson's administration. Few studies have investigated the possible connections between the first and second party systems.[9] Yet a closer analysis of the evidence reveals that the architects of the second party system did not construct their organizations out of whole cloth. Instead, they worked within a context of preexisting partisan identities that had an important effect on their efforts at party building. A study of the origins of the second party system in North Carolina must begin, therefore, with an examination of the events that led to the rise of organized parties during the 1790s, the factors that contributed to the "remarkable staying powers" of the Federalist party in the years after Jefferson's election, and the efforts that were made during the 1820s to ally Federalists and dissident Republicans in a crusade against the congressional caucus.[10]

One of the most important legacies of the earlier generation of political leaders was the articulation of a unique attitude toward government and society—a republican ideology. In recent years historians have become increasingly aware of the pervasive influence of republican ideology in the political culture of antebellum America.[11] Nineteenth-century Americans were deeply suspicious of any concentration of power, whether in the form of a caucus, an organized political party, or a chartered corporation. Although their views about the nature of the threat to republican government differed, Democrats and Whigs both portrayed themselves as foes of tyrannous concentrations of power; and each claimed that the preservation of liberty and equality depended on the defeat of the opposing party.

The development of organized parties thus proceeded within an ideological framework that was essentially antiparty in character. Yet few efforts have been made to explore the difficulties that party leaders faced in reconciling eighteenth-century republican ideology with the exigencies of nineteenth-century politics.[12] This study will reveal how popular suspicion of centralized power inhibited the development of effective party organization in North Carolina, especially in those parts of the state where one party enjoyed a monopoly of power. At the same time it will show how ambitious leaders in both parties exploited long-standing popular antipathy toward "management" and "caucus dictation" to promote their own political fortunes.

This study will also shed new light on the intriguing question of why the Whigs dominated the state during the 1830s and 1840s and why they lost power to the Democrats during the 1850s. Most accounts of the second party system in North Carolina have viewed the events of these decades within a progressive paradigm of party development.[13] Simply put, this interpretation claims that the political advantage almost invariably went "to the party which aggressively championed constructive, democratic reform." During the 1830s, the argument goes, it was the Whigs who presented the people of North Carolina with a constructive reform program. Without a progressive alternative of their own, the Democrats were no match for a party that stood for public schools, internal improvements, sound banks and currency, and the promotion of industry and agriculture. Unfortunately for the Whigs, however, their long years in power stimulated conservatism and, gradually, they "relaxed their zeal for the constructive policies which had made them the popular dominant party." At the same time the Democratic party found itself rejuvenated as new leaders came to the fore who were "determined to commit the party to a constructive, progressive program." Riding to power in 1850 on the issue of "free suffrage" (the removal of the fifty-acre property qualification for voters), the Democrats "gradually took over and even extended the Whig program of internal improvements, public education, and humanitarian reform."[14]

This viewpoint was expounded as early as 1896 in John Spencer Bassett's study of "Suffrage in the State of North Carolina," the first scholarly work to attribute the Whig downfall to the issue of free suffrage.[15] J. G. de Roulhac Hamilton's *Party Politics in North Carolina, 1835–1860*, written in 1916, developed the progressive interpretation even more fully. A Wilsonian Democrat, Hamilton was eager to trace the reformist pedigree of his party back to the antebellum period. In his view the Whigs were "progressive in actual policy as evidenced by their work of education and internal improvements" but aristocratic in spirit, with but "small confidence in the people or in their ability to rule, if indeed their attitude may not be properly described as contemptuous." Like Bassett, he attributed the success of the Democrats after 1850 to the popularity of the free-suffrage issue. Hamilton also emphasized the role of the suffrage reform movement in promoting a "new progressive spirit" within the Democratic party and in liberalizing its position on issues like internal improvements and public education.[16]

Two book-length studies of North Carolina's antebellum parties written during the 1930s provided additional details about state politics without, however, breaking any new interpretive ground. Like Hamilton's study, Clarence C. Norton's *The Democratic Party in Ante-Bellum North Carolina, 1835–1861* attributed the Democrats' success to their discovery of progressive leaders and issues. In Norton's view, "the years of defeat had taught them that ultra-conservatism does not satisfy the desire of the majority of the people for good government."[17] Herbert D. Pegg's *Whig Party in North Carolina*, written in 1932, praised the leaders of that party for presenting "a constructive program, looking towards the advancement of the economic and intellectual interests of the state." Unfortunately, according to Pegg, their long tenure in office eventually dampened the reformist zeal of the Whig leaders, so that by 1850 "the Whig party was decadent."[18]

Most of the research on antebellum North Carolina politics done since the 1930s has been biographical in nature, and the interpretive framework of these studies has adhered closely to the analyses of Hamilton, Norton, and Pegg. Biographies of Democratic leader William W. Holden by Edgar E. Folk and Horace W. Raper have characterized the editor as a man of "broadly democratic" principles who was instrumental in turning his party from conservatism to progressivism.[19] Biographical sketches of Democratic Governor David S. Reid by Paul A. Reid and Lindley S. Butler have reaffirmed the traditional image of Reid as an antebellum progressive whose free-suffrage program "marked a revolution in party politics."[20] Max R. Williams's dissertation on Whig leader William A. Graham has also endorsed the prevailing view that "the Whig Party which had prospered in the 1830's as the champion of democracy . . . had become by 1848 the bastion of conservatism." Like the biographers of Holden and Reid, Williams attributed the success of the Democrats to their ability to "shed the conservative mantle of Nathaniel Macon" and to adopt "progressive attitudes."[21]

Marc W. Kruman's recent study of North Carolina politics presents a much more sophisticated analysis of antebellum parties than the works of Hamilton, Norton, or Pegg, but Kruman fails to break away from the progressive paradigm developed in these pioneer studies. While recognizing the limitations of the Democrats' commitment to constitutional reform, he characterizes free suffrage as the issue that enabled party leaders to create "an effective image of the Whigs as aristocratic opponents of popular rights."[22] Kruman also makes the familiar point that, once in power, the Democrats emulated many of the progressive programs of the Whigs, particularly in regard to state-supported internal improvements.

This study will challenge almost every tenet of this time-honored view of political development in antebellum North Carolina. First, it will question the assumption that the decades before the Civil War marked "an era of unprecedented progress and reform."[23] If "progress" means nothing more than the construction of railroads and the establishment of public schools, then the years between 1815 and 1860 were, indeed, a progressive era. But the antebellum period also witnessed the rapid consolidation of the power of the slaveholding class, as improvements in transportation brought more farmers into the market economy and enabled the plantation system to spread westward from the coastal plain into the piedmont. As early as 1840, the slaveholding bloc in the general assembly achieved a major victory by changing the formula for apportioning the school fund from one based on white population to one based on federal population. During the 1850s eastern slaveholders in both parties consistently frustrated attempts by western reformers to democratize the structure of state and local government. On the eve of the Civil War, North Carolina's system of government remained one of the most undemocratic in the entire South.[24]

This study will confirm the existence of "progressive" and "conservative" attitudes in regard to issues like internal improvements, public schools, and constitutional reform. But it will also demonstrate that neither party had a monopoly on progressivism, either before or after 1850. From their beginnings both parties contained progressive western elements and conservative eastern elements. Because each party had to compete for voter support in all parts of the state, each could appear "conservative" at some times and "progressive" at others, depending on the section to which its strategists were appealing. Moreover, the progressive side did not invariably emerge triumphant in every contest. There is abundant evidence, for example, that the Democrats did not wrest the governorship from the Whigs in 1850 by appealing to the progressive inclinations of western reformers. Rather, they won it by pandering to the fears of conservative eastern slaveholders, who wished to preserve a constitutional system that protected their own sectional interests at the expense of the republican ideal of equality. Furthermore, the Democrats consolidated their power after 1850 not by articulating a progressive program of state development but, instead, by capitalizing on the growing sectional divisions within the Whig party, particularly over the issue of constitutional reform.

Although Democrats and Whigs divided sharply over a variety of policy issues, the leaders of both parties agreed about the importance of slavery in the economic and social life of the South. In the words of Herbert D. Pegg, both parties in the Old North State "were pro-slavery to the core."[25] Despite this broad consensus, Tarheel politicians constantly tried to exploit slavery-related issues for partisan advantage, and they consistently accused the opposition party of being in collusion with the abolitionists. As a topic of partisan discussion, slavery played an important role in practically every national campaign in North Carolina during the antebellum era. Yet there is little evidence that the continuous barrage of charges and countercharges had a significant impact on the outcome of these elections. Certainly North Carolina Whigs did not desert their party in droves during the 1850s as a result of the escalating national controversy over slavery. Indeed, thanks to eastern dissatisfaction with the steadily increasing taxes levied by the state's Democratic administrations, the Whigs were actually stronger in the slaveholding east at the end of the decade than they had been at its beginning.

The persistence of interparty competition during the critical decade of the 1850s had an important impact on the way that North Carolinians reacted to the alternatives of union and disunion during the secession crisis. Following the lead of their compatriots in the lower South, North Carolina Democrats attempted to use the power of their party organization to carry the state into the southern confederacy. At the same time, the strength of the Whig organization in North Carolina enabled leaders of that party to resist these efforts until Lincoln's call for troops united North Carolinians of all political persuasions in a determination to resist northern aggression. At one level the debate over secession was merely the latest in a long series of party battles over national issues. But the secession controversy also triggered a realignment of parties, as Democratic voters in many North Carolina counties refused to follow their leaders into the disunion camp. The advent of the secession crisis thus marked the end of one era in the state's political history and the beginning of another. For the issues and divisions arising out of that crisis would continue to shape the politics of the Old North State during the Civil War and Reconstruction years, and even beyond.

1 ✦ "A Proneness to Contention": Origins of Political Conflict in North Carolina

Six months in North Carolina was time enough to convince Josiah Martin, the new royal governor, that the task of governing the province would not be an easy one. "In this Country," he told the earl of Hillsborough early in 1772, "there prevails a proneness to contention without example."[1] Martin was referring specifically to the chronic disturbances that had convulsed the Carolina backcountry for more than a decade, culminating in a fierce two-hour battle between western "Regulators" and the eastern militia at Alamance on 16 May 1771. The Regulator movement, however, was merely the most recent in a long series of bitter political controversies that had plagued the province almost since its beginning. Few colonies would enter the American Revolution in such a divided and embittered condition. In few of the newly independent states would the animosities engendered during the long struggle against Britain provide the political organizers of the postwar era with more durable materials for the creation of mass-based parties.

Colonial North Carolinians had always been an individualistic, quarrelsome, and even violent people. During the proprietary period the colony's history had been punctuated by a series of disturbances with names such as Culpeper's Rebellion, Gibbs's Rebellion, and Cary's Usurpation. In the first half-century of settlement, six legally appointed governors were either deposed by a rival faction or prevented from entering the colony. Governor Alexander Spotswood of Virginia, who sent a company of Royal Marines to the Carolina proprietary in 1711 to suppress Cary's rebellion, observed that the people of North Carolina were so accustomed to turning out their governors that they had come to think they had a right to do so.[2] Forty years later Moravian Bishop August Gottlieb Spangenberg recorded in his diary that "if I am to say how I find things in North Carolina I must admit that there is much confusion. There is discord between the counties . . . [and] in some respects anarchy reigns."[3]

The situation had not changed significantly by the eve of the American Revolution. Indeed, rapid geographical expansion during the 1750s and 1760s intensified and prolonged the colony's political instability, as the settlers flocking into the western piedmont from Pennsylvania and other northern colonies complained about excessive taxation, corrupt sheriffs, and fee-gouging local officials. Initially a protest against the hegemony of unpopular local officials, the Regulator movement ultimately led its adherents to challenge the legitimacy of the provincial elite in the general assembly, who condoned these abuses of power and ignored the backcountry's demands for reform. Frustrated by their inability to achieve their goals through petition and negotiation, the Regulators eventually resorted to violence. Riots broke out in several piedmont counties, and in December 1770 the assembly adopted legislation allowing the governor to use military force to preserve order in the backcountry. The following spring eleven hundred well-equipped militia under the command of Governor William Tryon engaged two thousand Regulators on the banks of Alamance Creek in Orange County. Lacking discipline and leadership, the Regulators proved no match for Tryon's well-organized militia. The vanquished insurgents were court-martialed, and several were subsequently executed.[4]

The violent suppression of the Regulators at Alamance left a legacy of bitterness and hostility in the backcountry that boded ill for the efforts of the provincial elite to unite the people of North Carolina in resistance to British authority just a few years later. Backcountry inhabitants were inclined to look upon that authority not as an engine of oppression but as a source of protection against the rapacious behavior of their local enemies. Another group that had more to gain than to lose from the continuance of British authority were the Highland Scots who resided in the upper Cape Fear valley. Most of these settlers had come to North Carolina during the decade immediately preceding the Revolution. Among them were many former officers of the British army who were now retired on half pay. The wealthier immigrants still owned landed estates in Scotland, which would be forfeited should they join the rebellion. Both because of self-interest and because their recent arrival left them unacquainted with the points at issue between Britain and the colonies, the vast majority of Highlanders remained loyal to the Crown.[5]

To an extent far greater than in most other colonies, the American Revolution in North Carolina took on the character of a civil war. Although the British army entered the state briefly in 1780 and 1781, most of the revolutionary battles were fought between Patriot and Loyalist militia. It was a brutal conflict, and the slaughter was not confined exclusively or even primarily to formal battlefield encounters. Irregular bands of partisans on both sides murdered opposition leaders and destroyed the homes and property of their local enemies. The internecine conflict continued for almost a year after Cornwallis's surrender at Yorktown.[6]

Outsiders unfamiliar with the colony's turbulent past were shocked by the ferocity of the struggle. Nathanael Greene, the Quaker general who engaged Cornwallis at Guilford Courthouse in 1781, remarked that "the whigs and tories pursue one another with the most relentless fury killing and destroying each other whenever they meet. . . . The country is full of little armed parties who follow their resentments with little less than savage fury."[7] In the absence of effective institutions of authority in many parts of the state, rival groups resorted to violence as a means of redressing local grievances and settling old scores. Much of the bloodletting in North Carolina probably had little direct connection with the larger issues at stake in the struggle between Britain and her rebellious colonies.[8]

In addition to active Whigs and Tories, there was also a "great middle group of passive citizens who had no clear point of view, who hoped perhaps that one side or the other would win, but who wanted above all not to be disturbed."[9] In North Carolina this group included English Quakers and pietist and pacifist German settlers like the Moravians and Dunkards. During the course of the conflict, the revolutionary government alienated a substantial number of these neutral citizens. In particular, the Whig militia, which became the undisputed local arm of social and political control in the Carolina backcountry, tormented and intimidated those whom they suspected of being British sympathizers. "This campaign of terror transformed neutrals into loyalists and deepened the resentments of the disaffected."[10]

The conflicts and animosities engendered by the Revolution did not end suddenly in 1782 when the fighting stopped. Bitter controversy over the treatment of the Loyalists continued to inflame the passions of North Carolina's political leaders until the end of the decade. In the years immediately following the war, the North Carolina General Assembly passed a series of laws that prohibited former Loyalists from holding state or local office, continued the sale of confiscated property, and denied Loyalists the right to sue in the state courts for recovery of their property. Opposed to the Tory-baiters in the general assembly were a minority who favored a policy of leniency toward the former Loyalists. The leaders of the so-called Conservative faction had all been associated with the Patriot cause during the war, but many of them had relatives or close friends who had been prominent Loyalists. Moreover, as members of the state bar, they frequently found themselves representing Loyalists in matters involving the restitution of confiscated property and the collection of prewar debts. As urban dwellers, the Conservatives had also developed close ties with merchants in the coastal towns, and they generally supported measures favorable to the creditor class, such as the speedy redemption of paper currency and the repeal of the stay laws.[11]

The factional lines established during the debate over the treatment of Loyalists continued to hold firm during the contest over the ratification of the U.S. Constitution. Samuel Johnston, James Iredell, Archibald Maclaine, and other Conservatives organized and directed the campaign to mobilize public opinion behind the new charter of government, whereas Tory-baiters like Griffith Rutherford, Samuel Spencer, and Timothy Bloodworth provided leadership to the opponents of the Constitution. In 1787 the Conservatives secured enough support among uncommitted legislators in the general assembly to elevate Johnston to the governorship and to win approval for a ratifying convention. The Conservatives won another major victory in the first congressional elections, which were held in 1789. Supporters of the Constitution won three of the four seats in the House of Representatives, and the general assembly subsequently chose Johnston and another Conservative, Benjamin Hawkins, as North Carolina's first U.S. senators.[12]

Once the question of ratifying the Constitution had been settled, few issues of national politics remained to separate the leaders of the two North Carolina factions. Alexander Hamilton's proposal to refinance the federal debt and assume the obligations of the states was opposed not only by antifederalist Congressman Timothy Bloodworth but also by Johnston and the other Conservative leaders. Nor were North Carolinians easily reconciled to the doctrine of implied powers embodied in Hamilton's proposal to charter the Bank of the United States.[13] Not until the focus of partisan debate shifted from Hamiltonian finance to foreign policy did the Conservative faction in North Carolina develop a popular following and establish durable links with the national Federalist party.

More than any other event, the long controversy over the Jay Treaty was responsible for stimulating the creation of organized parties in North Carolina. The settlement negotiated by Chief Justice John Jay in 1794 contained a British promise to evacuate the forts illegally occupied on the American northwest frontier, but most of the other provisions favored Britain. The Republicans, as the opponents of the administration were now calling themselves, denounced the treaty as an abject surrender of American rights and honor. Hamilton and other Federalist leaders admitted that Jay's treaty was far from ideal but claimed that it was the best settlement obtainable and the only alternative to war.[14]

For the first time since the debate over the ratification of the Constitution, the leaders of the two North Carolina factions attempted to mobilize public opinion on an issue of national importance. As Federalism became increasingly associated in the public mind with a policy of peace and friendship toward Britain, popular support for the party began to coalesce.[15] In 1796 and 1797 Britain's enemy, France, stepped up its seizures of American merchant vessels in retaliation against the Jay Treaty and the election of John Adams. The French crisis and the alleged threat of the "Frenchified Democrats" to the national security provided the Federalists with powerful campaign issues during the midterm elections of 1798. Administration supporters won a majority of seats in the general assembly and elected William R. Davie as governor. In the congressional elections Federalist candidates captured four of the ten seats, and in three other districts antiadministration incumbents were replaced by less intransigent Republicans. Foreign affairs continued to provide the Federalists with campaign material during the presidential election of 1800. Federalist electors won majorities in four of the twelve districts, and Adams polled a respectable 44 percent of the popular vote.[16]

Conspicuously absent from Federalist rhetoric during the campaigns of 1798 and 1800 was any overt appeal to the interests of the commercial and financial classes. The merchants and professional men in the towns apparently voted Federalist in large numbers, but they were not sufficiently numerous in North Carolina to support a mass-based political party. In the rural areas of the state, where the vast majority of the population lived, there was little connection between political affiliation and economic status. Both parties derived the bulk of their popular support from small farmers living on the fringes of the market economy.[17]

Although Republican counties could be found in practically every part of the state, the stronghold of North Carolina Republicanism lay in the tier of northern counties along the Virginia border (see map 1). This area had been settled primarily by Virginians of English stock, who had subsequently developed strong economic ties with the Virginia market towns of Norfolk, Richmond, and Petersburg. Since the struggle for independence, most of the leading men in these counties had looked to Virginia for political leadership. Indeed, the Federalists frequently accused their opponents of mindless subservience to the politicians of the Old Dominion.[18]

In three congressional districts, all in the southern part of the state, the Federalists frequently found themselves in the majority. The Fayetteville district, comprising Cumberland County and several other counties in the upper Cape Fear valley and the southern piedmont, was one of the strongest bastions of Federalism in the country. With the exception of one two-year interval, the Federalists controlled this district continuously between 1795 and 1815. In no other district were the Federalists able to match this nearly unbroken string of victories. In two districts, however, they were strong enough to offer the Republicans vigorous competition and frequently to elect their own candidates. One such area of strength was the Salisbury district, comprising Rowan County and several other counties in the western piedmont. Federalists represented the district in the U.S. Congress from 1798 until 1803 and again from 1808 until 1815. The other Federalist stronghold was the New Bern district, comprising Craven County and several other counties in the southeastern coastal plain, which the party carried five times between 1798 and 1815.[19]

Significantly, all three districts had been centers of Tory activity during the Revolution. The counties of the upper Cape Fear had led all others in supplying men to Loyalist regiments and militia. As much as two-thirds of their population may have sympathized with

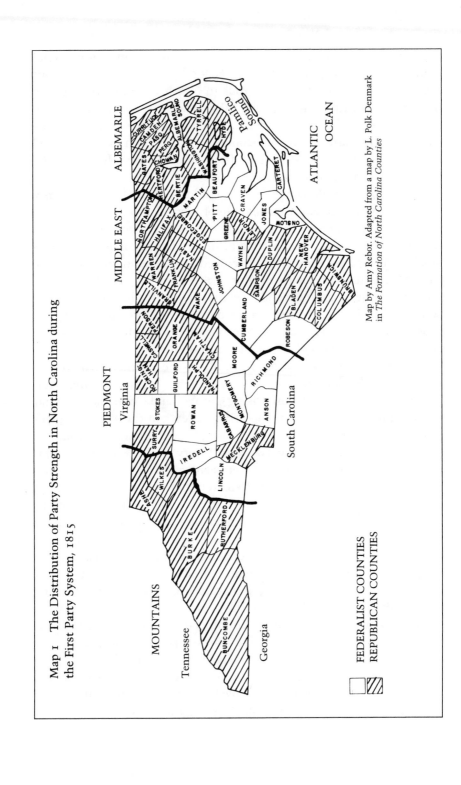

Map 1   The Distribution of Party Strength in North Carolina during the First Party System, 1815

Map by Amy Rebor. Adapted from a map by L. Polk Denmark in *The Formation of North Carolina Counties*

☐ FEDERALIST COUNTIES
▨ REPUBLICAN COUNTIES

PIEDMONT

MIDDLE EAST

ALBEMARLE

MOUNTAINS

Tennessee

Georgia

Virginia

South Carolina

ATLANTIC
OCEAN

Pamlico Sound
Albemarle Sound

ASHE
WILKES
BURKE
RUTHERFORD
BUNCOMBE
SURRY
STOKES
ROCKINGHAM
CASWELL
PERSON
GRANVILLE
WARREN
FRANKLIN
NASH
HALIFAX
NORTHAMPTON
EDGECOMBE
MARTIN
BERTIE
HERTFORD
GATES
CHOWAN
PERQ.
CAMDEN
CURRITUCK
PASQ.
TYRRELL
HYDE
BEAUFORT
PITT
GREENE
WAYNE
JOHNSTON
WAKE
ORANGE
GUILFORD
ROWAN
IREDELL
LINCOLN
MECKLENBURG
CABARRUS
MONTGOMERY
ANSON
RICHMOND
MOORE
CHATHAM
CUMBERLAND
SAMPSON
DUPLIN
JONES
CRAVEN
LENOIR
CARTERET
ONSLOW
NEW HANOVER
BLADEN
COLUMBUS
ROBESON
BRUNSWICK
JOHNSTON

the British. Rowan County, the largest and most populous county in the Salisbury district, had been a Regulator stronghold during the 1760s and a hotbed of loyalism a decade later. Likewise, the area between New Bern and Kinston had witnessed intense fighting between bands of Patriot and Loyalist partisans during the last year of the war.[20]

The prevalence of Federalism in those parts of the state where loyalism had been strongest suggests that the grass-roots party alignments of the Federalist era were continuations of political divisions that had emerged during the struggle for independence. As the descendant of one prominent Revolutionary leader pointed out: "The inhumanities and butcheries of the closing years of the long struggle left an indelible mark on the social conditions of the state. Fierce resentment and implacable hatred took possession of the contending factions."[21] The outbreak of war between Britain and France in 1793 served only to reinforce existing pro-British and anti-British sentiments within the electorate.

Grounded as they were in the lingering animosities of the eighteenth century, the early North Carolina parties offered few answers to the new problems that began confronting the state during the first decades of the nineteenth century. Federalists and Republicans failed to present the voters with alternatives on important state issues such as constitutional revision, internal improvements, judicial reform, tax policies, and the creation of new counties. These issues usually arrayed the wealthier plantation counties of the east against the poorer small-farm counties of the west, and votes on state issues in the general assembly tended to follow sectional rather than party lines.[22]

With their hopes for success pinned almost entirely on issues relating to foreign policy, Federalist fortunes alternately rose and fell as the prospect of American involvement in the European conflict increased and diminished. In 1800 the widespread fear that a Republican administration would plunge the country into war had led almost 45 percent of the electorate to vote for the New Englander John Adams instead of their fellow southerner Thomas Jefferson. Within a year after Jefferson's inauguration, however, the Treaty of Amiens temporarily ended the long war between Britain and France, and the Federalists' strength in North Carolina plummeted rapidly.[23]

The resumption of the European war in 1803 and the passage of the Embargo Act in 1807 gave a new lease on life to Federalism in North Carolina. Although the Federalists did not hesitate to blame the embargo for the declining prices of agricultural produce and the scarcity of currency, in their view the main threat posed by the embargo was not economic ruin but rather the horrors of another war with Britain.[24] The congressional elections of 1808 provided striking evidence of how effectively the fear of war worked to the advantage of the Federalists in North Carolina. In addition to carrying their stronghold in the Fayetteville district, the Federalists also captured the New Bern and Salisbury districts for the first time since 1800. Even more portentous for the future of Republican supremacy in North Carolina were the divisions that the embargo issue was beginning to create within the majority party itself. In the Hillsborough district, comprising Orange and several other piedmont counties, six-term incumbent Richard Stanford broke with his party over the issue. In the Tar River district centered on Edgecombe County William Kennedy, an antiembargo Republican, unseated Thomas Blount, the proadministration incumbent.[25]

The repeal of the Embargo Act in 1809 did not stop the Federalist resurgence or reverse the drift toward war. In the eyes of the Federalists, the declaration of war by Congress in June 1812 only confirmed their prediction that Republican policies would eventually embroil the nation in the European conflict. The political impact of the war quickly made itself felt in the Old North State, as the legislative elections of August 1812 produced a Federalist gain of ten seats in the North Carolina House of Commons and two in the North Carolina State Senate. The following spring Federalists captured three of the thirteen congressional seats and lost another by only thirty-six votes. In three other districts antiwar Republicans challenged supporters of the Madison administration. Altogether, five of the thirteen congressmen elected in 1813 were opponents of the war.[26]

By the time the general assembly convened in November 1813, opposition to the administration had become so intense that a joint committee submitted a report accusing the federal government of gross neglect. Administration supporters succeeded in postponing the report indefinitely, but by a majority of only one vote.[27] Had the war lasted much longer, it is possible that an alliance of Federalists and dissident Republicans might have replaced the Republicans as the majority party in North Carolina.

Instead, within three years after the end of the war with Britain, Federalism as an organized party was dead in North Carolina. Contrary to popular belief, however, Andrew Jackson's dramatic victory over the British at New Orleans in 1815 did not trigger a mass exodus of voters from the Federalist party. The Federalists held their own during the congressional and legislative elections of 1815 and, as late as 1816, they controlled almost two-fifths of the seats in the house of commons.[28] Federalism disappeared as an organized opposition party after 1816 not because the voters repudiated it, but rather because the party's leaders came to believe that their old organization could no longer serve as a useful means of advancing their political careers. From its inception Federalism had depended for political vitality on events in Europe over which the party's leaders had no control. The defeat of Napoleon at Waterloo signaled the end of the long series of wars that had plagued the Continent since the early 1790s. Foreign policy now became an arena for diplomats rather than politicians. Federalist leaders thus found themselves without an appealing national issue around which to unite their followers. For the politically ambitious, the best chance for advancement seemed to lie in casting aside old party labels and establishing new political connections.[29]

After offering token opposition to James Monroe in 1816, the Federalists abandoned the contest for the presidency and, except in a handful of states, ceased to compete as an organized party. The so-called Era of Good Feelings, as Charles S. Sydnor has pointed out, witnessed "the most complete one-party situation in the history of the nation."[30] Yet Federalism continued to persist as a unique political identity long after its collapse as an organized party. The proscription of Federalist politicians by the Monroe administration and the Republican-controlled state governments, along with the incessant Republican attacks upon them served to reinforce old partisan identities during the Era of Good Feelings. At the same time the lure of public office provided the incentive for Federalists in states like New York and Pennsylvania to form alliances with disaffected elements within the majority party. After 1820 the divisions arising within the Republican ranks over the successor to President Monroe also offered the Federalists an opportunity to reassert their influence on the national scene.[31]

In North Carolina most of the leading Republican politicians supported the candidacy of William H. Crawford, the Virginia-born secretary of the treasury. Veteran Senator Nathaniel Macon and ten of the state's thirteen congressmen endorsed Crawford, as did Bartlett Yancy, the longtime speaker of the state senate, and Joseph Gales, the influential editor of the *Raleigh Register*. Crawford's southern birth, his identification with the principles of strict construction and states' rights, and his support for a "plain, cheap, unostentatious administration" made him an attractive candidate to the conservative Republicans who dominated the state's politics.[32]

Until the sudden advent of the Jackson movement in early 1824, Crawford's principal opponent in North Carolina was Secretary of War John C. Calhoun. Despite his later association with the southern-rights movement, Calhoun's reputation during the 1820s rested primarily on his advocacy of federal aid for internal improvements and other programs of national development. Calhoun's unabashed nationalism frightened conservative Republicans like Romulus M. Saunders, who regarded the South Carolinian as "the most dangerous man in the Government."[33] On the other hand, it suited the inclinations of many politicians in underdeveloped parts of the state who desired improved transportation facilities and looked to the state or federal government to obtain the necessary funding. Charles Fisher, a former congressman and prominent Salisbury businessman, organized and directed the Calhoun campaign in North Carolina. At least four of the state's twelve newspapers, most notably the *Salisbury Western Carolinian* and the *Raleigh Star*, gave their editorial endorsement to the South Carolinian.[34]

At the beginning of the campaign Crawford appeared to have the decided advantage. The Georgian commanded widespread support among the established Republican leaders not only in his native South but also in key northern states such as New York, where Martin Van Buren and the Albany Regency were actively promoting his candidacy. Crawford was also expected to be the choice of the congressional caucus, and for almost twenty-five years nomination by the Republican caucus had proved tantamount to election. Well aware that their candidate's chances of winning caucus approval were hopeless, Calhoun's supporters adopted a strategy of denouncing the caucus system as aristocratic and antirepublican. On 2 December 1823 Fisher introduced a series of resolutions into the North Carolina House of Commons instructing the state's senators and requesting its congressmen to exert themselves to prevent a caucus nomination.

Fisher's resolutions provoked a memorable three-day debate during which both the caucus system and the qualifications of the presidential candidates were thoroughly discussed.[35]

Detractors of the prevailing system claimed that the caucus deprived ordinary voters of their constitutional right to choose the president and vested that power, instead, in a small group of self-appointed electors who were easily susceptible to the intrigues of corrupt political managers. According to Augustine H. Shepperd, a member from Stokes County, the caucus system had turned the election of the chief executive into "a mere matter of bargain and sale, by unauthorized individuals at Washington City." John Stanly, the Federalist member from New Bern, attributed the poor turnout at the two previous presidential elections to the deleterious effect of the caucus. The voters had no incentive to participate, said Stanly, "because they know the thing is already settled: Caucus management has usurped their rights."[36]

While the opponents of the caucus appealed to the antiauthoritarian tenets of eighteenth-century republican ideology, the pro-caucus argument addressed itself to the exigencies of nineteenth-century party politics. Defenders of the caucus accepted the reality of partisan conflict, and they justified the institution as a time-honored mechanism for promoting harmony within the majority party. As Thomas W. Blackledge of Beaufort County put it, the congressional caucus was "the only means of producing unanimity of sentiment and concert in action, among the Republicans." Without some formal means of nomination, the election of the president might well devolve upon the House of Representatives, where there would be far greater danger of intrigue and manipulation than in a congressional caucus. Even worse, the destruction of the caucus system might pave the way for "an incestuous union between the Federalists and discontented or deluded Republicans." According to Blackledge, this was the real motive behind the attacks on the caucus. In his opinion, Fisher was cynically appealing to long-standing Federalist prejudice against the congressional caucus "in order that, by uniting that party with a fragment of *soi di[s]ant* republicans, he may array a force sufficient to countervail the strength of the republican party" and "to elevate Calhoun to the presidency."[37]

These accusations were not entirely unfounded. The propriety of the congressional caucus had long been a bone of contention between

Federalists and Republicans in North Carolina.[38] Although the Federalist anticaucus argument was couched in the language of republican ideology, the party's antipathy toward the congressional caucus was more a product of practical politics than of ideology. Indeed, during the campaign of 1800 the Federalists themselves had been the first to use the congressional caucus, and the first attacks against it had come from Republicans who were unaware that their own congressional leaders had met secretly in Philadelphia to choose Aaron Burr as the party's vice-presidential candidate. The Republicans continued to employ the congressional caucus after 1800 because they found it to be a reasonably effective mechanism for unifying the party behind a single slate of candidates. The Federalists, on the other hand, quickly abandoned the caucus because their numbers in Congress became too small for such an institution to be truly representative of party opinion.[39]

Although the purpose of the congressional caucus was to promote party unity, disaffected elements within the Republican party frequently found it a convenient scapegoat for their own frustrated ambitions. In 1808, for example, supporters of both George Clinton and James Monroe denied the legitimacy of the caucus that had nominated James Madison for the presidency. Indeed, "all of the anticaucus arguments destined to gain wide currency in 1824 were enunciated at that time."[40] In 1812 dissident Republicans supporting the candidacy of De Witt Clinton again rejected the authority of the caucus and adopted an address to the voters that formally set forth their objections to that system of nomination.[41]

These anticaucus Republicans were not averse to seeking Federalist support. The promoters of both Monroe and George Clinton made overtures to the Federalists in 1808.[42] Four years later De Witt Clinton successfully solicited the support of antiwar Federalists, who refrained from nominating a presidential candidate of their own. With considerable justification Republicans loyal to President Madison claimed that Clinton was the candidate of a "coalition" of Federalists and dissident Republicans.[43] The Missouri crisis of 1819–21 reinforced the apprehensions of southern Republicans. To the consternation of southerners in Congress, a majority of northern congressmen from both parties steadfastly opposed the admission of Missouri into the Union as a slave state. Well aware of the role that prominent Federalists like Rufus King were playing in marshaling the opposition forces in Congress, southern Republicans believed that the Federalists were using the controversy as a wedge to split the Republican party along sectional lines in the hope of building a new antislavery party with the northern Republicans.[44] The passage of a series of compromise bills in 1821 resolved the dispute over Missouri but did not dispel fears of an alliance between Federalists and disgruntled Republicans.[44]

From the perspective of 1823 it was not unreasonable for North Carolina Republicans to regard the Fisher resolutions as yet another attempt to promote such an alliance. Although not a Federalist himself, Fisher represented one of the most solidly Federalist counties in the state, and his two ablest lieutenants in the debate were the Federalists John Stanly and James Iredell, Jr. The Federalist party had not competed in North Carolina elections since 1816, but suspicious Republicans like Blackledge were certain that its leaders were merely waiting for an opportune moment to reassert themselves. "The distinction . . . between the parties exists now, as broadly and distinctly as it did in 1800, or 1810," Blackledge warned his Republican colleagues in the house of commons. "For the present, the federalists have retired from the contest as hopeless; but . . . they have been beaten and not destroyed, overcome but not annihilated." For their part, Federalist leaders like Stanly and Iredell made no apologies for their earlier partisan proclivities. When Stanly proudly attested on the floor of the house of commons that "I thank God, I can say I am still a Federalist," he was articulating a sentiment that was undoubtedly shared by many others in his party.[45]

The alignment of votes on Fisher's anticaucus resolutions revealed that opposition to Crawford and the congressional caucus did indeed come primarily from legislators representing the Federalist counties and boroughs (see table 1.1). Whereas 70 percent of the commoners from Federalist constituencies supported Fisher's resolutions, 84 percent of the legislators from Republican constituencies opposed them. The solid Republican phalanx was broken only by the mountain delegation, where seven of the eleven members joined the Federalists in opposing the indefinite postponement of the resolutions.[46] The 82-to-46 vote in favor of postponement effectively killed the resolutions, but the vote underscored the potential for a successful coalition of Federalists and dissident Republicans organized around opposition to the congressional caucus.

Table 1.1 Alignment in the House of Commons on Fisher's Resolutions, 1823 (by percentage)

	Procaucus	Anticaucus
Legislators representing Federalist counties and boroughs (N = 47)	30	70
Legislators representing Republican counties and boroughs		
Albemarle (N = 22)	100	0
Middle east (N = 31)	90	10
Piedmont (N = 17)	82	18
Mountain (N = 11)	36	64
Total Republicans (N = 81)	84	16
Total legislators (N = 128)	64	36

Source: A. R. Newsome, ed., "Debate on the Fisher Resolutions," 325. For classification of Federalist and Republican counties, see Appendix.

The selection of rival electoral slates began less than two weeks after the defeat of Fisher's resolutions. On 24 December 1823 a caucus of about one hundred Republican legislators met in the chamber of the North Carolina State Senate, formed a ticket of fifteen Crawford electors, and established a central committee to direct the campaign. The selection of an anti-Crawford ticket began on 8 January 1824, when a public meeting in Beaufort County nominated William A. Blount as an elector on the "People's ticket." Although its promoters solicited the votes of all those opposed to the "caucus candidate," the movement was controlled by Charles Fisher and others sympathetic to the candidacy of Calhoun.[47]

By early February, however, it had already become clear that the success of the People's ticket was being jeopardized by the desire of many of Andrew Jackson's supporters to form their own electoral slate. The most influential Jacksonian in North Carolina was William Polk, a Federalist planter and businessman who had twice been a candidate for governor. Polk was a personal friend of William B. Lewis, one of Old Hickory's closest advisers. While visiting Lewis during the summer of 1823, he had seen a letter written by Jackson in 1816 that urged President-elect James Monroe to appoint two distinguished Federalists to his cabinet. Lewis assured Polk that Old Hickory was "disposed to reward merit wherever to be found" and would not "proscribe and persecute the Federalists because they differ with him in opinion." Jackson's nonpartisan stance attracted the support not only of Polk but also of other prominent Federalists in North Carolina and elsewhere throughout the nation.[48] A probable collision between the supporters of Jackson and Calhoun was averted when the South Carolinian withdrew from the presidential race early in March to run unopposed for the vice presidency. Polk and the other Jackson leaders quickly became reconciled to the People's ticket, and by the time of the election all but two of the People's electors had publicly pledged themselves to support Old Hickory.[49]

The presidential election of 1824 has frequently been portrayed as a contest of personalities, devoid of substantive issues. In North Carolina, however, the supporters of the two presidential contestants succeeded in raising the campaign above the level of personalities to encompass important issues relating to the survival of republican government. Throughout the campaign the supporters of the People's ticket repeatedly emphasized the threat that the caucus allegedly presented to the republican system of government. The editor of the *Salisbury Western Carolinian* announced that "the very existence of our republican government . . . depends upon the success or the failure of the present struggle of the people against the schemes and machinations of a caucusing, aristocratic combination of politicians in our country." The editor of the *Raleigh Star* agreed that "if we do not, at once, put an end to this usurpation . . . our government might still bear the *name* of a Republic; but the name would be all we could boast of." The voters should, accordingly, support Andrew Jackson as the candidate "most likely to unite the greatest number in opposition to the dangerous and aristocratical practice of *caucusing*." In a similar vein the editor of the *Fayetteville Observer* urged supporters of presidential candidate John Quincy Adams to remember that "our first object is to defeat the caucus usurpations. Our second to elect the man of our choice. If Jackson is chosen, we gain the first, and by far the most important of our objects."[50]

The supporters of Crawford also claimed that the fate of the Republic depended on the election of their candidate. They extolled the Georgian as a defender of "all those principles, which Jefferson has recommended and the people have sanctioned by their adoption and approval" and emphasized his commitment to an economical administration of the government. "The permanency of our Republican Institutions . . . require[s] that the spirit of prodigality and patronage in the General Government should be checked," the official Crawford address admonished the voters. As president, Crawford would oppose protective tariffs and federally supported internal improvements, along with "such other splendid schemes as are becoming the fashionable hobbies of the day."[51] Crawford's supporters also claimed that their candidate was the only reliable defender of the interests of the South. In an obvious reference to the recently settled Missouri controversy, the editor of the *Raleigh Register* urged those who wished "security against 'restrictions' on the states, whether as regards slavery or any thing else" to support Crawford as the southern candidate.[52]

On 11 November 1824 slightly more than 36,000 North Carolinians went to the polls. The People's ticket carried forty-two of the sixty-three counties and captured almost 57 percent of the vote (see map 2). The ticket scored majorities in all but four of the twenty-three Federalist counties, in all but two of the eleven counties bordering Albemarle Sound, and in all but one of the six counties in the far west. Crawford, on the other hand, did best in the Republican counties of the middle east and the northern piedmont, carrying two-thirds of the former and half of the latter (see table 1.2). Considering the unanimity with which the Republican leaders in North Carolina had supported Crawford, the ability of the People's ticket to poll ma-

Table 1.2   The Vote for President, 1824 (by percentage)

	Jackson	Crawford
Federalist counties	67 (19 counties)	33 (4 counties)
Republican counties		
Albemarle	68 (9 counties)	32 (2 counties)
Middle east	42 (5 counties)	58 (10 counties)
Piedmont	44 (4 counties)	56 (4 counties)
Mountain	75 (5 counties)	25 (1 county)
Total	51 (23 counties)	49 (17 counties)
All counties	57 (42 counties)	43 (21 counties)

Source: Albert R. Newsome, *The Presidential Election of 1824 in North Carolina*, 156.
For classification of Federalist and Republican counties, see Appendix.
Note: Percentages indicate each party's share of the total two-party vote.

Map 2   The Election of 1824 in North Carolina

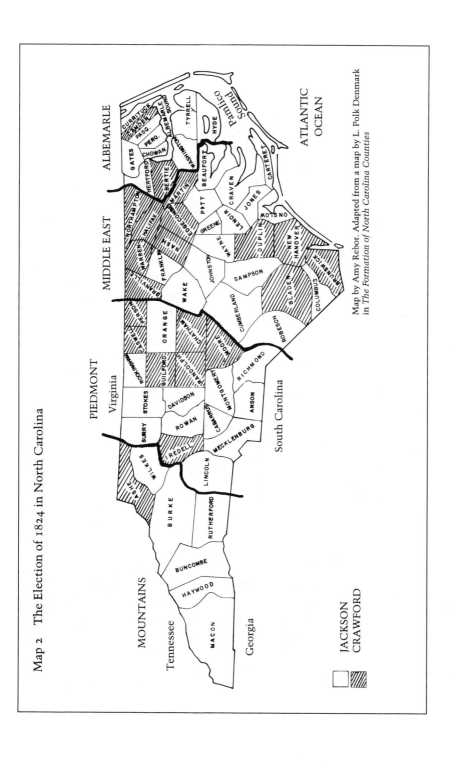

Map by Amy Rebor. Adapted from a map by L. Polk Denmark in *The Formation of North Carolina Counties*

jorities in two-thirds of the counties was nothing short of remarkable.[53]

An examination of the political antecedents of the strongest Crawford and Jackson counties provides support for the argument that the victorious Jackson coalition of 1824 was the product of an alliance between Federalists and antiestablishment Republicans. None of the seven counties where Crawford won more than 75 percent of the vote had been Federalist in political orientation, and only one of the thirteen counties that gave him over 60 percent of the vote had polled Federalist majorities during the first party system. On the other hand, Federalists comprised the majority in eight of the eighteen counties where the People's ticket polled over 75 percent of the vote. Of the ten non-Federalist counties that gave over 75 percent of their vote to Jackson, four were located in the far west, and the other six lay in the extreme northeastern part of the state. Significantly, only two of the eighteen strongest Jackson counties (both Federalist) were situated in the plantation-oriented middle east or in the to-bacco-growing counties along the Virginia border, whereas nine of the thirteen strongest Crawford counties were located in these regions.[54]

As a manifestation of disaffection within the Republican party, the Jackson coalition of 1824 can best be viewed as an alliance of the two extremes of North Carolina against the center. Both geographically and politically, the residents of the mountain and Albemarle regions were far removed from the centers of power in Raleigh. Since the adoption of the state constitution in 1776, a disproportionate number of the important state offices had been controlled by politicians residing in a handful of counties near the capital city. Effectively cut off from the centers of decision making, the voters in the extreme east and the far west were particularly susceptible to the appeals of the anticaucus crusaders against a system that favored political insiders at the expense of those on the fringes of power.[55]

Economic stagnation resulting from the lack of adequate transportation facilities reinforced the sense of political isolation among the residents of these remote counties. It is not surprising that local leaders there had proven far more willing than their counterparts in the wealthier plantation districts to support a policy of federal aid to internal improvements. In 1816 the congressmen from the mountain and Albemarle regions had voted against a majority of their colleagues in favor of Calhoun's bonus bill, which provided for the establishment of a permanent fund for internal improvements, and in 1824 the representative from the mountain district had supported Calhoun's general survey bill. Since 1815 local leaders in the Albemarle region had also been pushing hard for a federal survey to determine the practicality of cutting an inlet through the chain of sandbars that separated the counties along Albemarle Sound from the Atlantic Ocean.[56]

The internal improvements issue undoubtedly played a role in lining up support for the People's ticket in the underdeveloped counties of the extreme east and the far west. Crawford's supporters made no pretense that their candidate was sympathetic to the expenditure of federal funds on roads, canals, and inlets. On the other hand, Calhoun, the original candidate of the People's party, had built his reputation largely upon his advocacy of federally assisted internal improvements. Jackson's views were more problematic, and his supporters did not stress the issue during the campaign of 1824. But Old Hickory had voted in favor of the general survey bill, and his vote had been criticized by some of North Carolina's pro-Crawford congressmen. These attacks undoubtedly bolstered the image of Jackson as a supporter of internal improvements. It would be an exaggeration to claim that the improvements issue was the deciding factor in the election, but certainly it had the effect of reinforcing opposition to the governing establishment and its presidential favorite.[57]

The extent to which Jackson's personal popularity affected the outcome of the presidential election in North Carolina is a question that cannot be answered conclusively. Both the supporters and the detractors of Old Hickory readily acknowledged his appeal "among the more common and illiterate class of the community." Enemies of Jackson also complained that the general's popularity among militiamen in the western counties gave him an unfair advantage over Crawford. According to Robert Williamson, the Crawford elector from Lincoln County, "in almost every Captain's company the drums were beating and fifes whistling for the hero of New Orleans. The officers would treat their men, make them drunk, and then raise the war whoop for General Jackson." The supporters of Old Hickory were also more adept than their opponents at using mass meetings to stir up popular support for their candidate. "From Orange [County] inclusive to the Mountains," one observer noted, "there were meetings upon meetings of people at Law-days & Company musters, for the purpose of giving an expression of opinion on the subject of the next President; & General Jackson is always the man."[58]

There is other evidence, however, that casts doubt upon the traditional picture of the election of 1824 as a spontaneous outburst of popular enthusiasm for the Hero of New Orleans. For one thing, a majority of ordinary North Carolinians did not vote for Jackson—or for any other presidential contender—in 1824. Only 23 percent of the eligible voters cast their ballots for the People's ticket (compared to 17 percent for Crawford), and an indeterminate number of these voters preferred Calhoun or Adams to Jackson.[59] Equally important, recent scholarship has revealed that the sources of Jackson's appeal went considerably beyond his military reputation and his engaging personality. Throughout the campaign Jackson and his leading supporters lashed out vigorously against the malfeasance and corruption that supposedly prevailed in the highest echelons of Congress and the Monroe administration. The Letters of Wyoming, which were written as newspaper articles by John H. Eaton and later circulated widely in pamphlet form, provided a detailed exposé of the rampant corruption within the federal government. Unlike the other presidential contenders, who were either members of Monroe's cabinet, veteran congressmen, or both, Jackson had spent most of his career outside of Washington and thus stood "aloof from all the contemptible intrigue and management of the day."[60]

Like the crusade against the congressional caucus, Jackson's attacks upon government corruption found a particularly susceptible audience among ambitious politicians outside the ruling establishment. For their part, these political outsiders did not hesitate to call upon the voters to repudiate the authority of the established leaders. As Eaton remarked to William Polk, "heretofore in this Country the politicians & caucus and leading men, as they are termed, have ruled the affairs of this Country . . . the people for once are disposed to throw off the allegiance which the Leading men claim of them and to exercise for themselves rights which belong to them."[61]

Ironically, the Jackson coalition of 1824 bore more than a passing resemblance to the anti-Jackson party that rose to power in North Carolina during the 1830s. With but three exceptions the eighteen strongest Jackson counties of 1824 would provide the Whigs with large majorities a decade later. The gradual estrangement of the "original Jackson men" during the course of Old Hickory's administration is a phenomenon that historians of North Carolina parties have not explained satisfactorily.[62] A closer examination of political developments after 1824 reveals that the movement of Crawford's supporters into the Jackson coalition, and their victory in the ensuing struggle for power within the Jackson administration proved to be the most important factors in driving the president's earliest supporters out of his party.

The election of John Quincy Adams by the House of Representatives in January 1825 practically guaranteed that the Jacksonians would oppose the new administration. Old Hickory, who had received a plurality of the electoral votes, claimed that he had been cheated out of the presidency by a "corrupt bargain" between Adams and Henry Clay, and his supporters in Congress were quick to organize an antiadministration faction.[63] The friends of Crawford, on the other hand, did not immediately rush to join the opposition. Like Bartlett Yancy, most of Crawford's supporters initially believed that the most appropriate course of action would be to "attach ourselves to neither party—stand aloof—look on & see the prospect before us."[64]

Long before the end of Adams's term, however, the Crawfordites had turned decisively against the president. Committed as they were to economy in government and a strict construction of the Constitution, Crawford's supporters were thoroughly alarmed by the president's first annual message of December 1825, which called for a national program of internal improvements, a national university, and an astronomical observatory. Nathaniel Macon complained that the message "seems to claim all the power to the federal Government, which has heretofore produced so much debate, and which the election of Mr. Jefferson was supposed to have settled."[65] Conservatives like Macon were well aware that a latitudinarian construction of the Constitution could also be used to justify an attack upon slavery. Their concern about the safety of the South's peculiar institution undoubtedly accounted for much of their hostility toward Adams. By the spring of 1826 Congressman Willie P. Mangum was predicting that southerners of all political persuasions "will unite to put down Adams, & if they can get no better, they will take up Gen. Jackson for that purpose."[66]

At the national level, Martin Van Buren played a pivotal role in rallying Crawford's supporters behind Andrew Jackson. The New

York politician kept in close touch with Crawford's friends in North Carolina and nursed their grievances against the Adams administration. On 29 April 1827 Van Buren arrived in Raleigh after a trip to Georgia where he had conversed with Crawford himself. He remained in the City of Oaks for three days as a guest of Governor Hutchins G. Burton. Although there is no record of Van Buren's activities during his stay in Raleigh, the Little Magician undoubtedly facilitated the movement of the North Carolina Crawford men into the Jackson party.[67]

With most of the Jackson and Crawford men united against his reelection, the prospects for Adams carrying North Carolina in 1828 seemed bleak. Yet the president was not bereft of influential backers in the Old North State. By 1828 a few prominent Crawfordites like Lewis Williams and Joseph Gales had become active supporters of the administration. For editorial support Adams could count on Gales's *Raleigh Register*, as well as on other influential newspapers like the *Hillsborough Recorder* and the *New Bern Spectator*. Moreover, a sizable number of Federalist leaders, including former congressmen William Gaston, John Culpepper, and William Davidson, also lined up behind the president. On 20 December 1827 fifty-five of Adams's supporters assembled in Raleigh to nominate a slate of presidential electors and to appoint a central committee to coordinate the campaign.[68]

Four days after the meeting of the Adams convention, Andrew Jackson's supporters assembled at the county courthouse in Raleigh to nominate Jackson and Calhoun and to appoint their own central committee. The composition of the committee revealed that the Federalists and other original Jackson men continued to play the dominant role in the leadership of the Jackson party. Indeed, only one of the fourteen members had supported Crawford in 1824.[69]

The alliance between the two wings of the Jackson party was an uneasy one, and the Adams men tried hard to foment discord. Reminding the original Jackson men of the calumnies heaped upon their candidate by the Crawfordites in 1824, the editor of the *New Bern Spectator* claimed that Jackson's old enemies were now rallying to his support not because they honestly admired his talents but "because they believe he may be instrumental in promoting their views of office, and in gratifying their feelings of restless malignity." Whatever principles he may have stood for in 1824, Old Hickory was now merely "the puppet of . . . the master-spirits who make use of his name . . . to subserve their own personal aggrandizement." Few Jacksonians apparently paid attention to these charges in 1828, but the belief that he had fallen under the control of his former enemies would eventually drive many of Jackson's early supporters out of his party.[70]

In North Carolina, as elsewhere throughout the South, the election of 1828 resulted in a stunning victory for Andrew Jackson. He carried fifty-five of the state's sixty-three counties, winning all but four of the twenty-one that had voted against him in 1824. Adams received only 27 percent of the vote. One of the most curious features of the election was the dramatic increase in voter turnout. Despite the one-sided nature of the outcome, the total number of voters increased by almost 44 percent from the previous presidential election. Most of these new voters apparently supported President Adams, for the surge in participation was largest in the counties where Adams ran best. The increase amounted to almost 84 percent in the eight counties carried by Adams and almost 53 percent in the eighteen other counties where his percentage of the vote exceeded his statewide average. Six of the eight Adams counties had been Federalist strongholds a decade earlier, and in eleven of the seventeen other Federalist counties Adams's share of the vote was greater than his statewide average. Many Federalists who sat out the election in 1824 apparently took advantage of Adams's candidacy to reenter the political arena.[71]

The victorious Jackson coalition of 1828 was not so much a political party as an alliance of convenience, comprising a diverse group of politicians who had little in common except their distaste for the Adams administration. Federalists and Republicans, original Jackson men and Crawfordites, idealistic progressives like Archibald D. Murphey and hidebound conservatives like Nathaniel Macon, all found themselves together within the ranks of the Jacksonians. Hostility toward President Adams and the latitudinarian tendencies of his administration had thus far kept the coalition together, but it remained to be seen whether Old Hickory possessed the political dexterity to harmonize the disparate groups within his following.

Certainly the Federalists who had supported Jackson in 1824 and 1828 had no reason to complain about their treatment by the new administration. Unlike most of his Republican predecessors, Jackson had no compunction about appointing Federalists to federal offices, as long as they professed personal loyalty to him.[72] Ambitious Federalists also found that they could use their connection with Jackson as a springboard to other offices that would have been unattainable under the older system of politics. The career of James Iredell, Jr., of Chowan County is an excellent case in point. The son of a prominent North Carolina Federalist, Iredell began his political career in 1813 as a member of the house of commons from the borough of Edenton. As a leader of the anticaucus faction in the legislature of 1823, Iredell gained notoriety as one of the most outspoken supporters of Jackson and Calhoun. In 1827 he garnered enough support among his colleagues in the general assembly to win election as governor. A year later the legislature elevated him to the U.S. Senate.[73]

If Iredell typified the heights to which a Federalist politician could rise under the Jackson administration, he also exemplified the disillusionment that many Federalists and other original Jackson men came to experience before the end of Old Hickory's first term. By early 1832 Iredell was clearly disturbed by the growing influence of Martin Van Buren within the administration.[74] A close friend of John C. Calhoun, Iredell—like many of Jackson's early supporters—considered himself as loyal to Calhoun as to the president. The South Carolinian had been reelected to the vice presidency in 1828 as Jackson's running mate, and his supporters had every reason to believe that they would play a dominant role in the new administration. Yet, within a year after the election, policy differences over the tariff and the Bank of the United States, along with Jackson's belief that Calhoun was responsible for the unwillingness of some cabinet members to socialize with Peggy Eaton (the wife of his close friend and cabinet member John Eaton), had driven the two men far apart. As the vice president's stock in the Jackson administration declined, the influence of Secretary of State Van Buren grew proportionately. In April 1831 the turmoil within the Jackson administration culminated in the resignation of the entire cabinet. Although recent scholarship has cast doubt upon the notion that Van Buren was the precipitator of the cabinet dissolution, even those Democrats friendly to the New Yorker regarded the mass resignations as "a master stroke of policy" by which Van Buren had purged the administration of Calhoun's leading supporters.[75]

Among those ousted in the cabinet shakeup was Secretary of the

Navy John Branch, one of Jackson's earliest supporters in North Carolina. Branch was embittered by his forced resignation, and shortly after his return to North Carolina he issued a public letter attributing his misfortune to a "malign influence" surrounding the president. Branch went on to complain that Old Hickory was "gradually discarding from his counsels and friendship his old and long tried supporters, and throwing himself into the arms of persons whose cold hearted selfishness and artifices were played off upon him for *true* and faithful service." A few months later Branch published several other letters that specifically named Van Buren as the source of the "malign influence." According to Branch, this artful manipulator had somehow managed to make himself "the almost sole confidant and adviser of the President" and was now doing everything in his power "to drive from the Administration most of its old and long tried supporters."[76]

Branch was not the first North Carolinian to claim that Jackson was surrounded by a malign influence or that Van Buren was the guiding force behind that baneful influence. The Adams men had made similar charges during the campaign of 1828, but now for the first time this theme was being sounded by a leading supporter of the president. Moreover, it quickly became apparent that Branch was voicing the sentiments of many other original Jackson men, who were becoming increasingly concerned about Van Buren's influence over the president. From their viewpoint, the New Yorker seemed to personify the corrupt political manipulator who relied upon intrigue and management to promote his political fortunes. According to the editor of the *Western Carolinian*, Van Buren was "a man, whose whole life has been but one continued string of low and grovelling intrigue." Having failed to crush the Jackson party in 1824 by overt opposition, he was now seeking to destroy it from within by driving out the original Jackson men and "erecting upon its dismembered fragments, a Van Buren party, to be sustained by Caucuses, and the corrupt system of politics which he has been carrying on in New York for the last ten or fifteen years."[77]

Van Buren's nomination for the vice presidency by a national convention at Baltimore in May 1832 split the Jackson party in North Carolina and resulted in the formation of a rival ticket, with Judge Philip P. Barbour of Virginia as Jackson's running mate. The supporters of the Jackson–Van Buren ticket denounced the Barbourites as secret enemies of the president, whose real objective was to promote the disorganizing schemes of Calhoun and the nullifiers.[78] Since 1828 Calhoun and other leading South Carolina politicians had been claiming that each state had the constitutional right to declare a federal law null and void within its borders. Ostensibly aimed against the succession of protective tariffs enacted after 1815, the doctrine of nullification was also designed to protect the institution of slavery against attack by an antislavery majority in Congress. The most prominent proponent of nullification in North Carolina was Charles Fisher, the Salisbury politician who had directed Calhoun's presidential campaign in 1824. Although Fisher, Iredell, and other leading Calhoun supporters did, indeed, rally to the Barbour standard in 1832, the movement also claimed the loyalty of other Jackson men like William Polk, Edward B. Dudley, and Edward J. Hale, who were entirely out of sympathy with the doctrine of nullification. Barbour's supporters denied that they were motivated by hostility to Jackson himself or by a desire to divide his party. If any group could justly be suspected of insincerity in professing friendship to Jackson, they retorted, it was the Van Buren faction, who "in the contest of 1824 . . . not only opposed Gen. Jackson, but were his most virulent and unrelenting revilers and persecutors." Comparing the Baltimore convention with "the attempt which was made by Mr. Crawford's friends to juggle him into the Presidency . . . by caucuses" in 1824, the Barbour men reminded the voters that "this same Van Buren was one of the most active in that attempt."[79]

Despite vigorous efforts by the leaders of the two Jackson factions, fewer than thirty thousand North Carolinians went to the polls in 1832—only 60 percent of the number who voted in 1828. The regular Jackson ticket polled 71 percent of the vote, winning majorities in fifty-four counties and pluralities in two others, whereas the Barbour ticket garnered only 13 percent of the vote and carried only six counties. Henry Clay, the candidate of the National Republicans (as the anti-Jackson men were now calling themselves), won an equally disappointing 16 percent and carried only two counties. The low turnout and the poor showing of the Barbour ticket can be attributed, at least in part, to a last-minute announcement that the Virginian had withdrawn from the race. Many opponents of Van Buren apparently concluded that there was little point in voting and consequently sat out the election.[80]

The election of 1832 revealed the existence of a deep cleavage within the Jackson party in North Carolina. In less than a year after his reelection, Old Hickory's forceful response to South Carolina's attempt to nullify the protective tariff and his removal of the federal deposits from the Bank of the United States would complete the estrangement of the original Jackson men from the Democratic party. The events of the nullification crisis and the bank war have been frequently recounted, and recent scholarship has confirmed the notion that Jackson remained at the center of decision making throughout both controversies. Although he relied heavily at times on the advice of trusted counselors like Van Buren, Amos Kendall, and Francis P. Blair, "the president himself remained the hub of activity and generally initiated policy."[81]

From the viewpoint of the original Jackson men, however, the controversial policies of Old Hickory's second administration appeared to be fateful manifestations of "the errors into which he has been led by the artifice of the designing men who have wormed themselves into his affection and confidence." Skilled in the arts of flattery, management, and intrigue, this corrupt band of office seekers was manipulating the overly trusting president just as they had earlier managed the congressional caucus. At their behest Jackson had "banished from his councils all his old friends" and had replaced them with "those who opposed him until they discovered that he would have *rewards* at his disposal." The triumph of 1824 had proven illusory, and the real friends of Jackson had found themselves "read out of the Republican church, and their caucus opponents, by some species of magic, snugly seated in their places."[82]

For some erstwhile Jacksonians like Charles Fisher, the president's proclamation to the people of South Carolina in December 1832 and his force bill message a month later provided the occasion for a formal break with the administration. But instead of offering an opportunity for the creation of a mass-based opposition party, the nullification controversy divided the opponents of Jackson and temporarily enhanced the president's popularity in the Old North State. Although few Tarheels had any sympathy for the protective tariff, fewer still were willing to countenance a doctrine that threatened to sacrifice the Union in order to reduce the tariff. The minority position of the nullifiers became vividly apparent in December 1832, when the general assembly overwhelmingly approved a resolution denouncing the South Carolina doctrine as "revolutionary in its character" and "subversive of the constitution of the United States."[83]

Jackson's war against the Second Bank of the United States proved far more effective as a stimulus for the creation of an opposition party in North Carolina. In July 1832 he vetoed a bill that would have extended the bank's charter for another twenty years. The veto message, which was directed as much to the voters as to Congress, was an artfully constructed appeal to popular prejudice against banks and other chartered corporations. Ever since the Panic of 1819, when the banks in North Carolina had suspended their specie payments and less sound institutions in other states had closed their doors, public distrust of banks and bankers had run high. Between 1819 and 1832 the State Bank of North Carolina was almost continuously under attack from radicals who wanted to destroy the bank and imprison its officials, as well as from more moderate reformers who wished to replace it with another institution more susceptible to popular control. Jackson's antibank rhetoric thus struck a responsive chord among many elements within the North Carolina electorate, and except for the small coterie of National Republicans, few politicians criticized the president publicly for his stand against the "monster bank."[84]

Jackson's decision during the summer of 1833 to remove the federal deposits from the Bank of the United States proved to be another matter entirely. Almost as soon as it was announced, the policy was denounced not only by the National Republicans but also by many in the president's own party. His critics argued that the president had usurped a power that constitutionally belonged to Congress. By his extraordinary and unwarranted assumption of power over the public money, Jackson had set a dangerous precedent that threatened to transform the government from a republic to a despotism. "Whenever the purse and the sword shall become united in the same hands," warned Congressman Abraham Rencher, "and the people shall acquiesce in such a union, the days of American liberty are numbered."[85]

The National Republicans were angered, but probably not surprised, by the removal of the deposits. In their eyes, Old Hickory had always been a violent and impetuous man, "impatient of the wholesome restraints imposed by the Constitution," and the removal policy merely provided additional evidence of his lawless tendencies. On the other hand, those in Jackson's own party who condemned the removals were reluctant to concede that the Hero of New Orleans was by nature lawless or despotic. Like the editor of the *Raleigh Star*, they were more inclined to interpret the removal of the deposits as the misguided policy of a "confiding . . . honest and unsuspecting Chief . . . influenced by an irresponsible, ambitious, and designing cabal."[86]

The original Jackson men had no doubt that Martin Van Buren was the real architect of the removal policy. According to Congressman Rencher, the removal was a New York measure "brought about by the intrigues of the friends of Mr. Van Buren" and calculated to aggrandize the state banks of New York at the expense of the rest of the nation. Although personally innocent of impure motives or ambitious designs, the president had been "misled, fatally misled, by the ambitious and designing intriguers by whom, unfortunately, he is surrounded." It thus became the duty of true republicans to oppose these misguided policies, even if it meant opposing the president himself.[87]

Opponents of removal worked quickly to mobilize public opinion against the administration. On 26 December 1833 Henry Clay introduced a resolution into the U.S. Senate that censured Jackson for assuming authority and power not conferred by the Constitution. After three months of debate, the censure resolution was approved by a vote of twenty-six to twenty. Even before the final vote had been taken, antiadministration leaders in the Old North State had begun organizing public meetings to petition Congress to restore the deposits. The meetings provided the first formal occasion for the National Republicans and the antiremoval Democrats to act together politically, and their resolutions usually praised the conduct of Senator Willie P. Mangum, who had broken with the administration over this issue. By the end of March the editor of the *Raleigh Star* was apologizing to his readers that "such meetings are becoming so numerous that . . . we are therefore compelled to give them only a summary notice."[88]

Senator Mangum, meanwhile, was receiving numerous letters from his political allies, all claiming to discern a remarkable change of opinion among the followers of Jackson. Edward B. Dudley, who had been a Jackson elector in 1824 and 1828, told Mangum that "our

State is undergoing considerable change—General Jackson's tyranny & folly has alarmed & disgusted many of his old friends—among the intelligent part of the Community a Jacksonian is a *rare bird.*" Opponents of removal also pointed out that the controversy was attracting the attention of many voters who had not previously paid much attention to national politics. Spencer O'Brien, a Mangum ally from Granville County, told the senator that "we have never, before this time, felt the same interest, in the deliberation of Congress, as we [do] now. Men, who have, heretofore been indifferent or, rather, passive lookers on, in the great drama, are now beginning to inquire for themselves!" Like the Jay Treaty a generation earlier, the deposits controversy provided political organizers on both sides with an opportunity to reach out to the electorate and build grass-roots support.[89]

As early as February 1833 a few of Jackson's opponents in North Carolina were already calling themselves "Whigs."[90] However, it was not until after the furor over the deposits that the word "Whig" came to be widely used in the Old North State and throughout the nation to describe the disparate group of politicians who opposed the policies of Andrew Jackson. Supporters and opponents of President Jackson regarded the legislative elections of August 1834 as a test of strength between the contending factions. Senator Bedford Brown, who had remained loyal to Old Hickory, would be a candidate for reelection by the general assembly, and the Whigs were determined to replace Brown with an antiadministration senator. At the same time the Jacksonians were resolved not only to reelect Brown but to pass resolutions of instruction that would force Mangum to resign his seat. During the spring and early summer the leaders of both factions organized public meetings, which passed resolutions praising the conduct of one senator and denouncing the course of the other.[91]

In previous legislative elections local issues had overshadowed all other questions, but in 1834 the elections turned primarily on national issues. While acknowledging that local questions had influenced the outcome of some of the contests, the editor of the *Fayetteville Observer* pointed out that at no time "since the war, have [national] politics entered so much into our State Elections. It is perfectly notorious, that for many years, the people have not been so roused, as they are at present."[92] Each side claimed victory. Jacksonian newspapers estimated the administration majority to be somewhere between fifteen and fifty-four on joint ballot, whereas the Whig presses claimed a majority of at least fifteen, and perhaps as many as thirty seats.[93] The conflicting estimates revealed that the balance of power would lie with the minority of legislators who did not clearly identify with either faction during the campaign.

Three days after the general assembly convened on 17 November 1834, Senator Brown was reelected by a vote of 113 to 60. A week later Dr. John Potts, a Democrat from Edgecombe County, introduced resolutions instructing Brown and Mangum to vote for the expunging of Clay's censure resolutions. The Potts resolutions provoked a lengthy debate that occupied the attention of the legislators for an entire month. Not since the debate over Fisher's anticaucus resolutions a decade earlier had national politics so completely dominated the deliberations of the general assembly. On 11 December the house of commons passed the instruction resolutions by a vote of 69 to 57. Two weeks later the state senate approved them by a margin of 33 to 28. The alignment of votes in the house of commons revealed that antiadministration sentiment was strongest among legislators from the Federalist constituencies, the Albemarle Sound counties, and the mountain region—the three blocs that had been the strongest in their support for Old Hickory in 1824 (see table 1.3).[94]

Mangum's supporters advised him not to obey the instructions and not to resign his seat in the U.S. Senate. Even before the senator's return from Washington they began organizing public meetings that denounced the instruction resolutions and urged Mangum to pay no regard to them. In March 1835 the Whigs commenced preparations for a large subscription dinner in Mangum's honor at Raleigh. Party leaders in Salisbury, Fayetteville, Charlotte, and other towns also promoted public dinners or other large celebrations that Mangum was invited to attend.[95]

While Mangum's friends were honoring him with dinners and Fourth of July celebrations, Democrats and Whigs were campaigning hard for the August legislative elections. In May 1835 a Democratic convention in Baltimore had officially designated Martin Van Buren as Jackson's successor. Meanwhile, the Whigs in North Carolina and other southern states were lining up behind Senator Hugh Lawson White of Tennessee. The respective merits of the two presidential contenders were extensively discussed during the campaign, and the editors of the party presses classified the legislative candidates as "Van Buren men" or "White men," according to their presidential

Table 1.3   Alignment in the House of Commons on the Expunging
Resolutions, 1834 (by percentage)

	Pro-Jackson	Anti-Jackson
Legislators representing Federalist counties and boroughs $(N = 43)$	33	67
Legislators representing Republican counties and boroughs		
Albemarle $(N = 19)$	42	58
Middle east $(N = 32)$	78	22
Piedmont $(N = 16)$	81	19
Mountains $(N = 16)$	56	44
Legislators representing eastern counties $(N = 75)$	57	43
Legislators representing western counties $(N = 51)$	51	49
All legislators $(N = 126)$	55	45

Source: HJ, 1834–35, 189. For classification of Federalist and Republican counties, see Appendix. For the definition of "east" and "west," see note 51.

preference. As in 1834, both parties initially claimed victory, although by early September the Whigs conceded that the administration party would hold a small majority on joint ballot. The Whig editors attributed their party's defeat to the fact that many of the Democratic candidates had dodged the issue of the presidential succession and, instead, had taken shelter "under the wing of Gen Jackson."[96] Looking forward to the upcoming presidential campaign, the Whigs could take comfort in the knowledge that the name of Andrew Jackson would no longer be at the head of the Democratic ticket.

In North Carolina, as in the other states of the South, the early 1830s witnessed the rapid development of organized parties and a popular movement away from the party of Andrew Jackson. Historians have frequently attributed the rise of the Whig party in the South to the emergence of Martin Van Buren as Jackson's heir apparent. According to this interpretation, Van Buren's northern residence and his suspect views about slavery alienated important southern Democrats and ultimately drove them into the opposition.[97] There is certainly some validity to this argument. After 1834 most southern

Whigs refrained from criticizing Jackson personally, focusing their attacks instead on his hand-picked successor. And the enemies of Van Buren persistently denounced him as an unreliable defender of the South's peculiar institution. Nevertheless, the evidence for North Carolina does not support the conclusion that southern sectionalism was the driving force behind opposition to Van Buren. Popular support for the Whig party did not center in the counties with the most tangible interest in the preservation of slavery, but rather in the underdeveloped counties in the extreme eastern and western parts of the state and in Federalist counties throughout North Carolina.

For the voters in these counties, Van Buren was more than a symbol of northern antislavery. He was the principal exponent of the caucus system that had enabled a few men to control the politics of the Old North State and the entire nation until 1824. Once they realized that Van Buren and the other leading caucus supporters had become the dominant faction in the administration party, many of Jackson's earliest supporters abandoned his party and joined the National Republicans to form a new political coalition. Although the removal of the deposits provided the occasion for the formal break in 1834, that controversy was more a product than a cause of the split within the administration party. Indeed, the origins of the schism can be traced to the cabinet purge of April 1831, when it became clear that Van Buren's faction had won control of the Jackson party.

The importance of the deposits controversy lay in its impact on the ideological development of the two parties. It would not be an exaggeration to say that the basic character of both parties was shaped during the bank war of 1832–34. Jackson's veto message, with its appeal to long-standing popular prejudice against banks and paper money, signaled the onset of the Democrats' crusade against the financial aristocracy of bankers and speculators—symbolized by the Bank of the United States. For the Whigs, Jackson's unprecedented assertion of authority over the public revenues provided striking evidence of the extent to which the chief executive had succumbed to the machinations of the corrupt political managers by whom he was surrounded. In their attacks on the dictatorial policies of an overbearing chief executive and his coterie of sycophantic advisers, the Whigs were tapping the same vein of antiauthoritarianism that many of them had mined a decade earlier during the crusade against the congressional caucus.

The successive contests for the presidency and the factionalism within the upper echelons of the Jackson administration, important as they are to understanding the development of the second party system, cannot by themselves fully explain the genesis of parties in North Carolina. Deeply rooted social conflicts dating from the American Revolution, along with a widespread feeling of alienation among voters in the extreme parts of the state, formed the raw materials from which ambitious politicians constructed a winning coalition in 1824. Opposition to the congressional caucus—the device by which political insiders supposedly manipulated the electoral process—provided an ideal issue for bringing together voters and politicians who, for a variety of reasons, felt excluded from the centers of power and decision making.

Despite the development of increasingly elaborate techniques for mobilizing public opinion, the presidential contests of the 1820s and 1830s did not result in a steady rise in voter participation. Indeed, turnout reached a peak during the one-sided contest between Adams and Jackson in 1828, when 54 percent of the eligible voters went to the polls. This level of participation was not surpassed in a presidential election in North Carolina until 1840.[98] Voter participation during this period of party formation did not increase in direct proportion to the degree of interparty competition or to the growing sophistication of party machinery.

The relatively low turnout (declining to a mere 30 percent in 1832), the erratic fluctuations in the rate of turnout from one election to another, and the rapidly shifting patterns of grass-roots alignments all suggest that the factions that vied for popular favor in North Carolina between 1824 and 1834 were not fully developed political parties. Until 1834 their goal seems to have been focused exclusively on gaining control of the presidency, and even in presidential campaigns there was little systematic discussion of policy alternatives. Congressional elections during this period were generally not contested on a partisan basis. Despite Jackson's popularity in North Carolina, many of the men who were elected to the U.S. Congress regularly voted against the measures of his administration.[99] Moreover, partisanship did not usually extend to the level of legislative elections; and the factions that vied for supremacy in the general assembly had little relation to the divisions of opinion over national issues. Thus, at the same time that North Carolinians were rallying to the Jackson standard in presidential elections, the general assembly was elevating anti-Jackson leaders like Hutchins G. Burton and David L. Swain to the governorship.[100]

An important impetus toward the organization of mass-based parties in North Carolina and elsewhere throughout the South was the passage of Henry Clay's censure resolution by the U.S. Senate in early 1834. This unprecedented rebuke dealt "a savage blow to Jackson's pride," and it gave the president's supporters a powerful incentive to recapture the Senate and expunge the hated resolution.[101] In order to accomplish this objective the Democrats had to extend their organizing efforts to the local level and win control of the state legislatures, which had the power to elect the U.S. senators and, through the passage of instruction resolutions, to exert pressure on those senators who were not up for reelection. Thus the Democrats in North Carolina vigorously contested the legislative elections of 1834 in order to reelect Senator Brown and to instruct Senator Mangum out of his seat. The Whigs opposed these efforts with equal vigor. After 1834, candidates at all levels of government solicited popular support primarily on the basis of their positions on national issues, and the pattern of votes in legislative and congressional elections began to bear a close resemblance to the alignment in presidential elections.

The rapid growth in partisanship after 1834 made it increasingly difficult for candidates for local office to remain neutral about national issues. "Every one who equivocates in answering the question, whether he is for General Jackson's administration or against it, cannot be trusted . . . and should be rejected," the editor of the *Raleigh Standard* admonished his readers shortly before the legislative elections of 1835. Eleven years earlier the editor of the *Raleigh Register* had noted with satisfaction that "the Presidential Question is not pressed unnecessarily into the electioneering canvass" in local elections. "Our citizens," he said, "seem disposed to discard all political bias, and to unite in a wish to have representatives whom they believe will serve them with ability and faithfulness."[102] These contrasting remarks provide a striking indication of how partisanship had come to replace public service as the criterion for elective office.

One of the most distinctive features of the party system that emerged in North Carolina during the 1830s was its multisectional character. Even though easterners and westerners had been quarreling for decades over issues such as internal improvements and constitutional reform, the alignment of parties bore surprisingly little resemblance to these long-standing sectional divisions. Like the Federalists and Republicans of the previous generation, the two antebellum parties had bastions of popular support in both sections of the state. The cohesion, stability, and long-term viability of the parties depended upon the ability of their leaders to maintain harmonious relations between their eastern and western wings. Yet, even as party leaders throughout the state were reaching out for popular support, escalating sectional animosities were threatening to destroy the nascent party system at the very moment of its birth.

2 ✦ East versus West: State Sectionalism and Party Formation

Whatever measure of excitement may pervade this House while engaged in the discussion, gentlemen may rest assured, that little if any of that spirit will be found to possess their constituents at home.—Augustine H. Shepperd, Speech on Fisher's Anticaucus Resolutions, 1823

While the contest for the presidency occupied the attention of North Carolina's political elite during the 1820s and 1830s, a substantial portion of their constituents remained indifferent. Only 40 percent of the eligible voters participated in the presidential election of 1824, and the proportion of voters declined to a mere 30 percent in 1832.[1] The explanation for this widespread disinterest can be found, in large part, in the irrelevance of the incipient parties to the local concerns of the electorate. Oriented exclusively toward winning control of the presidency, the leaders of the contending factions failed to address important state issues like constitutional reform and internal improvements. Indeed, these issues divided the political elite along sectional rather than partisan lines, and their constant agitation during the 1820s and 1830s threatened the development of stable political parties. Not until the Constitutional Convention of 1835 had resolved the most fundamental differences between the sections did a viable party system emerge in North Carolina.

The indifference of many North Carolinians to national politics can be attributed to what one observer described as the "indirect and almost imperceptible operation . . . [of] the General Government . . . [on] the great body of the people."[2] Like all Americans during the years before the Civil War, North Carolinians lived under a three-tiered system of government, and most of the laws that affected their everyday lives were enacted by their state and local governments, not by the national government in Washington.

The most important agency of government in antebellum North Carolina was the county court, which exercised a wide variety of judicial, administrative, and legislative functions. The justices of the peace who served as members of these courts were appointed by the governor after being recommended by the county's delegation in the general assembly. Although a county could have many dozens of justices, only five of them were needed to transact the business of the court. The civil jurisdiction of the court included all suits of $100 or more, and its criminal jurisdiction extended to all cases in which punishment did not involve death or dismemberment. The court also had responsibility for building and operating local roads, bridges, and ferries; caring for the poor and unfortunate; constructing and maintaining the courthouse and other public buildings; binding out apprentices; settling estates; keeping birth, marriage, and land records; and licensing peddlers, taverns, and public mills. The county court also levied local taxes, which were generally several times higher than the prevailing state taxes.[3]

At the state level the powers of government were officially divided among the executive, legislature, and judiciary. The governor, who until 1836 was elected annually by the legislature, had little patronage and no veto power. By far the most important branch of government was the general assembly, which elected not only the governor but also the judges of the higher courts and numerous other state and local officials. Because of a popular aversion to taxes, the general assembly usually spent little beyond what was necessary to pay the salaries of the government officials. However, the legislature did promote state development indirectly by granting charters to banks, private academies, and river, canal, and turnpike companies. After 1815 the state also began making modest investments in the stock of internal improvement companies.[4]

The state constitution of 1776 guaranteed that the administration of government would be controlled by members of the landed class. Members of the house of commons were required to possess a freehold of at least one hundred acres, and state senators had to own at least three hundred acres. Besides confining officeholding exclusively to property holders, the constitution also gave a disproportionate share of power in the general assembly to the wealthier slaveholding counties of the east. Every county, regardless of population, was allowed two members in the house of commons and one in the state senate. This stipulation discriminated against the rapidly growing west, where counties were fewer but far more populous.[5]

Voting requirements were less stringent than the qualifications for officeholding. Every male taxpayer was entitled to vote for members of the lower house, for congressmen, and for presidential electors. Because nearly everyone paid the poll tax, the taxpaying requirement was tantamount to universal manhood suffrage. However, only voters possessing a freehold of at least fifty acres were allowed to vote for state senators, a requirement that disfranchised at least half the electorate.[6] Elections to the house of commons were vigorously contested and voter turnout was generally high. Even though the majority of voters remained indifferent in presidential elections, it was not unusual for two-thirds or even three-fourths of the electorate to participate in county elections.[7]

Until 1836 statewide campaigns for offices other than the president were unknown in North Carolina, and candidates for the general assembly were elected in totally autonomous elections in which issues and campaign techniques differed widely from one constituency to another. Within the legislature itself, however, the members of both houses organized themselves into factions for the purpose of distributing the spoils of office. Because of the abundance of offices at the disposal of the general assembly, and the even greater number of aspirants seeking to fill them, electioneering inevitably consumed a substantial portion of the time and attention of the legislature. Rival groups of veteran legislators each sponsored slates of candidates and actively courted the votes of new members and unaffiliated assemblymen.

Like the parties that vied for control of the federal government, the legislative factions tended to be bisectional in character. Influential easterners like Richard Dobbs Spaight, Jr., and John R. Donnell united with leading westerners like Romulus M. Saunders and Charles Fisher to divide the state offices among themselves, and their efforts were opposed by other bisectional coalitions composed of prominent easterners like John Owen and William Meares and westerners like David F. Caldwell and William J. Alexander. These factions seem to have been geared entirely toward electioneering. Once the elections were over, they did not serve as effective vehicles for the introduction and passage of legislation. Instead, on most important issues of state policy the members of the legislature divided into eastern and western blocs.[8]

A major bone of contention between easterners and westerners during the 1820s was the issue of state support for internal improvements. One of the most pressing economic problems besetting antebellum North Carolina was the lack of private investment capital to finance state development. For generations the state's woefully inadequate transportation facilities had kept most Tarheels confined to their own neighborhoods, had kept land prices low, had hampered the development of urban centers and a market economy, and had drained the profits of the state to merchants in Virginia and South Carolina. During the prosperous years immediately following the War of 1812, the general assembly, under the aggressive leadership of Senator Archibald D. Murphey, turned its attention for the first time to the matter of state aid for internal improvements. As chairman of the Committee on Internal Improvements, Murphey outlined his views in a series of reports that emphasized the importance of improving the state's river systems. In his later reports Murphey also recommended a system of turnpikes to carry the produce of the western counties eastward toward the navigable rivers. Between 1815 and 1835 the state invested almost $300,000 in various improvement projects, mostly in the form of loans and stock subscriptions to privately owned river, turnpike, and canal companies. These contributions were too modest to have much practical effect, but the general assembly did, at least, establish the beginnings of a program for state development.[9]

An examination of voting patterns in the house of commons reveals that sectional politics had as much influence as the enlightened patriotism of Murphey in the enactment of North Carolina's first significant internal improvement legislation. Although the eastern counties actually stood to benefit most from the river improvements suggested by Murphey, a majority of members from the eastern counties voted against the Murphey plan in 1815, 1817, and 1819. Most eastern legislators preferred to improve their imperfect river systems with private funds rather than set a precedent for state aid that might later result in the taxation of wealthy eastern residents for the benefit of their poorer western neighbors. Support for the Murphey plan was strongest among legislators from the western counties, where primitive mud roads—often impassable in the winter—provided the principal means of transportation.[10]

Conflicting economic interests between the east and the west inevitably fueled western dissatisfaction with the basis of legislative apportionment. When the framers of the state constitution established the county basis of representation in 1776, the white population of the two sections was roughly equal. In the years after the Revolution the west gained more rapidly in population than the east, and by 1815 a majority of the white population lived west of Raleigh. Yet the thirty-seven eastern counties continued to send 116 representatives to the general assembly, whereas the twenty-five western counties were allowed only 77 legislators.[11]

As early as 1801, westerners in the general assembly had introduced a resolution calling for a constitutional convention to amend the charter of government. The legislature voted on the issue five times between 1801 and 1808, and each time it defeated the convention bill by large majorities. The renewal of the controversy with Britain over neutral rights temporarily eclipsed the movement for state reform, and the convention question lay dormant until after the war. Although Federalist legislators, at least by 1815, were far more sympathetic toward constitutional reform than the Republicans, the Federalists never officially endorsed the idea of a convention for fear of losing popular support among voters in the east.[12]

For almost a decade after the War of 1812, practically every session of the general assembly considered—and voted down—western motions for constitutional revision.[13] The reform movement entered a more militant phase in 1820 with the establishment of the *Salisbury Western Carolinian*, one of the first newspapers to be published west of Raleigh. In their first issue of 13 June 1820, editors James Krider and Lemuel Bingham denounced the state government as "a complete aristocracy [in which] the few govern the many," and promised to devote their efforts to the cause of constitutional reform. In succeeding issues Krider and Bingham continued to stir up public opinion against "the aristocracy in the East" and threatened that westerners would, if necessary, call a constitutional convention without prior legislative approval.[14]

Unfortunately, the constitution of 1776 was silent about the means by which the state's fundamental laws could be altered. Until the early 1820s western reformers had been content to introduce convention bills into the general assembly, but in the face of continued eastern intransigence an increasing number began asserting the right of the people to disavow allegiance to an oppressive and unrepresentative government. In language reminiscent of the Declaration of Independence, a grand jury in Burke County asserted that "when those to whom the government of the people has been entrusted lose sight of the principles upon which it is founded . . . the people have a right to withdraw their confidence and to alter or amend the political compact by which they were united together."[15]

That these were not idle threats became apparent in December 1822, when a group of reform-minded legislators issued a call for a constitutional convention to assemble in Raleigh the following November. At the same time the western legislators established a central committee and county committees of correspondence to coordinate the selection of delegates. The reformers also issued an address denouncing the existing system of representation as "anti-republican, unjust, and oppressive" and calling for amendments that would "secure to every freeman of this state an equality of privileges and influence in the government."[16]

By 1822 the western bloc in the general assembly was beginning to take on many of the attributes of a political party. No longer content merely to introduce reform bills in the general assembly, westerners had organized to arouse public opinion and mobilize voter support behind their program of constitutional revision. The western leaders also articulated a republican ideology that transcended narrow appeals to sectional self-interest. A change in the structure of government was necessary, they claimed, not simply to give the west more power to promote its economic interests but also to vindicate the republican principles of majority rule and equal rights. As one group of reformers put it, "under a republican form of government, every citizen . . . is undeniably entitled to an equal participation in the rights and privileges of government and an equal degree of weight and influence in its administration." By denying the west its fair share of representation, easterners were denying the fundamental principle that "in republican governments the will of the majority, when fairly expressed, must and ought to prevail."[17]

On 10 November 1823 forty-seven delegates from twenty-four western counties met in convention to consider revisions in the state constitution. Among the delegates were most of the leading politicians of the west. Former congressman Charles Fisher, who would soon gain notoriety as the leader of the anticaucus forces, was present, as were U.S. Senator Montford Stokes, Congressman Romulus M. Saunders, former congressmen Thomas Settle and James S. Smith, and Bartlett Yancy, the longtime speaker of the state senate. After six days of deliberation, the convention approved a series of constitutional amendments that apportioned both houses of the legislature according to federal population (white population plus three-fifths of the slave population). The convention also called on the voters to elect delegates to a ratifying convention that would meet in Raleigh the following November. The convention agreed that its proposed amendments could be overridden by the general assembly, if that body should officially provide for a constitutional convention at its upcoming session. This stipulation, along with the fact that the reform convention was held immediately before the general assembly convened, suggests that the majority of the delegates were not plotting secession or revolution but rather were hoping to pressure the legislature into passing a reform bill of its own.[18]

The eastern-dominated general assembly remained oblivious to the reform demands of the westerners. Although resolutions were introduced calling for a popular referendum on the amendments suggested by the reform convention, the house of commons postponed them indefinitely by a decisive majority of forty-two votes.[19] After the session of 1823–24, the movement for a constitutional convention quickly subsided. In the legislative elections of 1824 only a few counties selected delegates to the proposed ratifying convention, and the delegates never assembled. Not until the 1830s would North Carolinians again give serious consideration to the matter of constitutional reform.

Historians have offered a variety of explanations to account for the sudden collapse of the convention movement of the 1820s, but insufficient attention has been given to the devastating impact of the revival of the contest for the presidency. Less than a week after the defeat of the reform resolutions, Charles Fisher introduced his anticaucus resolutions into the general assembly and sparked an acrimonious debate that shattered the unity of the reform bloc. Although many westerners joined Fisher in opposing the caucus, others, like Yancy and Saunders, defended the caucus and endorsed Crawford. In 1825 an anonymous correspondent of the *Western Carolinian*, who claimed to have served as a delegate to the Constitutional Convention of 1823, offered a perceptive analysis of the factors behind the failure of the reform movement. The correspondent pointed out that "the high excitement on the subject of the Presidential election" had created "considerable division of sentiment" among the friends of reform. Under the circumstances it was inevitable that "either one or the other, presidential or the convention question, would have acquired the ascendancy, and the other would have lost its interest. In order . . . that both might receive proper attention from the public, it was necessary to urge them only one at a time."[20]

Westerners like Fisher and Stokes, who supported constitutional reform but who also opposed Crawford and the caucus, found themselves in a dilemma. It was impossible for these reformers to crusade simultaneously against the antirepublican state constitution and the antirepublican congressional caucus, because many of their allies in the one crusade were their enemies in the other. In order to combat the threat posed to republican institutions by the caucus, it was necessary to join forces with like-minded easterners who held "aristocratic" and "antirepublican" views on the subject of state reform and to denounce westerners like Yancy and Saunders who supported the caucus. By choosing to focus their attention on the contest for the presidency, Fisher and the other anticaucus westerners effectively set back the cause of state reform for almost a decade.[21]

The publication of the census of 1830 sparked a renewed popular demand for constitutional revision. Although the white population of the west had for many years exceeded that of the east, the new census revealed that, for the first time, a majority of the total population lived west of Raleigh. In June 1831 the reform movement got an unexpected boost when a fire swept through the city of Raleigh, destroying the state house and most of the papers of the general assembly. The destruction of the capitol building emboldened the politicians from Fayetteville and some of the surrounding counties along the Cape Fear to agitate for the calling of a convention to move the state capital from Raleigh to Fayetteville. Westerners, who were largely indifferent about the location of the capital, offered to aid the Cape Fear legislators in exchange for their support for constitutional revision.[22]

The alliance between the west and the Cape Fear region was only partially successful. In the North Carolina General Assembly of 1831–32 the legislators managed to defeat a bill to appropriate funds for rebuilding the capitol in Raleigh. Seventy-four westerners combined with twenty-five members of the Cape Fear delegation and one other maverick easterner to vote down the measure. However, when westerners subsequently introduced a bill calling for a convention to consider both reapportionment and the relocation of the capital, only ten assemblymen from the Cape Fear joined the reformers and the bill was soundly defeated.[23]

During the debates over the convention bill, which consumed much of the attention of the general assembly in December and January, easterners made it clear that they considered the existing constitution to be already "as good . . . as the wisdom of man can make it." The patriots of the Revolution, they claimed, had given North Carolina a charter of government "uniform and permanent in its operations," and any alteration in its fundamental principles would certainly result in a change for the worse. Easterners denied that the west had experienced any real grievances or inconveniences under the existing system of legislative apportionment. Far from being a struggle for the vindication of republican principles, the reform movement—in the opinion of the east—was nothing more than a naked grab for power. "Give them the power they seek," predicted one easterner, "and, in all probability, you would, in a few years, see every dollar voted out of the Treasury, towards wild and unprofitable schemes of internal improvement, and an onerous system of taxation resorted to, in furtherance of the same policy. . . . Shall we run the risk of perpetual taxation, for the exclusive benefit of one section of the State only?" As this remark indicates, the issue of internal improvements was the driving force behind western support for—and eastern opposition to—constitutional reform.[24]

In the face of continued eastern intransigence in the general assembly, the reformers renewed their efforts to mobilize public opinion on behalf of a constitutional convention. On 4 January 1833 the friends of reform assembled at the Governor's Palace in Raleigh and voted to ask the sheriffs of each county to take a poll on the propriety of a convention. The meeting appointed a committee of four to prepare an address to the people and established county committees to coordinate the work of reform.[25]

Significantly, the chairman of the committee charged with the task of writing the reform address was an easterner. William Henry Haywood, Jr., a talented young Raleigh lawyer, had been one of the earliest supporters of Andrew Jackson in North Carolina and had served on the central Jackson committee in 1828 and in 1832. In 1831 the citizens of Wake County had elected him to the house of commons, but Haywood temporarily abandoned a promising legislative career after his constituents instructed him to vote against a constitutional convention. Shortly after the reform meeting of January 1833, Haywood wrote Vice President–elect Martin Van Buren for advice, inquiring whether it would be consistent with the correct principles of government for the people to meet in convention and alter the constitution without the consent of the legislature.[26]

Haywood's letter was indicative of the growing sense of desperation felt by moderate reformers who wished to observe legal procedures and yet not remain trapped forever within an unjust system of government. If Haywood hoped that the vice president would give his official blessing to constitutional reform, his hopes were dashed when Van Buren wisely refused to become embroiled in North Carolina's internal affairs. In an unsigned and undated response, the New Yorker told Haywood that he doubted whether there was any precedent for a constitutional convention without legislative approval. Only the gravest evil, he added, could possibly justify such a course of action.[27]

In August 1833 almost thirty thousand voters from thirty western counties cast their ballots in favor of a constitutional convention. Despite an eastern boycott of the unofficial referendum, the proconvention vote was still large enough to exceed the total statewide vote in the presidential election of the previous November. Shortly after the general assembly convened in November 1833, Governor David L. Swain, a reformer from Buncombe County, communicated the results of the poll to the legislators and urged them to take action. For the first time in its history the senate actually passed a convention bill, by a narrow margin of five votes, but the hopes of the reformers were again shattered when the house postponed the measure indefinitely by a majority of four votes.[28]

Two days before the legislature adjourned, the reformers held another meeting to coordinate strategy in preparation for the next legislative elections. An executive committee was appointed, and once again Haywood was selected to serve as chairman. The other members of the committee were Weston R. Gales, William A. Graham, William R. Hargrove, Romulus M. Saunders, and James Seawell. Significantly, all of the committeemen except Graham were easterners, and Graham's home town of Hillsborough was less than fifty miles west of Raleigh, the dividing point between the two sections. Although the members of the committee agreed on the necessity of state reform, their views on national politics differed widely. By 1834 Haywood and Saunders were two of the leading supporters of Van Buren in North Carolina. On the other hand, Gales, who had succeeded his father as the editor of the *Raleigh Register*, along with Graham and Seawell, who were serving in the general assembly, were three of the most vocal opponents of Jackson and his heir apparent.[29]

By 1834 the reform coalition in North Carolina was both bipartisan and bisectional. Even though the vast majority of eastern voters and lower-echelon politicians remained steadfastly opposed to making any concessions to the west, a growing number of newspaper editors and political leaders in the east were lining up in favor of constitutional reform. The editors of both Raleigh newspapers—the pro-Jackson *Constitutionalist* and the anti-Jackson *Register*—had publicly committed themselves to the cause of western rights, as had the editors of the *New Bern Spectator*, the *Fayetteville Observer*, the *Oxford Examiner*, and the *Edenton Gazette*.[30] In addition to Haywood and Saunders, prominent eastern Jacksonians supporting constitutional reform included Richard Dobbs Spaight, Jr., William Moseley, Ottway Burns, and William B. Lockhart. Among the eastern Whigs who were sympathetic to constitutional revision were William Gaston, Edward B. Dudley, Matthias Manly, and John McLeod.[31]

Although these eastern leaders held widely different views about national politics, most of them shared an urban orientation and a strong commitment to state-supported internal improvements. North Carolina's towns were small, even by antebellum standards. Yet these urban areas had a political importance far exceeding their rather modest number of inhabitants, and many of the leaders of the two emerging parties were lawyers, merchants, or newspaper editors residing at or near the county seats. While most rural easterners were content with a state government that merely preserved order and kept taxes low, their urban counterparts were eager to use the resources and power of the government to transform their sleepy towns into thriving commercial centers.

The advent of railroads in the early 1830s offered these urban boosters a particularly attractive means of economic development. In

July 1833, and again the following November, the supporters of state-financed internal improvements gathered in Raleigh to formulate a comprehensive plan of state development and to petition the general assembly for support. The report of the November meeting recommended an extensive program of railroad construction, which the delegates estimated would require an appropriation of $5 million. Once again, William H. Haywood, Jr., played a key role, serving as chairman of the general committee of the July convention and participating in the writing of both the July and the November addresses.[32]

By 1833 these town-oriented easterners were beginning to regard the western reformers as possible allies rather than as sectional enemies. At the same time they were becoming increasingly aggravated by the behavior of the rural-based conservatives, who comprised a majority of the eastern delegation in the general assembly. To the dismay of the railroad promoters, the legislature of 1833–34 proved as hostile to their program for economic development as it had to western demands for a constitutional convention. Although the legislators granted charters of incorporation to several railroad companies, they refused to appropriate any money to aid these fledgling corporations. The conservatives even managed to defeat a modest appropriation of $1,500 to conduct surveys of the proposed railroad routes.[33]

The eastern presses were almost unanimous in their condemnation of the obstructionists from their section. The Democratic editor of the *Fayetteville North Carolina Journal* bitterly castigated the legislators for presuming to dictate to the people of North Carolina, "telling the people . . . in so many words, you know nothing about your interests, you have not the capacity to judge for yourselves, and we will perform that office for you." The anti-Jackson editor of the *Oxford Examiner* was equally vehement in his denunciation of "the very reprehensible apathy, not to say stupidity of the Legislature." The editor of the *Wilmington Free Press* characterized the legislature as "a weak and incompetent assemblage of citizens . . . deep in a system of error."[34]

By the time the general assembly adjourned in January 1834, many proponents of internal improvements had reached the conclusion that no great work of state development would ever be undertaken until the constitution was revised to give the west a larger number of legislative seats. After condemning the legislature for its "utter dereliction, and disregard to the great interests of the community," the editor of the *Western Carolinian* admitted that he despaired "of seeing anything of importance, in the way of Internal Improvement, effected under the existing Constitution. . . . It is necessary, therefore, that we should strike at the root of the evil, and that we should devote our unceasing energies to the cause of Constitutional Reform."[35]

By 1834 many eastern leaders were also seriously concerned that westerners might resort to extralegal action if the legislature refused to endorse constitutional reform. Grand juries in the western counties of Burke, Lincoln, Rowan, and Wilkes went on record to declare that the people would be justified in taking revolutionary action if their demands continued to go unanswered.[36] Hamilton C. Jones, the militant editor of the *Salisbury Carolina Watchman*, warned that, should the general assembly fail to act, "we of the West are determined to go to work without the behest of that body." Recalling the experience of the western reformers a decade earlier, Jones added that "we are determined to try it before another hot Presidential contest shall come on to absorb State politics."[37]

The most forceful appeal to easterners for a sectional compromise came from the pen of William H. Haywood, Jr. In 1834 Haywood decided to run again for a seat in the house of commons, on a platform calling for a constitutional convention with carefully circumscribed powers. Haywood bluntly informed his constituents that they no longer had the power to prevent the assembling of a constitutional convention. The west, he told them, would call a convention regardless of whether the general assembly gave its formal approval. It was therefore "the plain dictate of duty and of common sense, to moderate and control the measure, while it is in our power to do it." If the westerners acted on their own, they would undoubtedly organize a convention without any limit to its powers of amendment, whereas the general assembly could, if it chose, construct a reform bill designed "to give the Convention as little power as possible, to alter the Constitution in as few particulars as possible." Although it was too late to forestall a convention, there was still time, said Haywood, "to *prevent the election of a Convention without limit to their powers*."[38]

During the spring and summer of 1834 the reformers flooded the state with tracts and pamphlets arguing the merits of constitutional revision. In some eastern counties reform candidates openly campaigned on behalf of a convention, and in many others reform-minded men of local influence attended political rallies and attempted to explain to the people the necessity of altering the constitution.[39] About twenty easterners sympathetic to reform won election to the general assembly, and on the last day of 1834 a convention bill drawn up by Haywood passed the house of commons by a vote of sixty-six to sixty-two. Three days later an amended version of Haywood's bill squeaked through the senate by a single vote. The house agreed to the senate amendments on 5 January 1835. After thirty-five years of repeated failure, the west had finally succeeded in winning legislative approval for a constitutional convention.[40]

It was no coincidence that the same session of the general assembly that passed the convention bill also witnessed the development of intense partisanship over the resolutions of instruction to Brown and Mangum. Nor was it purely happenstance that Whigs and Democrats found themselves working in unison to push the convention bill through the general assembly. By 1834 differences over national politics had produced a profound division within the governing elite of North Carolina, and, as the time approached to elect a successor to Andrew Jackson, the leaders of both parties were anxious to mobilize popular support behind their respective candidates. Yet the virulent sectional animosities that divided North Carolinians into easterners and westerners militated against the creation of stable, bisectional parties. The health of the nascent party system, as well as the peace and quiet of the state, thus depended on the successful resolution of the sectional crisis. Once the differences between east and west had been settled, predicted Charles Fisher, "local parties will . . . be merged into the great political parties of the country [and] . . . you will never more hear of East and West as parties."[41]

The convention bill that passed the general assembly in 1835 represented a compromise between the two sections. Rejecting the option of an open and unrestricted convention, the legislators themselves established the limits within which the convention would have to function. By forbidding the delegates to tamper with the property requirements for state senators and senatorial electors, the legislature guaranteed that North Carolina would continue to be governed by a landed elite. As an added assurance that control of the convention would not fall into the hands of propertyless demagogues, the legislature provided that no one could serve as a delegate unless he owned a freehold of at least one hundred acres.[42]

The general assembly also formulated the guidelines for legislative reapportionment. It ruled that the house of commons would contain between 90 and 120 members apportioned according to federal population, whereas the senate would contain between 34 and 50 members elected by tax districts. This arrangement left the wealthier eastern counties in control of the senate and gave the west considerably less influence in the house of commons than would have been the case had the seats been apportioned strictly according to white population. Finally, the legislature stipulated that the convention would not meet at all unless it was approved by a majority of the voters in a referendum. If a convention did assemble and enact constitutional revisions, these amendments would also have to be approved by a referendum before taking effect.[43]

Despite these numerous safeguards and qualifications, 87 percent of the easterners in the house of commons and 83 percent in the senate voted against the convention bill. On the other hand, 96 percent of the western assemblymen supported the bill in each house, even though its provisions were less favorable in certain respects than the reformers had hoped for. In the popular referendum held in May 1835, the convention was approved by a vote of 27,550 to 21,694. The alignment of votes for and against the convention mirrored the sectional cleavage within the general assembly. All but two of the western counties cast majorities in favor of the convention, and all but one of the eastern counties voted against it. In only a few of the eastern counties was the vote even close.[44]

The convention itself, which assembled in Raleigh on 4 June 1835, came as something of an anticlimax in view of the fact that the major question—the basis of legislative apportionment—had already been settled. The delegates did, however, inaugurate other important structural reforms by providing that the governor would henceforth be elected by popular vote for a period of two years and that the general assembly would meet biennially instead of annually. The convention also abolished the borough system of representation, which had allotted seven towns their own seats in the house of commons. It restricted the franchise by prohibiting free blacks from voting, but at the same time it liberalized the constitutional provision that had restricted officeholding to Protestants.[45]

The convention also adopted a system for making future amendments to the constitution. A committee appointed to study the matter recommended a plan by which amendments could be adopted by simple majorities in two successive legislatures, followed by a popular referendum. Easterners, however, succeeded in altering the committee's report to require a majority of three-fifths of the legislators in order to initiate the amendment process, followed by a two-thirds majority in the next legislature. The delegates also decided that no constitutional convention could again be called without the approval of two-thirds of the general assembly. Undoubtedly mindful of the narrow majorities by which the convention bill of 1835 had passed the legislature, one western delegate predicted that the requirement for larger majorities practically guaranteed that the constitution would never be amended again. Events would prove this prediction to be substantially correct.[46]

The convention adjourned on 11 July 1835; and four months later North Carolinians again went to the polls to decide whether to approve the proposed amendments. The division of the vote was almost identical to that in the earlier referendum, and the amendments were ratified by a majority of 5,165 votes. About 90 percent of the votes in favor of ratification were cast by westerners, whereas approximately 88 percent of the negative votes were cast by easterners.[47] Although the amendments were, in one sense, the product of a compromise in the general assembly between easterners and westerners, the referendum vote revealed that the vast majority of eastern voters remained adamantly opposed to constitutional reform.

Historians of antebellum North Carolina parties have generally viewed the struggle for constitutional reform during the 1830s as a partisan conflict. According to this interpretation, the Democrats, as the party of the slaveholding east, staunchly opposed efforts to alter the undemocratic framework of government. As the party of the more populous west, the Whigs eagerly embraced the cause of constitutional reform and thus became "the principal beneficiary of these reforms." "The increase in representation, which the west obtained in 1835, enabled the nascent Whig party to gain immediate ascendency in the state."[48]

The evidence presented in this chapter offers little support for this time-honored view. Indeed, the alignment of votes on the convention bill in the general assembly provides convincing evidence that the reform movement was bipartisan in character. Slightly less than half of the Democratic legislators cast their votes in favor of a convention, as did slightly more than half of the Whigs. Of the twenty eastern legislators who supported the convention against the wishes of their section, Democrats outnumbered Whigs by twelve to eight. Neither of the two parties could, or did, claim exclusive credit for championing constitutional reform.[49]

Nor did the change in the basis of legislative apportionment add significantly to the strength of the Whigs in the general assembly. Although westerners gained additional seats in both houses of the legislature, the biggest increases were not in the solidly Whig counties of the central piedmont and the mountain region, but rather in the heavily Democratic counties of Lincoln and Mecklenburg and in the hotly contested counties of Chatham, Orange, Stokes, and Surry, which frequently sent Democrats to the general assembly during the 1830s and 1840s. At the same time, the greatest loss of legislative seats was in the sparsely populated Albemarle region, which usually elected Whigs to the general assembly.[50]

This does not mean that the constitutional changes adopted in 1835 were totally irrelevant to the development of parties. Indeed, the provision for the popular election of the governor played an important role in shaping the contours of the new party system. The statewide campaign for the governorship required the effective coordination of numerous county campaigns and thus hastened the development of a strong central organization within each party. Shrewd observers like William Gaston recognized that the gubernatorial election would also stimulate the growth of partisanship among the electorate. As Gaston pointed out, "the election of governor coming on in a state so divided by parties will always be a party question. . . . To carry on this with success they must have concert—organization—discipline. Every man in the community becomes sooner or later enlisted, falls into his appropriate place in the ranks, and submits his will to the command of his party directors. This regular array made for one purpose is used for all—and the entire action of the state becomes party action."[51]

In this sense the passage of the convention bill in 1835 was really a victory for both North Carolina parties. By removing the explosive issue of legislative apportionment from the arena of politics, the constitutional amendments adopted by the convention allowed party leaders to unite on the basis of their position on national issues and ensured that national politics would not be overshadowed by divisive state issues. Even after 1835 the sectional blocs within each of the parties continued to maintain separate identities, and sectionalism continued to play an important role in determining alignments within the general assembly over issues like internal improvements. But state sectionalism did not seriously threaten the unity of either party until 1848, when Democratic gubernatorial candidate David S. Reid unwittingly reopened the Pandora's box of constitutional reform (see chapter 8).

The question of why the grass-roots divisions between Democrats and Whigs bore so little resemblance to the long-standing sectional divisions between easterners and westerners is one of the most intriguing questions about the second party system in antebellum North Carolina. The explanation for the growth of multisectional parties within a sectionally polarized political environment seems to lie in the fact that neither the east nor the west was a monolithic unit. Earlier partisan identities, local conflicts, and personal rivalries at the regional, county, and even subcounty level divided the political elite and played a significant role in conditioning the pattern of party alignment in North Carolina. Ironically, the end product of this kaleidoscopic pattern of local animosities and personal rivalries was a party system that was genuinely bisectional and statewide in character, despite the persistence of chronic conflict between east and west. No better explanation has been offered for this phenomenon than the one suggested by the editor of the *Raleigh Register* in 1849: "The members of every community have among themselves jealousies and heart-burnings . . . and the individuals of which it is composed, more naturally seek alliance with persons at a distance, with whom they have no such rivalry."[52]

By resolving the divisive issue of constitutional reform, the Convention of 1835 had laid the groundwork for the creation of mass parties. But the resolution of the sectional conflict did not automatically guarantee that efforts at party building would be successful. As long as a majority of North Carolinians continued to view party battles as mere scrambles for office or as abstract quarrels over issues that had little impact on their daily lives, politics would continue to be primarily the concern of the elite. Before party leaders could successfully cultivate a popular following, they first had to demonstrate the relevance of national politics to the hopes and aspirations of the average voter.

3 ✦ Whiggery Triumphant: The Creation of Mass Political Parties, 1834–1840

It has appeared to me that nothing short of touching their pocket, and that rudely, would induce the people or a considerable portion of them to doubt the infallibility of Jacksonism.—Samuel Hillman to Willie P. Mangum, 16 February 1834

The *Currency* and *pub[lic] Land* are the 2 strong questions with the people.— James Graham to William A. Graham, 8 April 1838

Between 1834 and 1840 an increasing number of ordinary North Carolinians began identifying with the two political parties. Prior to 1840, the high point of participation in a presidential election had come in 1828, when 54 percent of the voters went to the polls to choose between Jackson and Adams. By 1840 a phenomenal 84 percent of the voting population participated in national elections.[1] Both parties benefited from this increase, but most of the gains accrued to the Whigs. In 1840 the party captured the governorship for the third consecutive time, won commanding majorities in both houses of the general assembly, and delivered the electoral votes of North Carolina to the Whig presidential candidate. The Whigs would remain the majority party in the Old North State until the 1850s. In large part their success can be attributed to their adeptness in developing clear and explicit linkages between national issues and local concerns.

For many North Carolinians, particularly those living in the underdeveloped western half of the state, the most pressing local need was for a system of turnpikes and railroads to carry their agricultural products to market. The state was blessed with a good climate and abundant resources and yet, as Charles Fisher pointed out, thousands of its citizens were leaving each year, carrying off wealth and production capital, and keeping the value of land in a depressed state. In

Fisher's opinion, the answer to North Carolina's problems lay in the construction of a central railroad, which would usher in "a new era of brighter prospects" by bringing a market to every man's door, increasing the value of land, and checking the tide of emigration.[2]

After the War of 1812 reformers like Archibald D. Murphey and David L. Swain had promoted comprehensive programs for state assistance to internal improvements, but their plans had inevitably foundered on the reluctance of the general assembly to raise taxes or to create a large public debt. "The great obstacle to Internal Improvements in our State," Congressman Lewis Williams informed his constituents in 1835, "is the want of money; and the objection to borrowing it, is the difficulty of paying the interest." If North Carolina attempted to construct a system of improvements on borrowed money, one Whig legislator predicted, the tax rate would have to be increased fivefold simply to pay the interest. Should the general assembly be foolish enough to enact such an increase, the people "would pay the tax but once, and then turn out every member who voted for it, and the next Legislature would send the system to the winds."[3]

For those North Carolinians who wished to reap the benefits of internal improvements without bearing the burdens of taxation, the Whigs offered an attractive panacea in the form of Henry Clay's land bill. Early in 1833 the Kentucky senator had championed a bill to distribute the proceeds of federal land sales among the states for a period of five years. Clay's bill passed both houses by large majorities, but Jackson refused to sign it and the measure never became law. Anti-Jacksonians, like the editor of the *Raleigh Register*, claimed that Clay's bill would have given North Carolina over $130,000 a year—money enough to build railroads and improve other means of communication between the backcountry and the seaboard.[4]

By 1836 the idea of financing state development with federal land revenues had become a cardinal tenet of national policy for the Whigs in North Carolina. The public lands of the American West belonged collectively to all the states, they claimed, because these lands had either been ceded to Congress by the old states after the Revolution or had been purchased from France and Spain with federal monies. The Whigs reminded the voters that North Carolina had ceded many millions of acres of its own tramontane lands to the federal government during the postwar years. It was only fair that the proceeds from the national domain should be used as a common fund and not for the exclusive benefit of the new states.[5]

The Whigs repeatedly emphasized that the distribution of the public land revenues would enable North Carolina to build roads and schools "without one cent or burden, or tax of any kind upon the people." The editor of the *Register* went so far as to claim that the federal money flowing into North Carolina "would do away the necessity of any State tax." The editor painted a vivid picture of the benefits the state would derive from the judicious expenditure of this revenue. Within a decade, he predicted, "Rail Roads and Canals may be made to penetrate every section of the state; Public Schools be established in every neighborhood; the value of lands be enhanced ten fold; emigration be stopped; public and private prosperity reign in all our borders; and North Carolina take her stand among the first in character as she is now in population."[6]

Democratic strategists recognized the popularity of the land issue among the North Carolina voters and, indeed, even among many local leaders in their own party. But taking their cue from Jackson's veto of Clay's land bill, they claimed that the policy of distribution embodied a consolidating principle that would prove detrimental to the independence of the states. The editor of the *Raleigh North Carolina Constitutionalist* reminded his readers that "money is power, the more money the government has the more power it possesses; and already its gigantic arm overshadows the State authorities." Although superficially attractive, Clay's bill would ultimately place the states in vassalage to the federal government. "What sort of sovereigns would the States be," Congressman Thomas Hall asked his constituents, "if dependent on others for their revenue?" The Democrats claimed that the federal and state governments should each be the collector and disburser of its own revenue. If the federal government had a surplus of revenue, the proper course of action was to reduce the high tariffs that produced the surplus.[7]

While the Whigs were promising the voters roads, schools, and freedom from taxes, the Democrats were offering them constitutional abstractions. The Whigs effectively countered the Democrats' alternative of a reduced tariff by pointing out that the compromise tariff of 1833 forbade any change in the tariff rates until the next decade. In the meantime the federal government was confronted with an overflowing treasury—a certain invitation to "prodigality and corruption in those who administer it." The best way of preventing the accumulation of excessive power and influence on the part of the federal government, the Whigs argued, was to divide the surplus revenue among the states. Like the editor of the *Constitutionalist*, Whig Congressman Abraham Rencher told his constituents that "money is power," but Rencher drew an entirely different conclusion from this premise. Why, he asked, should the voters "place the whole of this tremendous power in the hands of the President of the United States?" It would be far better to "divide it equitably among the States, to enable them to maintain their ancient freedom, independence, and sovereignty."[8]

The political effectiveness of the distribution issue became apparent during the congressional elections of 1835. The Whigs campaigned vigorously on the issue of land policy, and they succeeded in capturing seven of the thirteen districts. Their most stunning victory came in the Third District, where Ebenezer Pettigrew unseated Thomas Hall, who had represented the district almost continuously for eighteen years. The other six Whigs who won election were all incumbents, but several of them were campaigning for the first time as avowedly anti-Jackson men. The editor of the *Register* claimed that, even without counting the two districts where the Whigs had run uncontested, his party had received 34,290 votes to only 22,680 for the Democrats.[9]

Federal land policy remained a hot political issue during the summer elections of 1836. Clay was again promoting his land bill in the U.S. Congress, and in May the bill had passed the Senate only to be tabled in the House. The six North Carolina congressmen who supported the bill were all Whigs, whereas the four who opposed it were Democrats. The Whigs claimed that the Democrats had effectively deprived the people of the Old North State of more than $1 million of their own money. The editor of the *Register* urged the voters, in the upcoming legislative elections, to "ask the Candidates for the Legislature, this question—'are you in favor of the distribution of the proceeds of the Public Lands?' . . . It is time that it should be made a TEST QUESTION."[10]

If the distribution issue was, indeed, the test question in the legislative elections of 1836, the outcome revealed the Whigs to be the victors in the debate over federal land policy. The party improved substantially over its showing in the two previous campaigns, winning a majority of seats in the senate and falling only two seats short of a majority in the house of commons. Even more encouraging to the Whigs than the results of the legislative elections was what one Democrat described as "the unexpected and somewhat disasterous result, of our election for governor."[11]

In accordance with the provision of the amended constitution, the voters of North Carolina were allowed for the first time to participate in the election of their governor. The Democratic candidate was incumbent Governor Richard Dobbs Spaight, Jr., and the Whig candidate was Edward B. Dudley, a wealthy Wilmington businessman who had previously represented his district in both the state legislature and the U.S. Congress. Neither candidate took an active part in the campaign, although Dudley did, at least, publish a letter of acceptance and speak to meetings of voters in New Bern and in Onslow County. Governor Spaight, on the other hand, never formally accepted his party's nomination and remained silent throughout the campaign. Incumbency proved to be no advantage for Spaight, and Dudley won the election by a majority of four thousand votes.[12]

The alignment of counties in the governor's election conformed to a pattern that had been familiar in North Carolina since the presidential contest of 1824 (see table 3.1). Dudley carried a majority of the Federalist counties and most of the counties in the Albemarle region, while Spaight ran strongest in plantation counties in the middle east and along the Virginia border. Spaight also won majorities in four sparsely populated counties in the extreme west, but Dudley carried the other four counties and garnered 62 percent of the vote in the

Table 3.1 The Vote for Governor, 1836 (by percentage)

	Dudley (Whig)	Spaight (Democrat)
Federalist counties	59 (12 counties)	41 (11 counties)
Republican counties		
Albemarle	65 (8 counties)	35 (3 counties)
Middle east	40 (5 counties)	60 (10 counties)
Piedmont	46 (3 counties)	54 (5 counties)
Mountains	62 (4 counties)	38 (4 counties)
Total	50 (20 counties)	50 (22 counties)
All counties	54 (32 counties)	46 (33 counties)

Source: Thomas E. Jeffrey, "The Second Party System in North Carolina," appendix A.
Note: Percentages indicate each candidate's share of the total two-party vote.

mountain region. Seven of the thirteen counties where Dudley polled more than 75 percent of the vote had been Federalist in political orientation, and all but one of the six other strong Whig counties were located in the Albemarle and mountain regions. On the other hand, six of the nine counties where Spaight won more than 75 percent of the vote were located in the middle east or along the Virginia border.[13]

The jubilant Whigs were quick to claim that Dudley's stunning victory in the August gubernatorial election augured certain defeat for Martin Van Buren in the November presidential election. The editor of the *Fayetteville Observer* proclaimed that "if ever there was an election [for governor] which was decided purely with reference to National politics, it was this." The editor of the *Greensboro Patriot* agreed that personal considerations had less to do with the outcome of the election "than any popular canvass we ever knew or heard of in the State. It was not Gov. Spaight and Gen. Dudley merely—it was the *Van* candidate and the *White* candidate." The Democrats, for their part, stoutly denied that Dudley's election was a referendum on the merits of the presidential candidates. According to the editor of the *Raleigh North Carolina Standard*, "other and false issues were placed before the people, to mislead their judgments and pervert their honest intentions"—issues that would have no effect in the November election.[14]

The outcome of the presidential election confirmed the Democrats' claim that the governor's election was not a reliable indicator of the strength of the two presidential candidates. Despite the Whig triumph of August, the Democrats won the November election with 53 percent of the popular vote. Voter turnout proved to be the main factor affecting the difference in outcome. Two-thirds of the electorate had participated in the contest for governor, but participation in the presidential election amounted to little more than a majority of the eligible voters. Both parties lost votes between August and November, but the decline in popular interest hurt the Whigs far more than the Democrats. Van Buren received about three thousand fewer votes than Spaight, whereas White won about ten thousand fewer votes than Dudley.[15] The Whigs had won the governor's contest by convincing a substantial number of voters who did not yet identify with either party that their policies were relevant to the interests of North Carolina. Their inability to persuade these voters to return to the polls in November accounts for their defeat in the presidential election.

The popularity of the land issue was undoubtedly an important factor behind the Whig victory in the gubernatorial election. By 1836 the Whigs were clearly on record in favor of a distribution of federal land revenues. In his inaugural address of December 1835, on the other hand, Governor Spaight had publicly announced his opposition to distribution. Spaight's chances for election were further diminished by the passage of the Deposit Act on 23 June 1836. This measure disbursed $28 million of the federal surplus among the states, ostensibly in the form of a loan subject to recall by the secretary of the treasury. Under the provisions of the act, North Carolina received almost $1.5 million—about nine times the amount of revenue collected in state taxes, land sales, and investments in 1836. Although the Deposit Act could not have passed Congress without Democratic votes, the Whigs did not hesitate to claim sole credit for the measure. The Whigs also charged that the Democrats planned to repeal the law once the election was over and that Spaight, if elected, would refuse to receive North Carolina's portion of the revenue. The editor of the *Fayetteville Observer* warned the voters not to "put the lamb in the keeping of the wolf."[16]

The Whigs also made a concerted effort to portray Spaight as an enemy of internal improvements. As a resident of New Bern, Spaight was more sympathetic to publicly financed internal improvements than most eastern Democrats, and the Democratic presses took pains to emphasize that the governor was not opposed to "a feasible scheme" of internal improvements. On the other hand, Spaight's long service in the general assembly offered the Whigs numerous opportunities to point to specific roll calls where the governor had voted against state aid. After the election, the Democratic editor of the *New Bern Carolina Sentinel* complained that "the impression has been studiously created that Gov. Spaight is the implacable opponent of Internal Improvement in every shape. On the other hand, General Dudley has been held up as a sort of patron of the Internal Improvement policy. . . . This very ground has assisted to elect him as much as any other."[17]

The internal improvements issue contributed to Dudley's margin of victory not only in the western counties, which desired railroad connections with eastern markets, but also in the northeastern counties bordering Albemarle Sound. For over two decades politicians in this region had been agitating for a federal or state appropriation to reopen the inlet at Nags Head in order to connect Albemarle Sound with the Atlantic Ocean. One proponent of the Nags Head project described the issue as "the *ne plus ultra* of public improvement" in the Albemarle counties, and even those who were unsympathetic to the idea admitted that it had "long been a favorite scheme with certain popularity-hunting politicians of our Legislature."[18]

Unfortunately for the Democrats, Spaight had voted many times in the general assembly against an appropriation for the inlet, and the Whigs exploited these votes during the campaign. Dudley, on the other hand, made a well-publicized tour of the Albemarle counties shortly before the election. There is no evidence that the Whig candidate actively promoted the inlet project during the tour, but his visit undoubtedly served to reinforce his image as a friend of internal improvements. And although Dudley himself was reticent about internal improvements during the campaign, his supporters in the Albemarle region certainly were not. According to the Democrats, the local Whig leaders had unabashedly promised that Nags Head would be cleared of its obstructions if Dudley won the governorship. Perhaps not surprisingly, the Whig candidate garnered a commanding 65 percent of the vote in the Albemarle counties.[19]

In certain parts of the state local issues worked to the advantage of the Democrats. A good example is the Cherokee removal issue, which produced overwhelming majorities for Spaight in the three counties in the extreme west where most of North Carolina's Cherokee population resided. According to the treaty signed at New Echota, Georgia, on 29 December 1835, the Cherokees agreed to relinquish their lands in western North Carolina and adjoining states in return for government transportation to new homes across the Mississippi. Unfortunately for the Whigs in the far west, Dudley had a conspicuous record of opposition to Cherokee removal. Even worse, he had issued a circular in 1830 suggesting that the Indian problem would solve itself if Cherokees were allowed to intermarry with whites. Democrats in the extreme west denounced Dudley as an amalgamationist, quoted his circular frequently during the campaign, and won heavy majorities in Haywood, Macon, and Yancey counties.[20]

The personal popularity of the two candidates also affected the result in certain counties. In his native Cape Fear region, for example, Dudley carried Columbus County and lost narrowly in Bladen County, even though succeeding Whig gubernatorial candidates never came close to carrying either of these counties. In his own Tar-Neuse region, on the other hand, Spaight won majorities in four Federalist counties that would frequently poll Whig majorities during the next decade. Although Spaight and Dudley undoubtedly picked up some "favorite son" votes in their home regions, the Whigs were probably correct in claiming that personal considerations had little impact on the overall result of the election.[21]

National issues and local interests both played a role in determining the outcome of the gubernatorial election in 1836. The most important factor behind the Whig success, however, was their policy of financing railroads, turnpikes, and other state improvements with the proceeds from federal land sales. It was not the issues of internal improvements or federal land policy by themselves that won the Old North State over to Whiggery, but rather the ability of party leaders to develop clear connections between national issues and local concerns. Although the Whigs portrayed themselves as the exclusive friends of improvement, leading Democrats like Richard Dobbs Spaight, Jr., William H. Haywood, Jr., Louis D. Henry, Thomas Loring, William D. Moseley, Romulus M. Saunders, and Robert Strange were also sympathetic to the cause of state development. What the Democratic party lacked in 1836 was not a commitment to internal improvements but rather an attractive alternative to the Whig program of financing state development with federal revenues.[22]

One month before the presidential election a disheartened Senator Bedford Brown told Martin Van Buren that "the Land Bill and the distribution of the surplus revenue, have been operating for some time, prejudicially, to our cause."[23] Sound political strategy might have suggested a continued emphasis by the Whigs on the land issue during the three months between the state and presidential elections. Instead, the distribution question faded into the background after the August elections. Indeed, from the very beginning of the long presidential campaign, the principal Whig charge against Van Buren was not that he was unsound on land policy but that he espoused principles that were detrimental to the slaveholding interests of the South.

Edward B. Dudley set the tone for the presidential campaign in his letter accepting the Whig nomination for governor. Instead of addressing state issues, Dudley's letter consisted entirely of an attack on Van Buren. "To say all in one sentence: He is not one of us. He is a Northern man in soul, in principle and in action, with no one feeling of sympathy or of interest for the South."[24] During the previous presidential campaign Dudley had been a leading supporter of Philip Barbour, and, in many respects, the Whig charges against Van Buren in 1836 resembled those of the Barbourites four years earlier. The New Yorker, it was claimed, favored a protective tariff that impoverished the southern farmer for the benefit of the northern manufacturer. In 1812 he had opposed the interests of the South by supporting De Witt Clinton for president. A decade later he had advocated the restriction of slavery in Missouri. In short, concluded a meeting of Orange County Whigs, Van Buren's entire political career was suggestive of "a hostility to the interests of the south which destroys all claim to our support, especially at this crisis."[25]

The crisis to which the Whigs were referring was the sudden and dramatic rise of militant abolitionism in the northern states. Prior to the 1830s there had been outspoken opponents of slavery in the South as well as in the North, and most antislavery men had advocated a policy of gradual emancipation with compensation to the slaveowners. On 1 January 1831 William Lloyd Garrison inaugurated a new, more militant phase in the antislavery movement by publishing the first issue of the *Liberator*, a newspaper dedicated to the policy of immediate and uncompensated emancipation. Eight months later a black preacher named Nat Turner masterminded a bloody but unsuccessful slave rebellion in Southampton County, Virginia, in which fifty-seven men, women, and children were killed. Widespread panic swept through North Carolina in the wake of the Turner Rebellion, as rumors spread that Wilmington had been destroyed, that Fayetteville was under attack, and that rampaging blacks were burning property and massacring entire families in many of the eastern counties. By the end of September the fear began to subside, but, in the meantime, at least eighteen blacks had been executed by the authorities or killed by mobs.[26]

In the midst of this excitement a copy of Garrison's *Liberator* was found in the Raleigh post office, and the probable connection between abolitionist propaganda and slave rebellion was not lost to North Carolina's political leaders. As the abolitionists continued to flood the mails with antislavery tracts and pamphlets, Tarheels began to look for ways to prevent the circulation of incendiary publications within their borders. In the North Carolina General Assembly of 1835 large majorities in both parties supported a series of resolutions calling upon the other states to pass laws against such publications and urging Congress to enact legislation to keep these materials out of the mails.[27]

By 1836 abolitionist societies were also deluging Congress with petitions and memorials urging the abolition of slavery in the District of Columbia. The South's political leaders warned that the abolition of slavery in the nation's capital would be merely the first step toward general emancipation. According to the editor of the *Register*, "all the Abolitionists now want is an entering wedge. This they seek, in the exercise by Congress of this contested right over the District—a right which no Southern man will admit." Responding to pressure by its southern members, the House of Representatives on 26 May 1836 adopted a "gag rule" directing that all such petitions be laid automatically on the table without being printed or referred to committee.[28]

During the campaign of 1836 North Carolina Whigs tried hard to make political capital on the issue of slavery in the District of Columbia. Party leaders claimed that the abolitionists were supporting Martin Van Buren because the Democratic candidate had acknowledged the constitutional right of Congress to legislate on slavery in the nation's capital. The Whigs repeatedly contrasted the heretical views of the Democratic candidate with the prosouthern opinions of Hugh Lawson White, their own nominee. Unlike Van Buren, White had unequivocally denied the constitutional power of Congress to abolish slavery in the District of Columbia and had promised that as president he would veto any bill to that effect.[29]

The Democrats spent much of the campaign of 1836 defending Van Buren's record on slavery and denouncing White as a sectional candidate whose election would threaten the existence of the Union. Party leaders claimed that the Whigs had grossly distorted Van Buren's position. Although acknowledging the theoretical power of Congress to legislate on slavery in the nation's capital, the Democratic candidate was unalterably opposed to the exercise of that power without the consent of the slaveholding states. Moreover, despite his northern birth, Van Buren was a national candidate who espoused the principles of Andrew Jackson and was supported by true Republicans in every state of the Union. White, on the other hand, was not even on the ballot in most of the northern states. According to the Democrats, the Tennessee senator had "lent his name to disunionists, for [the purpose of] forming a sectional party in the South, contrary to the warnings of experience and the advice of Washington."[30]

The Democrats also emphasized that White could not be elected president even if he received the electoral votes of every state where his name appeared on the ballot. A vote for White would, consequently, be a vote for "preventing an *election of President* by the *people.*" If Van Buren failed to win a majority of electoral votes, the election would be decided by the House of Representatives, where bribery and corruption would reign supreme. Or even worse, the White electors would cast their votes for William Henry Harrison, the candidate of the northern Whigs. And Harrison, the Democrats claimed, "not only believes that Congress possess the power to legislate on slavery, but that *it is their duty to do it.*"[31]

The Democratic argument against White's electability was a strong one, and this issue, along with the party's forceful appeal to the unionist sensibilities of the North Carolina electorate, proved sufficient to carry the state for Van Buren. In retrospect, it can be said that the Whigs probably blundered in shifting the focus of debate from the issue of land policy to that of slavery and southern rights. Some potential Whig voters may have considered the problem of slavery in the District of Columbia too remote to be a source of concern. Others may have been genuinely alarmed that a vote for White might be a vote against either the Union or the popular election of the president. In any event, the result was a substantial decline in voter participation and a victory for the Democrats.

The Democrats' triumph was short-lived, however, for in the congressional elections of August 1837 the Whigs increased their majority in the House of Representatives, winning eight of the thirteen seats. The Democrats undoubtedly were hurt by the onset of a financial crisis in the spring of 1837, which led the three banks of North Carolina to stop redeeming their notes in specie. The Whigs blamed the Panic of 1837 on the destruction of the Bank of the United States, the promulgation of the Specie Circular, and other Democratic "experiments" upon the currency.[32] With considerable justification the Democrats attributed their poor showing in 1837 to the "pecuniary distress." At the same time they were optimistic that their party would recover its standing among the voters once the crisis had ended. "The Democratic Republicans labored under many disadvantages in this last election," acknowledged Thomas Loring of the *Raleigh Standard*, "[but] on future occasions, when the temporary mists of error shall have passed away, North Carolina will be found Democratic Republican to the core."[33]

Although the economy slowly recovered during 1838, the state elections that summer did not result in a concomitant increase in Democratic strength. The party's prospects for success in the governor's election were probably doomed from the start by the inability of its leaders to agree on a suitable standard-bearer. Indeed, Loring, who edited the state's leading Democratic newspaper, initially opposed the intrusion of partisanship into the governor's election and suggested that his party offer no opposition to the Whig incumbent. "In the selection of *State officers*," Loring reasoned, "we should ask what were their opinions of *State matters*. . . . If the official conduct of the Executive officer of the State is unexceptionable, it certainly gives him claims to a re-election." According to Loring, Governor Dudley's policies had given "no dissatisfaction . . . to the citizens of the State." Thus, it made no sense for the Democrats to contest his reelection on partisan grounds.[34]

The belief that public service should be the criterion of elective office was certainly consistent with the tenets of republican ideology. Yet in an era of intense and growing partisanship, Loring's position was already an anachronism. Those Democrats who disagreed with Loring retorted that Dudley's views on national politics were sufficiently obnoxious to justify an opposition candidate, regardless of his position on state issues. Indeed, they added, the Democrats could not support Dudley without abandoning the principles upon which their own party had been founded. The debate between Loring and his critics came close to causing an open rift within the party. In a series of articles published in the *Tarborough Press* during February and March 1838, one angry Democrat bitterly assailed Loring for attempting "to *barter, control* and *transfer*" his party "to the support of . . . [a] Federalist, *Whig, Bank man*."[35]

By early summer Loring and other leading Democrats had concluded that the nomination of an official standard-bearer was a necessary prerequisite to the restoration of party harmony. On 30 June 1838, only a month before the election, Democratic leaders in Raleigh took the initiative by organizing a public meeting in Wake County and offering the nomination to John Branch. One week later Branch formally accepted the offer. The Whigs, and probably many Democrats as well, were flabbergasted by the choice. The former navy secretary had been one of the first North Carolinians to oppose the "malign influence" of Martin Van Buren, and the Whigs had considered him to be a member of their own party. The Whigs were quick to cite the surprise nomination as evidence of the opportunism and desperation of their opponents. Afraid to put forth one of their own, the Democrats, they claimed, had cynically given their endorsement to a man whom they had repeatedly declared to be unworthy of the confidence of the people, a man more obnoxious to Jackson than almost any other man in the Union.[36]

The Raleigh Democrats made a serious blunder in nominating Branch without consulting with party members in other parts of the state. Instead of unifying the party, the nomination antagonized these local leaders, and many of them refused to acknowledge Branch as the official candidate. After the election the editor of the *Western Carolinian* remarked that "it is notorious that the administration party in no section of the State rallied on Mr. Branch. The truth is, the nomination made in Wake County turned out to be unadvised, without concert, and certainly highly impolitic. . . . The consequence is that he has been badly beaten."[37]

Indeed, the election resulted in a landslide for the Whigs, as Dudley won more than 64 percent of the two-party vote. No antebellum governor would ever again come close to winning by such a margin. Yet the proportion of eligible voters who cast their ballots for Dudley in 1838 (36.0 percent) was almost identical to his share in 1836 (35.9 percent). Few Democrats who had voted for Spaight in 1836 defected to the Whigs two years later, but almost 10,000 Spaight voters sat out the election. The drop in the Democratic vote for governor also hurt the party in the legislative elections. The Whigs won majorities in both houses of the general assembly, and for the first time the state government was completely under their control.[38]

The distribution of the vote in 1838 conformed closely to the pattern that had prevailed in North Carolina since 1824 (see table 3.2). Dudley did best in the Federalist counties, in the Albemarle Sound region, and in the far west. Indeed, no election during the antebellum period so graphically demonstrates the relationship between

Table 3.2   The Vote for Governor, 1838 (by percentage)

	Dudley (Whig)	Branch (Democrat)
Federalist counties	74 (23 counties)	26 (1 county)
Republican counties		
Albemarle	70 (10 counties)	30 (1 county)
Middle east	47 (6 counties)	53 (9 counties)
Piedmont	60 (5 counties)	40 (3 counties)
Mountains	65 (5 counties)	35 (3 counties)
Total	58 (26 counties)	42 (16 counties)
All counties	64 (49 counties)	36 (17 counties)

Source: Thomas E. Jeffrey, "The Second Party System in North Carolina," appendix A.
Note: Percentages indicate each candidate's share of the total two-party vote.

Whiggery and Federalism. Dudley carried all but one of the twenty-four Federalist counties and garnered an astounding 74 percent of their vote. He did almost as well in the Albemarle counties, where he won majorities in ten of the eleven counties and received 70 percent of the vote. Branch, on the other hand, did best in the plantation counties of the middle east, where he won 53 percent of the vote. The Democratic candidate also carried three of the eight piedmont counties and came within one percentage point of winning a fourth. The persistence of the Cherokee removal issue was responsible for heavy Democratic majorities in the extreme western counties of Macon, Haywood, and Yancey.[39]

Although badly defeated in the governor's election, the Democrats could at least take comfort in the belief that the disgruntled voters who sat out the election would come back to their party in time for the presidential election in 1840. The congressional elections of 1839 seemed to bear out these hopes. The Democrats picked up three seats in the House of Representatives, gaining control of eight of the state's thirteen congressional seats.[40] The North Carolina Democrats were also heartened by the return of John C. Calhoun to the Democratic fold. In 1837 the South Carolinian had publicly endorsed Van Buren's proposal for an independent treasury, and early in 1840 he completed his rapprochement with his former enemy. Some of Calhoun's North Carolina supporters, most notably Charles Fisher and Samuel T. Sawyer, also broke with the Whigs and campaigned actively for Van Buren and the Democrats.[41]

On the other hand, the Democrats' hopes for delivering the Old North State to Van Buren were severely dampened by a sharp drop in commodity prices during the fall of 1839. The rapid deflation resulted in a new financial crisis, as banks throughout the nation once again began curtailing loans and suspending specie payments. The drop in prices also meant that North Carolina farmers received substantially less money for their produce and that loans contracted during a period when money was cheap would have to be paid back in dollars that were increasingly scarce.[42]

Modern scholarship has attributed the crisis of 1839 and the ensuing depression primarily to international market forces beyond the control of the Jackson–Van Buren administrations.[43] The Whigs, however, were quick to blame the hard times on the misguided financial policies of Old Hickory and his successor. Some Whigs went even further, claiming that the nation's economic difficulties resulted not merely from incompetence and mismanagement, but also from an "avowed determination to *destroy credit . . . reduce the wages of labor . . .* [and] *destroy paper currency.*"[44]

The Whigs had been criticizing the financial policies of the national Democratic administrations since 1834, but the flush times of the mid-thirties had seemed to belie their predictions of impending economic doom. Party leaders had accordingly downplayed the banking issue during the presidential campaign of 1836. With the onset of the depression, however, banking and currency again became central issues, and by 1840 one shrewd Whig was advising his party to campaign hard on financial issues. "The Hard Times, the *Reduction of Wages* and *prices of produce and property* & stagnation of business will do much to awaken & inform the people," predicted Congressman James Graham. "The People should be reminded continually of this. Van Buren has had and now has a Majority in both branches of Congress and must be responsible for the present state [of] things."[45]

Van Buren's answer to the financial troubles of the nation consisted principally in removing the federal government's funds from the unsound and increasingly unpopular "pet banks" handpicked by Jackson and establishing federal depositories entirely independent of the state banks. After failing several times in Congress, an indepen dent treasury bill finally became law in June 1840. To win the support of Calhoun and other hard-money men, Van Buren agreed to incorporate a "specie clause" stipulating that federal receipts and disbursements could be made only in gold, silver, or paper issued by authority of the federal government. State bank notes would no longer be receivable as payment for land purchases or tariff duties.[46]

The Whigs roundly denounced the independent treasury as a measure that would lead to political despotism and economic ruin. They were especially vociferous in their denunciation of the specie clause, claiming that its deflationary impact would fall most heavily "upon the poor, and those who are in moderate circumstances and owe money." Indeed, according to the Whigs, the only beneficiaries of the measure would be the wealthy creditors, who always profited from falling prices, and the federal officeholders, whose salaries would remain fixed and whose real buying power would consequently increase.[47]

From the viewpoint of the Whigs, the Van Buren administration was responsible for the depression, and its "relief" measures would serve only to make the rich richer. The Democrats, on the other hand, denied that their banking and currency policies had anything to do with the hard times. One Democratic orator complained that the Whigs had unjustly attributed "the evident distress of the country . . . to the Administration when it properly lay at the door of the Banks." According to the Democrats, the state banks had irresponsibly overissued their notes and then, after the damage had been done, callously refused to redeem their paper in specie.[48]

The Whigs had a ready response to this argument. The state banks might, indeed, be at fault, but their misdeeds were the direct result of the Democratic policy of favoring pet banks with federal revenue. The editor of the *Register* sarcastically commented on the hypocrisy of the Democrats in condemning a banking system that they had done so much to create. The Whigs, he reminded his readers, had consistently warned about the inevitable consequences of "this mighty league of 'Pets'" and on numerous occasions had predicted that "this high-handed attempt to connect monied corporations with political schemes would inflict disgrace and embarrassment upon the country." Now the Democrats were denouncing their own policies and acknowledging that their opponents had been right all along. But instead of admitting their error, the party's leaders were promoting "yet another untried Experiment" in the form of the independent treasury.[49]

By 1840 the partisan debate over banking and currency had become much more than an argument over abstract constitutional principles. The Panic of 1837 and its aftermath had demonstrated that banking policy could have very tangible economic consequences. Although Democratic and Whig explanations of the financial crisis differed sharply from one another, neither party attributed the hard times to the operations of impersonal market forces. Each, in its own way, was making the argument that a direct relationship existed between party politics and the economic well-being of the people. By nominating Van Buren for a second term in 1840, the Democrats practically guaranteed that the economic policies of his administration would become the central issue in the presidential campaign.

In December 1839 the Whigs held their first national convention at Harrisburg, Pennsylvania, and selected William Henry Harrison as their presidential standard-bearer. Many Whig leaders undoubtedly hoped that they could exploit the military reputation of their candidate in the same way that the Democrats had previously capitalized on the heroic deeds of Old Hickory. Although he was not a statesman of the caliber of Daniel Webster or Henry Clay, Harrison was a veteran politician with many political connections and few political enemies. Moreover, as the candidate of the northern Whigs in 1836, he had demonstrated his vote-getting capacity by holding his own against Van Buren in the Middle States and in the Old Northwest. North Carolina's Whig leaders had supported Clay in the Harrisburg convention, but they quickly warmed to Harrison's candidacy and campaigned vigorously on his behalf.[50]

In many respects the campaign of 1840 was a replay of the two previous presidential contests. All the familiar charges against Van Buren were repeated to prove that he was hostile to the interests of the South. This time the Whigs also made some effort to exploit the president's acknowledged opposition to the distribution of public land sales revenue. George E. Badger, a rising Whig star who was soon to become secretary of the navy, accused Van Buren of using the public lands to buy the votes of the western states in which they were situated, thus "making a present of the share of North Carolina to these States." Badger and other Whig orators also paid considerable attention to the military exploits of "Old Tippecanoe," whom they characterized as a "gallant soldier and inflexible patriot."[51]

Party leaders were not content, however, to portray Harrison as merely a military hero. According to the Whigs, he espoused all the principles that their party had been advocating since 1834. If elected, Harrison would not allow the executive to become the source of legislation, as Jackson and Van Buren had. He would limit his veto to bills that were clearly unconstitutional or that encroached upon the rights of individuals or of the states. He would disclaim all power to control the public money and would never attempt to influence the outcome of elections. He would confine his tenure to one term, would never use his office for purely partisan purposes, and would never remove anyone from office without apprising them of the causes of their removal. As for specific policies, the Whigs claimed that Harrison opposed the abolitionists and the independent treasury, supported the distribution of public land revenues, endorsed the compromise tariff of 1833, and stood overall for "a strict construction of the constitution."[52]

The Democrats, for their part, placed considerable emphasis on the issue of banking policy during the campaign. Indeed, the address of the Democratic central committee, which was published in the *Raleigh Standard* in June 1840 and was subsequently circulated in pamphlet form throughout the state, devoted its attention almost entirely to issues of banking and currency. Claiming that "the great issue is one between 'The *People* and the *Bank*,'" the Democratic address was filled with tirades against "Bank interest and Bank power . . . Bank oppression and Bank dishonesty." The address also attempted to demonstrate that "the *Harrison party* is in fact the *Bank party*." According to the Democratic committeemen, the refusal of the North Carolina Whigs to openly advocate the bank's recharter was in itself conclusive evidence of a secret conspiracy "to fix upon this country an irreversible Bank dynasty."[53]

The leaders of both parties agreed that the August state elections, which one Democratic editor described as "a mere skirmish to that which awaits us in November," would provide an accurate measure of public opinion in regard to the presidential contest.[54] Branch's disastrous defeat two years earlier had convinced both parties of the necessity for a state convention to select their gubernatorial standard-bearer. The Whig convention nominated John M. Morehead, a lawyer and businessman from Guilford County. Like Dudley, he had served several times as a Jackson elector before his break with the administration in 1834. The Democrats gave their party's official endorsement to Romulus M. Saunders, a perennial office seeker who was then serving as a judge on the state superior court. Both candidates broke precedent by campaigning extensively in virtually every part of the state. In their campaign speeches each concentrated primarily on the merits of the two presidential candidates. National politics also dominated most of the legislative elections. After the elections, the editor of the *Fayetteville Observer* remarked that "there never was an election in this State in which National politics was brought to bear to a greater extent than in the one just past. In no county, that we have heard of, was there a single candidate elected except on party grounds, and those who ran as neutral, taking neither side in politics, received comparatively, no votes at all."[55]

Until 1842 the various counties in North Carolina did not vote on the same day. State elections were held over a period of two weeks, beginning on the last Thursday of July and continuing until the second Thursday in August. Long before the final vote had been tabulated, however, it became apparent that the Whigs had won a sweeping victory in both the gubernatorial and the legislative elections. Morehead defeated Saunders by a majority of over 8,500 votes, winning more than 55 percent of the two-party vote. The Whigs' gains in the legislative elections were even more impressive. The party again carried both houses of the general assembly, winning a majority of thirty-two seats in the house of commons and six in the senate. The jubilant Whigs interpreted the election as a vindication of the national principles of their party. As the editor of the *Register* put it, "the State has gone for HARRISON and REFORM by a tremendous majority."[56]

The distribution of the gubernatorial vote in 1840 was similar to the pattern that had prevailed in 1836 and 1838 (see table 3.3). Once again the Whigs carried a majority of the Federalist and Albemarle Sound counties, while the Democrats did best in the counties of the middle east and the northern piedmont. The most significant difference from the two previous elections was Morehead's impressive showing in the mountain counties. He carried seven of the nine counties, most of them by lopsided majorities, and came within two

Table 3.3   The Vote for Governor, 1840 (by percentage)

	Morehead (Whig)	Saunders (Democrat)
Federalist counties	59 (17 counties)	41 (7 counties)
Republican counties		
Albemarle	64 (9 counties)	36 (2 counties)
Middle east	37 (4 counties)	63 (11 counties)
Piedmont	49 (4 counties)	51 (4 counties)
Mountains	72 (7 counties)	28 (2 counties)
Total	53 (24 counties)	47 (19 counties)
All counties	55 (41 counties)	45 (26 counties)

Source: Thomas E. Jeffrey, "The Second Party System in North Carolina," appendix A.
Note: Percentages indicate each candidate's share of the total two-party vote.

percentage points of winning the other two. The Democrats attributed the Whig gains to Morehead's western residence and to his reputation as a promoter of western rights. Undoubtedly, the disappearance of the Cherokee removal issue also contributed to the dramatic increase in the Whig vote in the far western counties of Haywood, Macon, and Yancey.[57]

In addition to the large Whig majorities in the far west, there were several other important changes in the distribution of the vote between 1836 and 1840. The defection of Charles Fisher and other Calhoun supporters produced substantial gains for the Democrats in four of the five counties in Fisher's congressional district. The significant increase in the Democratic vote in the eastern counties of Granville, Northampton, Perquimans, and Washington can probably also be attributed to the return of Calhoun supporters to the Democratic fold. In none of these eight counties, however, was the drop in the Whig vote sufficient to throw it into the Democratic column.[58]

The Whig prediction that Morehead's victory was a certain indication of Harrison's upcoming triumph in the presidential race proved to be accurate. Indeed, the party's showing in November was even more impressive. Harrison received about 1,200 more votes than Morehead, while Van Buren's vote was more than 2,000 below that of Saunders. Thus the outcome differed significantly from that of 1836, when the Whigs had won the state elections only to lose the presidential contest a few months later. The main difference between the two presidential elections was in voter turnout. Although the number of eligible voters increased by only 1,300 between 1836 and 1840, the number of Whig voters increased by over 22,000. Few, if any, of these converts to Whiggery had been Van Buren supporters in 1836, for the Little Magician's vote also increased by almost 7,000 between the two elections. Both parties succeeded in mobilizing a far larger proportion of the electorate than ever before. Indeed, by 1840 almost 85 percent of North Carolina's eligible voters were politically active.[59]

Some of this increase can be attributed to the development and refinement of new campaign techniques. Both parties staged political dinners, barbecues, mass rallies, and parades, which provided the voters with a variety of opportunities for eating, drinking, music, and oratory.[60] However, the voters who were attracted to the parties by these techniques did not divide equally between the Democrats and the Whigs. Ordinary North Carolinians may have enjoyed a drink and a free meal at election time, but when it came time for them to make a choice between the two parties, more often than not it was the Whigs who reaped the benefits.

The debate over Jackson's removal of the deposits in 1834 had provided the formal occasion for National Republicans, Barbourites, and other dissident Jacksonians to coalesce into the Whig party, but the deposits issue by itself cannot account for the extraordinarily high voter turnout after 1836 or for the series of Whig victories that continued almost uninterrupted until 1850. Between 1834 and 1840 the Whigs managed to expand their base of popular support and become the majority party in the Old North State. They accomplished this by winning previously uncommitted voters to their party rather than by making converts among Democratic voters. In the years following the deposits controversy, Whig leaders found new ways to make their policies relevant to an increasing number of voters. Their promise to give the state a fair share of the public land sale proceeds appealed to voters in underdeveloped areas throughout North Carolina. Their slogan of "retrenchment and reform" also attracted previously uncommitted voters who believed that the Democrats' policies had caused the financial crisis and who hoped that a Whig administration would restore the economy to its proper balance.

The evidence for North Carolina does not offer much support for the argument that the slavery issue was the driving force in southern politics during the 1830s.[61] Undeniably, the status of the South's peculiar institution loomed large in the rhetoric of the two parties. Whigs and Democrats both claimed that their opponents' presidential candidate was supported by northern abolitionists and that he championed policies that were detrimental to the slaveholding interests of the South. At the same time both parties made efforts to present their own candidates as friendly to slavery and to southern interests. But these appeals to sectional self-interest did not appreciably affect the outcome of the elections or induce significant numbers of new voters to the polls. Indeed, the sharp contrast in voter turnout in the state and national elections of 1836 revealed that a far greater number of North Carolina voters responded to issues that touched their pocketbooks than to the mutually contradictory claims about slavery and southern rights. With the onset of the financial crisis in 1837, the slavery issue receded into the background, and both parties devoted their primary attention to banking policy and to the condition of the economy. The dramatic increase in the popular vote in 1840 can be attributed to the success of the Whig party in capitalizing on the hard times and bringing previously uncommitted voters to the polls.

The Whig leaders interpreted their stunning triumph in 1840 as a vindication of correct principles. There were many ordinary voters, however, who also expected certain tangible results from the party's victory. They anticipated that the national Whig administration would restore the prosperity that they had enjoyed during most of the 1830s and that the state administration would build schools, railroads, and turnpikes, and at the same time keep taxes low. It remained to be seen whether accomplishments could keep pace with expectations.

4 ✦ Cliques, Caucuses, and Conventions: Political Parties and the Organizational Dilemma

The chief element of strength which the Whigs possess is the goodness of their cause. On this they rely too much, and have, hitherto, done but little in the way of organization.—*Raleigh Register*, 18 October 1836

The Whigs had their *Central Committee of office-holders at Raleigh*, while the Democrats had no Committee, no organization whatever—they relied on *truth* and *truth* alone; soberly and righteously administered to the people.— *North Carolina Standard*, 17 August 1842

By 1840 both Democrats and Whigs in North Carolina had come to accept the necessity of party organization as a means of promoting harmony, ensuring a full turnout at elections, and discouraging independent candidates. Both parties established national conventions to nominate their presidential candidates, state conventions to choose their gubernatorial standard-bearers, district conventions to select congressional candidates and presidential electors, and county conventions to determine candidates for the general assembly. In addition, a hierarchy of national, state, and local committees had responsibility for coordinating the various campaigns, plotting strategy, raising money, and disseminating political information to the voters.

Yet, despite these organizational efforts, neither the Democrats nor the Whigs managed to develop party machinery that completely fulfilled their goals and expectations. The leaders of both parties frequently complained that their own followers were lax, apathetic, and undisciplined, while those of their opponents were supposedly well organized and thoroughly drilled. After each election the editors of the partisan presses pointed out numerous examples of counties where their party had been late in announcing its candidates or where it had more than a sufficient number in the field. Leaders in remote parts of the state distrusted the central organization in Raleigh and frequently complained that party affairs were controlled by a "Raleigh Clique." Similarly, neighborhood leaders living in rural areas of the various counties often aired charges of domination and dictation by a "courthouse clique" located at the county seat.

The organizational problems of the North Carolina parties resulted largely from the difficulties of reconciling eighteenth-century republican ideology with the exigencies of nineteenth-century party politics. The tenets of traditional republicanism suggested a multiplicity of self-nominated candidates, yet political reality demanded the establishment of legislative caucuses and nominating conventions to narrow the party's choice to one official nominee. Whereas republican ideology placed the highest premium upon a candidate's virtue and his willingness to sacrifice personal interests for the public good, party leaders placed the greatest value upon a candidate's popularity and his willingness to subordinate his own views to the official positions of the party. Republican thinking was premised on the idea of an independent electorate freely selecting the most qualified among the contenders for office, but the stability of the party system was predicated on the ability of party activists to persuade the voters to support the official standard-bearer regardless of their personal preferences.

Most important, eighteenth-century republicanism had been imbued with a distrust of centralized authority and a belief that liberty was continually being threatened by concentrations of power. Yet the difficulties of coordinating myriad individual state and county campaigns eventually led to the establishment of central committees and other mechanisms of central control. It is unclear whether a majority of the voters in antebellum North Carolina ever fully accepted the legitimacy of the machinery established by the leaders of the two parties. Certainly the widespread popular suspicion of centralized power inhibited the development of effective party organization and led to frequent charges of "intrigue," "management," and "caucus dictation."

The leaders of the Whig party in North Carolina were slower than the Democrats to acknowledge the need for nominating conventions and other appurtenances of party organization. This reluctance was not a by-product of evangelical antipartyism, as some historians of the northern parties have suggested.[1] Rather, it was a result of the party's long-standing aversion to caucuses. In 1824 most of the future leaders of the North Carolina Whig party had crusaded against the efforts of the congressional caucus to "dictate" the choice of president. Four years later these leaders had again raised the issues of intrigue and management in their campaign against the "corrupt bargain" supposedly engineered by President Adams and Henry Clay. The 1832 nomination of Martin Van Buren as vice president had provided the occasion for many of them to set up a separate Jackson ticket in opposition to the choice of the "Baltimore caucus." Not surprisingly, the call for another national convention in 1835 to nominate Van Buren for the presidency set off a new round of charges that the convention system was nothing more than "King Caucus" in disguise.

The resolutions adopted by a Whig meeting in Davidson County in April 1835 were typical of Whig expressions of hostility toward conventions. The resolutions denounced the upcoming Baltimore convention as "nothing but a *Caucus*, got up at the instance of the office holders and office seekers—without consultation with the great body of the people, not in obedience to their will—but to bias and control that will . . . to destroy the freedom of elections, and to perpetuate their own power." Like the discredited congressional caucus, the national nominating convention was viewed as an antirepublican institution whose real object was to dictate to the people their choice for president. A Whig meeting in Rowan County characterized the Baltimore convention as an "attempt to subvert the Constitution of the country—to take from the People the right of choosing their own President, and to transfer it to an irresponsible CAUCUS, composed of interested Office-holders and Office-seekers."[2]

The Whigs pointed out that the acknowledged purpose of the Baltimore convention was not to select a Democratic candidate from among a multitude of contenders, but rather to give a stamp of approval to Jackson's own handpicked successor. The Whigs characterized the convention as a "packed jury" composed only of those "who have already made up their minds to support the *heir apparent*." To the Whigs it was only logical that Van Buren, with his long experience in management and intrigue, should be the choice of the Baltimore caucus. "It is perfectly consistent for the friends of the Caucus now to support Mr. Van Buren," John M. Morehead told a Whig meeting in Stokes County, "as he was the Chairman of the Congressional Caucus in 1823, which nominated Mr. Crawford." Morehead, who had thrice been an elector on the Jackson ticket, assured his audience that "he had voted for Gen. Jackson in 1824, 1828, and in 1832 against *King Caucus*, and that he would vote for Judge White and against King Caucus in 1836."[3]

The Democrats denied the charge that the Baltimore convention was a trick to foist Van Buren upon a gullible electorate. Yet, ironically, party leaders defended the national nominating convention with the same arguments that Crawford's supporters had used in 1824 to justify the congressional caucus. They claimed that a convention was the only effective means of concentrating the strength of the Republican party and preventing an election by the House of Representatives. A meeting of Nash County Democrats warned that if the election were again thrown into the House, "that body by opening the door to fraud and management, may impose upon the country a President who is not the choice of a majority of the people."[4]

In addition to defending the propriety of a national convention, the Democrats took the offensive by denouncing the manner in which the opposition's presidential candidate had been presented to the voters. In December 1834 a group of Tennessee congressmen had picked Senator Hugh Lawson White as their choice to oppose Van Buren. White had subsequently been endorsed by legislative caucuses and public meetings in most of the southern states, including North Carolina. The Democrats charged the Whigs with hypocrisy in claiming to be opposed to caucuses while, at the same time, submitting to caucus dictation. The editor of the *Standard* contrasted Van Buren's nomination "by democratic Delegates, called together by the people themselves" with White's selection "in the first instance, by a little *caucus* at Washington City, and afterwards by legislative caucuses." The editor asked his readers, "Whose, now, is the 'caucus' candidate?"[5]

Probably more effective than these mutual charges of caucus dictation was the Democrats' argument that White could not win enough electoral votes to elect him president even if he carried all the states where his name appeared on the ballot. The Whigs did not effectively rebut this argument, and after Van Buren's victory over the three opposition candidates in 1836, leading Whigs throughout the nation were convinced that the party's failure to unite behind a single candidate had been the main cause of their defeat. In order to concentrate the strength of their party in 1840, the Whig leaders decided to emulate the tactics of the opposition and hold a national convention.[6]

In May 1838 the Whig members of Congress officially issued a call for a convention to meet in Harrisburg, Pennsylvania, late in 1839. Henry Clay, who had been soundly defeated by Jackson in 1832, was eager for another try at the presidency, and his aspirations were supported by a majority of southern Whigs, including those in North Carolina. Shortly after the call for a national convention, Clay asked former senator Willie P. Mangum for help in persuading the North Carolina party to overcome its "repugnance to Conventions" and to send a full delegation to Harrisburg. The Kentuckian argued that "the more general, fair and respectable the composition of the Convention may be, the greater will be the influence of any recommendation that shall issue from it." Undoubtedly Clay also realized that he could not hope to win the nomination for himself without a full turnout by the southern states.[7]

The leading Whigs in North Carolina quickly responded to Clay's initiative. On 11 June 1838 Weston R. Gales, the editor of the *Raleigh Register*, publicly called upon the Whig voters in the Old North State to hold primary meetings and elect delegates to the Harrisburg convention. Gales justified his party's call for a national convention with arguments similar to those used by the Democrats in 1832 and 1836. A convention, he argued, was the only effective means of achieving concert and harmony among the friends of good government. Moreover, the experience of 1836 had demonstrated the folly of having more than one standard-bearer. Gales assured his readers that "the Whigs intend to profit by past reverses—they will bring forward but one candidate, and that candidate will be elected, be he whom he may."[8]

Not all Whigs embraced the Harrisburg convention with as much enthusiasm as did Gales. Some, like the anonymous correspondent of the *Western Carolinian*, asked "on what grounds can the Whigs justify a CAUCUS at Harrisburg, when they have most loudly condemned a similar one, held in Baltimore?" Others, like the powerful eastern leader James W. Bryan, supported the call for a convention but did not rule out the possibility of a separate Clay ticket in North Carolina should the Harrisburg delegates fail to nominate the Kentuckian. The twelve North Carolina delegates supported Clay to the very end, but after considerable maneuvering both on the convention floor and within the nominating committee, the Sage of Ashland was cast aside in favor of William Henry Harrison. North Carolina Whigs were initially less than ecstatic with the choice, but the party presses dutifully called on the voters to abandon their personal preferences and support the official nominee.[9]

After 1839 the Whigs would never again challenge the legitimacy of a national nominating convention. Indeed, the behavior of the party leaders suggests how easily republican ideology could yield to political expediency whenever the two came into direct conflict. Leading Whigs in North Carolina denounced the convention system as long as they believed that they could make political capital by appealing to popular suspicion of caucuses and other mechanisms of central control. But they abandoned their objections to party organization as soon as they realized that it could be used to serve their own partisan purposes.

The Democrats had been quicker than their opponents to accept the convention system as a legitimate means of selecting the party's presidential candidates. Neither party, however, initially saw the need for a state convention to concentrate party sentiment behind its candidate for governor. In 1836 the leaders of both parties reached a consensus by less formal means, and each party adopted the strategy of holding county meetings to ratify the leaders' choice. During the early months of 1836 at least thirty-four Democratic meetings publicly endorsed the candidacy of Richard Dobbs Spaight, Jr., who had been elected governor the year before by the general assembly. On 10 March 1836 the editor of the *Raleigh Standard* placed Spaight's name on his masthead and boasted that the governor's nomination had been the result of a spontaneous outburst of "public opinion—unwarped by *central* influence, and untainted by the promptings of nightly conclaves of members of assembly."[10]

The reference to "nightly conclaves" was an unmistakable allusion to the meeting of Whig legislators and other party leaders on the evening of 22 December 1835, immediately after the adjournment of the general assembly. Although the Whig leaders did not officially nominate a gubernatorial candidate, they agreed informally that evening to support Edward B. Dudley. Dudley's impeccable Jacksonian pedigree made him a more attractive candidate than his main rival,

William B. Meares, a Federalist and supporter of John Quincy Adams, whom the Whig legislators had run against Spaight in 1835. With some justification the editor of the *Standard* charged that the Whigs had "elbowed Mr. Meares out of the way, and caucussed Gen. Dudley into his shoes." Dudley was officially nominated by a meeting of Wake County Whigs on 30 January 1836. By the beginning of June at least forty-six county meetings had endorsed his candidacy.[11]

Although neither gubernatorial nomination in 1836 resulted from a spontaneous outburst of public opinion, both candidates at least could claim the support of the majority of party activists throughout the state. This was not the case in 1838, when the Democrats chose John Branch to oppose Dudley. As mentioned earlier, many leading Democrats were at first reluctant to make the governor's election a partisan issue in a nonpresidential year. Even after deciding to field a candidate, the Raleigh leaders rejected the option of a state convention. Instead, they followed the precedent established in 1836 and nominated Branch at a meeting of the Wake County Democrats. This time, however, a partywide consensus had not been achieved in advance, and many local Democratic leaders refused to acknowledge the legitimacy of the nomination. The editor of the *Fayetteville North Carolina Journal* expressed the sentiments of these dissidents when he declared after the election that "Branch *was not* the candidate of the Republican party in North Carolina."[12]

Just as their defeat in the presidential election of 1836 had convinced the Whigs of the necessity of holding a national nominating convention, so too the debacle of 1838 convinced the Democratic leaders that county meetings were not suitable vehicles for uniting party sentiment behind a gubernatorial candidate. Shortly before the adjournment of the general assembly in January 1839, the Democratic legislators adopted resolutions recommending that a convention be held "to nominate a candidate for Governor, and for other purposes connected with the success of the Democratic party in this State." The Whig legislators also recommended that a convention be called to choose a successor to retiring Governor Dudley.[13]

Both conventions were poorly attended. Only thirty-six of the sixty-seven counties were represented in the Whig convention, which met in Raleigh on 12 November 1839 and nominated John M. Morehead for governor. Only thirty-five counties sent delegates to the Democratic convention, which met two months later to choose

Romulus M. Saunders as the party standard-bearer. Most of those who attended the conventions resided in counties near the state capital. Few delegates from the extreme eastern and western parts of the state chose to journey to Raleigh at a time of year when the roads were at their worst.[14]

As in 1836, the leaders of both parties had already reached a consensus on their candidates, and like the county meetings four years earlier, the state convention merely ratified a choice that had already been made. With some justification each party charged that their opponent's candidate had actually been selected by a "caucus." The Democratic editor of the *Western Carolinian* characterized the Whig convention as a "ridiculous farce" and wondered "why so many federal Lawyers and Doctors went down to Raleigh to ratify the *night act* of old 'King Caucus.'" The Whig editor of the *Carolina Watchman* was equally convinced that Saunders's nomination had been fixed in advance by an "irresponsible cabal at Raleigh." As evidence, he pointed out that the nomination had been announced by newspapers in Lincolnton and Salisbury on the very day of the convention, well before the editors could have officially learned the identity of their party's nominee.[15]

In 1840 a consensus among party leaders had been reached well in advance of the state convention. However, this was not always the case in subsequent years. In 1843 a caucus of Whig legislators failed to agree informally upon a candidate to succeed Morehead, and the delegates to the Whig convention considered a number of candidates before settling on former senator William A. Graham. In 1848 several prominent Whigs were mentioned as possible successors to Graham, who acknowledged that "the selection of a Candidate will depend rather on the composition of the Convention than on any decisive demonstration of public sentiment beforehand." The Whig convention of 1854 considered the qualifications of at least three aspirants before finally agreeing upon former congressman Alfred Dockery.[16]

Several of the Democratic state conventions also acted as decision-making bodies. For example, the delegates to the convention of 1846 debated the strengths and weaknesses of five possible nominees before selecting Greene W. Caldwell to oppose Governor Graham. In all of these cases, however, the actual choice was made secretly by a nominating committee or by a poll of the delegates in advance of the convention so that the official convention vote could convey the fiction of unanimity. Only once during the antebellum era did the contenders for the gubernatorial nomination carry their fight to the floor of the convention—in 1858, when the Democratic convention chose John W. Ellis by a narrow margin over William W. Holden.[17]

Neither party in North Carolina used conventions to give the ordinary farmer, laborer, or mechanic a voice in selecting candidates for the state's highest elective office. On the other hand, state conventions were not merely cosmetic devices created by cynical party leaders to delude gullible voters with the illusion of democratic procedures. Instead, they served the important purpose of bringing together local leaders from various parts of the state and thus imparting legitimacy to the party choice. As the editor of the *Standard* put it, a convention nomination enabled the party's gubernatorial candidate to "go before the people with the stamp of general party recognition and authority upon him." A state convention also served as a means of arbitrating and reconciling sectional differences within the party. According to the editor of the *Wilmington Journal*, "a Convention puts to rest any little jealousies which may exist between different sections of the State. The man upon whom the choice of the [Democratic] Convention might fall, will be almost certain to carry with him through the contest the enthusiastic support of every Democrat in the State. Whereas if he was brought before the people in any other way, there might be some room for dissention."[18]

Both parties in North Carolina also adopted the convention system to nominate candidates for the U.S. Congress. As early as 1835, district conventions assembled to select candidates in at least five congressional districts, and the practice became even more widespread in the following years.[19] The effectiveness of the congressional nominating convention varied in proportion to the degree of interparty competition in the various districts. In districts where parties were closely matched or where the minority party had at least a chance of winning the election, conventions were generally accepted as a political necessity. In districts where the minority party was too weak to field opposition, the convention was less effective as a means of settling intraparty disputes. In such districts rival candidates from the same party often ran against each other without the sanction of a convention nomination, and even a formal nomination did not guarantee that the official party candidate would run unopposed. Indeed, in districts where one party overwhelmingly dominated, the legitimacy of the convention system often became a major campaign issue in its own right.

The difficulties experienced by the Democrats in the Tar River district in 1847 provide an excellent example of the organizational problems that party leaders faced in uncompetitive districts. In 1846 the Whig general assembly had grouped six strongly Democratic counties in the northern coastal plain into a single congressional district. Five Democrats, including one incumbent congressman and two former congressmen, announced their candidacy. One of the Democratic aspirants was Henry Irwin Toole, a Tarboro lawyer who had previously sought the congressional nomination in 1843 and 1845. Both times a district convention had rejected Toole in favor of another Democrat. In 1845 Toole's supporters had publicly denounced the convention as a "packed caucus," and Toole had remained in the race until the Whigs, hoping to capitalize on a divided Democratic vote, decided to field a candidate of their own. Rather than bear the odium of a Whig victory, Toole finally withdrew.[20]

Running in 1847 in a less competitive district, Toole announced that he had no intention of abiding by a convention decision. Instead, he made the legitimacy of the convention system the major issue in his campaign, arguing that conventions were inherently antirepublican because their proceedings were invariably controlled by "a few second-rate politicians near the Court houses and villages of the several Counties." According to Toole, the convention managers habitually selected "some leading, honest and substantial country gentleman" as honorary president, in order to give a veneer of respectability to the proceedings. A secretary and nominating committee were then appointed in the same manner, "except that one at least of the contrivers of the meeting, who has a string of Resolutions in his pocket ready cut and dried for the occasion, is placed on the committee. *Of course* they are adopted unanimously—*of course* they are published in the newspapers . . . as the sentiments of large masses of free and enlightened citizens. . . . Thus do small politicians, who wish to be considered and affect to be party leaders, cover themselves with the mantle of the people—that *real* people whose voice they pretend to speak, whose rights they will not scruple to betray."[21]

Like numerous other frustrated aspirants, Toole advocated a return to a simpler and allegedly purer era when the people elected their representatives without the trammels of party organization or the "little tricks of little politicians." Comparing party conventions to the discredited congressional caucus, Toole appealed to the voters in his district to awaken to "the dangers which these caucuses threaten to your constitutional rights" and to unite as they had done in 1824 to put down "this irresponsible mode of *dictating* to the people for whom they should vote." Despite his appeal to anticonvention sentiment, Toole lost the election to incumbent Congressman John R. J. Daniel.[22]

There was certainly some truth in Toole's criticisms of antebellum party conventions. Undoubtedly the long and densely worded resolutions adopted by most of these conventions had been composed well in advance of the meeting to be presented "cut and dried" to the delegates, and it is probable that the nominees of many district conventions had been determined before the delegates ever assembled. Some conventions were poorly attended, and even the well-attended ones may not have faithfully represented the sentiments of all the voters for whom the delegates presumed to speak. At the same time, however, one must wonder, as did the editor of the *Wilmington Journal* on another occasion, "how many of those who are now furiously denouncing the convention would have refused its nomination?"[23] Toole had twice submitted his claims to a party convention and, on at least one occasion, he had come very close to winning its endorsement. His opposition to the convention system in 1847 can be attributed as much to thwarted ambition as to an ideological aversion to party organization. Moreover, despite Toole's claims to the contrary, there is no evidence that the convention system was any less democratic than the older system of self-nomination and informal selection by local notables that it replaced.

The experience of the Democrats in the Tar River district suggests that conventions could sometimes be divisive rather than unifying influences on the North Carolina parties. In more competitive districts, however, conventions did serve to prevent the minority party from capitalizing upon an overabundance of candidates within the majority party. Only once during the antebellum period did an excessive number of candidates produce a Whig victory in a Democratic congressional district, and no Democrat ever won election in a Whig district for that reason.[24] Moreover, for the Democrats at least, a convention nomination carried with it an authority and sanction that exerted a powerful influence over the party faithful. Although independent Democrats often campaigned against the convention nominee in districts where the Whigs were too weak to field an opposition candidate, not once did a Democratic insurgent ever manage to defeat the regular candidate.

In heavily Whig districts, on the other hand, a convention nomination was not invariably a guarantee of success. In 1839, for example, an official endorsement by a convention in Asheboro did not prove sufficient to elect Pleasant Henderson over Charles Fisher, who ran as an independent Whig. Indeed, Henderson may have been handicapped by the charge that he had been nominated at Asheboro "by a few caucus managers."[25] Another convention nomination at Asheboro in 1845 did not lend sufficient legitimacy to the candidacy of Jonathan Worth to enable him to triumph over Alfred Dockery, his independent Whig opponent. Like Toole and Fisher, Dockery made the propriety of a nominating convention a major issue in his campaign. In more competitive districts, however, the convention system did prevent the divisive effect of independent Whig candidates. When a Whig district convention again rejected Dockery in 1849, the former congressman reluctantly acquiesced in the decision. Running in a new district where the Democrats were much stronger, Dockery realized that a multiplicity of Whig candidates would inevitably result in a victory for the opposition.[26]

Both parties also used conventions to nominate candidates for seats in the general assembly. The convention system proved least effective as a vehicle for selecting official party candidates at the county level. In those counties where the parties were competitive, conventions did function with reasonable efficiency as a means of settling disagreements among rival aspirants. However, most North Carolina counties tended to identify strongly with one party, and attempts by party leaders to impose the convention system in such counties were frequently met with charges of "caucus dictation."[27]

Few counties with overwhelming Whig majorities used conventions to nominate candidates for the general assembly. Instead, a multitude of self-nominated Whig candidates competed among themselves for the legislative seats, and the editors of the party presses generally took a position of neutrality. The editor of the *Greensboro Patriot*, for example, described his attitude as "the more the merrier." On one occasion he characterized the seven Whig candidates from Guilford as "a clever set of gentlemen" and expressed his regret that only three could be chosen. The editor of the *North Carolina Argus* voiced a similar opinion in regard to the Whig candidates who competed for the legislative seats from Anson County. "We don't care who whips [whom] in this fight," he declared, "for all are equally well qualified—all will make good representatives."[28]

Some of the strong Democratic counties also continued to adhere to the old republican ideal of self-nominated candidates. In Duplin County, according to one Democratic editor, "party opinion being nearly altogether of one and the same hue . . . and it therefore being thought unnecessary to hold conventions, patriotic gentlemen who are willing to make so many and so great sacrifices for their country, nominate and announce themselves." Other heavily Democratic counties initially attempted to use conventions but later abandoned them as divisive and ineffective. In Stokes County, for example, one local leader remarked that "the abortive results in attempting to hold conventions . . . have so prejudiced the party against them, that it would not do to try it again soon."[29]

The absence of a convention system in these small electoral districts increased the possibility of a minority candidate entering the race in order to capitalize on a divided majority vote. When such a danger seemed to exist, party leaders tried to pressure the weaker candidates to withdraw. In Anson County, for example, six aspiring Whigs announced themselves during the spring of 1860 as candidates for the county's two seats in the house of commons. By late May two Whigs had already abandoned the race, and a third dropped out early in July. By the time the election took place in August, only three Whig candidates remained in the contest. In Anson, at least, this system of trial heats in advance of the general election proved to be more effective than a convention in narrowing the field of candidates to an acceptable number.[30]

While the Whig leaders preferred to rely on informal means to limit the number of legislative candidates, the Democrats tried to impose the convention system on many of the counties where they enjoyed large majorities. In such cases independent Democrats frequently announced themselves as candidates, and the propriety of the nominating convention often became the major campaign issue. In New Hanover County, for example, William S. Larkins offered himself as a candidate for state senator in 1852, in opposition to the convention nominee, whom Larkins's supporters characterized as "the selected candidate of an 'irresponsible cabal.'" The friends of Larkins urged their fellow citizens "to put a stop to this political *garotte*— conventions, we mean—especially in New Hanover, where we can expect no opposition from the Whigs." The dissidents predicted that "the freemen of New Hanover County will not again submit to dictation, altho' backed by the formidable name of Convention."[31]

A persistent theme among opponents of county conventions was that their nominations were controlled by a clique of party leaders at the county seat. Such charges were often initiated by disappointed aspirants from the majority party and then eagerly picked up by editors of the opposition presses. The Whig editor of the *Salem People's Press*, for example, claimed that the Democracy of Forsyth County was controlled by a "'knot of politicians,' whose head-quarters is at the court-house . . . a 'clique,' who strive, not only to manufacture public opinion for the people, but even go so far as to threaten refractory members of the Democratic party with the *political lash*, if they do not readily acquiesce in the decisions of the 'clique,' as agreed upon in *caucus*, and promulgated in convention!"[32]

Understandably, the leaders of the majority party took pains to deny the existence of a courthouse clique. The Democratic editor of the *Tarboro Southerner* claimed that the "Tarboro Clique" existed only in "the fertile imagination of some one, peculiarly fond of starting humbugs." The Democratic editor of the *Winston Western Sentinel* asserted that the "mere idea of such a thing as a courthouse clique is ridiculous and absurd." Similarly, the editor of the *Washington Whig* deprecated the efforts of the Democrats in Beaufort County "to gull the people, by crying Caucus—Caucus—Caucus, wherever they go, and to magnify the county meeting that nominated the Whig Candidates into something wonderful and dangerous."[33]

It would be a mistake, however, to dismiss these charges of town domination as nothing more than the fabrications of disappointed aspirants and opportunistic editors. Although antebellum North Carolina was a predominantly rural state, party affairs at the county level tended to be dominated by small groups of lawyers, newspaper editors, planters, and businessmen who lived near the county seat and whose business and legal affairs brought them into frequent contact with one another. The editor of the *Raleigh Standard* remarked that "there is always to be found a bevy of noisy village politicians in every little town."[34] It was these village politicians who chose the time for the meeting of the county convention, composed the long addresses and resolutions, and exercised a disproportionate influence over the choice of their party's legislative candidates.

On the other hand, these local party managers were not oblivious to public opinion, as opponents of the convention system often argued. Indeed, popularity and family connections were important considerations in the choice of suitable legislative candidates. On occasions where dissatisfaction arose with the convention's nominee, the fault did not always lie with the party managers. Few nominations probably satisfied all of the numerous neighborhood chieftains in a county. Sometimes such men failed to attend the convention themselves and then loudly complained that it had ignored their wishes. Local aspirants with a limited following sometimes expected the nomination for themselves even though their candidacy would lend little strength to the party ticket. Occasionally a neighborhood would divide its loyalties among several aspiring politicians, and the party managers hesitated to alienate one local leader by nominating a candidate favored by another.[35]

If an abstract devotion to democracy was not sufficient to impel party leaders to respect public opinion, a healthy recognition of their own self-interest almost certainly supplied the deficiency. In counties where the party balance was close, an unpopular nomination could mean defeat for the entire legislative ticket. And even in areas where the majority party monopolized power, a nominee who did not enjoy the support of a large portion of his constituency invited insurgency and intraparty wrangling. Thus, the editor of the *Wilmington Journal* implored his Democratic readers "for heavens sake . . . make it a point that the Convention shall be full, and composed of men who have conferred with the people, and can therefore represent them."[36]

Although attempts by local opposition leaders to make capital on the charge of town domination could have an impact on individual county campaigns, the overall effect on the balance of parties in North Carolina was probably negligible. More important in its influence on the outcome of statewide campaigns was the widespread belief that the parties were controlled at the state level by a clique of politicians in Raleigh. The institutional embodiment of the so-called Raleigh Clique was the state central committee, which directed the statewide campaigns for president and governor and coordinated the legislative and congressional campaigns. Until 1848 the Whig central committee was composed exclusively of officeholders, newspaper editors, and lawyers living in or near Raleigh. The Democratic committee was officially composed of members from each congressional district, but the preponderance of members from Wake and other nearby counties, together with a low quorum, enabled politicians residing near Raleigh to carry on the business of the committee.[37]

The first central committees were appointed in 1835 by party leaders in the general assembly. After 1839 they were selected by the biennial state conventions. Through its control of the Raleigh newspapers and its biennial address to the people, the central committee set the tone for each campaign by determining which issues the party would stress and which it would ignore. Committee members kept themselves informed of party activities in the various counties, encouraged local leaders to select candidates at an early date, secured and distributed campaign literature, sent out speakers to remote parts of the state, and made efforts to avert local party divisions and independent candidacies.[38]

Although the individuals comprising the committees varied somewhat from one campaign to the next, there was sufficient continuity of membership to permit the identification of many of the "movers and shakers" within each party. The Whig committee of 1840, for example, consisted of eight members: William H. Battle, John H. Bryan, Weston R. Gales, George W. Haywood, Thomas J. Lemay, Hugh McQueen, Charles Manly, and Henry W. Miller. Gales and Lemay were, respectively, the editors of the *Raleigh Register* and the *Raleigh Star*, North Carolina's leading Whig newspapers. The other members were attorneys who had moved to Raleigh to practice law. Only Gales, who served as a member of the general assembly in 1836, and Manly, who became governor in 1848, held a popularly elected office between 1836 and 1860. On the other hand, many of the committeemen benefited from patronage positions at the disposal of the Whig-controlled general assembly. Battle, a native of Edgecombe County, served as reporter to the state supreme court from 1834 until 1839, as judge of the superior court from 1840 until 1852, and as justice of the state supreme court from 1852 until 1867. McQueen, a native of Chatham County, was North Carolina's attorney general from 1840 until 1842. Manly, another native of Chatham, was clerk of the house of commons almost continuously from 1830 until 1848.[39]

Because the Democratic committee was nominally composed of members from all parts of the state, it is more difficult to identify its active members. One of the most influential Democrats on the committee was undoubtedly William H. Haywood, Jr., who served from 1836 until 1842. Haywood had been one of the organizers of the Jackson party during the 1820s, but, unlike many original Jackson men, he remained loyal to Old Hickory after 1834. Haywood retired from the house of commons in 1837 and never again held a popularly elected office. He did, however, accept an appointment as U.S. district attorney from the Van Buren administration, and in 1842 the general assembly elevated him to the U.S. Senate. Other Democrats who played a leading role on the committee were Louis D. Henry, a native of New Jersey, who practiced law in Fayetteville and ran as the party's candidate for governor in 1842; Thomas Loring, a native of Massachusetts, who edited the *Raleigh Standard* from 1837 until 1843; and James B. Shepard, a native of New Bern, who succeeded Haywood as U.S. attorney in 1840 and ran for governor in 1846.[40]

After 1843 the most influential Democrat on the central committee was William W. Holden, Loring's successor as editor of the *Standard*. The illegitimate son of a Hillsborough grist-mill operator, Holden began his journalistic career as a Whig, serving as an apprentice and typesetter for the *Hillsborough Recorder*, the *Milton Chronicle*, and the *Raleigh Star*. Despite his lack of formal education, Holden studied law while working with Thomas Lemay of the *Star*, and in 1841 he received his license. A year later the young Whig asked Senator William A. Graham for a loan to purchase a controlling interest in the *Star*. Graham turned him down, and Holden subsequently approached James B. Shepard, who arranged the necessary funds for him to assume both the ownership and the editorship of the *Standard*. Some Democrats were initially skeptical about Holden's commitment to Democratic principles, but the new editor approached his task with the zeal of a convert and quickly won over his critics. Indeed, Holden proved to be a brilliant editor and a master political strategist, and he played a central role in making the Democrats the majority party in North Carolina during the 1850s.[41]

An association with the Raleigh central committee frequently proved a stepping-stone to higher political office. Two of North Carolina's U.S. senators, along with several of its governors and gubernatorial candidates, were active members of the central committee. Numerous other gubernatorial and senatorial nominees were politicians who lived in Raleigh, in Wake County, or in a handful of other nearby counties. The widespread—and not entirely unfounded —belief that Raleigh-based politicians were monopolizing the important state offices fueled popular resentment against the Raleigh Clique and, on more than one occasion, wreaked havoc on the efforts of party leaders to unite their forces behind their official standard-bearers.

The Democrats were the first to feel the deleterious effects of the Raleigh Clique issue. In 1838 the Raleigh Democrats had injudiciously nominated John Branch without consulting with party leaders in other parts of the state, and local Democratic leaders bitterly complained about this high-handed action. Even before Branch's nomination, dissidents had warned their party to be on guard against "the intrigue and treachery of a few . . . at Raleigh . . . who are trying to establish a central power to dictate and to give law and rule to the balance of the freemen of this State." The Raleigh Clique issue undoubtedly was a major factor behind Branch's disastrous defeat in 1838.[42]

The gubernatorial nominating convention, which was adopted by both parties shortly after Branch's defeat, was intended to forestall such charges of central influence. But the Raleigh Clique issue returned to plague the Democrats in 1846, when their convention failed to accomplish its function of selecting a gubernatorial candidate. Most of the Democratic delegates who assembled in Raleigh on 8 January 1846 expected the convention to tender the nomination to Charles Fisher, the mercurial ex-Whig from Salisbury who had been a driving force in North Carolina politics since the campaign of 1824. Shortly before the convention, however, Fisher flabbergasted his political friends by refusing to become a candidate. The delegates subsequently gave the nomination to former congressman Greene W. Caldwell, who, as it turned out, had no intention of giving up his lucrative appointment as superintendent of the U.S. mint at Charlotte. On 20 January Caldwell formally declined the nomination on grounds of ill health and "the condition of my private matters."[43]

In the absence of a call by the central committee for another state convention, county meetings in Anson, Catawba, Lincoln, Mecklenburg, and Union nominated Walter F. Leak, a wealthy manufacturer from Richmond County, who agreed to become a candidate. Ignoring these expressions of sentiment, the Raleigh-based members of the central committee subsequently designated one of their own, James B. Shepard, as the Democratic nominee. Leak refused to accept the legitimacy of the nomination. Instead, he issued a sharply worded circular condemning the behavior of the "Raleigh Clique." Characterizing the nomination as "a naked assumption of power," Leak lambasted the "political wire-workers in and about the city of Raleigh, who now, as heretofore, really seem impressed with the belief that Raleigh, like Paris, is the State, and that every citizen must bow to their dictation." For his part, Leak pledged, he would "be dictated to by no such irresponsible clique."[44]

Leak's circular was published first in the *Fayetteville Observer* and then in other Whig newspapers throughout the state. Not surprisingly, the Whig editors quickly took up the charge that Leak was being bullied by a power-hungry clique at Raleigh. "We shall see," exclaimed the editor of the *Register*, "whether Mr. Leake [sic] and his friends are to be whipped into the ranks, by the managers about Raleigh, who think that THEY *are the party*, and can put up, or put down, whomsoever they please." The Whig presses also published numerous extracts from local Democratic newspapers and county meetings denouncing Shepard and the Raleigh Clique.[45] Undoubtedly aware that a divided Democratic vote would inevitably result in the reelection of Governor Graham, Leak eventually agreed to abide by a nomination made by the full membership of the central committee. After the full committee reaffirmed the nomination of Shepard, Leak withdrew from the race. But the stigma of the Raleigh Clique remained on Shepard's candidacy, and the friends of Leak gave him only grudging support.[46] Not surprisingly, the election resulted in a landslide victory for Governor Graham. As in 1838, many disgruntled Democrats simply sat out the election.[47]

The Whig leaders at the state capital had not hesitated to sound the changes on the Raleigh Clique theme during the campaign of 1846. They soon learned that the issue was a double-edged sword. Both William A. Graham and his predecessor, John M. Morehead, lived in counties to the west of Raleigh, and Whigs in the extreme east expected that the party's gubernatorial nominee in 1848 would come from their part of the state. Many eastern Whigs favored the candidacy of former congressman Edward Stanly, who actively campaigned for the nomination. However, other prominent easterners like Kenneth Rayner, Andrew Joyner, James W. Bryan, Frederick Hill, and William Washington also had their share of supporters. Because of the inability of the eastern Whigs to unite on a single candidate from their section, the Whig state convention chose Charles Manly as a compromise candidate.[48]

The choice proved to be an injudicious one. Manly had served his party capably for many years, and he had been prominently mentioned for the nomination four years earlier. But the smooth-talking clerk of the house of commons had never held an elective office and, even worse, he was a long-time member of the Whig central committee. Manly's nomination antagonized many Whigs in the east. William Valentine, a lawyer from Hertford County, characterized him as "a gentleman whom no body suspected they would nominate" and added that "I can't help from thinking that his nomination was obtained by central influence." The editor of the *Washington Whig* claimed that "the whole East are deeply mortified at this result."[49]

The Democrats were quick to capitalize on the belief that Manly's nomination had been engineered by a few party managers in Raleigh. According to William W. Holden, "the preferences of Eastern Whigs were set aside, and Raleigh was declared to be *the East*." Holden was convinced that Manly would be a weak candidate. "It is *certain*," he told Congressman Abraham Venable shortly after the Whig convention, "that the dissatisfaction in the East at his nomination is deep and wide-spread."[50] Indeed, the charge of "central influence" did considerable damage to Manly in the east, where the Whig share of the governor's vote dropped sharply from the previous election. Manly won the election, but by a majority of only 854 votes. Two years later the Raleigh Clique issue would contribute to the victory of David S. Reid, North Carolina's first popularly elected Democratic governor.[51]

The difficulties experienced by the parties in uniting their forces behind their gubernatorial candidates were paralleled by the chronic intraparty wrangling over the choice of North Carolina's U.S. senators. From the 1830s until the end of the antebellum era, both parties used the legislative caucus to nominate their senatorial candidates. This institution was not totally unfamiliar to the leaders of the two antebellum parties. Earlier in the century Republican legislators had occasionally used the caucus to select their candidates for governor and senator. But this device seems to have been employed only intermittently, and Tarheel Republicans never developed the sophisticated machinery that was characteristic of Republican parties in most of the northern states. The Federalists, for their part, consistently expressed disdain for all caucuses, legislative as well as congressional.[52] With the reemergence of partisanship in the mid-1830s, however, both legislative parties quickly turned to the caucus as a means of uniting their strength behind a single senatorial candidate. Still, some ambitious politicians refused to accept the authority of the caucus, and recurring complaints that a few political insiders manipulated the caucus to their own advantage served to reinforce popular resentment against the Raleigh Clique.

The legislative caucus was first used by the Democrats in 1836 to nominate a successor to Willie P. Mangum, who had resigned his seat after Van Buren carried North Carolina in the presidential election. The party controlled the general assembly by a majority of only two seats, and no Democrat could hope for success without the backing of his entire party. Despite the pressing need for party unity, the first Democratic caucus failed to agree on a candidate. A second caucus, held a few days later, agreed to tender the nomination to Robert Strange, a Fayetteville lawyer. On the floor of the general assembly, party lines held firm, and all but two of the legislators gave their votes either to Strange or to John Owen, the Whig candidate.[53]

Despite some difficulties, the legislative caucus of 1836 ultimately fulfilled its function of narrowing the field of Democratic candidates to one. Six years later, however, when the Democrats enjoyed considerably larger majorities in both houses, the caucus failed to avert a factional fight on the floor of the general assembly. Indeed, Romulus M. Saunders, who lost the caucus nomination to former senator Bedford Brown, made a major issue of "the malign influence" that supposedly had "controlled and directed" the deliberations of the caucus. As Saunders put it, "the *big lawyers* were against me," and the Democratic legislators had lacked the firmness to resist "this secret influence against me." Saunders also claimed that the legislators had been pressured by the "wire-workers in Washington City," who had let it be known that Brown was their choice.[54]

After his defeat in the caucus, Saunders carried his case to the floor of the general assembly, where he received thirty-six votes on the first ballot, compared to fifty-six for Brown and seventy for William A. Graham, the Whig incumbent. Because all three candidates repeatedly fell short of the eighty-six votes required for election, the balloting continued for a period of two weeks. On the eighth ballot most of the Whigs threw their support to Saunders, who came within eight votes of election. Faced with the prospect of a senator beholden to the Whigs for his election, the Democrats quickly closed ranks and agreed to set both Brown and Saunders aside in favor of William H. Haywood, Jr., who was subsequently elected. The Democrats did not get another opportunity to elect a U.S. senator until 1852, and, once again, Saunders played the role of spoiler. This time, however, the party was unable to unite on a compromise candidate, and after more than one hundred ballots the general assembly adjourned without filling the vacancy.[55]

The Whigs, who controlled the general assembly for most of the period between 1836 and 1850, fared little better in uniting their party behind their senatorial candidates. The Democratic incumbents, Bedford Brown and Robert Strange, had both resigned after their party's defeat in the presidential election of 1840, and the Whigs that year had an unprecedented opportunity to elect two U.S. senators. The most formidable contender was former senator Willie P. Mangum, who had resigned his seat four years earlier and was now eager for a political comeback. The Whigs generally agreed that Mangum should be one of their nominees, and most of the competition centered on the choice of a candidate to fill the two years remaining in Strange's term. Among the aspirants from the east were former congressman William B. Shepard of Pasquotank and former governor John Owen of Bladen. The most prominent candidate from the west was former governor David L. Swain of Buncombe. Other western contenders included Congressman Lewis Williams of Surry and former congressman Augustine H. Shepperd of Stokes.[56]

As expected, Mangum easily won the caucus nomination for the full six-year term. But to the surprise of many, the other nominee was William A. Graham, the speaker of the house of commons. Totally ignoring the concept of geographical balance, the Whigs had unabashedly selected two men who were residents of the same county and who lived only a few miles from Raleigh. Residents of the remote counties of the extreme east and the far west had long been resentful of the power of the central counties, and in 1840 William B. Shepard, the candidate of the Albemarle region, lashed out bitterly against his fellow Whig legislators for submitting blindly to "the dictates . . . of King Caucus." According to Shepard, the caucus system practically guaranteed that politicians from the seaboard counties would be permanently excluded from high office. "Should it be persisted in, the people on the seaboard had as well not send members here. They are now geographically in a minority, but when matters are done openly . . . we have some security in the power of decency and the sense of shame. Not so, however, if we must obey King Caucus."[57]

One of the most outspoken defenders of the legislative caucus in 1840 was Thomas L. Clingman of Buncombe County, who delivered a long speech in the state senate in defense of his party's choice of Mangum and Graham.[58] By the end of the decade, however, Clingman himself had become the most outspoken Whig opponent of the legislative caucus. One of the most controversial characters in the history of antebellum North Carolina, Clingman spent the first dozen years of his political career helping to build the Whig party in the Old North State, and the next dozen systematically trying to tear it down (see chapter 11). Clingman's attitude toward the legislative caucus changed dramatically once he found it to be an obstacle to his own senatorial ambition. He first competed for his party's senatorial nomination in 1846, only to lose out to George E. Badger. A brilliant and distinguished lawyer, Badger had served briefly as secretary of the navy in the Harrison and Tyler administrations. Like Charles Manly, however, he was a resident of Raleigh and a member of the Whig central committee, and he had not held an elective office in thirty years. In 1848 Clingman again challenged Badger unsuccessfully for the Senate seat, and, like other disappointed aspirants, he convinced himself that his ambitions had been thwarted by a small faction of "central managers."[59]

In a public letter to his constituents, which he published shortly after the senatorial election, Clingman summarized his case against the Raleigh Clique. The western leader pointed out that the heavy Whig majorities in the mountain counties invariably supplied the winning margin in state elections. Yet when the time came to distribute the political rewards, the "central clique" in Raleigh "most modestly make arrangements for dividing among their favorites all the offices in the state." According to Clingman, the central managers maintained their ascendancy within the party through their manipulation of the legislative caucus. By threats, promises, and appeals to the generosity, vanity, and party loyalty of the "plain, honest, sensible men" in the legislature, the party managers inevitably succeeded in nominating the candidate of their choice "just as the dullest gamester, when he has the privilege of shuffling the pack to his liking, is able to turn up a particular card."[60]

There is little evidence to support Clingman's charge that the Raleigh Whigs were deliberately conspiring to exclude westerners from important state offices. Defenders of the legislative caucus claimed that the preponderance of Raleigh-based senators was a natural result of their central location, which gave them numerous opportunities to become acquainted with other party leaders and develop political support. According to the editor of the *Register*: "Their central position gives them relations with the extremities, which a man residing remotely from the Seat of Government cannot have with his fellow-citizens in other quarters." The editor denied, however, that "there is any concert of action at the centre, to despoil or injure the extremities."[61]

At the same time, it is undeniably true that a disproportionate share of North Carolina's antebellum senators lived in the vicinity of the state capital. The six senators who served between 1834 and 1854 all resided in four contiguous counties near the center of the state. Not until the election of Asa Biggs in 1854 did either party select a senator who lived more than one hundred miles from Raleigh. Although there is no evidence of a conspiracy to exclude outsiders like Shepard and Clingman from the state's highest offices, Whig leaders certainly did exhibit insensitivity to the aspirations of such leaders. The Raleigh Whigs would ultimately pay dearly for their unwillingness to reward talented outsiders like Clingman.

Throughout the antebellum years Democrats as well as Whigs consistently experienced difficulties in selecting candidates at all levels of government. These difficulties were, in large part, an outgrowth of the organizational dilemma that beset both parties in North Carolina. In order to mobilize their supporters behind a single slate of candidates, the parties established sophisticated machinery at the state and even at the county level. Yet the widespread belief that party managers in Raleigh and at the county seats manipulated this machinery to the disadvantage of outsiders meant that the deliberations of party conventions and caucuses would frequently be accompanied by charges of "central influence" and "caucus dictation." Instead of promoting unity, party machinery could, ironically, become a major source of discord. And, as the governor's elections of 1838, 1846, and 1848 revealed, the burden of an unpopular standard-bearer could have an adverse effect on a party's standing at the polls. At the same time, however, too much emphasis should not be placed on the organizational dilemma as an explanation for long-term changes in the balance of parties in North Carolina. Both parties were equally afflicted by the problem, and the ability of the Democrats to rebound quickly after Shepard's disastrous defeat in 1846 suggests that the impact of the organizational issue could be quite transitory.

One of the ways in which the antebellum party system differed from that of the Federalist era was in its considerably more sophisticated organizational structure. Yet historians have disagreed about the role that organization played in mobilizing voter support for the parties.[62] Most studies of North Carolina parties have emphasized the importance of effective party machinery and have attributed the success of the Whigs during the 1830s and 1840s at least in part to their superior organization.[63] This argument is based on two assumptions, both of which are arguable: first, that superior organization invariably has a positive impact on the political fortunes of a party; and second, that the Whigs were, in fact, better organized than their opponents.

The evidence presented in this chapter suggests that sophisticated party machinery was not invariably a source of strength; indeed, at times it could become a liability. Nor is there much evidence to support the claim that the North Carolina Whigs were better organized than their opponents. The two parties developed almost identical organizational structures, and the Democrats were actually more successful than the Whigs in extending party machinery to the county level. Whether the Whigs used their machinery more effectively than the Democrats is a question that cannot be answered conclusively. Certainly the Democrats were quick to attribute their opponents' success to their superior organization—along with their adeptness at vilification, misrepresentation, and slander. The Whigs, on the other hand, never attributed their success to superior organization, ascribing it instead to "the goodness of their cause."[64] Each point of view was, of course, congruent with partisan self-interest.

The Democrats found it far more satisfactory to blame their successive electoral defeats on extraneous factors like party organization than to acknowledge that the policies espoused by their opponents might seem more attractive to the voters. Ironically, historians have uncritically accepted an image of superior Whig organization that was initially created by the Democrats for their own partisan purposes.

In contrast to a faction or a junto, a fully developed party is more than merely a set of individuals with similar outlooks or beliefs. It is an institution with "a life—and goals—of its own." Indeed, like all institutionalized organizations, "its pre-eminent goal is survival."[65] Historians have often characterized the antebellum parties as "electoral machines" whose primary function was to nominate candidates, conduct campaigns, and win elections.[66] The concept of electoral machines provides a highly useful approach to analyzing the behavior of antebellum North Carolina parties. For example, it explains why the Whigs campaigned vigorously against the presidential nominating convention in 1836, only to embrace it four years later. The attitude of the party leaders during the two campaigns may not have been ideologically consistent, but it certainly was consistent with their primary goal of electoral success.

The concept of electoral machines can easily lead to a cynical view of parties as nothing more than "great hoaxes" created to gull a credulous electorate.[67] Yet this viewpoint is every bit as simplistic as the antithetical position that parties are primarily embodiments of abstract, enduring principles. As one insightful student of antebellum politics has pointed out, party leaders never had the luxury of saying or doing anything they pleased. On the contrary, they "had to operate within defined limits set by the party's understandings, traditions, principles, and distinctive outlook."[68] The electoral machines of the antebellum era functioned within the boundaries of a definite and circumscribed political culture. To comprehend the essence of the second party system and the roots of the intense partisan loyalties so characteristic of the antebellum era, it is necessary to examine the ideological contexts within which the two parties operated.

5 ✦ "Measures, Not Men": Ideology and Political Culture in Antebellum North Carolina

Remember one thing, brother Democrats, that in contests of this sort *men* are as nothing, and that *principles* are everything.—*North Carolina Standard*, 18 April 1846

It is *office*, OFFICE, for which the Loco Foco leaders pant. . . . Freedom, country, national glory, are all as dust in the balance, compared with the delights of office.—*Raleigh Register*, 7 August 1850

Did the two antebellum parties embody two fundamentally different views about the relationship between government and society, or were the party battles of the Jacksonian era nothing more than "a stage duel with tin swords"? In his classic study of politics and society in the antebellum South, Charles S. Sydnor concluded that the parties did not offer meaningful alternatives to the voters and that "the chief activity of Southern politicians in the 1830's and 1840's consisted in struggles for local place and power rather than in contests over any principles that differentiated the national parties." According to Sydnor, the rank-and-file southern voter was "unable to see much difference between Whigs and Democrats" and, therefore, "made his choice on the basis of minor events and insignificant words."[1]

This view of southern politics has fallen increasingly into disfavor among historians. In a ground-breaking article published in 1954, Charles G. Sellers challenged both the Sydnor thesis and the older view that the Whig party in the South embodied the states'-rights philosophy of the great planters. Sellers pointed out that like their northern counterparts, southern Whigs fought with the Democrats over a variety of economic issues relating to banking and financial policy. Far from being a stage duel fought with tin swords, the drama of southern politics unfolded in an arena "full of the resounding clash of solid interests and opposing ideologies."[2]

Recent studies of the second American party system have elaborated upon Sellers's interpretation to present a picture of partisan conflict over a wide range of national and state issues. At the national level the Whigs supported a policy of active governmental intervention in the economy and endorsed such measures as a national bank, a protective tariff, federal internal improvements, and the distribution of federal land revenues. At the state level the Whigs favored the chartering of banks and other corporations, state aid to internal improvements, public education, and other policies designed to promote the common weal. The Democrats, on the other hand, endorsed the doctrine of the negative state by opposing a national bank, a protective tariff, internal improvements, and distribution. The various state Democratic organizations also moved in the direction of negative government by restricting the privileges of state banks, opposing the chartering of corporations, and denying the power of government to promote internal improvements. The parties thus presented real alternatives to the voters, and the resulting electoral alignments "represented real and abiding differences of attitude and opinion."[3]

An analysis of the rhetoric of the two North Carolina parties confirms the argument that Democrats and Whigs disagreed sharply over a number of specific policies at both the national and state levels. In particular, the parties held contrasting views about the proper relationship between the executive and legislative branches of the national government and about the role that banks and corporations should play in the economic and political life of the nation. Ideologically, however, the party conflict in North Carolina was not a struggle between proponents of positive and negative government. Both parties advocated principles of strict construction, states' rights, and negative government at the national level, while at the state level leading Democrats as well as Whigs supported a policy of state-financed internal improvements and public schools. Moreover, the leaders of both parties articulated and defended their own policies, and attacked those of their opponents, within the context of a commonly shared republican ideology.

In recent years historians of pre–Civil War politics have become increasingly sensitive to the pervasive influence of republican ideology in the political culture of antebellum America. Initially articulated in the mid-eighteenth century to justify colonial resistance to Britain, the idea of republicanism meant more than merely the absence of monarchy. It also embodied a unique attitude toward the relationship between government and society. According to republican theory, the main purpose of government was to safeguard individual liberties from concentrations of arbitrary power. The vitality of republican government depended upon the virtue of its citizens and upon the willingness of its leaders to sacrifice their personal interest to the public good. Because of their dependence upon the rectitude of their citizens and officeholders, republics were considered to be frail institutions, easily susceptible to subversion by corrupt and selfish rulers who put their own self-interest ahead of the public interest. The only preventive was constant vigilance on the part of the people.

Among the electorate, republican ideology produced a widespread distrust of authority and a suspicion of all concentrations of power, whether in the form of a caucus, an organized political party, or a chartered corporation. Republican ideology also led to a paranoid outlook on politics and a tendency on the part of politicians to discuss almost every issue in terms of its implications for the future of republican government. Instead of viewing their opponents as honest but misguided patriots, party leaders characterized them as enemies of the republic and denounced their policies as conspiratorial efforts to destroy liberty and to promote aristocratic privilege. Words like "corruption," "tyranny," "aristocracy," and "dictation" pervaded the rhetoric of both antebellum parties.[4]

There is abundant evidence that the leaders of the two North Carolina parties were thoroughly imbued in the ideology of republicanism. Indeed, republican theory provided the framework within which they viewed both their own actions and the conduct of their opponents. Newspaper editors and party orators repeatedly warned of the fragility of liberty and the need for the people to watch constantly over the actions of their rulers. "Power is constantly stealing from the many into the hands of the few," one Whig editor reminded his readers. "The few in their turn are soon reduced to ONE, who becomes the supreme ruler. This is the natural principle of progression from republicanism to despotism. Let us therefore guard against its influence."[5]

Unfortunately for the friends of liberty, the enemies of republican institutions were often clever men who disguised their true intentions by mouthing platitudes about the rights of the people, even as they conspired to subvert those rights. "The enemies of popular rights," warned Charles Fisher, "like the great enemy of the human soul, are always at work, secretly and in the dark; they come upon us like a thief in the night and while we sleep they steal away our liberty." Internal subversion thus presented a greater threat to the viability of republican government than did military force. As one candidate for Congress pointed out: "There is more danger to our institutions from FRAUD than FORCE. All military usurpations must be violent, and therefore cannot succeed until the great body of the people consent. It may happen, however, that whilst the people remain attached to their liberties, they may be cheated into an involuntary surrender of them by the arts and intrigues of unprincipled politicians."[6]

Although the leaders of the two parties claimed to be devoted to popular rights, a close examination of their rhetoric reveals a pessimistic attitude about the ability of ordinary citizens by themselves to preserve their liberties, surrounded as they were by scores of designing politicians. The average citizen might be basically well meaning, but he was also extremely gullible and, therefore, easy prey for flattering demagogues. According to one Whig editor: "The great majority of the people are both honest and patriotic, but many of them are over credulous, and are too easily imposed upon by low selfish politicians, whose only chance of distinction springs from the credulity of those on whom they practice." Another Whig agreed that "it is indeed a lamentable but political truth, that . . . [the people] are too confiding in their public functionaries, forgetting the maxims of Republican Governments—that liberty is only secured to the people by their constant watch over . . . the acts of their public men."[7]

Democratic leaders also subscribed to this dim view of the people's ability to protect themselves against the secret enemies of republicanism. How else could the steady succession of Whig victories be explained if not by the ability of opposition leaders to deceive the honest yeomanry? In an address to the "reflecting men" of Northampton County delivered shortly after the state elections of 1836, Congressman Jesse A. Bynum complained that the Whigs had "succeeded in deluding many of the best men of the county" by means of "the grossest falsehoods and misrepresentations." Bynum warned his listeners that, in the upcoming presidential election, the opposition would continue its efforts "to delude and carry off the plain and honest men of that heretofore plain republican county. To dazzle the eyes of the plain, farming men of the county."[8]

Despite their frequent lip service to the sovereignty of the people, the leaders of both parties held an essentially elitist view of the nature of politics and the role of parties. Believing that "the common, well meaning classes of our country . . . only err from the want of necessary light to guide them in the paths of political wisdom," party leaders justified their organizations as the necessary means of enlightening public opinion and protecting "the good and honest, but too *confiding* people of North Carolina" from unscrupulous demagogues and from their own worst instincts.[9]

Both parties claimed that the preservation of liberty depended upon the election of men with correct principles. Each argued that its own principles would promote republican government and that the principles espoused by the other party would destroy it. But Democrats and Whigs in the Old North State actually held similar views about the role of the national government and its relationship to the states. The two parties did not present the voters with a clear choice between an activist federal government and a policy of laissez-faire. Instead, the leaders of each party claimed to support a policy of minimal government and argued that the policies of their opponents would inordinately increase the power of the federal government, destroy the independence of the states, and lead inevitably to aristocracy and despotism.

The Whig view of government was ably summarized in a letter by Congressman James Graham to his constituents in 1843. According to Graham, the purpose of government was to protect the lives, liberty, and property of the people, "but not to transfer one man's labor to another without his consent." Government should not attempt to reallocate the resources of society by imposing taxes on one class of citizens for the benefit of another. Graham promised the voters that he would do his best to ensure that the government was "so administered as to award equal justice to all, and exclusive privileges to none. . . . I will not legislate for the advantage of the few at the expense of the many." The congressman also assured his constituents that he did not favor high taxes or extravagant expenditures. "No more money should be collected from the pockets of the people, than is necessary for a wise and economical administration of Government." Although the Democrats might have questioned the sincerity of Graham's beliefs, none would have challenged his views about the role of government.[10]

In North Carolina Whigs as well as Democrats went on record in favor of "a strict construction of the Constitution—no unnecessary taxation—a cheap and economical Government."[11] The leaders of both parties believed that an overflowing federal treasury was a curse rather than a blessing, because an excess of revenue would lead inevitably to extravagance, corruption, and the loss of liberty. According to Congressman Charles Shepard: "He who is sincerely anxious for honest rulers, and is opposed to daring usurpation, must strive to keep the Government poor, and frown upon every scheme of extravagance." The editor of the *Hillsborough Recorder* agreed that "liberty is not half so much endangered by the assaults of open violence as from the covert and insidious operations of a corrupt government (and such every government may become) in dealing out largesses and bribes from the public treasury."[12]

During the 1830s the Whigs repeatedly pointed to the dangers of a large federal surplus as one of the reasons for distributing public land revenues among the states. The Democrats countered that the best way of reducing revenue was to lower the tariff, but they too were alarmed and embarrassed by the surplus that had accumulated by 1836, and all but one of North Carolina's Democratic congressmen joined the Whigs in voting for the Deposit Act. By the end of 1837, however, the collapse of the land boom and the abrupt decline in imports and tariff revenues had turned the surplus into a deficit of over $12 million, and expenditures continued to exceed revenues in every year but one until 1844.[13]

The Whigs were quick to attribute the growing federal deficits to the corruption and extravagance of the Van Buren administration. Campaigning in 1840 upon a program of "retrenchment and reform," the Whigs accused Van Buren of presiding over "one of the MOST CORRUPT Administrations ever in power" and claimed that he was trying his best "to imitate the royal magnificence of the eastern monarchs." Party leaders were particularly critical of Van Buren's expenditures for furnishing the East Room of the White House, and they cited these expenses as evidence that the president was attempting "to convert the Chief Magistrate's house into a regal palace."[14] Needless to say, the Democrats immediately turned the tables on their opponents after the Whigs gained control of Congress and the presidency in 1841. The Democratic platform of 1842 denounced the Whigs for not carrying out their promises of retrenchment and for practicing extravagance while preaching economy.[15]

To a modern reader these charges and countercharges of extravagance may seem quite petty and, in some cases, downright mean spirited. Indeed, even some of the Democrats balked when their party attempted to make an issue of the $3,000 spent on President Harrison's funeral in 1841.[16] Such overtly partisan attacks probably persuaded few voters who were not already prepared to be convinced. Yet it is unlikely that the issues of extravagance and corruption would have played so large a role in the rhetoric of the two parties if these themes had not struck a responsive chord in the minds of the voters. In the political culture of antebellum North Carolina, money was power. And the extravagant disbursement of the people's money carried the threat not only of financial ruin but also of the destruction of the republic itself.

While claiming to support a strict construction of the federal constitution and a severely circumscribed national government, leading spokesmen in both parties acknowledged the right of the state government to use its power and resources to promote the public welfare. Not all North Carolinians agreed that the state should use its revenues to construct railroads, turnpikes, and other improved transportation facilities. Indeed, many Tarheels were vehemently opposed to any efforts to involve the state in investments that they considered extravagant and unprofitable. Much of this anti-improvement sentiment was concentrated in the wealthy plantation counties of the middle east, which already had adequate connections with the market towns and stood to derive little direct benefit from an ambitious program of state development. A majority of legislators from these counties consistently voted against measures to invest state money in the stock of internal improvement companies.[17]

The middle east was one of the strongholds of the North Carolina Democracy, and many Democratic voters staunchly opposed the concept of state aid to internal improvements. This does not mean, however, that the party itself objected to positive government at the state level. Indeed, Democratic leaders such as William H. Haywood, Jr., Romulus M. Saunders, Robert Strange, Louis D. Henry, Lewis H. Marsteller, James B. Shepard, and William D. Moseley were in the

vanguard of the movement for state-supported internal improvements. These eastern leaders resided in the commercial towns of
Fayetteville, New Bern, Raleigh, and Wilmington, and their constituents desired improved transportation connections with the interior.
Western Democrats such as Charles Fisher, Michael Hoke, Samuel
Flemming, William W. Avery, and William H. Thomas also desired
state aid to build railroads and turnpikes to link their communities
with eastern markets.[18]

Leading Democrats played a prominent role at the numerous internal improvements conventions that were held during the 1830s to
promote the idea of state involvement in economic development. At
the Raleigh convention of November 1833, for example, Strange
drafted a memorial to the general assembly recommending a $5 mil-
lion program of internal development to be financed by a state loan.
Haywood, Henry, and at least twenty-seven other prominent Democrats also participated in the deliberations of the convention. In 1838
another convention assembled in Raleigh, this time under the chair-
manship of Saunders. A committee report signed by Saunders, Henry,
and Marsteller recommended a $3 million loan to finance internal
improvements. Also in attendance at the convention were Haywood,
Shepard, and other important Democratic leaders.[19]

Divided as they were over the issue, the Democrats did not mention internal improvements in their official party platform until
1854. However, leading spokesmen for the party went on record numerous times in support of positive government. The editor of the
Raleigh North Carolina Constitutionalist, the organ of the state
party until 1834, argued that "any investment . . . of the funds of the
State which has for its object the advancement of the general prosperity and happiness of the people, must be commendable. It is upon
this principle that appropriations are made by governments for the
promotion of literature and science. It is upon this principle that all
expenses of government are incurred." Robert Strange, who drafted
the memorial of the internal improvements convention of 1833, expressed similar sentiments. According to Strange, republican governments "were not devised only that their citizens might be safe, but
that they might be happy. Whatever man singly is incompetent to
perform for his individual happiness, society was formed that it
might be accomplished by united effort." Although internal improvements undertaken by the national government were unwise and inex-

pedient, "internal improvement within the limits of each particular State, if not its duty, is at least its own exclusive right."[20]

Historians of North Carolina politics have frequently pointed to the Democratic campaign against the financially troubled Raleigh & Gaston Railroad during the 1840s as evidence that the party opposed a policy of state assistance to economic development. Under the vigorous leadership of William W. Holden and the *Raleigh Standard*, the Democrats tried hard to convince the voters that the successive Whig administrations had driven the state to the verge of bankruptcy through their involvement with railroads (see chapter 7).[21] But it is important not to confuse the natural tendency of the out-party to rail at the extravagant policies of the in-party with an ideological opposition to positive government. Even at the height of the railroad controversy Holden denied that he opposed the concept of state aid in itself. "We are not ourself hostile to the course of improvement, *prudently* conducted," the editor asserted in 1844. "*But we are opposed to any increase of our State Debt. . . . We say let the existing Rail Road debt be paid off first.*" Not all Democratic editors were willing to endorse Holden's demand for a moratorium on state spending. "The first duty of a wise and good government," the editor of the *Fayetteville North Carolinian* admonished his readers, "is to make good roads—and thus foster its agricultural interests." If Holden happened to believe that the state was too deeply in debt to construct additional improvements, "that is but the opinion of the *Standard*; we think differently."[22]

The Whigs proved just as adept as their opponents at playing politics with the internal improvements issue. Numerous examples can be cited of Whig editors accusing leading Democrats of endorsing "extravagant," "reckless," and "injudicious" schemes of internal improvements. Indeed, the Democrats frequently complained of "Whig Editors who, to suit their own party schemes, have denounced leading democrats for their votes to improve the state."[23] Yet no historian has mistaken this Whig tactic for an ideological opposition to state development. In the case of both parties it is necessary to distinguish between ideology and opportunistic partisan rhetoric.

An analysis of partisan responses to other state issues also casts doubt on the argument that North Carolina parties disagreed sharply about the proper relationship between government and society. One of the most enduring myths in the historiography of antebellum

North Carolina politics is that the two parties divided over the issue of state-supported public schools. According to this interpretation, the Whigs were "practically a unit in advocating the establishment of a system of public schools," while the Democrats "manifested little . . . interest . . . in the matter of giving to the state a creditable educational system."[24] In reality, however, there was a bipartisan commitment to public education. Early in 1839 a bill to establish a system of public schools passed the general assembly by an almost unanimous vote. What little opposition there was came principally from the Whigs. A popular referendum the following August revealed a similar pattern of bipartisan support. Only seven counties—five Democratic and two Whig—voted against the school law.[25]

The existence of a bipartisan consensus on public schools did not prevent parties from agitating the issue. Indeed, the Whigs tried hard to convince the voters that they were the exclusive friends of the new school law, and they vilified the Democrats as its enemies. According to the Whig editor of the *New Bern Spectator*, the Democrats were "using every heartless and wicked argument" against the school law "merely because the bill was passed by a Whig legislature, and because they know that it would have been passed and in effectual operation years ago, had the Whigs had the ascendancy."[26] The Democrats did not allow such statements to go unchallenged. After pointing out that the voters in several solidly Democratic counties had registered almost unanimous support for the school law, Thomas Loring of the *Raleigh Standard* bitterly castigated the Whigs for "their falsehoods about the vote on the school bill. They strive to make it a party matter, and would induce the people to believe that the Democrats, as a party, oppose Free Schools, while the Federalists [Whigs] support them."[27] Despite the efforts of Loring and others to set the record straight, the image of a progressive Whig party struggling against the Democrats' opposition and indifference to establish a public school system for North Carolina has persisted into the twentieth century.

An examination of party attitudes toward other social issues fails to reveal a consistent pattern of support for, or opposition to, positive government at the state level. In 1840, for example, 54 percent of the Whigs in the house of commons voted in favor of a bill to establish a penitentiary, as did 39 percent of the Democrats. Depending on one's point of view, this evidence can be interpreted in different ways. It suggests that Whigs tended more than Democrats to support a policy of government activism, but it also indicates that legislators in both parties were deeply divided over the penitentiary issue. In 1844, to cite another example, an overwhelming 85 percent of the Whigs in the lower house supported a bill to charter a school for the deaf and dumb, compared to only 36 percent of the Democrats. This vote seems to offer more clear-cut evidence of a Whig commitment to positive government. Yet the Democrats could not have been unequivocally opposed to a school for the handicapped because two years later, when the legislature voted on appropriating funds for the institution, large majorities in both parties supported the measure.[28]

An analysis of roll-call votes in the general assembly on issues like the penitentiary and the school for the deaf and dumb demonstrates rather convincingly that more Whigs than Democrats usually voted in favor of government support. But these differences often blur into insignificance once the roll calls are cross-tabulated to account for the influence of section as well as party. In the case of the penitentiary bill, for example, the bloc that provided the strongest support for the measure was actually the western Democrats (69 percent), followed in turn by the western Whigs (60 percent), the eastern Whigs (43 percent), and the eastern Democrats (24 percent).

If an examination of legislative roll calls provides less than conclusive evidence of a sharp partisan division over social issues, an analysis of partisan rhetoric fails to supply the deficiency. Although the North Carolina General Assembly voted numerous times during the antebellum years on measures such as a penitentiary, an insane asylum, a medical board, schools for the handicapped, and loans to private academies, these issues were almost never discussed in the party platforms, on the hustings, or in the party presses. They simply were not matters of partisan concern.[29]

The dichotomy between positive and negative liberalism posited by recent historians of the second party system thus has only limited application to North Carolina. At neither the state nor the federal level is there much evidence of a sharp partisan cleavage between advocates of an activist government and supporters of laissez-faire. This does not mean, however, that consensus was the dominant force in antebellum North Carolina politics. On the contrary, the parties disagreed vigorously over a number of specific policy issues. Most of these differences related to the power of the president and to the role that banks and corporations should play in the economic and political life of the nation.

One point upon which all Whigs could agree was that the nation's chief executive had become far too powerful and that this accretion of power threatened the very existence of republican government. The Whig platforms of the 1840s constantly alluded to the dangers of executive power and advocated such remedies as a one-term presidency and the limitation of the president's veto power to legislation that was clearly unconstitutional. Party leaders also professed alarm at the growing patronage power of the president and warned that "the power and patronage of the General Government must be restricted to narrower limits or liberty will but too soon exist only in name." The Whigs claimed that the irresponsible use of this power had already created an army of greedy officeholders dependent upon the executive for their livelihood. These pensioners on the public bounty were continually attempting "to control the freedom of elections, and to dictate to the people who shall be their next President."[30]

The Whig emphasis on the growing power of the president was not empty rhetoric designed to hold together a group of politicians who were unable to agree on any substantive policies. Rather, it was a response to what one historian has called the "genuine institutional growth of the presidency under Jackson."[31] By using his veto power to negate legislation for reasons of expediency rather than constitutionality, and by claiming to do so in his capacity as the representative and spokesman of all the people, Old Hickory transformed the office of the president and significantly altered the relationship between the executive and Congress. If the opposition exaggerated the extent of the removals from office during his administration, it is nonetheless true that Jackson dismissed far more officeholders than his immediate predecessors and that he did so for reasons not always related to their fitness for office. And undoubtedly the Whigs were genuinely alarmed by Jackson's unprecedented claim of authority to transfer the federal revenues to the state banks without the consent of Congress.

Far from advocating an increase in the power of the government, Whig ideology was fundamentally antipower in character. The editor of the *Raleigh Register* claimed that the leaders of his party "project no visionary schemes, are satisfied with power actually granted, and would never transcend the limits of the Constitution, to gratify personal views or party purposes." On another occasion the editor reminded his readers that "the name Whig made its appearance in North Carolina, when *power* first began to encroach on the rights of the people. . . . The name implies opposition to misused power, and we glory, as does every true Whig, in the name." According to the Whigs, it was the Democrats who advocated "the increase of the strength of Government, which would take the political power from the many, and transfer it to the few."[32]

If the Whigs were the ideological heirs to the long-standing fears of republican subversion that had fueled the anticaucus movement of the 1820s, their opponents were the principal beneficiaries of the wave of antibanking sentiment that had swept across the nation following the Panic of 1819. From the viewpoint of the Democrats, the real danger to the Republic lay not in a despotic chief executive and an aristocracy of officeholders, but rather in a monied aristocracy composed of banks and other privileged corporations in alliance with unprincipled and opportunistic politicians. For the Democrats, the Bank of the United States was the symbol of this emerging aristocracy of finance, and Jackson's destruction of the "monster bank" was proof of their party's opposition to dangerous concentrations of financial power.

In appealing to popular hostility toward banking institutions, the Democrats were tapping a vein of sentiment with deep roots in the political soil of North Carolina. As Whig Governor Edward B. Dudley observed, "a very great number of our population . . . are distrustful of Corporations of any kind & are ready to oppose masses of wealth in corporations or individuals at the polls or elsewhere."[33] This popular aversion to banks was primarily a reaction to the specific policies that had been pursued by the state's own banking institutions during the 1820s. The years immediately following the War of 1812 had witnessed a rapid expansion of bank notes in North Carolina and throughout the nation. The Second Bank of the United States, which had been chartered by Congress in 1816, initially supported this expansion of credit, but a sudden reversal of policy in 1818 forced the state banks to begin calling in their notes. This action, together with a sharp drop in cotton prices, produced a financial panic. Suddenly faced with an unusually high demand for hard money, the state banks suspended specie payments. Farmers, merchants, and others who had

borrowed heavily during a period of inflation were now forced to re-
pay their debts during a period of currency scarcity.[34]

As the impact of the hard times increasingly made itself felt, public opinion in North Carolina turned decisively against the state
banks. During the early 1820s Governor John Branch led the outcry
against the banks, attributing the nation's financial distress to the
"unreasonable multiplication of banks, and the excessive issue of
their paper far beyond their capacity to redeem."[35] Although Branch's
solution to the bank problem was tighter regulation and a strictly
enforced requirement that bank notes be redeemable in specie, less-
enlightened antibank crusaders denounced all banks as irresponsible
monopolies whose only purpose was to enrich a few stockholders at
the expense of the rest of the population. As one antibank philoso-
pher put it, "all banks . . . are monied monopolies, tending to make
profit to those who do not labor, out of the means of those who do . . .
tending to create a privileged order unuseful and pernicious to society; tending to destroy liberty, and create a power unfriendly to human happiness; tending, inevitably, to an unfeeling monied aristocracy . . . [and] the destruction of the best hopes of man, here and
hereafter."[36]

Antibank fever in North Carolina reached a crescendo in 1828
when the general assembly, under the leadership of Robert Potter,
appointed a joint committee to investigate the affairs of the state
banks. Potter was a hotheaded politician who had made a career
crusading against banks. A minority report submitted by Potter recommended that the charters of the state's three banks be revoked and
that criminal proceedings be instituted against their officials. The
majority report conceded that some of the practices of the state banks
were technically in violation of their charters but denied that there
had been any criminal intent on the part of their officials. Potter's bill
directing the attorney general to begin proceedings against the banks
was defeated in the house of commons by the vote of the speaker.
Stunned by their narrow escape, the directors of the three banks
agreed to surrender their charters and close their affairs.[37]

The Bank of the United States largely escaped the opprobrium
directed against the state banks during the 1820s. Early in 1832 James
Iredell, Jr., told Senator Willie P. Mangum that "whether right or
wrong, that Bank is at this time very popular in our State—I believe,
indeed I know, it has done us vast good and as yet we have felt no

evils from it—where is the check upon the State Banks, if not to be found here!! I mean not theoretically but practically?" As Iredell's remarks suggest, many North Carolinians did not view the Bank of the United States as merely a state bank writ large but rather saw it as an agency whose operations had acted to restrain irresponsible banking practices at the state level. Prior to the introduction of the recharter bill in 1832, a majority of Democratic leaders in North Carolina probably agreed with William H. Haywood, Jr., that "the Bank might not be so *dangerous* & mischievous as is supposed by many."[38]

Although most of North Carolina's congressmen voted against the recharter bill in 1832, it was not until the controversy over the deposits a year later that the Democrats turned decisively against the Bank of the United States. Charles R. Ramsay, editor of the *Raleigh Constitutionalist*, typified the Jacksonian who could see the menace presented by the bank, but only after Jackson had opened his eyes for him. In September 1833 Ramsay admitted that "we have heretofore expressed ourself in favor of a National Bank, as essential to the maintenance of a sound currency and as furnishing important commercial facilities to the country. . . . And there was a time when we were solicitous for a renewal of the charter of the present institution; but we must confess that subsequent developements [*sic*] have created a great revolution in our feelings upon this subject."[39]

Once Jackson had shown them the way, the North Carolina Democrats dutifully followed in his path. After 1833 the party consistently denounced the bank as an unlawful concentration of economic power and "a dangerous engine to the liberties of the country." Unchecked by public opinion, the bank had the power to make money plentiful or scarce, prices high or low, and the value of all property uncertain. Even worse, by extending its loans to members of Congress and by buying newspaper editors, the bank had acquired a political influence that threatened the very existence of republican government. Democrats repeatedly characterized the bank as "a great electioneering machine" that had illegally used the vast funds at its command "in order to controul elections and regulate public opinion."[40]

Although the Democrats persistently accused their opponents of conspiring to recharter the Bank of the United States, the Whigs initially refused to acknowledge any desire to revive the dead "monster." Indeed, as late as the presidential election of 1840 the Whigs in North Carolina hesitated to come out forthrightly in favor of recharter. In response to Democratic charges that Harrison supported the bank, George Badger stated categorically that "his opinions . . . are against a Bank." But Badger cleverly left the door open to the possibility of a Whig-dominated Congress subsequently rechartering the bank. According to Badger, Tippecanoe would respect the prerogatives of the legislative branch, despite his own personal predilections. Should "unequivocal manifestations of public opinion" lead the people's representatives to recharter the bank, Harrison would not try to interpose his own will against the national will.[41]

Just as the Jackson–Van Buren men had been willing to follow their leaders into the antibank camp in 1833, so too the vast majority of Tarheel Whigs responded to the leadership of Henry Clay after their party won control of the federal government in 1841. Unlike some Whigs, Clay had never given up hope of rechartering a national bank, and the Whig landslide in 1840 guaranteed that there would be a sympathetic Congress and a president committed to the doctrine of executive restraint. During the first session of the Twenty-seventh Congress, the Whigs in the North Carolina delegation voted unanimously in favor of both of Clay's bank bills. When John Tyler (who had become president after Harrison's death in April 1841) vetoed the two bills, North Carolina's congressmen joined the other Whigs in voting to expel the recalcitrant chief executive from the party.[42]

By 1841 the propriety of reestablishing the Bank of the United States had become the chief bone of contention between the two parties in North Carolina. The Whigs campaigned vigorously for a national bank during the state elections of 1842, and two years later the Whig state convention adopted a resolution supporting a national bank as the best means of collecting and disbursing the public revenues and furnishing a currency of uniform value throughout the nation. After the Democrats regained control of the federal government in 1844, however, the Whigs gradually lost hope of rechartering the bank. The passage of the Independent Treasury Act in 1846 resulted in neither the financial chaos nor the executive despotism predicted by the Whigs, and by the end of the decade banking policy had ceased to be an important political issue in North Carolina.[43]

The partisan debate over banking was never a clear-cut struggle between proponents of positive government and advocates of laissez-faire. Although the Democrats repeatedly denounced the Bank of the United States as an unholy alliance between banking and government, the Whigs levied the same criticism against the independent treasury. According to the Whigs, the independent treasury would give the executive enormous power over the nation's currency without any of the restrictions or guidelines that would be included in a charter incorporating a national bank. Even worse, it would place the public money in the hands of corrupt officials appointed by the chief executive and removable at his will. The editor of the *Raleigh Register* warned his readers that the independent treasury would inevitably result in the creation of "a fearful and tremendous power, that ought never to exist in any country." Instead of divorcing the federal government from the banks, as the Democrats were claiming, the independent treasury would be, in effect, "a great Government Bank under the control of the President, which would confer on him despotic power."[44]

The Democrats denied that the independent treasury was a government bank, but they ruefully acknowledged the political efficacy of the charge. One Democratic leader admitted that there were at least one thousand voters in his own congressional district who "at this moment believe that the [Van Buren] Administration is trying to establish a Government Bank."[45] Moreover, in their defense of the independent treasury the Democrats came dangerously close to contradicting their own principles of limited government. Although party leaders repeatedly justified the measure as a means of extricating the federal government from its previous involvement with banks, they were also sensitive to Whig charges that the agency would be powerless to control the practices of the state banks. The Democrats never suggested that the federal government should totally abdicate responsibility for regulating the nation's banking system. Instead, they argued that the requirements of the specie clause would act indirectly to discipline the banks by forcing them to redeem their notes in hard money. The independent treasury would thus keep the state banks honest and guarantee a uniform circulating medium without involving the federal government in any direct way with the banking system.[46]

Despite their differences over the propriety of a national bank, the leaders of both parties claimed to support a properly regulated system of state banks and to oppose irresponsible and unsound banking practices. The debate over banking policy was not so much a dispute over positive versus negative government as it was an argument over the role that banks and paper money should play in the economy. While most Whigs accepted banks and paper money as necessary appurtenances in an expanding market economy, many Democrats viewed banks as, at best, necessary evils and considered gold and silver to be the only legitimate circulating media. Certainly there were few Democratic counterparts to the correspondent of the *Raleigh Register* who pointed out that banks lent money at low interest, allowed the funds of widows and orphans to draw honest dividends, and protected the people against sharpers and speculators. On the other hand, one would be hard put to find a Whig equivalent to the correspondent of the *Raleigh Standard* who pronounced gold and silver to be "the only money God ever made" or to the correspondent who believed that the distress and demoralization of the people rose and fell "in an exact ratio to the amount of paper money which they have suffered to be manufactured by the Banks." A voter who believed that all banks were agencies of the monied aristocracy and that God did his own business exclusively in hard money would have little reason to vote for candidates of the Whig party.[47]

Divergent views about the role of business corporations paralleled the party differences over banking and paper money. While the Whigs were inclined to accept corporations as necessary agents in an expanding economy, the Democrats were constantly trying to throw legislative roadblocks in their path. An examination of roll-call votes in the general assembly reveals that most Whigs consistently voted against efforts to make the personal property of stockholders liable for corporate debts and also voted against provisions that would give the legislature the right to repeal corporate charters. An overwhelming majority of Democrats, on the other hand, opposed efforts to restrict the liability of manufacturing and transportation companies to the assets of the corporation itself.[48]

Most Democrats considered all corporations to be dangerous concentrations of economic power and were thus inclined to prescribe strict limits on their activities. Democrats were particularly fearful that the special legal privileges granted to corporations would, in time, allow them to "absorb in themselves all political and commercial influence." For this reason Democrats opposed any attempt by the state legislature to give corporate institutions economic advantages that were denied to the average citizen. "Government has no proper connexion with corporations," admonished one Democratic orator, "and should be entirely separate from the moneyed influence."[49]

The Whigs, in general, took a more favorable attitude toward the role of corporations in promoting economic development. In their view, a paramount public interest justified the granting of certain legal rights, such as limited liability, to corporations. Few men of moderate fortunes would invest in corporate enterprises, they argued, if business failure also carried with it the danger of personal ruin. Far from being agents of the "monied influence," corporations provided the means by which men of middling circumstances could pool their resources and compete effectively with wealthy capitalists. Corporations thus served as "the powerful instruments with which a democratic people of small individual fortunes, have accomplished what elsewhere required the accumulated wealth of centuries and all the patronage of wealth and honor to effect."[50]

Party differences over banks, paper money, and corporate privileges reflected a deep-seated ambivalence among antebellum voters about the direction of economic development in nineteenth-century America. Americans welcomed the opportunities offered by an expanding economy, but they also feared the huge concentrations of economic power that seemed to accompany the rise of industry and the commercialization of agriculture. As Marvin Meyers has pointed out, Americans wanted to have it both ways. They "wanted to preserve the virtues of a simple agrarian republic without sacrificing the rewards and conveniences of modern capitalism." The divergent appeals of the Whigs and Democrats were directed not toward two competing social groups but rather toward two conflicting impulses within the same American psyche. While the Whigs "spoke to the explicit hopes of Americans . . . [the] Jacksonians addressed their diffuse fears and resentments."[51]

Aside from banking policy and the related issues of paper money and corporate privileges, the issue that aroused the most animated discussion in North Carolina during the 1830s and 1840s was the tariff. Yet, ironically, the two parties never presented the voters with a clear choice between a protective tariff and a tariff designed solely for revenue. In a state whose economic pursuits were predominantly agricultural, neither party was sympathetic to a protective tariff that would primarily benefit the industrialists of the North. Thus the North Carolina congressional delegation voted unanimously against protective tariff bills in 1816, 1824, and 1828, and as late as 1844 the editor of the *Raleigh Register* could remark that "the public man does not exist, nor the party, that asks or desires 'a Tariff for protection *merely*, and not for revenue.'"[52]

Until 1842 both parties pledged to abide by the compromise tariff of 1833, which provided for a gradual reduction of tariff duties over a ten-year period. Each party, however, tried to make political capital by accusing the other of secretly plotting to reinstitute the protective tariff. In 1840, for example, the Democrats claimed that Harrison favored a policy of protection and predicted that, if the Whigs gained power, one of their first priorities would be to reestablish high tariff rates "to obtain a surplus to carry out their scheme of a splendid Government." The Whigs retorted that Harrison was far more sound on the tariff issue than Van Buren, who had voted for the protective tariffs of 1824 and 1828 and had proven himself to be "foremost among those who carry furthest the Protective System."[53]

By 1842 the steadily increasing federal deficits had convinced many Whigs in Congress of the need for an increase in the tariff rates. After unsuccessfully attempting to enact a tariff bill incorporating the principle of distribution, party leaders settled on a bill that raised the tariff duties to the level of the tariff of 1832. Among the North Carolina Whigs, however, sectional self-interest took precedence over partisan loyalty. Although five of the eight Whigs from the Old North State had been willing to support a tariff bill containing a distribution feature, all eight voted against the bill that finally did pass Congress. Ironically, the Whig-sponsored tariff would have gone down to defeat except for the support it received from northern Democrats.[54]

Although the tariff of 1842 passed Congress too late to have an impact on the North Carolina state elections that year, the tariff did become a major political issue two years later. The Democratic state convention of 1844 urged a "tariff of duties laid solely with a view to the raising of . . . revenue" and condemned the tariff of 1842 for violating this principle.[55] Two years earlier the North Carolina Whigs had done their best to prevent the passage of the tariff bill. But in 1844 party leaders were aggressively promoting the presidential candidacy of Henry Clay, who had been one of the chief architects of the new tariff law, and this time sectional self-interest took a back seat to party loyalty. Thus William A. Graham, who had voted against the tariff in the U.S. Senate and was now running for governor, justified the measure as a necessary source of revenue. Graham admitted that the tariff contained some protective features, but he made a distinction between a purely protective tariff, which he opposed, and a revenue tariff with "incidental protection."[56]

The Democrats did not challenge Graham's concept of "incidental protection" in 1844 because their own presidential candidate, James K. Polk, had publicly gone on record in support of the same policy. According to William W. Holden of the *Raleigh Standard*, the Tennessean supported a revenue tariff but would sanction "such moderate discriminating duties as would . . . afford reasonable incidental protection to our home industry." Holden conceded that "no tariff can be laid without enuring to the benefit of one interest or another" and that, consequently, some discrimination would necessarily accompany any tariff measure. He denied, however, that the Democratic position on the tariff issue was identical to that of the Whigs, remarking somewhat lamely that whereas his own party believed in a policy of "discrimination for all," the Whigs supported discrimination "merely for the aristocratic capitalist of the North."[57]

It is unlikely that partisan arguments like these won any converts to the Democratic party in 1844. Democrats and Whigs may have disagreed about whether the tariff of 1842 was actually a protective tariff or merely a revenue tariff with "incidental protection," but both parties had committed themselves to the latter policy, and their official positions on the tariff issue were virtually indistinguishable. Once in power, however, President Polk and other leading Democrats quickly revealed their determination to push hard for a significant reduction in the tariff duties. In April 1846 North Carolina Congressman James I. McKay introduced a tariff bill incorporating the views of Polk and Secretary of the Treasury Robert J. Walker. Three months later the so-called Walker tariff passed Congress. Although most southern Whigs had opposed an increase in the tariff rates in 1842, all but two of them voted against a Democrat-sponsored reduction in 1846. On the other hand, except for the Pennsylvania delegation, the vast majority of northern Democrats supported the Walker tariff, even though many of them had voted in 1842 to increase the tariff rates. The Walker tariff failed to fulfill the dire predictions of the Whigs that it would lead to economic prostration and a bankrupt treasury. Indeed, the reduction in tariff rates did nothing to impede the process of economic recovery, which had begun in late 1843 and continued unabated until the latter part of the 1850s. By the end of the 1840s the tariff was no longer an important political issue in North Carolina.[58]

Although the issues of banking and tariff policy occupied much of the attention of party leaders during the 1830s and 1840s, the issue most consistently emphasized in the platforms of the North Carolina Whig party was the distribution of public land sale proceeds. When the Whigs adopted their first official platform in 1842, the party specifically endorsed the short-lived Distribution Act that had passed Congress in September 1841. A distribution plank appeared again in the Whig platforms of 1844 and 1846. Party leaders had always acknowledged that it would be impolitic to distribute federal revenues in time of war, and, not surprisingly, the advent of the Mexican War temporarily eclipsed the issue. By the early 1850s, however, distribution had again become an important part of the Whig program.[59]

The Democrats, for their part, opposed distribution much less vigorously than the Whigs supported it. Their platform of 1844 argued that distribution would be impolitic in view of the increasing national debt and the exhausted state of the treasury, but the other state platforms adopted during the 1840s ignored the issue. Behind the façade of party unity were many Democrats who quietly agreed with the Whigs that North Carolina was entitled to a share of the proceeds from the sale of lands in the American West. Throughout the 1840s the Democratic leadership managed to preserve party harmony by downplaying land policy, emphasizing instead their opposition to the Bank of the United States and their support of the independent treasury. During the next decade, however, the land issue would produce an open schism within the party.[60]

On the issue of federal support for internal improvements, which was hotly debated on the floor of Congress throughout the antebellum era, most North Carolinians were of one mind—at least in theory. During the first decade after the War of 1812, some of North Carolina's congressmen, especially those from the Albemarle region and the far west, had shown an inclination to support a policy of federal assistance. As it became increasingly apparent that the Old North State would derive no direct benefit from this outpouring of federal largesse, North Carolina's political leaders turned decisively against the idea of federally supported internal improvements. In

Congress the North Carolina representatives, Whigs as well as Democrats, repeatedly voted against measures to appropriate federal monies for the construction of railroads, canals, and turnpikes. Of course, opposition to federally supported improvements did not necessarily signify hostility to the cause of improvement itself. For the Whigs at least, the distribution of federal revenues among the states seemed a far more equitable means of achieving the goal of improvement than a policy of direct federal support that discriminated against the older seaboard states in favor of the rapidly developing states of the American West.[61]

Although theoretically committed to oppose a policy of federal aid, the Whigs were always prepared to make an exception in the case of the proposed inlet at Nags Head. William B. Shepard, who represented the interests of the Albemarle region in both the state and national legislatures for over twenty-five years, claimed that the federal government had a duty to improve the nation's harbors and inlets, even though it had no power to build turnpikes or canals. "The work at Nags head," he declared, "is an improvement strictly national in its character, and is far removed from all contested questions about internal improvement by the General Government."[62]

Not all Democrats were willing to agree with Shepard's distinction. Congressman Thomas Hall reminded his constituents that the U.S. Constitution said nothing about the power of Congress to improve harbors or inlets, and he wryly observed that a congressional appropriation for Nags Head might not be able to compete against the inexorable workings of the Gulf Stream, the Atlantic Ocean, and Albemarle Sound. Hall may have been right about both the Constitution and the Gulf Stream, but his constituents replaced him with a Whig who had more faith in the ability of federal money to connect Albemarle Sound with the ocean. Although the larger issue of federal support for internal improvements never became an important topic of party debate in North Carolina, the Nags Head issue was an important influence in keeping the northeastern counties in the Whig column.[63]

In North Carolina, as throughout the United States, party leaders divided over a set of economic issues relating to banking, tariff, and land policies. Whigs consistently supported the distribution of public land proceeds, and by 1841 had come out in favor of rechartering a national bank. Although committed against the idea of a protective tariff, party leaders defended the protective features of the tariff of 1842 and condemned the Democrat-sponsored Walker tariff. The Democrats, for their part, consistently opposed the recharter of the Bank of the United States, vigorously defended the independent treasury, vehemently condemned the tariff of 1842, and with considerably less vehemence opposed the policy of distributing public land proceeds. In addition to these specific economic issues, party leaders also held widely divergent views about the powers of the chief executive and the role of banks and corporations in the economic life of the nation.

Despite the existence of sharp policy differences, Whigs and Democrats in the Old North State did not offer the voters clear-cut alternatives on the role of government in promoting economic and social development. At the state level neither party took an unambiguous stand for or against active government. On some issues, such as the establishment of a public school system, there was a pattern of bipartisan support. On other issues, like the penitentiary, there was no intraparty consensus among either Whigs or Democrats. On the issue of state support for internal improvements, leading Democrats as well as Whigs explicitly endorsed a policy of government activism.

On the other hand, both parties in North Carolina espoused a policy of strict construction, states' rights, and negative government at the federal level. Of course, this argument cuts against the grain of much of what historians have recently said about the character of the two antebellum parties and the nature of partisan competition. Many of their generalizations have been grounded in a close analysis of partisan behavior in the U.S. Congress and in the state legislatures. The question naturally arises: Does not much of their evidence refute the claims made in this chapter? After all, North Carolina Whig congressmen consistently voted with their fellow partisans in favor of such measures as a national bank, a distribution of land revenues, and (at least in 1846) a protective tariff. Does not their support for these policies prove, ipso facto, that Whig leaders throughout the nation shared an ideological commitment to positive government?

Certainly there were antebellum North Carolinians who argued that support for a national bank and for a distribution of land revenues was tantamount to support for a "strong and splendid Government."[64] But such arguments invariably came from Democrats who were trying to discredit these policies; they never emanated from the

Whigs themselves. Indeed, according to the Whigs, it was the Democrats who were spawning an incestuous union between government and banking, first through their support for the "pet banks" and later through their proposal for a "government bank" or independent treasury. As for distribution, the Whigs argued that an overflowing federal treasury was the real source of corruption, consolidation, and despotism, and that dispersal of the federal revenues among the states was the best means of averting the danger of a consolidated national government.

Whatever the merits of these arguments, an analysis of Whig rhetoric offers little support for the notion that the party explicitly endorsed a policy of positive government. Nor does such an analysis confirm the claim that parties at the state level held conflicting attitudes toward the role of government. Again, there were antebellum North Carolinians who argued that the Whigs stood forthrightly behind a policy of internal improvements and public schools and that the Democrats were, at best, indifferent toward the success of these policies. Yet this interpretation of party conflict was invariably put forth by the Whigs to serve their own partisan purposes; it was repeatedly denied by the Democrats. Historians must be wary of accepting at face value the images that one party creates of the other.

The North Carolina case also suggests some of the pitfalls of attempting to infer comprehensive belief systems from legislative voting data. Roll-call analysis can serve as a useful tool for identifying salient points of partisan disagreement. But the alignment of votes on a particular policy measure can be the product of myriad influences, and partisan divisions within the U.S. Congress or the state legislature are not always reliable indicators of ideological divisons at the grass roots. For example, the unwillingness of North Carolina's Whig congressmen to join the Polk administration in dismantling the Whig-sponsored tariff of 1842 is hardly evidence that Tarheel Whigs were ideologically committed to a protective tariff. Nor are alignments in the general assembly on measures such as a penitentiary, a school for the deaf and dumb, and an insane asylum necessarily suggestive of how the parties' rank and file felt about such matters. Significantly, when the people of North Carolina were offered an opportunity to register their opinion on the penitentiary issue, the voters in both parties overwhelmingly rejected "positive government."[65]

To deny that the two North Carolina parties differed over the proper role of government is not to say that party battles lacked ideo-logical content. Indeed, the partisan debate took place within the framework of a republican ideology that transcended and even over-shadowed the specific policy matters at stake. Democrats argued that the Whig banking and tariff policies were part of a conspiracy by the monied aristocracy to consolidate the power of the central govern-ment and to gain special privileges and distinctions at the expense of the rest of the community. Similarly, the Whigs told their constitu-ents that Democratic measures such as the independent treasury were elements in a conspiracy to corrupt elections and to create a clique of officeholders and office seekers dependent on the president rather than the people for their livelihood. Both parties characterized the electoral battles of the day as momentous struggles for the sur-vival of republican government, and each claimed that the preserva-tion of liberty depended upon the defeat of the opposition.

A recognition of the central role of republican ideology in the political culture of antebellum North Carolina provides the key to understanding why the economic issues debated by the two parties had meaning and significance even to those voters who may not have been keenly interested in, or even aware of, the specific policy ques-tions at stake. However, republican ideology does little by itself to explain why a majority of voters in some North Carolina counties equated the menace to republicanism with banks and paper money, while a majority in other counties identified it with executive usur-pation and the independent treasury. Did the ordinary voter choose his party on the basis of its position on these issues? Or did most voters choose their party for other reasons and then look to their leaders for "correct" opinions about partisan issues? What, precisely, was the relationship between the divergent party programs and the actual pattern of grass-roots voting alignments?

6 ✦ Tories, Federalists, and Bank Men: The Social Bases of Party Allegiance

It is alike curious and instructive to trace the rise and progress of the names of the present Federal party. In 1772 many of them were Tories. . . . In 1812 Peace and Submission men. . . . In 1826 National Republicans. . . . And in 1844 *Coons* and Clay men.—*North Carolina Standard*, 11 September 1844

The question of why antebellum southerners divided their political allegiance between the two parties in almost equal numbers is one that has intrigued historians for generations. Earlier scholars tended to view the political behavior of antebellum voters as a reflection of broad socioeconomic divisions within the electorate. According to this interpretation, the Whigs constituted the "broadcloth and silk stocking party embracing a large part of the wealth, intelligence, and blue blood of the South." The Democrats, on the other hand, appealed mainly to small farmers and artisans in poorer areas with fewer slaves.[1]

Two recent studies of antebellum politics have refined and elaborated upon this model of political behavior. In a brilliant and provocative examination of politics and parties in Alabama, J. Mills Thornton argues that Whig counties tended to be more affluent, more deeply involved in commercial activities, and, therefore, more oriented toward a market economy than were their Democratic counterparts. The favorable attitude of Alabama Whigs toward banks, railroads, and other corporations, and the opposition of Democrats to these appurtenances of a market economy reflected the parties' divergent sources of electoral support. Harry L. Watson's intensive investigation of party alignments in Cumberland County, North Carolina, reached similar conclusions. The Whigs, he claims, were strongest among merchants and other professional men in the county seat of Fayetteville and among planters in the wealthiest, most commercially oriented parts of the rural hinterland. The Democrats, on the other hand, were strongest among small farmers in the poorer, more remote sandhills precincts. As in Alabama, the ideological divisions between the parties paralleled their different social bases. Whigs extolled the virtues of commercial expansion and urban growth, whereas Democrats distrusted the market economy and feared the consequences of economic development.[2]

At the same time that these studies of southern politics have been reconfirming the economic model of political behavior, recent studies of voter behavior in the northern states have seriously questioned the significance of economic issues as determinants of grassroots party alignments. Practitioners of the so-called ethnocultural school point out that few antebellum voters had access to nonpartisan or independent sources of information about economic issues. They knew only what their local leaders and newspaper editors told them. According to this model of political behavior, voters chose their parties according to group antagonisms that had little to do with the economic programs of the two parties. Having made their choice, they then followed the views of their leaders on partisan economic issues.[3]

Unfortunately, few antebellum voters left records of why they chose one party over the other, and the problem of voter motivation is one that historians will never resolve conclusively. The evidence for North Carolina suggests that some voters, particularly those living in towns and in underdeveloped areas of the state, responded favorably to the Whig program of promoting economic growth through banks, corporations, and publicly financed internal improvements. However, there is also evidence supporting the argument of those historians who claim that voter behavior was primarily a reflection of local group antagonisms rather than a response to the specific policy alternatives presented by the two parties. Earlier political divisions between Federalists and Republicans, and even between Tories and Patriots, continued to influence the pattern of party alignment in North Carolina until the end of the antebellum era.

Certainly there is evidence suggesting that many North Carolina voters lacked the ability to make independent judgments about the divergent economic programs of the two parties. Indeed, the Old North State had a notorious and long-standing reputation for backwardness. Until the last three decades of the antebellum period the state government was committed principally to keeping taxes low, and it did little to promote the development of public education. As late as 1840, one-third of the adult white population was illiterate. The northern traveler Frederick Law Olmsted remarked in 1856 that "North Carolina has a proverbial reputation for the ignorance and torpidity of her people." Educated North Carolinians like Archibald D. Murphey sometimes made even less generous remarks about the character of their state's population.[4]

In their correspondence, if not always on the hustings, political leaders frequently made a distinction between "the intelligent part of the community" or the "reading and reflecting men," on the one hand, and the "more common and illiterate class of the community" or the "unreading portion," on the other.[5] It seems likely that the "unreading portion" of the population was heavily dependent on the more educated political elite for information about issues as complex as banking and tariff policy. Indeed, even the "reading and reflecting men" admitted to being confused by the intricacies of these issues. The Democratic editor of the *Fayetteville Journal* acknowledged that "we have always looked upon financial and political economy as among the most perplexing subjects which could be submitted to the human mind, little understood by even those who pretended to some knowledge of them." Whig Congressman James Graham concurred that "every thing which appertains to regulating or controuling the currency is difficult and delicate and but few of our most talented men understand it's [*sic*] practical operation and effects." Whether the activities of the Bank of the United States had been helpful or harmful to the country, and whether the independent treasury was a measure to dissociate the government from the banking system or an insidious "government bank" in its own right were questions that could not easily be answered on their merits by an uneducated electorate.[6]

Equally perplexing was the issue of tariff policy. Whigs defended the tariff of 1842 as a measure designed primarily to raise revenue, whereas Democrats argued that it was really a protective tariff designed to take money from the pockets of the farmers to enrich the manufacturers. Few voters possessed the economic sophistication to resolve this argument. As Congressman Graham pointed out in 1843: "The tariff (or the rate of duties put on foreign goods imported) is one of the most difficult and complicated subjects in political economy. It embraces *a table of duties on five or six hundred articles, all in one bill*, and the arguments and reasons on each one of which are just as different as the nature and description of the articles." Even in the midst of the nullification crisis, antitariff crusaders had privately admitted that few voters could perceive a direct connection between tariff policy and their own economic welfare. "The great misfortune of this Tariff system," one North Carolinian told Senator Willie P. Mangum in 1832, "is that its *modus operandi* is insidious and deceptive—you and I perhaps may understand it, but the great mass of the people are profoundly ignorant of its true and real character. . . . They want light to enable them to judge correctly."[7]

Both parties, of course, endeavored to enlighten the voters as to their true interests, but their mutually contradictory arguments undoubtedly led the average voter to look for guidance to neighborhood leaders whom he knew and trusted. The leaders of both parties readily acknowledged the power and influence of the neighborhood leaders. As the editor of the *Raleigh Register* acidly remarked: "Every neighborhood has its political leader, always ready to aid in the diffusion of error and misrepresentation, and whose vocation it is, by means like these, to gain converts!" In a more positive vein, Congressman Graham advised his younger brother of the importance of actively courting these local leaders. "Very much may be done," he said, "by enlisting certain influential persons. And if the *first* man in the Neighbourhood be against us, try the *Second*, and divide the influence."[8]

The leaders of both parties took great pains to solicit the support of neighborhood leaders. Members of Congress, for example, constantly requested their lieutenants in the various counties to send them lists of influential persons and their post offices. One such list, containing the names of sixty-one of "the most respectable & influencing men, in the different neighborhoods" was sent to Senator Willie P. Mangum by William D. Amis of Northampton County in June 1834.[9] Influential men like the ones on Amis's list were the principal recipients of the speeches, committee reports, and other government documents that Mangum and other North Carolina congressmen circulated widely throughout the state. These local leaders also comprised the readership of the party newspapers, whose densely worded arguments were unmistakably addressed to an educated elite.

The entire voting population of antebellum North Carolina cannot be neatly bifurcated into "influential men" and their loyal followers. Undoubtedly there were many ordinary North Carolinians who thought and acted for themselves and who stubbornly resisted any efforts to be dictated to by their social betters.[10] Nevertheless, the task of building popular support for the local party organization was, in no small part, a matter of cultivating and maintaining the goodwill of the neighborhood leaders.

In the towns and villages most of these community leaders may well have chosen their party on the basis of a rational appraisal of their economic interests. The Whigs consistently defended banks and corporations as necessary and desirable economic institutions, while the Democrats repeatedly denounced them as "monied aristocracies." Under the circumstances, it is not surprising that the majority of bankers, businessmen, and other professionals living in urban areas were inclined to support the party that supported them.

The Democrats were quick to acknowledge the towns of North Carolina as the bastions of their political enemies. According to the Democratic editor of the *Washington* (N.C.) *Republican*: "The strength of their party resides in the towns & villages and country shops. . . . whilst on the contrary the Republicans generally, are plain, laborious, hardworking people . . . engaged in the agricultural or mechanical pursuits." The Democrats also agreed that most members of the business class did not support their party. "The Democracy of this town and County have a hard *row to weed*," one Democrat from the thriving town of Wilmington told Governor David S. Reid in 1854. "Three Banks, a Rail Road Company and the influence of all the Steam Mills and Turpentine Distilleries arrayed against us."[11]

Recent scholarship has corroborated the contemporary impression that the majority of business and professional men in North Carolina supported the Whigs. In Cumberland County, for example, almost two-thirds of the merchants with a known party preference in 1835 were Whigs. In addition, over 70 percent of the directors and officers of banking, railroad, and other Cumberland business corporations were affiliated with the Whigs. Lawyers and newspaper editors also seem to have preferred the Whigs to the Democrats. In 1850 one-third of the Whig members of the general assembly were lawyers, compared to only one-sixth of the Democratic members. Of the twenty-three newspapers published in North Carolina in 1836, all but six were Whig in political orientation. The number of Democratic presses increased considerably during the next two decades, but as late as 1856 the Whigs still controlled almost two-thirds of the newspapers.[12]

An examination of the political behavior of North Carolina towns also lends credence to the claim that urban dwellers tended to vote Whig. In 1860 there were fifteen towns in North Carolina with a population of over one thousand. Subcounty voting returns are incomplete and widely scattered, but a search of local newspapers uncovered information about twelve of the towns for at least one gubernatorial election between 1840 and 1852. In all but three of the counties the Whigs' percentage of the town vote exceeded their percentage of the rural vote.[13]

Merchants, bankers, lawyers, and other professional men figured prominently in the leadership of the Whig party in North Carolina, but the majority of the party's rank and file were undoubtedly farmers or farm laborers. In 1840 agriculture employed over 90 percent of the state's work force. A decade later almost four-fifths of the working population were still either farmers or farm laborers.[14] It is unlikely that these rural voters were as intensely concerned about issues of banking and currency as were the bankers, merchants, and other businessmen in the towns. "If our State was polled," former governor Edward B. Dudley remarked in 1841, "a very great number of our population would be found to be very indifferent on the subject. . . . None but business men think or care for such matters, & they are not a majority in our State."[15]

The generalization that the Whigs were strongest in market-oriented plantation areas has only limited validity for North Carolina (see map 3). Although the Whigs comprised the majority in some wealthy tobacco- and cotton-growing counties along the Roanoke River, most of the plantation counties of the middle east identified politically with the Democrats. In the piedmont the Democrats habitually polled majorities in the tobacco-producing counties along the Virginia border, which had easy access to markets in Richmond and Petersburg, whereas the Whigs controlled most of the counties in the central piedmont, which struggled to send their wheat and other farm products to faraway markets in Fayetteville and South Carolina. In the mountain region, the most isolated and self-sufficient part of the state, the Whigs also polled heavy majorities during the 1840s.

This does not mean that economic issues had no impact what-

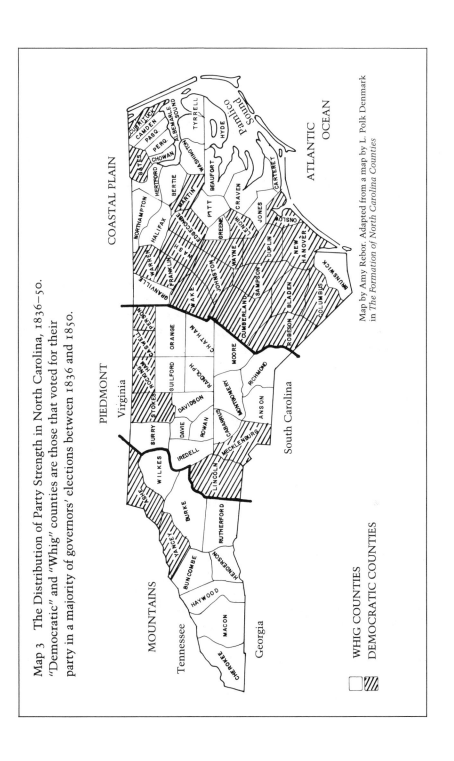

Map 3 The Distribution of Party Strength in North Carolina, 1836–50. "Democratic" and "Whig" counties are those that voted for their party in a majority of governors' elections between 1836 and 1850.

Map by Amy Rebor. Adapted from a map by L. Polk Denmark in *The Formation of North Carolina Counties*

WHIG COUNTIES
DEMOCRATIC COUNTIES

ever on the process of party formation in the rural areas of the Old North State. As we have seen, many voters in underdeveloped parts of the state responded favorably to the Whig program of financing internal improvements with federal land proceeds. Although the issues of banking and tariff policy were extraordinarily complex and the party positions on each were mutually contradictory, the positions of the parties on land policy were sharply defined and distinguishable to most voters. There is also evidence that many Tarheel voters reacted positively to the Whig argument that the financial policies of the Jackson and Van Buren administrations were responsible for the financial problems that beset the nation after 1837.

At the same time there were probably many local leaders and ordinary voters in the rural precincts who were swayed by noneconomic issues, although the impact of such issues on party alignment is impossible to measure. Some North Carolinians who had voted for Andrew Jackson during the 1820s and 1830s undoubtedly continued to support his party in the years that followed, despite the defection of many of the leading "original Jackson men." On the other hand, there is evidence that some Tarheels were genuinely concerned that Old Hickory's unprecedented assertion of executive power threatened the checks and balances established by the Constitution. The economic ramifications of banking policy may have been difficult to comprehend, but the constitutional questions presented by Jackson's removal of the deposits were ones on which any intelligent voter could take a stand.[16]

Although some voting behavior was issue oriented, there is also evidence to support the claim of ethnocultural historians that the Democrats and Whigs built much of their popular support on local rivalries, social cleavages, and group identities that long antedated the emergence of the parties as formal institutions. Aside from the Albemarle Sound region and the far west, the main bastion of Whig strength in North Carolina lay in the counties of the central piedmont and the southeastern coastal plain, where Loyalist sentiment had been strong during the Revolution and where Federalism had prevailed throughout the early years of the Republic. Democrats, on the other hand, were strong in the counties near the Virginia border, in the middle east, in the lower Cape Fear region, and in the area around Charlotte near the South Carolina border, where loyalism had been weak or nonexistent during the Revolution and where the Republican party had dominated earlier in the nineteenth century.[17]

It thus seems likely that the divisions engendered by the struggle for independence continued to influence the pattern of party alignment even as late as the 1840s. The Democrats frequently claimed that whenever a surviving Tory of the Revolution was to be found, he was certain in every instance to belong to the Whig party. Democratic orators and newspaper editors almost invariably called their opponents "Federalists," refusing to dignify them with the Whig label. As the editor of the *Raleigh Register* acknowledged in 1844, the appellation "Federalist" was "the obnoxious epithet applied to the Whig Party, from the chief wire-worker down to the lowest scullion."[18] Of course, partisan rhetoric by itself proves nothing about the bases of party alignment. But in conjunction with other evidence, the prevalence of the words "Tory" and "Federalist" in the rhetoric of the parties suggests that memories of the struggle for independence, and of the party battles between Federalists and Republicans continued to inflame the passions and influence the votes of North Carolinians during the antebellum era.

As evidence that Whiggery was nothing more than Federalism in disguise, the Democrats frequently claimed that their opponents espoused exactly the same principles as the old Federalist party. As one Democratic orator explained, "the same principles of strong and splendid Government, and of latitudinous construction, are arrayed against those of a plain and economical Government and strict construction; and the same contempt of the popular power, alternately smothered and triumphant, displays itself in a party which, no matter how often it may change its name, never loses its original identity. The present Whig party and the old Federal party are one and the same."[19]

The Democrats did not content themselves, however, with merely arguing that a continuity in philosophy existed between Federalists and Whigs. They also contended that a majority of Federalist leaders and even Federalist voters were now swearing allegiance to the Whig party. Democrats occasionally admitted that a few former Federalists who had seen the error of their ways had gravitated to the Jackson party. But for every such individual there were many more in the Whig ranks. "Looking abroad over the Union, we find nearly all the old Hartford Convention Federalists opposed to Mr. Van Buren and the Democracy," the editor of the *Standard* remarked in 1836. "And particularly is such the fact in North Carolina. In most of those counties where opposition to the War & Federalism prevailed in 1812–15, 'new-born Whigism' is strong *now*."[20]

The Whigs denied these charges about their paternity and challenged their opponents' efforts to preempt the Republican label. The Whig coalition was much broader than the old Federalist coalition had been, and the party stood to gain little by openly acknowledging its Federalist antecedents. "Our friends should hold on and use that word *Republican*," the son of one Federalist legislator advised his brother in 1840. "It is an expressive and potent word; & we should appropriate it to our own Cause. It is a host before the people."[21]

In addition to claiming a pure Republican pedigree, the Whigs frequently attempted to turn the tables on their opponents by pointing out prominent Democrats with Federalist backgrounds. Roger Taney, James Buchanan, Louis McLane, and Levi Woodbury were often mentioned as examples of Federalists who held powerful positions in the Democratic national administration. Unlike their opponents, however, the Whigs rarely tried to cast aspersions on the principles of Federalism or on the motives of those who had once supported that party. The editor of the *Register* claimed that both of the early parties had been wise and patriotic. "Their contest was for great principles, and not a petty scrambling for men and offices. Who would not rather be a Federalist of the old school, than a Patent Rucker Loco Foco of the present day?"[22] When the Whigs made efforts to link Democracy with Federalism, it was in order to demonstrate the hypocrisy and opportunism of a party that campaigned against Federalists while secretly trying to elevate them to office.

That the issue of Federalism could become a double-edged sword for the Democrats became vividly apparent in 1842, when the party nominated Louis D. Henry, a former Federalist from Cumberland County, as its candidate for governor. Well aware that Henry's Federalist antecedents were too conspicuous to ignore, the Democrats tried to defuse the issue early in the campaign by pointing out that their candidate had long ago renounced his Federalist principles. The editor of the *Fayetteville North Carolinian* optimistically predicted that "the pitiful charge that he acted with the Federal party, when a mere boy of unripened judgment, will have no effect on liberal minds."[23]

Unfortunately for the Democrats, Henry had clung to his Federalist principles until well into manhood, and the Whigs immediately made the candidate's Federalist background a major campaign issue. In response to the claim that Henry's Federalism had been a boyhood infatuation, the editor of the *Hillsborough Recorder* sarcastically retorted that "Mr. Henry was a Federalist until he was pretty well grown—a lad of some thirty-five or forty years of age." According to the Whigs, his conversion to the Democratic party could be attributed solely to his desire to participate in the spoils of office. Referring to Henry's recent appointment as a federal commissioner under a treaty with Spain, one correspondent of the *Register* noted that "yes, he changed, and he got *the change* for changing. He got near six thousand dollars not long after that change, out of the public treasury. . . . He never had the opportunity of seeing such sights as that, when he had the federal scales in his eyes."[24]

Henry lost the gubernatorial election to incumbent John M. Morehead in a year in which popular dissatisfaction with the Whigs produced substantial Democratic majorities in both houses of the general assembly. Although it would be an exaggeration to attribute Henry's defeat solely or even primarily to his Federalist antecedents, the Democrats certainly did not win any votes for their ticket by nominating a prominent ex-Federalist as their standard-bearer. Henry's candidacy merely provided the Whigs with additional campaign ammunition by lending credence to their charge that the Democrats were an unscrupulous band of office seekers "composed of the most heterogeneous materials . . . holding no principle in common."[25]

The epithet "Tory" was also a popular term in the lexicon of North Carolina politics. Particularly in those parts of the state where the Loyalists had been strong, Democrats and Whigs each accused the other of being the descendants of Tories. One Democratic meeting in Lincoln County, for example, resolved that "the application to itself of the term 'Whig' by the party which numbers among its most zealous advocates those who were *Tories* in the last War, is an impudent assumption and shameless desecration of a name 'sacred to the Heroes of the Revolution.'"[26] The Whigs, understandably, denied the presence of Tory blood in their lineage. In response to a correspondent of the *Western Carolinian*, who claimed that most of the people of Guilford County had been Tories during the war, an irate correspondent of the *Greensboro Patriot* penned a lengthy rebuttal and denounced the perpetrator of the charge as "a *base liar* and *unprincipled scoundrel.*" "No honest man," he added, "who knows any thing about the history of Guilford, would so far forget himself as to be guilty of such foul and contemptible slander."[27]

The Whigs were not averse to levying the same charge of Toryism against their opponents. In reply to yet another reference to "Tory Guilford," this one appearing in the *Lincoln Courier*, a correspondent of the *Patriot* retorted that the Democrats of Lincoln should be the last to cast aspersions on the Revolutionary loyalties of Guilford. "That word *Whig* . . . was never popular in the neighborhood of the Lincoln Courier man; and the way in which these Guilford Whigs lent a helping hand to the Patriots [in several Revolution battles] . . . must excuse to some extent the bitterness of Lincoln now towards Guilford and Whiggery."[28]

These charges and countercharges of Toryism generally had only local impact. In 1844, however, the Revolutionary antecedents of the various presidential and gubernatorial candidates became a major campaign issue in North Carolina. The "battle of the grandfathers" began when the Whigs learned that Ezekiel Polk, the grandfather of Democratic presidential candidate James K. Polk, had taken protection from the British after Cornwallis invaded Mecklenburg County in 1780. Despite the Whig charges, there is no evidence that Ezekiel Polk had really been a Tory or even a British sympathizer during the war. Like many other wealthy North Carolinians, he had placed himself under British protection in order to save his estate from destruction. In the view of the Whigs, however, the behavior of the elder Polk was tantamount to Toryism, and the nomination of his descendant served as yet another example of the inconsistency and hypocrisy of "the party who takes pleasure in calling their opponents British Whigs and the descendants of Tories."[29]

The Democrats took the Whig charges quite seriously, and during the campaign they published numerous affidavits, testimonials, and other documentary evidence that proved, at least to their satisfaction, that Ezekiel Polk had been a sterling Patriot during the war.[30] Party leaders also tried to take the offensive by claiming that the ancestors of William A. Graham, the Whig gubernatorial candidate, had been "as bitter Tories as ever wore a red coat, or took protection under British power." Not to be outdone, the Whigs counterattacked with charges that the grandfather of Michael Hoke, Graham's Democratic opponent, had fought on the British side at the battle of Ramsour's Mill.[31] The painstaking efforts made by both parties to pin the Tory label on their opponents, and to refute the accusations made against their own candidates, suggest that many North Carolinians had not yet forgotten the bitter animosities occasioned by the struggle for independence.

An analysis of partisan rhetoric cannot, by itself, provide conclusive evidence that earlier political divisions continued to influence the pattern of party alignment during the 1840s. However, it is reasonable to expect that some relationship may exist between the image that a party projects to the electorate and the characteristics of the voting groups who support that party. Just as a majority of bankers, merchants, and other businessmen in North Carolina chose not to support the party that habitually denounced banks and corporations, it seems likely that many Federalists and descendants of Federalists might have hesitated to vote for a party that persistently ridiculed Federalist principles. One might also suppose that many ordinary Federalist voters took the Democrats at their word when they repeatedly claimed that Whiggery and Federalism were identical.

Fortunately, it is not necessary to infer political behavior merely from partisan rhetoric. An examination of the political antecedents of several Democratic and Whig counties in different parts of the state lends additional support to the hypothesis that the political conflicts of the Revolutionary War generation played a role in conditioning the party alignments of the antebellum era.

The political behavior of two contiguous staple-producing counties in the Tar-Neuse region of eastern North Carolina provides an excellent illustration of how community conflict influenced the pattern of voting behavior in antebellum North Carolina. Throughout the 1840s the Whigs were the majority party in Greene County, while in nearby Lenoir County the Whigs were always a hopeless minority. It is unlikely that the divergent political loyalties of the residents of Greene and Lenoir were the product of conflicting economic interests. Both counties were wealthy, at least by North Carolina standards. With relatively easy access to the market town of New Bern, the political leaders of both counties were reluctant to give their support to a program of state-assisted internal improvements. Thus, in the North Carolina General Assembly the Whig commoner from

Greene voted just as consistently against internal improvement measures as did his Democratic colleague from Lenoir.[32]

Instead of being a response to clashing economic interests, party alignments in Greene and Lenoir reflected a traditional enmity with roots as far back as the colonial period. Both counties had originally been part of colonial Dobbs County. During the Revolution most of the inhabitants of lower Dobbs (Lenoir) sided with the Patriots, but a considerable amount of disaffection existed in the upper part of the county (Greene). Indeed, an association of citizens in upper Dobbs resisted the draft, insulted Patriot officers, and wounded officials who were trying to apprehend deserters. Three of Dobbs's seven militia companies deserted to the British. After the Revolution the citizens of Dobbs were again bitterly divided, this time over the ratification of the U.S. Constitution. In the election of delegates to the Hillsborough convention in 1788, a riot occurred while the ballots were being counted, and, as a result, neither faction was seated at the convention. In 1791 the citizens of lower Dobbs petitioned the general assembly for a division of the county, citing as their principal reason the lawlessness and general unrest among the people in the northern half of the county. It is not surprising that the advent of organized parties during the 1790s left the residents of the two counties on opposite sides of the political fence. In the three congressional elections between 1803 and 1810 for which county-level returns can be found, Lenoir consistently voted Republican, whereas Greene just as consistently supported the Federalists.[33]

The political behavior of the residents of the contiguous counties of Mecklenburg and Cabarrus in the southern piedmont reveals a similar pattern of endemic community conflict. During the antebellum period Mecklenburg supported the Democratic candidate for governor in all thirteen elections between 1836 and 1860, whereas Cabarrus gave majorities to the Whigs in every one of these elections. Again, these divergent political loyalties can be traced back to community rivalries dating from the colonial period. In the case of Mecklenburg and Cabarrus, ethnic divisions also played a significant role in conditioning the pattern of political behavior.

In the years before the Revolution Mecklenburg had been a center of Scotch-Irish immigration and, unlike many other parts of the piedmont, it was staunchly Patriot during the struggle for independence. Lord Cornwallis, who had firsthand information on the subject, described Mecklenburg as "the most rebellious section in America." The British general was referring specifically to the area around Charlotte, the county seat, which was the nucleus of the Scotch-Irish settlement. Prerevolutionary Mecklenburg also had an important German minority, which had settled in the northeastern part of the county. During the 1760s the Germans had come into conflict with their Scotch-Irish neighbors over the location of the county seat. The two communities clashed again early in the Revolution when some of the German settlers sent a Loyalist address to the royal governor. Shortly after the end of the war, the Germans demanded their own county, and in 1792 Cabarrus was formed from northeast Mecklenburg. During the first party system the Scotch-Irish in Mecklenburg generally supported the Republicans, while the Germans in Cabarrus usually gave majorities to the Federalists. In 1813, for example, the Republican candidate for Congress won 70 percent of the vote in Mecklenburg but only 19 percent in Cabarrus.[34]

Despite their claims to the contrary, Whiggery in the Old North State often thrived in communities that had identified with the Tories during the Revolution.[35] One of the centers of Toryism in the North Carolina piedmont had been in Rowan County, along the bend of the Yadkin River in what is now northeast Davie County. Most of the early settlers in that part of the county were of English stock, although there was also a substantial contingent of Germans. Unlike Mecklenburg, however, there were few Scotch-Irish. The leading family in the community were the Bryans, a Quaker family who had come into the county from Pennsylvania. During the Revolution Samuel Bryan, the son of the settlement's founder, played a leading role in organizing support for the British in the Yadkin River area. Although there are no precinct-level returns for the early 1800s, it is likely that the residents along the bend of the Yadkin supplied many of the votes that enabled the Federalists to poll large majorities in Rowan County. The scattered precinct-level returns for the 1840s reveal that the voters in northeast Davie County were virtually unanimous in their support for the Whigs. In the gubernatorial election of 1842, for example, the Whig candidate won 95 percent of the votes cast in northeast Davie, even though the Democratic candidate received almost half of the votes in the remaining parts of the county.[36]

Whereas the Whigs tended to predominate in areas with large numbers of Loyalists, the Democrats were often strongest in communities where Tories had been rare or nonexistent. The residents of Warren County, where 85 percent of the voters usually supported the Democratic ticket, liked to boast that there had been no Tories in their county during the Revolution.[37] Similarly, an early historian of Caswell County pointed out that there had been no battles fought in his county during the struggle for independence. Moreover, unlike most of the piedmont counties, Caswell was ethnically homogeneous. The county had been settled during the 1750s by immigrants from Orange and Culpeper counties in Virginia, and its earliest booster pointed out with great pride that "we have no *Spumy* Irishmen, revolutionizing Frenchmen, nor *Speculating* Scotchmen among us." The absence of community conflict in counties like Warren and Caswell was probably an important factor behind their monolithic political behavior.[38]

The case studies presented in this chapter suggest that ethnocultural conflict may have played just as important a role in conditioning the pattern of party alignment in North Carolina as it did in the northern states. In the Old North State, however, the main wave of immigration came during the the period between 1740 and 1775, when tens of thousands of Germans, Scotch-Irish, and Highland Scots, along with smaller numbers of Lowland Scots, Irish, Welsh, Swiss, and French settlers moved into the piedmont and the upper Cape Fear valley. Although much more research needs to be done before conclusive generalizations can be made, it seems likely that divergent responses to the Revolution, to the policies of the newly established state government, and to the appeals of the Federalist and Republican parties may have been a manifestation of ethnocultural conflict.

Long-established and ethnically homogeneous counties that had been settled by Virginians and South Carolinians of English ancestry during the seventeenth and early eighteenth centuries tended to be the strongest in their support for independence, and they later became the bastions of the Republican party. On the other hand, Toryism and Federalism tended to prevail in counties that were ethnically heterogeneous. The non-English groups were not uniformly hostile to the Revolution or to the post–Revolutionary War state governments. Indeed, the Scotch-Irish, who settled in Mecklenburg and neighboring counties seem to have been almost unanimous in their support for independence. However, other ethnic groups like the Highland Scots and the Germans, along with Quakers and other settlers of English stock who moved into the Carolina backcountry from Pennsylvania, seem to have been partial to Toryism or neutralism during the Revolution, and to Federalism during the first party system, especially in areas where they came into conflict with the Scotch-Irish.[39]

It thus seems quite likely that the clash of cultures played a significant role in shaping the contours of the party system in North Carolina. The final wave of immigration arrived much earlier there than it did in the North, and there were no substantial additions to the state's population after the 1770s. Yet to argue that white North Carolinians during the antebellum era were "a remarkably homogeneous people in their nativity,"[40] is to subscribe to a "melting-pot" theory of ethnicity that has been largely discredited by practitioners of the new social history. Ethnic distinctions in North Carolina did not disappear within a generation. For more than half a century after the Revolution, Gaelic was as commonly spoken as English on the streets of Fayetteville and in the sandhills precincts in Cumberland, Richmond, and Robeson counties. Indeed, according to one historian of the Highland Scots, "the old ones spoke little else."[41] The Germans, for their part, were notorious for their "clannishness"—or for what a more sympathetic observer might call their desire to maintain their distinctive ethnic identity. German settlers in the Carolina backcountry tended to congregate in their own neighborhoods and to retain their ancient customs and language. As late as 1826, the minutes of the North Carolina Lutheran Synod were printed in German as well as English. And the German language continued to be used for church services in some communities in Rowan and Cabarrus counties until the 1840s.[42]

Like ethnic minorities elsewhere throughout the nation, the German and Scottish immigrants in North Carolina were initially the objects of suspicion and discrimination on the part of the host culture. As one historian of early southern parties has pointed out, "there is little doubt that the eastern Englishmen viewed these newcomers, with their different language, religion, and culture, as hardly the equals of old-stock colonists. . . . Facing such treatment by the dominant political group . . . the minority nationalities naturally would react by giving their support to the local opposition group—the Federalist party."[43]

In a larger sense, the pattern of party alignment in North Carolina seems to have been a manifestation of what one historian has described as endemic conflict between the "core" and the "periphery." According to this model of political behavior, the core is the dominant cultural group seeking to maintain or extend its values over the out-groups or minorities (the periphery), which, in turn, resist the political, economic, and cultural hegemony of the core.[44] In North Carolina the core was composed of planters of English stock living in counties in the middle east and along the Virginia border, who led the state during the Revolution and dominated the government until the 1820s. Unlike their counterparts in some of the northern states, the core group in North Carolina did not espouse a policy of government activism; instead, they supported a policy of miminal public services that enabled the government to keep taxes low. By the 1820s the periphery had come to include not only the Federalists, who comprised perhaps a third of the state's population, but also the residents of the extreme northeast and the far west, who had been largely excluded from the process of government. Many of the voters in these counties were dissatisfied with a policy of laissez-faire and desired a more active government that would provide them with improved transportation facilities.

Opposition to the caucus—the institution by which the in-group had supposedly exercised its control over government—provided the rallying cry that brought the diverse collection of out-groups together in 1824 to carry the Old North State for the People's party. During the early 1830s the nascent Whig party presented themselves as the ideological heirs of the People's party by attacking the "Baltimore caucus" that had nominated Van Buren for the presidency and by emphasizing Van Buren's own links with the discredited congressional caucus. On a more positive note, the Whigs cultivated the support of voters in the periphery by promising them a system of internal improvements that could be effected without the burden of additional state taxes.

Ironically, once the Whigs had become an institutionalized political party, they accepted the necessity of the presidential nominating convention and established a central committee at Raleigh to direct the activities of the party. During the 1840s another conflict between the periphery and the core was fought out within the Whig party itself, as spokesmen for the periphery, like William B. Shepard and Thomas L. Clingman, challenged the authority of the legislative caucus and the hegemony of the Raleigh-based politicians who monopolized the highest state offices.

The Democrats, for their part, continued to derive the bulk of their popular support from counties in the middle east and along the Virginia border. While opposition to the caucus provided the rallying cry for the Whigs during the 1830s, the Democrats tried to unite their forces behind their opposition to the Federalist menace. Their incessant warnings about the danger of a Federalist revival, and their persistent efforts to link Federalism with Whiggery, were not merely hyperbolic flourishes without intrinsic political meaning. Had the Democrats succeeded in convincing the North Carolina electorate that they were the only legitimate heirs of the Republicans, they would quite possibly have become the majority party.

Despite the rise of new issues and new party organizations during the 1830s, politics in the Old North State continued to be conditioned by long-standing rivalries and earlier group identities. National issues like the Bank of the United States, the tariff, and land policy may have dominated the platforms and other official pronouncements of the Democrats and Whigs, but the second party system in North Carolina had roots that antedated both the emergence of these issues and the establishment of organized parties.

7 ✦ National Issues and Local Interests: North Carolina, 1840–1848

A national bank, a tariff, a distribution of the public lands, in a word, federal politics have been the constant, unchanged, and unchangeable text.—*Hillsborough Recorder*, 14 March 1844

There are always side issues in many of the counties which seriously affect the result of elections, but which the public abroad are unable to comprehend.—*Wilmington Herald*, 12 August 1856

Throughout the 1840s the Whigs were unquestionably the majority party in North Carolina. The party monopolized the governor's office, electing John M. Morehead in 1840 and 1842, William A. Graham in 1844 and 1846, and Charles Manly in 1848, by percentages ranging from 55.3 percent in 1840 to 50.5 percent in 1848. The party also controlled the general assembly on joint ballot in every legislative session except that of 1842. Whig successes in presidential elections paralleled their victories in state contests. In 1840, 1844, and 1848 the party delivered North Carolina's electoral votes to Whig presidential candidates Harrison, Clay, and Taylor.

Despite this nearly unbroken chain of victories, the balance between the parties was actually quite close. Only twice during the decade did the Whig gubernatorial candidate garner as much as 55 percent of the vote—in 1840, when Morehead rode to victory on a wave of popular revulsion against the depression and the financial policies of the Van Buren administration, and in 1846, when Graham reaped the benefits of incumbency and a divided opposition. Except for 1840, when the party enjoyed a majority of thirty-six seats on joint ballot, Whig control of the general assembly was precarious. In 1842 the Democrats controlled both houses with a majority of twenty-eight seats. In 1844 a shift of only eleven seats would have given the Democrats control. In 1846 the party was only eight seats short of a majority, and in 1848 a shift of only three seats would have enabled the Democrats to organize the legislature (see figures 7.1 and 7.2).[1]

As might be expected, given the tenacity of party loyalties, split-ticket voting in North Carolina was the exception rather than the rule, especially during presidential election years. In 1840, for example, only two of the counties carried by the Whigs in the gubernatorial election chose Democrats to represent them in the house of commons. Only three counties giving majorities to the Democratic gubernatorial candidate sent Whig commoners to the legislature. Four years later Democratic legislative candidates scored victories in only four Whig counties, whereas Whig legislators were victorious in only two Democratic counties.[2]

As the party out of power, the Democrats fared considerably better in off-year elections. In 1842 Democratic candidates for the house of commons won legislative seats in eleven counties that gave majorities to the Whig candidate for governor. Indeed, ticket splitting that

Figure 7.1 Party Affiliation in the North Carolina House of Commons, 1836–50. *Source:* Thomas E. Jeffrey, "Internal Improvements and Political Parties in Antebellum North Carolina," table 1.

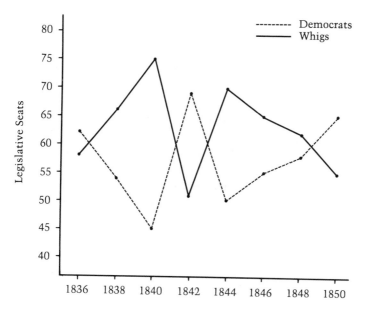

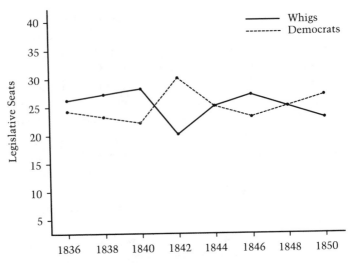

Figure 7.2   Party Affiliation in the North Carolina Senate, 1836–50. *Sources:* Legislative returns in *Raleigh Register,* 6 September 1836, 10 September 1838; *Fayetteville Observer,* 26 August 1840; *Raleigh Standard,* 14 September 1842; *Fayetteville Observer,* 21 August 1844; *Raleigh Standard,* 9 September 1846; *Greensboro Patriot,* 25 November 1848; *Raleigh Standard,* 28 August 1850. For special elections to fill vacancies caused by the death of several senators-elect, see Herbert D. Pegg, *The Whig Party in North Carolina,* pp. 74, 121–27.

year was extensive enough to give the Democrats control of both houses of the general assembly, despite Morehead's victory in the governor's race. In 1846 Democratic candidates for the lower house won victories in ten counties that were carried by William A. Graham, and Graham's landslide victory in the governor's race was not duplicated by lopsided Whig majorities in the general assembly.[3]

Party competition in state elections tended to focus primarily upon national issues. This was particularly true for the gubernatorial elections, and the parties attached great significance to these elections as barometers of the relative strength of the two parties. According to the editor of the *Hillsborough Recorder:* "The vote for Governor may be considered as testing the strength of parties in this county, that being strictly a party question." The editor of the *Register* agreed that "every man, of the slightest degree of intelligence, knows that the election for Governor is the only fair test. . . .

[because] in an election for Governor, the Candidates are voted for in special reference to their opinions on subjects of National Politics."[4]

National issues also frequently dominated the legislative elections, as is attested by numerous complaints that the parties did not pay sufficient attention to local concerns. As one candidate for the general assembly pointed out: "It is too common for candidates for the Legislature, to consume their whole time in the discussion of national politics, and pay no regard to State matters at all." A correspondent of the *Recorder* agreed that national politics had been "the constant, unchanged, and unchangeable text" in legislative elections. The correspondent admonished candidates for the legislature "to take care of the interest of North Carolina . . . [and] not to be eternally ding donging in the ears of the people federal politics."[5]

Historians of antebellum North Carolina have sometimes criticized the parties for what one scholar has called their "absurd absorption . . . in national politics" and their "complete inattention to the needs of the state."[6] Such criticism ignores the vital role that national issues played in the functioning of the second party system. Whigs and Democrats emphasized national issues during the 1840s because these were the issues over which the leaders of the two parties could agree to disagree. The revival of the contest for the presidency and the controversial financial policies of the Jackson administration had provided the original impetus for the creation of organized parties in North Carolina. In the years after Old Hickory's retirement, national issues continued to separate Whigs from Democratic candidates and to provide the activists in both parties with a sense of identity and cohesion.

An emphasis on national politics might, indeed, be the surest way to maintain harmony and cohesion within the party. However, viable parties need to win elections as well as remain cohesive, and political underdogs in the various counties often tried to increase their chances for success by downplaying their national partisan identities and emphasizing their personal qualifications and local issues of immediate concern to their constituents. In local elections many politicians probably acted upon the strategy suggested by Charles Fisher, who counseled that "in counties where we are in the minority politically, let our friends make the *issues* as much as possible on *local* questions."[7]

An examination of campaign circulars, local newspapers, and the correspondence of party leaders reveals that it was generally the candidate of the minority party who urged the voters to place local issues and public service above partisanship in state elections. In heavily Democratic New Hanover County, for example, the two Whig candidates for the house of commons in 1844 admonished the electorate that "the proper inquiry in State elections about a candidate is not what does he think of Bank, Sub-Treasury, Tariff, Distribution, &c; but is he *honest*? is he *capable*? what does he think about *State affairs*?" Minority candidates frequently presented themselves as "no-party" men and promised, if elected, to carry out the will of their constituents without reference to "party considerations." Thus, W. P. Richards, a Democratic candidate for the house of commons in the Whig bastion of Davidson County, pledged that "should I be elected, so far as legislation is concerned, I shall be neither a Democrat nor Whig, but a Commoner of Davidson, ready to advocate her best interest, and defend the same, irrespective of any party considerations whatever."[8]

The career of William H. Thomas, one of the leaders of the Democratic party in the far west, provides an excellent case study of how minority candidates could sometimes win election by avoiding too close an identification with strictly partisan issues. From 1848 until 1860 Thomas represented the counties of Haywood, Macon, and Cherokee in the state senate, even though his district generally polled majorities for the Whigs in the governor's election. Thomas failed to win election on his first try for office in 1846, but his campaign circular for that year offers much insight into the strategy that later enabled him to compete successfully in a Whig-dominated district. Although the state Democratic platform for 1846 concentrated on national issues such as the independent treasury and the Mexican War, Thomas's own circular ignored these issues and focused instead on local questions such as the turnpike from Raleigh to the Georgia line, relief for insolvent debtors, and a state penitentiary. Indeed, the circular did not even identify Thomas as a Democrat. Avoiding all reference to national politics and partisan concerns, the candidate told the voters that "*National* and *State politics* should, in my opinion, be kept as *separate* as possible."[9]

William W. Avery of Burke County was another western Democrat who proved adept at capitalizing on personal connections and local issues to win elections with Whig votes. The son of Isaac T.

Avery, one of the organizers of the Whig party in western North Carolina, the younger Avery won election to the house of commons in 1842 at the same time that his party's gubernatorial candidate was garnering a paltry 21 percent of the vote in Burke. The Whigs attributed Avery's success to his numerous Whig connections and to a popular belief that, if elected, he would go to the legislature untrammeled, unpledged, and free to act according to his own judgment. The Whigs also claimed that throughout the campaign Avery had steadfastly refused to acknowledge that he was a Democrat.[10]

In some of the Democratic counties there were Whigs who proved equally adept at winning legislative elections. One of the more successful practitioners of the art was John E. Thomas, who represented Franklin County in the house of commons in 1842 and in the state senate in 1846. While taking advantage of endemic factional divisions within the local Democratic party, Thomas carefully cultivated his image as a "no-party" man. Thus, one Franklin Democrat acknowledged that Thomas "laboured hard to convince the democrats that so far as state politicks are concerned, he is no party man, that if elected he would accommodate his legislative action to the public weal regardless of party bias."[11]

The issue of county division provides an excellent example of how both parties tried to capitalize on local issues in counties where they were in a minority. As North Carolina counties—particularly those in the west—gradually became more populated, and as settlement spread beyond the environs of the county seat, a movement usually arose to divide the county and create a new seat of government. Understandably, neither party at the state level took a position for or against the division of counties. Yet this reticence did not prevent party leaders at the local level from attempting to exploit prodivision sentiment for partisan advantage. In heavily Whig Rutherford County, for example, the Democratic candidates for the general assembly in 1844 attempted to win additional votes by supporting county division. As one Rutherford Whig perceptively remarked: "The Democratic Candidates . . . are thus endeavouring to draw off public attention from National politicks." The Democrats failed to make any gains in Rutherford that year, but in normally Democratic Ashe County the Whigs did manage to pick up a legislative seat by appealing to prodivision sentiment. After the election, one Ashe Democrat emphasized that the opposition victory did not represent a repudiation of the Democratic party. "The late elections here were carried by a stratagem, based on a local question . . . and not by any political change."[12]

Both parties also tried to capitalize on the issue of internal improvements in county elections. In those parts of the state where railroads and other improvements were unpopular, the Whigs proved just as willing as the Democrats to exploit anti-improvement sentiment for partisan advantage. In Franklin County, for example, perennial Whig candidate John E. Thomas tried hard in 1844 to make political capital on the support that Michael Hoke, the Democratic gubernatorial candidate, had allegedly given to the Raleigh & Gaston Railroad. After the election, one Franklin Democrat complained that "against Col. Hoke the most despicable means were used a few days before the election. His Rail Road votes were magnified and distorted in sections of the county particularly hostile to such institutions . . . and every device [was] used to persuade the democrats to assume a neutral ground."[13]

The editors of the partisan presses sometimes warned the voters to be wary of "no-party" men campaigning on local issues. In an editorial entitled "Democrats, Beware!" the editor of the *Standard* cautioned his readers that "in the Counties where they are in the minority . . . [the Whigs] will use all their well known artifices to get their candidates elected on the *no party* plan." Whig leaders, like the editor of the *Register*, also admonished the party faithful: "Let not a victory be gained over you, in any County, on Local questions." Although both parties denounced such tactics when used by the opposition, neither was averse to employing them for its own partisan advantage.[14]

The partisan uses to which issues like internal improvements and county division could be put suggest that, in legislative elections at least, the parties were not invariably unresponsive to the local interests of their constituents. Instead of preventing partisan discussion of local affairs, the absence of official party positions on such matters allowed candidates at the local level the flexibility to assume any position that conviction or political expediency might dictate. But the ability of local parties to agitate these issues did not guarantee that they could subsequently translate their campaign rhetoric into public policy. A legislative candidate might successfully exploit public sentiment on internal improvements or county division and use it to defeat his opponent. However, he could not depend on his fellow partisans in the general assembly to help him deliver on his campaign promises.

Few close observers of politics would have disagreed with the editor of the *Register* that "in county elections . . . local questions frequently form the pivot on which the issue turns."[15] A purely local issue like county division, on which the parties could not take a consistent statewide position, usually had little more than local and transitory impact on the overall balance of parties. Yet the same logic that led the minority party to capitalize on local concerns in county elections also propelled the leaders of the North Carolina Democratic party on an elusive search for attractive state issues that might enable them to overcome their opponents' statewide majority without threatening their own internal unity.

The midterm elections of 1842 provide an excellent example of the possibilities that state issues presented to the minority party in North Carolina. Although the Whigs succeeded in reelecting Governor Morehead that year, they lost control of both houses of the general assembly. According to the editor of the *Register*, the party's legislative losses could be attributed to "the agitation of questions of State and local policy." The editor of the *Observer* agreed that his party's defeat was not a repudiation of the national principles espoused by the Whig party. Instead, he claimed, "local causes have contributed to defeat many Whig candidates. . . . By seizing hold of the strong side of public opinion, in regard to some local matter, and using it as a hobby to electioneer with, (thus turning the issue from National politics to matters of a local nature,) they have been enabled to get Locos elected in some of the strongest Whig counties in the State."[16]

One issue consistently emphasized by the Democrats during the campaign of 1842 was the "unholy alliance" between the Whigs and the state banks. Banking policy had been an important political issue in North Carolina since the 1820s, and even though the public uproar against the state banks had diminished after they had agreed to surrender their charters in 1828, many antibank men probably continued to harbor resentment against their successors, which were chartered by the general assembly during the early 1830s. For most of the decade, however, the Democratic leaders centered their fire on the Bank of the United States, and when they spoke at all about the new state banks it was usually in tones of guarded approval.[17]

The Democratic attitude toward the North Carolina banks became more critical after they joined others throughout the nation in suspending specie payments following the Panic of 1837. Specie payments were suspended from May 1837 until August 1838, and again from October 1839 until September 1842. In a speech delivered one month after the second round of suspensions, William H. Haywood, Jr., sharply criticized the banks' conduct as a clear violation of their charter obligations. Haywood also accused the Whigs of tamely submitting to "Bank usurpations" and promised that if a Democratic governor and legislature were elected in 1840, they would conduct an investigation into the specie suspensions.[18]

Chiefly in response to this Democratic criticism, the North Carolina General Assembly of 1840 appointed a special committee to investigate the conduct of the state banks. The final report, which was signed by Bartholomew F. Moore, a Whig from Halifax County, defended the specie suspensions and concluded that the banks had conducted their business with "laudable zeal for the public welfare" and not in pursuit of the private gain of their stockholders.[19] The Democrats denounced the committee's report as a whitewash and condemned the Whigs in the general assembly for their "abject obsequiousness" in refusing to hold the banks accountable "for their agency in the past and present distress of the people."[20]

By 1842 the state banks of North Carolina had joined the Bank of the United States in the Democratic lexicon as engines of special privilege and threats to the existence of republican government. Louis D. Henry, the Democratic candidate for governor, set the tone for the campaign that year in his letter of acceptance, which rejected the findings of the legislative committee and condemned "the corrupt confederation between the great leaders of the Whig party and the United States Bank, with the affiliated local Banks." According to Henry, the financial problems of the nation could be attributed directly to the paper money system and to "the Whig leaders, who for party purposes, gave efficacy and moral power to the evil tendencies of the system." Democratic editors echoed Henry's denunciations, characterizing banks as "anti-republican monopolies" and demanding that they resume specie payments "or *go into liquidation!*"[21]

In 1840 the Whigs had won many uncommitted voters to their party by emphasizing the alleged connection between the country's financial distress and the economic policies of the Jackson and Van Buren administrations. In 1842, however, party leaders found themselves on the defensive, as the Democrats attributed the continued low prices and scarcity of money to the refusal of the state banks to redeem their paper. Three months before the summer elections, Priestly H. Mangum, the brother of North Carolina's senior senator, confided to Senator William A. Graham his "misgivings as to the complexion of our next Legislature." "I fear the result," he told Graham, "because the 'floating Capital' of the Country . . . may likely be carried by the force of the senseless cry of our opponents on the score of *the promise of better times* not being redeemed. . . . The pecuniary pressure of the day will hurt us more than any thing else."[22]

Rather than defend the unpopular specie suspensions, the Whigs accused the Democrats of being inconsistent and opportunistic on the banking issue. The editor of the *Register* asserted that "the Whigs are as much opposed to Bank frauds and Bank mismanagement as any party. . . . They go for *improving* the Banking system, and hold their political opponents responsible for the frauds and corruption which have crept into it." Whig editors claimed that most of the unsound and mismanaged banks in the country had been chartered by Democratic legislatures over Whig opposition, whereas well-managed state banks, such as those in New England, were usually the products of Whig legislation.[23]

The Whigs took particular delight in exposing the multitudinous banking connections of the opposition's principal antibank crusader. Like many other leaders of the North Carolina Democratic party, Louis D. Henry came from an urban background that contrasted sharply with the rural orientation of most of the party's voters. A lawyer by profession, he had spent much of his career as a director of the Fayetteville branch of the Bank of the United States and as an attorney for the local branch of the Bank of the State of North Carolina. The Democratic candidate also owned stock in the Bank of Cape Fear in Wilmington, in the Bank of New Bern, and in various banks in Louisiana and Ohio. The Whigs did not hesitate to point out the inconsistency between Henry's past record of service to banks and his present denunciation of the banking system. Governor Morehead dryly observed that his opponent seemed quite fond of the company of the "thieves, rogues and swindlers" he was denouncing so furiously on the stump.[24]

Henry lost the governor's election, but the Democrats did manage for the first time since 1835 to win control of both houses of the general assembly. It is difficult to assess the extent to which the issue of state banking contributed to the party's success in the legislative elections, but many Democrats in the new general assembly undoubtedly interpreted the result as a mandate against the banks. The legislature spent several months debating a series of antibank resolutions but, to the dismay of the militant antibank crusaders, no punitive measure won approval in either house. A bill that would have required banks suspending specie payments to forfeit their charters did win the approval of 69 percent of the Democrats in the state senate, but almost a third of the party voted with the Whigs to defeat the measure. In the house of commons antibank Democrats were unable to persuade even a majority of their fellow partisans to vote for punitive legislation.[25]

Fifteen years earlier the officials of the state banks had voluntarily agreed to surrender their charters rather than endure the continual harassment of antibank men like Robert Potter. Early in January 1843 the principal stockholders of the Bank of the State of North Carolina again offered to relinquish their charter if the general assembly so requested. A resolution to that effect, introduced by Cadwallader Jones of Orange County, passed the house of commons by a strict party vote on 7 January. The senate tabled Jones's resolution but adopted a similarly worded substitute, which the house subsequently tabled. Despite all their blustering and threats, the antibank party, as the Whigs sarcastically pointed out, "failed to kill the *monster* when it was in their power."[26]

It is not difficult to understand why the Democratic majority in the general assembly found themselves unable to accept the surrender of the bank's charter. As one Democratic editor acknowledged, if the state bank began rapidly calling in its outstanding loans, the result would have been an unprecedented degree of financial distress, which the Whigs would certainly have blamed on their opponents.[27] Equally important, North Carolina derived over a third of its annual revenue from the dividends that the state received from its own holdings of bank stock—dividends that the banks continued to pay even during the specie suspensions. According to the editor of the *Register*, the state had received $317,000 in revenue from the state bank since 1835, and another $233,000 from its stock in the Bank of Cape Fear. Could any reasonable person, he asked, argue that "the State's connection with the Banks, which has saved them from increased taxation, has been so unprofitable as to render a dissolution of the copartnership desirable?"[28]

Although the Democrats' refusal to pay the political price of destroying the state's banking system is readily understandable, it is not so easy to comprehend why the party failed to honor its pledge to conduct a thoroughgoing investigation of the banks. A bill establishing a joint investigating committee passed the house of commons without a dissenting vote on 30 December 1842, but three days later the bill was reconsidered and tabled by the Democrats against virtually unanimous Whig opposition. The Whigs claimed that their opponents' refusal to conduct an investigation was proof that "they do not themselves believe the charges which, for political effect, they have heretofore countenanced and circulated." Certainly this is an explanation that cannot be ruled out.[29]

The Democrats' antibank campaign of 1842 illustrates the pitfalls, as well as the possibilities, that state issues presented to the parties in North Carolina. By identifying their opponents with the unpopular policies of the state banks, the Democrats may have temporarily won new voters to their party, but their inability to translate antibank rhetoric into meaningful policy ultimately caused the party a great deal of embarrassment. Leading Democrats such as former governor Richard D. Spaight, Jr., privately denounced the antibank Democrats in the general assembly for their unseemly behavior. After the party lost control of the legislature in the state elections of 1844, one Democratic editor even acknowledged that his party "deserved the loss of power there, for they did not know how to use it when they had it in 1842 & 43."[30]

Instead of unifying and strengthening the Democrats, the antibank campaign divided the party and ultimately cost it the services of its leading editor. Unlike many Democrats, Thomas Loring of the *Raleigh Standard* had never joined wholeheartedly in the antibank campaign. Although he was ready to support "a cool and dispassionate investigation of the affairs of all the Banks," Loring denied that their officials were corrupt or dishonest, and he characterized the state bank as "one of the soundest and best managed Institutions in the Union." As the legislative session of 1842 progressed, it became increasingly apparent that Loring was more concerned about the radical tendencies of the antibank legislators in his own party than he was about any infractions that might have been committed by the state banks. When Cadwallader Jones introduced his resolution to accept the surrender of the bank's charter and to place its funds in the hands of agents appointed by the legislature, Loring denounced the measure as a "jacobinical encroachment upon the rights of private property" and rejoiced when the senate laid the resolution on the table.[31]

By mid-January 1843 the columns of the *Standard* were filled with vituperative attacks on the "destructives" and "madmen" in the Democratic party, who would destroy a sound and stable banking system "merely to verify their electioneering slang." Not surprisingly, several antibank legislators and newspaper editors responded in kind by denouncing the *Standard* as a "bank organ" and characterizing its editor as "a traitor in the camp, openly fomenting discord and division among those who should be his friends." On 31 May 1843 Loring announced that he was resigning as editor of the *Standard* to become editor of the *Independent*, a newspaper that would, as its name implied, be "independent of party bias." The following year the *Independent* endorsed Henry Clay for president and William A. Graham for governor, and Loring completed his journey from the Democratic party to the Whig party.[32]

The public debate between Loring and his critics was not simply a dispute about the merits of North Carolina's banking system. The controversy also reflected a deep-seated disagreement within the Democratic party about the role that state issues should play in the conduct of partisan campaigns. In Loring's view, the two parties existed because of fundamental differences regarding the policies of the national government. The editor denied that a consensus existed within his party on state issues, and he argued that such issues were not, therefore, the proper objects of party contention. Acting upon the belief that the parties should tolerate differences of opinion over matters of state policy, Loring expressed surprise and dismay that some Democrats were willing to read him out of the party for voicing "an *opinion* unconnected with politics."[33]

The propriety of introducing state issues into the party debate was also discussed in 1842 in connection with the matter of state aid to the financially troubled Raleigh & Gaston Railroad. Designed to connect the state capital with the Virginia markets of Norfolk and Petersburg, the Raleigh & Gaston had been incorporated in 1835 with a capital stock of $800,000. Construction began in 1836 and was completed four years later at a cost of $1,600,000. Because even the staunchest advocates of internal improvements were reluctant to provide state support to a project that would divert traffic away from North Carolina's market towns and increase the state's economic dependence on Virginia, the railroad had received no state aid and had been constructed entirely with private funds. In 1838, however, the general assembly agreed to guarantee $500,000 of the railroad's bonds in return for a mortgage on the property of the railroad. Two years later the legislature endorsed an additional $300,000 in bonds. The initial guarantee had passed the house of commons by the narrow margin of fifty-four to fifty-two, with 70 percent of the Whigs and 29 percent of the Democrats in support. The vote to endorse the additional bonds in 1840 was even more partisan. Only eight of the fifty-three legislators supporting the bill were Democrats, whereas that party supplied twenty-eight of the forty-two negative votes.[34]

The Raleigh & Gaston loan became an issue in the state elections of 1842. Again, it was gubernatorial candidate Louis D. Henry who set the tone for the campaign by denouncing the Whigs for saddling the state with "gambling debts—for mad schemes of Internal Improvement." The Fayetteville lawyer, who had a long and conspicuous record as a proponent of state aid for internal improvements, did not repudiate the concept of government assistance itself. Instead, he centered his fire on the decision of the general assembly to guarantee the bonds of the Raleigh & Gaston. Henry was particularly critical of the 1840 guarantee, claiming that it had been made without proper security because the railroad's assets were already mortgaged under the provisions of the earlier loan. Given the precarious financial condition of the railroad, the state would, according to the Democrats, probably have to pay the principal on the bonds once it fell due. With few resources available, North Carolina was now confronted with the prospect of repudiation and disgrace.[35]

Again, however, it was Loring who blunted the force of the Democrats' attack by refusing to join the antirailroad compaign. In March 1840 Loring had hailed the completion of the Raleigh & Gaston as "a most splendid specimen of the triumph of art over the obstacles of nature." Later that year he had given his editorial endorsement to the bond guarantee. Now, in 1842, the editor publicly took his party to task for trying to make political capital on the plight of the Raleigh & Gaston. "We see no good that can arise from causeless carping and inconsiderate revilings against our Rail Roads," said Loring. "They have difficulties enough to contend with, without being exposed to groundless censure." The editor reminded his Democratic readers that the proimprovement ranks were "composed of men of all parties," and he admonished them not to mix the issue of internal improvements "with national party politics."[36]

The Whigs, for their part, adopted the strategy of denouncing the Democratic gubernatorial candidate as a rabid promoter of reckless improvement schemes, who was cynically exploiting anti-improvement sentiment for partisan advantage. A correspondent of the *Register* accused Henry of having "sanctioned unequivocally, the most extravagant plans of Internal Improvement." As evidence, he pointed to Henry's membership in the Raleigh convention of 1838, which had recommended a state loan of $3 million to finance a comprehensive program of state development.[37] In his speeches at Wilmington and Fayetteville, Governor Morehead contrasted Henry's present position with his earlier "willingness, nay eagerness, to run the State in debt." Moreover, in a debate with the Democratic candidate at Fayetteville, Morehead extracted from Henry the damaging admission that he was a bondholder in the very railroad that his party was denouncing for insolvency and mismanagement.[38]

Henry's own prominent role as a supporter of state aid to railroads probably neutralized the internal-improvements issue in the governor's election. On the other hand, the unpopularity of the Raleigh & Gaston undoubtedly did help the Democrats in the legislative elections. The editor of the *Fayetteville Observer* claimed that the Whigs had lost three seats in Granville County and one in Brunswick County on account of the Democratic outcry against the railroad. Governor Morehead also attributed his party's loss of the general assembly to Democratic exploitation of the Raleigh & Gaston issue. "The Raleigh & Gaston Rail Road seems to have a fatality attending any connection with it," Morehead wrote a supporter shortly after the summer elections. "All most every friend it had in the last Legislature, has been sacrificed politically by his vote in its favor wherever there was a doubtful contest."[39]

The hapless Raleigh & Gaston continued to be a topic of partisan debate during the campaign of 1844. On 1 January 1843 the railroad defaulted on its interest payments, and the state treasurer immediately took over responsibility for meeting the railroad's debts. By the end of 1844 the state had paid out more than $90,000 in interest on the state-endorsed bonds. This sum amounted to over 20 percent of total state expenditures for 1843 and 1844. With expenditures exceeding revenues by almost $63,000, the state treasury was in a genuinely precarious position.[40]

Five months after the announcement of the Raleigh & Gaston's default, Thomas Loring sold the *Raleigh Standard* to William W. Holden. Unlike his predecessor, Holden was not averse to injecting state issues into the arena of politics. Indeed, the new editor directed many of his partisan barbs at the state debt that had been incurred during eight years of Whig administration. "The people cannot shut their eyes to the fact that the Whigs have plunged the State in debt hundreds of thousands of dollars," he declared two weeks before the 1844 state elections. "This is the result of Whig legislation. How do you like it? Will you have more of it? . . . Do you wish to pay additional taxes on your land and your negroes, in order that your Whig Representatives in the Legislature may have the pleasure of voting to sustain insolvent corporations?"[41]

The default of the Raleigh & Gaston and the increasing state debt each had possibilities as campaign issues for the Democrats in 1844. However, the party blunted the force of its attack by nominating Michael Hoke, a wealthy iron manufacturer from Lincoln County, as the gubernatorial standard-bearer. Hoke had a conspicuous reputation as a supporter of railroads and other state improvements, and the Whigs immediately pointed to his legislative record as evidence that he was a proponent of extravagant and visionary schemes of improvement.[42]

The Whigs also made much of the dismal record of the Democrats in the general assembly of 1842–43. The editor of the *Register* reminded his readers that, after blaming the Whigs for the hard times, the Democratic majority had adjourned without passing a single measure of relief. The editor also hammered away at the failure of the Democrats to carry out their promises to discipline the state banks. "Before they got into power," he remarked, "they denounced these Institutions as the 'manufactories of rogues and swindlers, and guilty of every species of evil.' Upon getting into power, they find them sound and well managed, and furnishing an excellent currency. . . . And so might we take up all the prominent measures of reform promised on the 'Stump' but forgotten or neglected in the legislative Halls."[43]

The election of 1844 resulted in a dramatic comeback for the Whigs, especially in the legislative elections, where they picked up twenty seats in the house of commons and five in the senate to regain their ascendancy in the general assembly. In addition, William A. Graham defeated Michael Hoke to continue the Whigs' uninterrupted tenure in the governor's office. The summer elections, together with the subsequent victory of Clay in the North Carolina presidential contest, offered conclusive proof that the Old North State remained, as the editor of the *Register* put it, "Whig to the core!"[44]

The elections also revealed that the Democrats had failed to make political capital on the new issue of Texas annexation. After the nomination of James K. Polk as the Democratic presidential candidate, North Carolina Democrats became vigorous supporters of immediate annexation. Even before the Tennessean's nomination, Holden had warned his readers that "we must have Texas very soon, or lose her forever." Democrats like Holden emphasized the danger of an unannexed Texas falling under the influence of the British. If Britain succeeded in turning Texas into a satellite, the result would almost certainly be the abolition of slavery, not only in Texas but in the entire South as well.[45]

The Whigs, on the other hand, opposed the idea of immediate annexation. Although they did not rule out the possibility of eventually acquiring Texas, Graham and other Whig spokesmen emphasized the probability that premature annexation would result in a war with Mexico, which had never recognized the independence of its former province. "Let us first set our own house in order," admonished Graham, "improve our great nation, and in due time we shall have Texas without war, and without a violation of honor."[46] The Whigs denied that immediate annexation was necessary to prevent Britain from turning Texas into a satellite. In their view, the real danger to the Union lay not in the imagined threat of British power along the southern border but rather in the possibility that irresponsible demagogues "under the guise of . . . a patriotic love of Texas" would

involve the nation in an unjust war for the benefit of "land speculators, bond holders, stockjobbers and disunionists."[47]

Neither party claimed that the election of 1844 was a referendum
on the Texas issue. Holden ruefully remarked after the election that
the Whigs had obtained thousands of votes from citizens who favored
annexation and who believed that the Whigs were not inveterately
hostile to the acquisition of Texas. "On this question more than all
others, perhaps, in the campaign, did they dodge and equivocate,"
Holden declared. "And even now they dare not claim their victory as
a triumph over Texas."[48] To acknowledge that the Whigs equivocated
on the Texas issue is not to say that the party failed to offer the voters
a distinct and discernible alternative to the Democratic position on
annexation. While the Democrats were advocating the immediate acquisition of Texas as both necessary and desirable, the Whigs were
urging a policy of patience and caution that, for the time being at
least, meant allowing Texas to remain an independent republic.

Throughout the debate over Texas the Democrats displayed a
greater concern about the threat of British power than about the danger of war with Mexico. The annexation of Texas by a joint resolution
of the U.S. Congress on 1 March 1845 did not immediately provoke
hostilities with Mexico, and the members of the Democratic convention that met in Raleigh on 8 January 1846 could not resist boasting
that Polk's policies had falsified "the prediction of our opponents,
that the annexation of Texas would most certainly produce a foreign
war."[49] Ironically, only five days after the adoption of this resolution,
Polk ordered Zachary Taylor to proceed from Corpus Christi to the
disputed territory between the Nueces and Rio Grande rivers. On 11
May 1846 the president sent a special message to Congress accusing
Mexico of shedding American blood upon American soil and recommending a declaration of war. Unfortunately for the Democrats, the
war that Polk hoped would be brought to a "speedy and successful
termination" dragged on for almost two years and became a major
topic of party debate in North Carolina and throughout the nation.[50]

In North Carolina the news of the war arrived as the counties
were nominating legislative tickets for the August elections. The resolutions adopted by the Whigs of Guilford County, under the leadership of former governor John M. Morehead, typified the party's views
on the origin of the war. While promising to "stand by our Country in
war as well as in peace," the Guilford Whigs decried "the rashness

and imprudence of the Executive in involving our Government in war with Mexico."[51] The Whigs took pains to make it clear that they would do nothing to obstruct the war effort, but they did not hide their belief that the conflict was both unnecessary and unconstitutional.

One recent study of the second American party system has argued that the economic issues of the 1830s became less salient and relevant with the return of prosperity in the mid-1840s, and that the leaders of the two parties searched for new issues to reinforce the attachment of the electorate. The annexation of Texas and the ensuing war with Mexico thus gave a lease on life to the party system by creating a new set of issues over which the two parties could agree to disagree.[52] The evidence for North Carolina tends to support this argument. By 1848 the focus of partisan debate had shifted from national economic issues like the Bank of the United States and the tariff to questions of war and territorial expansion. The Whig platform for that year made no specific reference to any of the old issues of the Jacksonian era, whereas the Democratic platform claimed that Polk's domestic policies had been "so eminently successful that many of the . . . opposition pretend to be ready to abandon . . . [the] old issues and now defy us to meet them on the question of the war."[53]

Although the Democrats might laud the success of the Polk administration's domestic policies, the outbreak of war with Mexico undoubtedly put them on the defensive in North Carolina. Party leaders had consistently made light of Whig predictions that annexation meant war with Mexico, and now events had proven the Whigs to be the better prophets. Indeed, the Whigs were confident that "the war question properly managed may be made to break the democrats."[54] For their part, the Democrats were not willing to rely totally on national issues for political success in 1846. As in 1844, many party leaders hoped that political capital might be made on the endemic financial problems of the hapless Raleigh & Gaston.

Once again the plight of the bankrupt railroad seemed to have genuine campaign potential for the Democrats. In January 1845 the general assembly had authorized Governor Graham to institute foreclosure proceedings on the railroad, to sue its stockholders for payment of the 1840 bonds, and to bid on the property of the railroad at not more than $300,000 plus the accrued interest on the 1840 bonds.

On 29 December 1845 Graham bought the road for $363,000, and three days later the state formally took possession. In the meantime, North Carolina continued to pay about $45,000 annually in interest on the guaranteed bonds.[55]

The Democrats again accused their opponents of recklessly involving the state in thousands of dollars of debt for the benefit of insolvent corporations. Assuming that the state would be liable not only for the interest payments but also for the principal, once it fell due, party spokesmen calculated that North Carolina's connection with the Raleigh & Gaston would eventually cost almost $1.4 million. Such an extravagant amount could be raised only by increasing taxes or by taking money from the public school fund. The Democrats were especially critical of Graham for adding to the state's liabilities by bidding the maximum allowable sum for the railroad when he could almost certainly have bought it for much less. In short, according to one Democratic candidate for the legislature, Graham and his party had placed "a load of debt upon the tax-paying people that years of toil and sweat only can remove."[56]

In response to these charges, Graham and the other Whig leaders again made the point that the record of the Democrats on internal improvements belied their claim that the Whigs were entirely responsible for North Carolina's involvement with the railroads. In a speech at Elizabeth City the governor made the familiar argument that Haywood, Strange, Saunders, Henry, and other prominent Democrats had been staunch advocates of state support for internal improvements during the 1830s. The leading men of both parties had sanctioned the railroads, and if the state should unfortunately become embarrassed on account of its connection with them, the parties must both share the blame.[57] The editor of the *Register* reminded his readers that the Democrats had held the balance of power on improvement measures in the legislatures of 1838 and 1840. Had the entire party voted against the two loans to the Raleigh & Gaston, neither measure would have become law. "We now boldly ask— 'Who, by their *votes* and *acts*, have involved the State in debt for the Raleigh and Gaston Road?' And we emphatically answer, *the* DEMOCRATIC *members of the Legislatures of 1838 and 1840*! . . . It was in their power to have SAVED the State, BUT THEY WOULD NOT!!!"[58]

Once again the Democrats inadvertently gave force to these arguments by nominating a gubernatorial candidate who was closely associated with the internal improvements movement. The editor of the *Register* pointed out that Democratic candidate James B. Shepard had been a member of the Raleigh convention of 1838 and had supported a motion recommending a state loan for $500,000 in Raleigh & Gaston bonds. Even worse from the standpoint of the Democrats, the Whigs discovered that Shepard owned $5,000 worth of stock in the Raleigh & Gaston and thus was one of the individuals whom Governor Graham was planning to sue for payment of the 1840 bonds. In a speech at Kinston Graham acidly remarked that Shepard was not the proper person to be elected governor because the people were not in the habit of electing judges to decide their own cases.[59]

On the pages of the *Standard*, William W. Holden vigorously denied that Shepard was a stockholder in the Raleigh & Gaston, but the editor's explanation certainly did nothing to help the Democratic cause. Admitting that Shepard had once owned fifty shares of Raleigh & Gaston stock, Holden pointed out that the Democratic candidate had sold his stock in May 1845. The purchaser was none other than Holden himself, although the editor had subsequently transferred the stock to another Raleigh resident. The Whigs naturally charged the two Democrats with double-dealing. A correspondent of the *Register* declared that Shepard "has been connected with Rail Roads and Banks, ever since he cut loose from the apron-strings, until a few months ago, when he made a family arrangement with the Editor of the 'Standard.'" The correspondent accused the candidate of selling his stock to escape liability for the company's debts and condemned the sale as "an attempt . . . to chisel the Old North State." He also pointed out that Governor Graham, unlike his opponent, had no personal interest in the Raleigh & Gaston. "He never tried for six years to make money out of the Road, and when the last hope was gone, then impose his Stock on a simple or overgenerous friend, and call it a SALE!"[60]

The summer elections of 1846 proved disastrous for the Democrats. Graham trounced Shepard by a margin of almost eight thousand votes, winning 55 percent of the two-party vote. In addition, the Whigs won clear majorities in both houses of the general assembly for the first time since 1840. Shortly after the election, the editor of the *Register* observed that the Democrats had introduced the Raleigh & Gaston issue "as the grand cardinal principle of state policy, upon which the Election was to turn." The result, however, had again proven that the Democratic doctrines were "too disorganizing and ruinous, too much at enmity with the principles upon which our Government is founded, to receive the sanction of a majority of the People of North Carolina."[61]

Holden, on the other hand, attributed the opposition's success to "base, secret, and abominable Whig lies and Whig slanders," to the war with Mexico, and to the apathy of the Democrats in certain parts of the state.[62] Certainly, however, he and many other Democrats must finally have begun to realize the ineffectiveness of the Raleigh & Gaston loan as a campaign issue, as well as the folly of campaigning against railroads with standard-bearers who had conspicuous records as railroad supporters. Indeed, by the end of 1848 Holden had reversed his opposition to railroads and had become an outspoken advocate of state aid. In words reminiscent of those of Thomas Loring six years earlier, the editor of the *Standard* now admonished his Democratic readers that "party spirit and party interests have nothing to do with this work."[63]

Holden's conversion to the cause of internal improvements marked the end of an era in North Carolina politics. Never again would the Democrats attempt to wage a statewide campaign against North Carolina's railroad system. Did the issue of railroad relief represent a clash of conflicting ideologies, or can it best be understood in terms of two "electoral machines" competing for political advantage? One recent study of party politics in North Carolina has placed great importance on the ideological dimension of the railroad issue, characterizing that issue as "the major catalyst for partisan disagreement" in the Old North State. According to this interpretation, the divergent views of the parties on railroad relief reflected deep-seated differences about the role of government in promoting economic development and even about the desirability of the market economy itself. Democratic hostility toward railroads supposedly began to dissipate, however, once North Carolina emerged from the long depression of the 1840s and began "enjoying a taste of prosperity. . . . Many who had resisted the charms of the market economy now succumbed to them." Thus, by the middle of the 1850s "both Democrats and Whigs in North Carolina had come to accept Whiggish notions of the relationship of government and society."[64]

This interpretation of party conflict founders on the matter of timing. It makes no sense to attribute catalytic qualities to an issue of five years' duration whose emergence postdated the creation of organized parties by almost a decade. Nor does the economic recovery, which actually began in 1843, adequately explain why Democratic attacks against the Raleigh & Gaston ceased after 1846. It seems more reasonable to argue that the Democrats introduced the railroad issue in 1842 not because the party was ideologically opposed to positive government or to a market economy but because Democratic strategists saw the plight of the hapless Raleigh & Gaston as a potentially effective campaign issue. The party's success in the legislative elections that year, along with the railroad's default on its interest payments, encouraged the Democrats to pursue the issue during the next two state campaigns. By 1848, however, party leaders had abandoned the railroad issue because by then it had conspicuously failed to produce the desired results.

The personal background of the Democratic gubernatorial candidates undercut the party's efforts to exploit the railroad issue during the 1840s. Henry, Hoke, and Shepard were all talented leaders who were thoroughly committed to the national programs of the Democratic party. But they were also urban dwellers who were closely associated with the manufacturing and commercial interests of their towns, and all three had long-standing and conspicuous records as supporters of internal improvements. Henry and Shepard also had personal investments in railroad stocks and bonds, including the railroad that their party was denouncing for being bankrupt, mismanaged, and insolvent. Instead of defending their own record on internal improvements, the Whigs deftly changed the issue to focus on the extravagant schemes of improvement allegedly advocated by their opponents.

It seems unlikely that a party ideologically opposed to a market economy would have chosen men like Henry, Hoke, and Shepard to be their standard-bearers. Undoubtedly these leaders were in many respects "exceptional" Democrats. The majority of Democratic voters did not own stock in banks or railroads and were not involved in manufacturing enterprises. The same can also be said about the vast majority of Whig voters. Both parties were led by exceptional men who were intimately involved in the workings of the market economy. Despite their sometimes acerbic campaign rhetoric, the leaders of the Democratic party were not prepared to alter the status quo radically. Certainly the Democrats had the legislative muscle to mount a radical challenge during the session of 1842–43. Had they chosen to do so, the party could have destroyed the state bank by accepting the surrender of its charter, and they could have crippled the nascent railroad system by voting down all relief measures. But the legislative session actually witnessed no major departures in state policy.

As the summer elections of 1848 approached, not even the most partisan Democrat would have denied that, after twelve years in power, the Whigs still commanded the loyalty of a majority of voters in the Old North State. Neither the agitation of state issues like the Raleigh & Gaston nor the introduction of new national issues like the annexation of Texas seemed sufficient to draw the people of North Carolina away from their Whig moorings. When the Democratic state convention nominated ex-congressman David S. Reid as their gubernatorial standard-bearer in April 1848, the war with Mexico had just ended, and Reid's opponent, Charles Manly, looked forward to the ensuing debate on the unpopular foreign policy of the Polk administration. Few, even among the Democrats, could have suspected that Reid was about to raise an issue that would unleash the forces of state sectionalism and profoundly transform the politics of North Carolina.

8 ✦ Democracy Triumphant: "Free Suffrage" and the Revival of State Sectionalism

I trust Sir, the day is not far distant when this unpatriotic cry of eastern and western prejudices—eastern and western influences—shall cease to be heard in our land.—Robert G. A. Love, speech in the North Carolina House of Commons, 1849

By a fair compromise with our Western friends, after a controversy of thirty years, our fundamental law . . . was settled. That controversy can never be renewed without injury to us.—William A. Graham to the editor of the *Newbernian*, 13 July 1848

During the 1820s and 1830s the acrimonious sectional controversy between the east and the west had played a major role in shaping the contours of politics in the Old North State. By satisfying the most pressing western demands for reform, the constitutional amendments adopted in 1835 had alleviated this long-standing animosity and had made it possible for the leaders of the nascent Whig and Democratic parties to build statewide coalitions. Yet even after 1835, the tensions between North Carolina's two disparate halves never lay far beneath the surface. In the chambers of the general assembly, sectional passions frequently flared as easterners and westerners divided over internal improvements, the apportionment of the public school fund, the creation of new counties, and other measures of state policy. Although the parties generally refrained from agitating these sectional issues in their statewide campaigns, neither was averse to appealing to sectional prejudices whenever its strategists thought that they could win votes by doing so.

By a tacit agreement between the parties, one issue was singled out as being entirely beyond the limits of permissible discussion. Under no circumstances, either in the legislature or on the hustings, should any question be raised about the terms of the sectional compact that had been forged by the Constitutional Convention of 1835. The leaders of both parties agreed that any effort to secure additional amendments to the state constitution was certain to unleash the disruptive forces that had threatened to tear the state apart during the 1820s and 1830s. For over a dozen years the two parties adhered faithfully to this unwritten rule of North Carolina politics and scrupulously avoided any discussion of constitutional change. When David S. Reid breached the agreement in 1848 by advocating a rather minor modification in the suffrage requirements, he unwittingly reopened the Pandora's box of constitutional reform and released the spirits that his fellow partisans had been striving to control. The second party system in North Carolina would never be the same thereafter.

Even before 1848, sectional cross-pressures had already weakened the hold of the Whigs on North Carolina. Both antebellum parties were coalitions of easterners and westerners (see table 8.1), and each experienced difficulties in reconciling the interests of its two sectional wings. During the 1840s, however, the Whigs were more vulnerable to sectional pressures than their opponents, because as the governing party they had the responsibility for enacting specific policies that would satisfy the competing blocs within the party.

Table 8.1 Party Strength in the North Carolina House of Commons, 1836–48

	Whig members			Democratic members		
	East	West	Total	East	West	Total
1836	22	36	58	37	25	62
1838	25	41	66	34	20	54
1840	30	45	75	29	16	45
1842	17	34	51	42	27	69
1844	25	45	70	33	17	50
1846	23	42	65	35	20	55
1848	23	39	62	35	23	58

Source: Thomas E. Jeffrey, "Internal Improvements and Political Parties in Antebellum North Carolina," table 1.

Table 8.2   Vote in the House of Commons on Aid to Existing Railroads, 1836–40 (affirmative percentage by party and section)

	Whigs			Democrats				
	East	West	Total	East	West	Total	East	West
Wilmington & Raleigh and Fayetteville & Western subscription (1836)	70	94	85	40	65	51	53	83
Raleigh & Gaston relief (1838)	30	92	70	24	35	29	27	72
Wilmington & Raleigh relief (1840)	48	89	74	9	13	11	30	69
Raleigh & Gaston relief (1840)	46	100	76	21	25	22	34	80

Sources: HJ, 1836–37, 487–88; HJ, 1838–39, 527–28; HJ, 1840–41, 541–42, 717–18.

One of the most vexatious issues involved the question of state aid to internal improvements. By 1838 western Whigs were thoroughly committed to the completion of the two existing railroads—the Wilmington & Raleigh and the Raleigh & Gaston—which they viewed as the first segments of a statewide transportation network (see table 8.2).[1] Eastern Whigs, on the other hand, took a much different view of these two railroads. In 1836 a large majority of eastern Whigs had voted in favor of a state appropriation to the Wilmington & Raleigh. However, when the railroad began experiencing financial difficulties after the Panic of 1837, a majority of eastern Whigs voted against measures to guarantee the railroad's bonds. Eastern Whigs also objected to measures designed to provide relief to the struggling Raleigh & Gaston, a railroad that they believed would siphon off the commercial wealth of the state to markets in Virginia.[2]

The two wings of the Whig party also disagreed about the propriety of additional improvement projects. Western Whigs were particularly interested in the construction of the Fayetteville & Western, a railroad that had been chartered in 1833 to connect the counties of the piedmont with the market town of Fayetteville on the Cape Fear. Western legislators, especially in the mountain region, were also anxious to secure state aid for the construction or improvement of local roads and turnpikes. Eastern Whigs, for their part, were reluctant to invest the scarce resources of the state in purely local improvement schemes that would have no direct benefit to their constituents. Many legislators from the southeastern counties were willing to support the Fayetteville & Western, but only in return for western support of the North Carolina Central Railroad, a project designed to link the ports of Beaufort and New Bern with the capital city of Raleigh. Whigs in the extreme northeastern counties tended to be indifferent toward both of these railroad schemes, but many Whigs in the Albemarle region were ready to vote for these projects in exchange for a legislative appropriation for the reopening of Roanoke Inlet.[3]

The ability of the Whigs to reconcile these numerous sectional interests was severely limited by their policy of financing state development exclusively with North Carolina's share of federal land sale proceeds. The Deposit Act had provided the state with almost $1.5 million in federal money in 1836, but the financial panic that began the following year prevented the influx of additional revenue from Washington. The deepening economic depression also discouraged private investment in transportation projects. Thus, even though the general assembly agreed in 1836 to purchase two-fifths of the stock in the proposed Fayetteville & Western and North Carolina Central railroads, the inability of private investors to subscribe the remaining stock prevented the organization of the companies. Given the troubled economic situation and the unwillingness of the private sector to assume the task of improvement, only state intervention on a massive scale could have provided the financial resources necessary to satisfy the demands of all the elements in the Whig party. But this would have required a substantial increase in state taxes or the creation of a large state debt—alternatives that were anathema to a majority in both parties.[4]

A rift in the Whig party over internal improvements first manifested itself during the legislative session of 1838–39, when pro-improvement western Whigs took the lead in defeating a proposal for a state subscription of stock in the North Carolina Central Railroad (see table 8.3). Western Whigs apparently feared that state involvement in the central railroad would jeopardize the success of their own Fayetteville & Western scheme, and they counted on the popularity of the Fayetteville railroad among western Democrats to offset any losses that might result from antagonizing their eastern colleagues. This calculation eventually proved to be correct, but only after the

Table 8.3   Vote in the House of Commons on Internal Improvement Projects, 1838 (affirmative percentage by party and section)

	Whigs			Democrats				
	East	West	Total	East	West	Total	East	West
North Carolina Central railroad subscription	48	5	20	21	26	23	32	12
Fayetteville & Western subscription (four-fifths)	9	54	37	3	20	10	6	39
Fayetteville & Western subscription (three-fourths)	27	92	67	13	50	27	19	77
Fayetteville & Western subscription (three-fifths)	30	100	74	23	55	36	26	85
Roanoke Inlet Company subscription	59	32	42	7	5	6	29	23

Sources: HJ, 1838–39, 524–25, 488–89, 490–91, 525–26, 501–2.

railroad's promoters agreed to scale down their initial demands. As reported by the House Committee on Internal Improvements, the Fayettteville & Western bill contained a provision for a state subscription of four-fifths of the railroad's stock. Even within the western Whig delegation, a substantial minority of legislators balked at this attempt to finance the railroad almost entirely with state funds, and the house struck this provision from the bill. A motion to substitute a three-fourths stock subscription also failed to win approval in the house. However, when the railroad's supporters finally agreed to reduce the state subscription to three-fifths, the bill passed easily. This still amounted to a generous infusion of state aid, but not enough to persuade private investors to purchase the remaining stock. As a result, the Fayetteville & Western Railroad was never built.[5]

In addition to voting against state aid for the central railroad, western Whigs also helped to defeat a bill that would have authorized a state subscription of stock in the Roanoke Inlet Company. Eastern

Whigs eventually succeeded in adding an amendment to the Fayette-ville & Western bill to provide for a survey and report upon the feasibility and probable cost of reopening the inlet, but this compromise did not prove entirely satisfactory. Eight of the thirteen eastern Whigs who had supported the inlet bill in the house of commons later voted against the Fayetteville & Western. Indeed, not one of the major improvement proposals before the legislature of 1838, aside from the Roanoke Inlet bill, received the endorsement of a majority of eastern Whigs.[6]

Intraparty differences over internal improvements reached a high-water mark during the legislative session of 1840–41, when westerners helped to defeat another bill for state assistance to the Roanoke Inlet Company. Northeastern Whigs, under the leadership of William B. Shepard of Pasquotank, retaliated by voting against a bill to appropriate $300,000 for the construction of a turnpike from Raleigh to the mountains. In a bitter diatribe on the floor of the state senate, Shepard charged that "we of the East have been met by our Western brethren with an intense selfishness, that exceeds anything I have hitherto met with in the history of Legislation."[7]

Thomas L. Clingman, who had introduced the turnpike bill in the state senate, responded to Shepard's accusations with an equally caustic speech. The Buncombe County Whig pointed out that most of the votes against the inlet bill had been cast by anti-improvement Democrats from the east. Instead of denouncing the real authors of his discomfort, Shepard was recklessly venting his disappointment and anger on the west. Clingman went on to charge that the legislators from the east, not those from his own section, were the ones really guilty of a lack of generosity. In support of this argument he pointed out that during the previous legislative session not a single easterner had supported the bill to purchase stock in the turnpike between Rutherfordton and Asheville—a measure that would have directly benefited Clingman's own constituents. Yet the legislators from the west had not tried to retaliate, but instead had voted almost unanimously in favor of the construction of railroads, the improvement of rivers, and other developmental projects in the east. Far from having monopolized the benefits of internal improvements, the west had received almost nothing.[8]

Clingman's use of the facts was highly selective, but it is true nonetheless that the people of the west failed to benefit significantly

from North Carolina's early internal improvement program. The
votes of the western Whigs in the legislatures of 1836 and 1838 had
been instrumental in providing state assistance for the completion of
the Raleigh & Gaston and the Wilmington & Raleigh railroads. But
these railroads lay entirely in the east and by themselves could be of
no direct benefit to western residents. Of all the proposed railroads,
only the Fayetteville & Western was designed to traverse the counties
of the west. Yet easterners had refused to supply the degree of state
aid that was necessary to organize the company and begin construction. A program of generous support for western turnpikes might
have compensated for the lack of an east-west railroad, but eastern
Whigs like Shepard repeatedly sabotaged plans to construct a state
road from Raleigh to the Tennessee line. Not until 1848 did the general assembly finally give its approval to the idea of an east-west high-
way across the mountains.[9]

Throughout most of the 1840s the continuing depression and the
necessity of shoring up the shaky financial foundations of the two
existing railroads militated against the introduction of costly new
schemes of internal improvement. The general assembly did, however, consider numerous bills to provide assistance to local improvement projects, particularly in the mountain region. By 1844 a majority of eastern Whigs had abandoned their opposition to these local
projects and were voting along with their western colleagues in favor
of modest state appropriations (see table 8.4). At the same time the
western Democrats, who earlier had been quite sympathetic toward
local improvement projects, reversed their position and joined eastern Democrats in opposing them. Only western Democrats from the
mountain region continued to vote consistently in favor of local improvements. By the end of the decade, the propriety of state support
for internal improvements seemed well on its way to becoming a
strictly partisan issue. However, the course of events would soon reveal that the intraparty consensus on internal improvements was
more apparent than real.

An analysis of legislative roll-call votes reveals that section and
party both played a role in shaping alignments on internal improvements in the North Carolina General Assembly. In the case of both
parties, westerners consistently gave more support than easterners to
state-financed internal improvements. However, the roll calls also indicate that the Whigs in each sectional delegation were substantially

Table 8.4 Vote in the House of Commons on Aid to Roads and Turnpikes, 1836–46 (affirmative percentage by party and section)

	Whigs			Democrats				
	East	West	Total	East	West	Total	East	West
1836								
Macon County road	33	84	67	7	86	41	16	85
Yancey County road	20	59	45	8	88	40	12	70
1840								
Rutherford-Buncombe turnpike	30	98	74	7	73	31	18	91
1842								
Rutherford-Buncombe turnpike	42	97	82	3	27	13	13	66
Buncombe County road	25	93	74	3	18	8	8	62
Wilkesboro-Jefferson road	15	63	49	10	61	33	12	62
1844								
Rutherford-Buncombe turnpike	78	90	86	7	18	11	38	69
Buncombe County road	63	83	78	0	31	10	24	71
Cherokee County road	88	87	87	10	27	16	31	74
Macon County road	52	85	73	3	23	9	24	70
1846								
Cherokee County road	69	63	64	13	15	13	31	47
Buncombe County road	88	72	76	23	21	22	46	55
Morganton-Yorkville (S.C.) turnpike	100	97	98	14	22	18	49	70

Sources: HJ, 1836–37, 445, 491; HJ, 1840–41, 528–29; HJ, 1842–43, 692–93, 721–22, 553–54; HJ, 1844–45, 612–13, 509–10, 648–49, 681–82; HJ, 1846–47, 478–79, 491, 550.

more inclined to vote for improvement bills than the Democrats. Thus, the proportion of eastern Whigs voting in favor of internal improvements exceeded the proportion of eastern Democrats on all of the twenty-two roll calls presented in the tables. And the percentage of western Whigs voting favorably on such measures surpassed the percentage of western Democrats on all but three roll calls.

What the roll calls do not substantiate is the existence of mono-

Table 8.5 Vote on Internal Improvement Measures in County Delegations Containing Members from Both Parties, 1836–46

Year	County	Party	Roll calls			
			Party line	Consensus	Divided	No vote
1836	Chatham	2W/1D	0	2	1	0
	Guilford	2W/1D	1*	2	0	0
	Orange	3W/1D	1	0	1	1
	Stokes	2W/1D	1*	2	0	0
	Wake	1W/2D	0	0	1	2
	Total		3	6	3	3
1838	Bertie	1W/1D	0	6	0	0
	Granville	2W/1D	0	5	1	0
	Johnston	1W/1D	0	6	0	0
	Northampton	1W/1D	0	5	0	1
	Stokes	2W/1D	1*	5	0	0
	Total		1	27	1	1
1840	Johnston	1W/1D	0	3	0	0
	Orange	3W/1D	0	1	2	0
	Robeson	1W/1D	3	0	0	0
	Stokes	2W/1D	2	1	0	0
	Total		5	5	2	0
1842	Beaufort	1W/1D	1*	2	0	0
	Burke	2W/1D	0	3	0	0
	Chatham	2W/1D	1	2	0	0
	Franklin	1W/1D	0	1	0	2
	Granville	1W/2D	2	0	0	1
	Northampton	1W/1D	1*	1	0	1
	Orange	1W/3D	0	1	2	0
	Total		5	10	2	4
1844	Granville	1W/2D	2	0	0	2
	Johnston	1W/1D	0	3	0	1
	Rowan	1W/1D	1	1	0	2
	Stokes	1W/2D	4	0	0	0
	Surry	1W/2D	2	1	1	0
	Total		9	5	1	5
1846	Granville	1W/2D	0	0	0	3
	Johnston	1W/1D	0	1	0	2
	Orange	3W/1D	1	0	2	0
	Rowan	1W/1D	2*	0	0	1

Table 8.5—*Continued*

Year	County	Party	Roll calls			
			Party line	Consensus	Divided	No vote
	Stokes	1W/2D	3	0	0	0
	Surry	2W/1D	1	1	1	0
	Total		7	2	3	6
Total			30	55	12	19

Sources: Roll calls cited in tables 8.2, 8.3, and 8.4.

Note: Party-line roll calls are those in which Whig and Democratic legislators were arrayed on opposite sides. Consensus roll calls are those in which Whig and Democratic legislators voted on the same side. Divided roll calls are those in which legislators from the same party voted on opposite sides. "No vote" indicates roll calls in which one party did not vote.

*Whig(s) voted against internal improvements; Democrat(s) voted in favor.

lithic party positions for and against internal improvements. Although Whigs were more likely than Democrats to support a policy of government assistance, a majority of eastern Whigs voted against state aid on almost three-fifths of the roll calls, while a majority of western Democrats supported such aid on almost a third of them. An analysis of the behavior of individual county delegations containing members from both parties provides additional evidence that the legislative parties did not vote monolithically on internal improvement measures (see table 8.5). Overall, Whigs and Democrats in these divided delegations were almost twice as likely to vote together on improvement measures than to split along party lines. And even in delegations where party-line voting prevailed, in almost one-fourth of the cases it was the Democrats—and not the Whigs—who voted on the proimprovement side of the issue. A number of generalizations can undoubtedly be derived from an examination of these legislative roll calls, but the most salient fact is that both parties were internally divided over the issue of internal improvements.[10]

The difficulties experienced by the parties in developing a coherent policy on internal improvements were paralleled by the chronic intraparty wrangling over the distribution of the public school fund. In 1838 the general assembly had established a system of public schools to provide free education to all white children. According to the provisions of the school law, the county courts were responsible for laying off school districts and appointing district committees. Any district that supplied a school building and raised twenty dollars in taxes would receive twice that amount in state aid. Two years later the general assembly considered a supplementary bill that was designed to expand and modify some of the provisions of the original school law. As initially introduced into the senate, the new bill provided for the apportionment of the school fund among the counties according to their white population. However, a bipartisan coalition of eastern senators succeeded in amending the bill to provide for apportionment according to federal population (white population plus three-fifths of the slave population). Except for David S. Reid, who represented a slaveholding district on the Virginia border, the western senators from both parties unanimously opposed the amendment.[11]

From the viewpoint of the westerners, distribution of the school money according to federal population would be a gross injustice because such a formula would allot a disproportionate share of the state's scarce resources to the wealthier plantation counties, which needed financial aid the least. Moreover, it made no sense to factor in the slave population, because only white children were allowed to attend the schools. Under the federal basis of apportionment, claimed one western lawmaker, "we find that the Counties having the fewest number of children to educate, receive the largest portion of this fund; and the Counties having the greatest number, receive the smallest!"[12]

These arguments failed to sway eastern legislators either in 1840 or in subsequent sessions of the general assembly. In 1840 the western legislators in the house of commons attempted to restore the white basis of apportionment by striking out the phrase "federal population" from the senate bill, but the motion was defeated by a vote of sixty-two to fifty-two. Only one easterner in the entire house voted with the western bloc, and only seven westerners, all from counties with a substantial proportion of slaves, voted against the majority in their section.

The school fund continued to be an important political issue in North Carolina throughout the 1840s, as western legislators in each session of the general assembly tried unsuccessfully to restore the white basis of apportionment (see table 8.6). During the session of 1850–51 Charles Manly, the recently defeated Whig governor, took the side of the west and denounced the act of 1841 in his last message

Table 8.6   Vote in the House of Commons on the Distribution of the
School Fund According to White Population, 1840–46
(affirmative percentage by party and section)

	Whigs			Democrats				
	East	West	Total	East	West	Total	East	West
1840	3	89	55	0	86	29	2	88
1842	8	88	55	0	90	41	3	89
1844	0	65	44	3	77	26	2	68
1846	0	75	57	4	53	25	3	67

Sources: HJ, 1840–41, 654–55; HJ, 1842–43, 994; HJ, 1844–45, 732–33; HJ, 1846–47, 552.

to the general assembly. According to Manly, the public school fund had been "designed for the education, not of the rich, nor of the poor, exclusively, but for all the white children of the State alike." The fund ought, therefore, "to be divided equally amongst them, whether their residence happens to be, or not to be, in a community holding slaves and free negroes."[13]

Manly's forceful appeal to justice and equality emboldened westerners to adopt a more aggressive strategy. Several times during the 1840s Whigs in the general assembly had introduced bills to create an office of superintendent of public schools in order to provide central direction to North Carolina's nascent school system. On the surface this was a sectionally innocuous issue. Indeed, it was one of the few state issues on which Democrats could unite wholeheartedly against the Whigs.[14] By 1850, however, western Whigs were ready to use the superintendent issue as a bargaining chip to extract concessions from eastern Whigs on the apportionment issue. Thus, when Calvin H. Wiley introduced a superintendent bill into the house of commons, westerners offered an amendment providing that "the distribution of the Common School Fund according to the Federal population be repealed and that hereafter that fund shall be distributed according to the number of white children." To the dismay of the reformers, however, the eastern Whigs joined the eastern Democrats in voting unanimously to reject the amendment. The western Whigs retaliated by voting with the Democrats against Wiley's unamended bill, and the measure was resoundingly defeated.[15]

Two years later, western Whigs pursued the same strategy and again refused to support a superintendent bill without a provision for the apportionment of the school fund according to white population. This time, however, a significant minority of Democrats under the leadership of John W. Cuningham, a close personal friend of Wiley, provided enough votes to push the bill through the assembly, despite the opposition of the western Whigs. Wiley thus realized his long-standing goal of establishing central direction for North Carolina's public school system. Until the end of the antebellum era, however, the wealthy eastern counties would continue to receive the lion's share of the school money.[16]

Another issue that consistently produced an east-west division within the general assembly was the propriety of creating new counties in the rapidly growing areas of the west. Between 1836 and 1860, each session of the legislature considered numerous bills to divide old counties and to create new ones. A large majority of easterners in both parties generally voted against such measures (see table 8.7). One western legislator aptly characterized the east's reluctance to create new counties as "a relic of that sectional prejudice which excited such a powerful influence over the minds of many, before the constitutional reform of 1835." Until the constitution was amended, each county had been allotted one senator and two commoners, and an increase in the number of western counties would necessarily result in a diminution of eastern power in the legislature.[17]

Table 8.7 Vote in the House of Commons on the Creation of New Counties, 1836–42 (affirmative percentage by party and section)

	Whigs			Democrats				
County	East	West	Total	East	West	Total	East	West
Jefferson (1836)	5	77	51	3	76	34	4	77
Henderson (1838)	52	100	83	24	100	52	36	100
Jefferson (1838)	17	95	67	15	100	49	16	97
McDowell (1838)	13	89	61	6	100	40	9	93
Cleveland (1838)	13	85	57	6	100	42	9	90
Union (1840)	29	98	77	7	63	28	16	88
McDowell (1842)	25	97	73	16	77	41	19	88

Sources: HJ, 1836–37, 290; HJ, 1838–39, 343–44, 347–48, 363, 380–81; HJ, 1840–41, 454–55; HJ, 1842–43, 551.

After 1835 there was no such compelling reason to oppose an increase in the number of counties. Yet easterners remained unsympathetic to the needs of the west, where residents often had to travel many days over rough terrain and poor roads in order to attend the county courts and the regimental musters. According to one western legislator, those in the east who were blessed with railroads, steamboats, and other modern transportation facilities "know nothing of our difficulties, locked in, as we are, by our towering mountains and majestic rivers." The legislator went on to emphasize that the refusal to create new counties meant more than merely personal inconvenience for the people of the west. "Unless you extend to us this relief," he warned, "our progress to prosperity and wealth must be greatly retarded, and our usefulness and happiness much impaired." Despite the entreaties of westerners, easterners in both parties continued to oppose new counties until the end of the antebellum era.[18]

Divided as they were over important state issues such as internal improvements, the school fund, and the creation of new counties, the leaders of the North Carolina parties generally preferred to emphasize cohesive national issues in their statewide campaigns. One veteran of the second party system accurately characterized the rationale behind this strategy when he remarked that "owing to the local sectional troubles between the East and the West, the leaders of both parties had long sought to avoid State issues and trust rather to National topics for popular discussion."[19]

State issues were never entirely absent from antebellum political campaigns. Indeed, precisely because their constituents were intensely interested in these issues, party leaders were constantly tempted to exploit them. Thus, the sectionally innocuous issue of state banking became a major topic of partisan debate during the early 1840s, although the outcome of the debate ultimately proved disastrous for the Democrats, who had initially raised the issue. During the mid-1840s Democratic strategists also tried to make political capital on the issue of relief for the Raleigh & Gaston Railroad.

At first glance the Raleigh & Gaston issue might seem an exception to the general tendency of the parties to avoid divisive sectional issues in their state campaigns. The manner in which the Democrats exploited this issue, however, provides an excellent example of how party strategists could sometimes direct potentially explosive sectional issues into safer partisan channels. Even at the height of the railroad controversy the Democratic leadership carefully refrained from an all-out attack on the concept of state-supported improvements. Such an attack would undoubtedly have alienated substantial numbers of Democratic voters in the west. By limiting their fire to one particularly unpopular and financially beleaguered eastern railroad, party leaders were able to capitalize on anti-improvement sentiment in the east while maintaining their support among prorailroad Democrats in the west.

Such a strategy allowed western Democrats like John W. Ellis to join enthusiastically in the attack against the Raleigh & Gaston without abandoning their commitment to state-supported railroads. Indeed, Ellis's main argument was that the Whig policy of pampering Raleigh's insolvent railroad had jeopardized the success of internal improvements in the west. According to Ellis, these "extravagant donations to an almost exclusively local work" had resulted in a neglect of more worthy projects and had "postponed the work of Internal Improvement in North Carolina for ten years to come." In Ellis's view, the Raleigh & Gaston issue offered proof that the Democrats were the only party genuinely devoted to internal improvements. "The democrats of North Carolina . . . are now and will continue to be in favor of a system of Improvements throughout the whole extent of the State . . . [whereas] the Whig party in our Legislature has adopted an unimportant part of it, and upon that lavished all the treasure of the State." By tailoring their arguments to the peculiar interests of each section, the Democrats managed to exploit the Raleigh & Gaston issue and still maintain harmony between their eastern and western wings.[20]

Although they usually refrained from raising explicitly sectional issues in their state campaigns, party strategists were not averse to appealing in a more general way to long-standing sectional prejudices. After John M. Morehead won the governor's election in 1840, for example, the Democrats complained that Morehead's western supporters had urged the people of that section to vote for him as the "western candidate" at the same time that eastern Whigs were exhorting their constituents to bury old sectional prejudices. In addition, the Democrats claimed that Morehead's residence in Guilford County and his extensive law practice in the western counties had given him a decided advantage in that part of the state over his "eastern" opponent, Romulus M. Saunders. The significant increase in the Whig percentage of the vote in the counties of the far west lends credence to

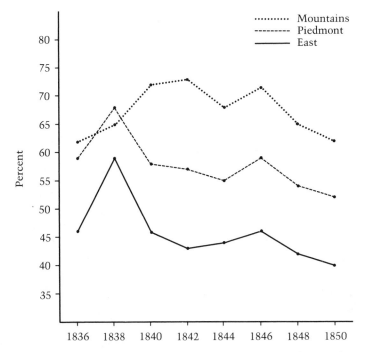

Figure 8.1 Whig Percentage of the Vote in North Carolina Gubernatorial Elections, 1836–50. *Source:* County voting returns, in Thomas E. Jeffrey, "The Second Party System in North Carolina," appendix A.

the Democratic claim that Morehead's western identity was a valuable asset for his party in that region. In the eastern counties, on the other hand, Morehead failed to improve upon the showing of his eastern Whig predecessor (see figure 8.1).[21]

After losing four successive elections with eastern candidates, the Democrats decided to nominate a westerner as their standard-bearer in 1844. Michael Hoke, a legislator from Lincoln County, proved to be an ideal choice. Acknowledging Hoke's reputation as a witty and entertaining stump speaker, one Whig pointed out that "his social swagering manner is well calculated to captivate & please the unlettered men of the mountains." Equally important, Hoke—like Morehead—was widely known in the west because of his law practice, and he could boast of many political opponents who were also his personal friends. Hoke traveled extensively throughout the western counties during the campaign and tried hard to persuade Whig voters that the governor's election should be nonpartisan. According to Whig lawyer Bayles M. Edney, Hoke's argument was "that the Election is peculiarly local, & has nothing to do with National politics, that a generous Whig might well, without any sort of impropriety, vote for Mr. Clay, & Mike Hoke."[22]

The Democratic strategists in Raleigh did not rely exclusively on Hoke's personal popularity to win western voters to their cause. About one month before the election, the party issued a circular entitled *Plain Thoughts for the West*, which was distributed widely throughout the western counties. According to the Whigs, the circular was written by Senator William H. Haywood, Jr., and was printed by William W. Holden at the office of the *Raleigh Standard*. It is not surprising that the tract never appeared in the *Standard* itself. The Democratic organ had a wide readership among eastern Democrats, yet *Plain Thoughts* was little more than a blatant appeal for westerners to support Hoke as the "western candidate."[23]

The main argument of *Plain Thoughts* was that Hoke had devoted his entire career to protecting western rights and defending western interests, and that he deserved the support of all westerners regardless of their party preference. The circular pointed out that Hoke had voted for the convention bill in the North Carolina General Assembly of 1834–35 and that—unlike his opponent, William A. Graham—he had voted in the convention to give the people the right to elect their governor. That same year he had defended the interests of those financially beleaguered settlers who had purchased Cherokee lands in Cherokee, Macon, and Haywood counties, and he had successfully prevented the state government from demanding immediate payment on their bonds. As a member of the general assembly in 1834, Hoke had also voted in favor of David L. Swain, who, although a Whig, was considered by many to be the western candidate for governor. In short, Hoke had consistently "been true to all parties in the West; all parties in the West should now prove true to MICHAEL HOKE, the western candidate for Governor!"[24]

The results of the gubernatorial election revealed that the western strategy had been at least partially successful for the Democrats. Hoke lost the hotly contested election, but he received a respectable 48 percent of the vote—the most impressive showing up to that time for a Democratic gubernatorial candidate. Not surprisingly, the Democrats' greatest gains were in the far west, particularly in the counties of Haywood, Henderson, Macon, and Rutherford, where the Whig vote dropped fifteen percentage points from the previous election. The Whigs made no secret of their belief that the circulation of *Plain Thoughts* had contributed significantly to Hoke's strong showing in the west. According to the editor of the *Hillsborough Recorder*, "these tracts were artfully written to effect the purpose intended. . . . After reading them, it is very easy to account for the falling off in the Whig vote for Governor."[25]

Although the Democrats could take pride in their impressive gains in the western counties, their strategy may have been counterproductive in the eastern counties. Hoke improved on Louis D. Henry's 1842 vote in only eighteen of the fifty counties between Guilford and the seacoast, whereas Graham surpassed Morehead's percentage in twenty-nine of these piedmont and eastern counties. Overall, the Whig gains in the east tended to balance Democratic increases in the far west, and Hoke's 48.1 percent of the popular vote was only a slight improvement over Henry's 47.6 percent. Moreover, despite Hoke's gains in the west, the Democratic candidate failed to carry a single county west of Guilford that had not been carried by the easterner Henry in 1842. Indeed, Hoke actually lost one far western county (Ashe) that Henry had won two years earlier.

The results of the legislative elections in August and the national election in November revealed another deficiency in the western strategy—its inability to translate Hoke's personal popularity into votes for other Democratic candidates. The Democrats lost an unprecedented twenty-four seats in the general assembly, which enabled the Whigs to reassert their control over that body (see figure 8.2). In the presidential election, James K. Polk received about 1,500 votes fewer than Hoke, while Clay garnered about 1,600 more votes than Graham. Thus, most of the Whigs who defected to Hoke in August probably returned to the fold in time for the November presidential election.[26]

Still, the Democratic leaders were gratified by Hoke's strong showing, and in 1846 they again looked west for a candidate to challenge Governor Graham. Their first choice was Charles Fisher, the Salisbury politician who had first gained notoriety during the anticaucus campaign of 1824. Fisher's popularity in the west would undoubtedly have made him a formidable contender, but shortly before the meeting of the Democratic state convention he startled the party

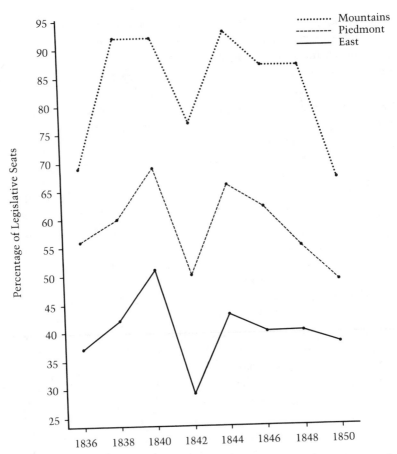

Figure 8.2   Whig Strength in the North Carolina House of Commons, 1836–50. *Source:* Thomas E. Jeffrey, "Internal Improvements and Political Parties in Antebellum North Carolina," table 1.

leaders by refusing to become a candidate. The convention subsequently tendered the nomination to another westerner, Greene W. Caldwell, who also declined to become a candidate. After some hesitation, the party's central committee finally gave the nomination to James B. Shepard of Raleigh.[27]

Shepard's status as an easterner resulted in an abrupt change of strategy. Shepard began his campaign in the eastern counties and repeatedly attacked Governor Graham for being an "advocate of Western improvements and interests" to the detriment of the taxpayers of the east. Eastern Whigs, like the editor of the *Raleigh Register*, sharply criticized the Democratic candidate for "labouring to revive the exploded prejudices between the East and the West." Perhaps remembering how Hoke's image as a "western man" had worked against him in the eastern counties, the editor warned the Democrats that Shepard's tactics might backfire. "The *Western* people," he predicted, "will be very apt to recollect, when Mr. Shepard visits them, that the gravest charge he has against Gov. Graham, is that he is the 'sole advocate of Western interests.'" For a variety of reasons Shepard proved to be a weak candidate, and he failed to make significant inroads in either section.[28]

Two years later the Democrats again chose a popular western politician as their standard-bearer. And, once again, the party leaders had to struggle to persuade a reluctant candidate to accept their nomination. Like Greene W. Caldwell, the party's would-be nominee in 1846, David S. Reid of Rockingham County had not been consulted in advance about the nomination. Upon receiving word that he was the choice of the Democratic convention, Reid penned a letter of declination to William W. Holden. Reid's letter was intended for publication in the *Standard*, but Holden wisely withheld it and induced the reluctant nominee to come to Raleigh and confer with him and other party leaders.[29]

Reid subsequently agreed to accept the nomination on the condition that he be allowed to campaign in favor of removing the fifty-acre freehold requirement for voters in state senatorial elections. Many of the Raleigh Democrats had serious reservations about the propriety of raising this issue. A change in the suffrage requirements would necessitate an amendment to the state constitution, and the leaders of both parties had agreed that the subject of constitutional revision was beyond the pale of legitimate political discussion. On the other hand, the Democratic leaders no doubt remembered how Caldwell's unwillingness to accept the nomination two years earlier had resulted in a debacle for the party in the governor's election. Another refusal could have equally disastrous results. If the Democrats were to have any hope of capturing the governorship, they would have to accept Reid's conditions, even though it meant violating the unwritten rule of North Carolina politics. Primarily at the urging of Holden, the party leaders agreed to allow Reid to campaign for "free suffrage."[30]

The issue was first broached publicly in a debate between Reid and his Whig opponent, Charles Manly, at Beaufort on 10 May 1848. Manly began with a speech condemning the domestic and foreign policies of the Polk administration, and he probably expected Reid to focus on the same national issues. Instead, Reid replied briefly to Manly's points and then startled his opponent by advocating the repeal of the fifty-acre suffrage qualification. The flabbergasted Whig candidate asked for a day's time to think over the issue and subsequently declared his opposition to any modification in the state constitution.[31]

The issue of suffrage reform divided the leaders of both parties. Despite their initial hesitation, most leading Democrats eventually rallied behind the call for suffrage reform—some no doubt because of conviction, others because free suffrage seemed an attractive issue with genuine vote-getting potential. However, a few Democratic leaders, most notably Weldon N. Edwards, remained adamantly opposed to a change in the suffrage requirements. Indeed, Edwards proved instrumental in delaying the passage of the suffrage amendment until 1857. The Whigs, for their part, were even more divided than the Democrats over the merits of suffrage reform. A few party organs, like the *Raleigh Register* and the *Wilmington Commercial*, followed Manly's lead and announced their opposition to constitutional change, while several Whig newspapers in the west explicitly endorsed free suffrage. The editors of most of the Whig presses tried to maintain a position of neutrality.[32]

Although their opinions about the propriety of suffrage reform varied, the Whigs were united in their belief that the free-suffrage issue, as raised by Reid, was merely the latest in a long series of Democratic efforts to distract the attention of the electorate from that party's unpopular position on national issues. "Is it possible," the editor of the *Greensboro Patriot* sarcastically inquired, "that gentlemen doubt the strength of their chosen positions on the tariff, currency, public lands? Upon the justice, necessity, constitutionality and *expenses* of the Mexican War?" The editor of the *Register* agreed that "Mr. Reid, satisfied of the unpopularity of the War, is endeavoring to divert attention from it, and ring in upon the People some new issue . . . without any wish or disposition to effect . . . that which he advocates."[33]

Conservative eastern Whigs opposed free suffrage primarily because they feared that the agitation of the issue would inevitably lead to demands for other, even more radical revisions in the constitution. Once the unwritten rule of North Carolina politics was violated, neither party would be able to limit the discussion to suffrage reform alone. "If we *begin* to alter, where is it to end!" one Whig candidate for the legislature asked. "It has *begun* with Mr. Reid's proposition— Does any man believe it will stop there? . . . The next assault may be made upon the *Federal Basis* of the House of Commons, and the present principle of dividing off Senatorial Districts." In a letter to the editor of the *Newbernian* under the pen name "A Citizen," Governor Graham argued that free suffrage carried with it an egalitarian dynamic that would culminate in an effort to remove all the protections granted by the state constitution to the rights of property. "If property should not be considered in the qualification of voters, it surely follows, that it is entitled to no weight in laying off communities of voters, or districts," said Graham. "If the amendment of Mr. Reid is to prevail, it must of course be accompanied with a change of the basis of representation in the Senate from taxation, to White population."[34]

Of course, easterners would not give up their constitutional privileges without a fight. Thus, the practical effect of free suffrage, according to its Whig opponents, would be the revival of the bitter sectional controversy that had been put to rest by the constitutional compromises of 1835. Although the Democrats might pretend that free suffrage was "a contest between the freeholder and nonfreeholder," said Graham, "resolve it into its true elements, and it becomes a contest between the free White men of the mountains, and his fellow citizens of the lowlands. . . . The proposition of Mr. Reid attempts to break up the Compromises of the Constitution, and to deprive our section of the State, of the guarantees which that instrument affords us." From the viewpoint of the Whigs, free suffrage was a spurious reform "instigated by a few corrupt partisans, who, for the sake of a political triumph would break up the solemn covenant so lately entered into and ratified between the East and the West, and sow the dragons teeth of discord over the quiet soil of the State."[35]

In their efforts to prevent the revival of sectional animosities, Governor Graham and the other Whig leaders were undoubtedly as concerned about the health of their party as they were about the peace and quiet of the state. From its inception the Whig party in North Carolina had been a heterogeneous collection of easterners and westerners. Until 1848 party leaders had kept these two wings in harmony by ignoring divisive sectional issues. The negative reaction of Graham, Manly, and other Whigs toward free suffrage did not result so much from an objection to the measure itself as from a fear that the introduction of constitutional reform into the political arena would disrupt the delicate sectional balance within their party. It was not long before the course of events confirmed these expectations.

The election of 1848 witnessed the closest gubernatorial contest in the history of North Carolina's second party system. Although the Whigs won the governorship for the seventh consecutive time, Reid captured an impressive 49.5 percent of the vote and fell less than 1,000 votes short of a majority. Undoubtedly the free-suffrage issue contributed to Reid's strong showing. The outcome of the November presidential election, however, revealed that an attractive national candidate could still put the Old North State solidly in the Whig column. Zachary Taylor defeated Lewis Cass in North Carolina by a margin of almost 8,500 votes. Taylor received about 1,400 more votes than Manly had garnered in the governor's election, whereas Cass polled 6,400 fewer votes than Reid. Although state issues may have weakened the Whig hold on North Carolina by 1848, in national elections the loyalty of its Whig majority remained unshaken.[36]

Yet events would prove that the Whig party could no longer ignore the divisive issue of constitutional reform. Although they had been too politically astute to discuss the matter in public during the campaign of 1848, eastern Whigs were well aware that the real threat to the status quo in North Carolina came not from Reid and the Democrats but from the western wing of their own party. The western Whigs did not initiate the crusade for suffrage reform, but they were quick to recognize its appeal among the small farmers who comprised their constituency. Spokesmen for western Whiggery like Congressman Thomas L. Clingman endorsed the principle of free suffrage in 1848 while at the same time urging the voters not to support Reid on account of this issue. Indeed, the western Whigs were not averse to chastizing the Democratic candidate for failing to pursue his egalitarian argument to its logical conclusion. If the principle of political equality dictated that all citizens should vote equally, as Reid was claiming, did it not also follow that all voters should be equally represented in the general assembly? And that the legislative districts should be laid out according to white population rather than property and wealth? And that property requirements should be eliminated for officeholders as well as for voters?[37]

By the time the newly elected legislators assembled in Raleigh for the convening of the general assembly, a majority of western Whigs was already prepared to go beyond free suffrage and to challenge all of the sectional compromises that had been worked out by the Constitutional Convention of 1835. For the first time in more than a dozen years, the general assembly considered a variety of constitutional reform measures, ranging from a free-suffrage bill to a new convention with unlimited powers of amendment. Early in the session a bipartisan bloc of easterners in the house of commons signaled their adamant opposition to radical reform by voting to reject, on its first reading, a bill that would apportion both houses according to white population and abolish the property qualifications required for members of the general assembly (see table 8.8). Because most bills were allowed to pass their first reading without a formal vote, many reformers must have viewed this rejection as a high-handed attempt by the east to stifle debate and foreclose all discussion of constitutional revisions. Western legislators introduced several other reform bills during the course of the session, but all their efforts to democratize the structure of government succumbed to the solid eastern phalanx.

Table 8.8   Vote in the House of Commons on Constitutional Reform, 1848 (affirmative percentage by party and section)

	Whigs			Democrats				
	East	West	Total	East	West	Total	East	West
Abolition of property qualifications, and apportionment according to white population	5	95	62	0	55	23	2	80
Apportionment according to white population	0	86	55	0	37	14	0	70
Constitutional convention	8	59	45	0	20	7	2	47

Sources: HJ, 1848–49, 494, 651, 757.

By the end of the session it had become apparent that the Whig party was seriously divided over the issue of constitutional reform. This lack of intraparty consensus was nothing new. Eastern and western Whigs had disagreed about a variety of state issues throughout the 1830s and 1840s. Prior to 1848 these sectional differences had not imposed unbearable strains upon party unity because neither sectional wing had tried to make its own position a test of party orthodoxy. However, as Whig legislators from the west returned to their constituencies early in 1849, they carried with them more than the usual amount of irritation at the conduct of their eastern allies. For more than a decade North Carolina's unequal system of legislative apportionment had enabled easterners in both parties to frustrate western efforts to construct internal improvements, to distribute the school fund equitably, and to create new counties. By 1850 many western Whigs had come to the conclusion that the enactment of state policies favorable to their section depended upon the establishment of a more representative framework of government. To accomplish this goal the North Carolina Whig party would have to abandon its traditional reticence on state issues and publicly commit itself to the cause of constitutional reform.

As the summer elections of 1850 approached and the county conventions assembled to pass resolutions and nominate candidates for the general assembly, the western Whigs began formally serving notice that they expected the state party to turn its attention away from the national issues that had played so prominent a role in the political debate. The convention of the Buncombe County Whigs summarized the rebellious attitude of the western reformers, declaring that "nothing has so seriously retarded the prosperity, and hindered the advancement of our State, as the practice of making national politics the sole test in all State elections." The convention went on to resolve that "there are questions of state policy, which we regard as of more importance to us at this time, than any of the old issues of national politics which have heretofore divided the two great political parties of this country. . . . In the selection of persons to fill offices in the state government . . . we prefer those who are right on state questions."[38]

By the time the Whig state convention assembled on 10 June 1850, it had become apparent that the party's platform would somehow have to come to grips with these widespread demands for reform. The resolutions finally adopted by the convention were carefully written—in the words of one Democratic editor—"to catch the Anti-reform Whigs of the East, and the Reform Whigs of the West."[39] The party did not come out directly in favor of free suffrage, but the Whigs did express their willingness to abide by the results of a popular referendum on the subject. In another concession to western reform sentiment, the Whigs called on the people to decide by referendum whether justices of the county courts, state judges, and other appointive officials should be elected directly by the voters. On the other hand, the platform made no mention of popular dissatisfaction in the west with the basis of legislative representation, and it said nothing about the propriety of calling another constitutional convention.[40]

The Whig party in 1850 was seriously divided not only in its attitude toward constitutional reform but also in its choice of a gubernatorial standard-bearer. By the spring of 1850 a substantial number of eastern Whigs had publicly voiced their opposition to the renomination of Governor Manly. During the six months preceding the Whig state convention, eastern editors had suggested a number of alternative candidates, and several county conventions had nominated William B. Shepard of Pasquotank as their choice for governor. A correspondent of the *Elizabeth City Old North State* summarized the case of the eastern Whigs against the renomination of Manly. "Many thought his nomination [in 1848] effected through the influence of a few central leaders to honor an undeserving favorite," the correspondent remarked. "If he is again nominated, this feeling, so widely diffused through the State, will defeat his election."[41]

The embattled governor was not without his share of powerful supporters within the party. On 23 January the editor of the *Raleigh Register* reminded his readers of the Whig tradition of nominating their incumbent governors for a second term, and he cautioned against the "distracting tendency" of discussing alternative candidates. In February the editors of the *Greensboro Patriot* and the *Asheville Highland Messenger* endorsed Manly, and other Whig presses soon fell in line. During the late winter and early spring, local conventions in numerous counties, including at least fourteen in the east, recommended Manly's renomination. Opponents of the governor were also handicapped by the refusal of Shepard and other eastern leaders to campaign actively for the nomination. By the time the Whig state convention assembled in June, Manly's renomination had become a foregone conclusion.[42]

The Democrats again selected David S. Reid as their standard-bearer. Ignoring the growing western demands for a complete over-haul of the state constitution, Reid continued to campaign on the narrow issue of free suffrage. In the west the Whigs tried hard to con-vince the voters that Reid was really an enemy of western interests, despite his advocacy of suffrage reform. "In order to judge of the real depth and extent of his sympathies with our people," said the editor of the *Patriot*, "we are not to look alone at his *professions* about free suffrage or anything else, but to his *votes* in the Legislature. . . . In the matters of internal improvement—dividing large counties—and dis-tributing the common school money, his votes in the Legislature have been almost uniformly against the wishes and interests cher-ished in the Western portion of the State." From the viewpoint of the western Whigs, Reid's persistent opposition to western interests on these vital issues more than offset his affirmative stance on the mat-ter of suffrage reform.[43]

Governor Manly, meanwhile, had wisely backed off from his ear-lier opposition to free suffrage and was now promising to abide by the results of the referendum that had been recommended by his party. However, Manly quickly committed a series of blunders that would ultimately cost him the election. The governor's troubles began dur-ing a speech at Wentworth on 29 June 1850, when he made some ambiguous remarks about the basis of legislative apportionment. A few Democrats in the audience interpreted his comments as an in-dication that Manly had given in to western demands for a change in the basis of representation. An overjoyed William W. Holden was convinced that the Wentworth incident, if properly exploited, could swing the governor's election to the Democrats. If the people of the east could be persuaded to believe that the Whig governor actually did favor a change in the basis, Holden told Reid, "Manly must lose thou-sands."[44]

On the pages of Holden's *Standard*, free suffrage quickly took a back seat to the issue of legislative apportionment as the editor ham-mered away at Manly's alleged support for a change in the basis. In 1848 the Whigs had accused Reid of stirring up sectional animosities, but now it was Holden's turn to accuse the opposition of recklessly jeopardizing the sacred constitutional compromises in order to win votes in the west. According to Holden: "The question of political power was settled in the Convention of 1835 . . . and *Col. Reid is opposed to disturbing it.* What he demands is, that every man who votes for the Commons may be allowed to vote for the Senate also; but Gov. Manly goes beyond this, and advocates . . . the abolition of the basis on which great questions of political power were permanently settled in Convention, in 1835!"[45]

The editors of the eastern Whig presses were quick to react to Holden's accusations. Seaton Gales, the editor of the *Raleigh Register*, denounced the white-basis charge as "a miserable party trick, calculated and designed to injure Gov. Manly in the East!" At the same time that they were publicly disavowing the white-basis charge, Gales and other eastern editors were privately urging Manly, who was then campaigning in the west, to send them a written denial. On 12 July 1850 Manly wrote a letter to that effect from Wilkesboro, which was circulated in an extra edition of the *Raleigh Times*. Five days later he sent similar statements to Gales and to Edward J. Hale, the editor of the *Fayetteville Observer*. The letter to Gales was published in an extra edition of the *Register* as well as in the regular issue of 31 July.[46]

While the Whig editors were trying to limit the political impact of the apportionment issue, Holden was continuing to make political capital in the east, this time on the school-fund issue. During his tour of the west Manly had expressed a sympathetic attitude toward western demands for a more equitable distribution of the public school money. By thus taking a public stand on a sensitive issue that previous Whig candidates had avoided, Manly gave his enemies a powerful weapon to use against him in the east. To easterners, Whigs as well as Democrats, Manly's position on the school fund was tantamount to sectional heresy. "If Gov. Manly's wishes in this respect should prevail," Holden predicted, "the [eastern] Counties . . . would at once lose *thousands* of dollars they are now receiving; and this money would go to Counties that do not pay more than half the taxes of those mentioned above." Adroitly linking the school-fund issue with the question of legislative apportionment, the editor warned that "the *principle* that would be thus established might be the entering wedge for destroying the present basis of the Senate and the Commons."[47]

Holden's blatant appeal to the prejudices of conservative east-erners marked a significant departure from the western strategy pursued by the Democrats during previous gubernatorial campaigns. Moreover, instead of sidestepping delicate sectional issues like the school fund and the basis of apportionment, as he and other Democratic strategists had done in the past, Holden was now confronting these issues head-on. Holden's strategy was based on the premise that a large increase in the Democratic vote in the eastern and central counties would more than compensate for any losses that his party might incur in the far west. The editor thus assured Reid that the Whigs "must lose by it in the East, and it cannot affect you in the West."[48]

Holden also hoped to neutralize Manly's appeal in the far west by campaigning hard on the issue of the Raleigh Clique. Two years earlier the Democratic editor had done all that he could to exploit the widespread belief among eastern Whigs that Manly's nomination had been secured through improper "central influence." Now, in 1850 Holden reminded the voters that "the East and the West *both* [have] been neglected and slighted, in order that the 'Clique' might be pampered, petted, and promoted. Who defeated William B. Shepard for Senator? The *'Clique.'* Who defeated Thomas L. Clingman? The *'Clique.'* Who put these distinguished statesmen under the ban, and would forever exclude them from such posts . . . of profit and honor? *This same 'Clique.'*" Holden skillfully linked the issue of central dictation with Manly's earlier opposition to free suffrage, claiming that "this Central Whig Power, which has . . . monopolized nearly all the offices of trust and profit, *could not be for this general Reform without being against itself.*"[49]

The Raleigh Clique issue, coupled with the Democratic exploitation of the white-basis and school-fund issues, were the important factors behind Reid's victory in 1850. East of the mountains the Democratic percentage of the vote increased in forty-two of the sixty counties. The party's most impressive gain was in Washington County in the Albemarle region, where Josiah Collins, the local Whig leader, publicly came out in opposition to Governor Manly, primarily because of his position on the school fund. The Democrats' share of the vote in Washington increased from a mere 34 percent in 1848 to an astounding 61 percent in 1850. Reid also carried the wealthy plantation counties of Halifax and Northampton, which had never before supported a Democrat in a governor's election. Slaves made up a substantial majority of the population in both counties, and they would have been among the heaviest losers had the basis of legislative apportionment been changed to white population.[50]

The free-suffrage issue, on the other hand, did not contribute significantly to the Democratic victory in 1850. Indeed, Reid's percentage of the vote actually declined from the previous election in all but three of the mountain counties where suffrage reform was most popular. Most of Reid's gains in that section were confined to the one county of Rutherford, where local Whig leaders believed that Manly had improperly used his influence as governor to route the recently chartered western turnpike by way of Burke County rather than through Rutherford. Prominent Rutherford Whigs like Thomas A. Hayden, the editor of the *Rutherfordton Mountain Banner*, took the stump against Manly, and the Whig proportion of the vote dropped from 74 percent in 1848 to a mere 35 percent in 1850.[51] Elsewhere in the mountain region, Manly's reputation as a supporter of internal improvements, his position on the school fund, and his alleged support for the white basis of representation served to offset Reid's reputation as the "father of free suffrage."[52] On balance, the evidence suggests that the Democrats won the governorship in 1850 not by appealing to the progressive inclinations of western reformers but by pandering to the fears of conservative easterners, who wished to preserve the unequitable system for apportioning legislative seats and distributing the school fund.

Reid defeated Manly by a majority of almost three thousand votes and thus became North Carolina's first popularly elected Democratic governor. The Democrats also gained seven seats in the house of commons and two in the state senate, which gave them a comfortable majority of fourteen seats on joint ballot. Manly's unpopularity in the eastern and central parts of the state probably contributed to the Democratic victory in the legislative elections. It would be a mistake, however, to conclude that dissatisfaction with Governor Manly was the sole, or even the most important, factor behind his party's loss of the general assembly. In many counties the Whig legislative candidates also had to contend with the unpopularity of the recently chartered North Carolina Railroad.

During the session of 1848–49 the general assembly had granted a charter of incorporation to a railroad that would traverse the state in a westerly direction from Goldsboro to Salisbury and then turn south to Charlotte. Even more important, the usually parsimonious legislators had voted for a state subscription of two-thirds of the capital stock of $3 million. The North Carolina Railroad bill passed the house of commons by a vote of sixty to fifty-two, and squeaked through the senate by an even narrower one-vote margin. Although more Whigs than Democrats supported the measure, the North Carolina Railroad Act was a bipartisan effort. Three-fourths of the Whigs in the house of commons supported the bill, but the proposal would have gone down to defeat in the lower house had not a third of the Democrats also voted in its favor. In the senate the bill passed only because of the tie-breaking vote of Calvin Graves, the Democratic speaker.[53]

Ironically, most of the Democratic support for the North Carolina Railroad came from the party's eastern wing. While 40 percent of the eastern Democrats voted in favor of the bill, only two of the twenty-one Democrats from the piedmont supported the measure. Even the piedmont Whigs, who normally gave overwhelming support to railroad bills, were divided over the proposal, and almost a third of them ultimately voted against it. These piedmont legislators were not opposed in principle to the construction of a railroad through their section, but they favored a rival project that would run in a north-south direction through Salisbury to connect with a Virginia railroad at Danville and a South Carolina line at Charlotte. The financial backers of the so-called Danville connection were even willing to construct the road without a subsidy from the state. All they wanted from the general assembly was a charter of incorporation. Although it would cost the state no money, easterners in both parties regarded the Danville connection with alarm. Whatever their differences over the propriety of state aid to internal improvements, eastern Whigs and Democrats were united in their opposition to any railroad that would carry the commerce of the west to markets in Virginia and South Carolina.[54]

Largely because of the threat posed by the Danville connection, eastern Democrats supported the North Carolina Railroad bill in sufficient numbers to secure its passage. Yet, in many counties east of the mountains, Democrats or "independent Whigs" campaigned against the railroad in 1850 and, in some cases, even promised to work for the repeal of its charter. In Halifax County disgruntled

Whigs who opposed the favorable vote that their commoners had given on the railroad bill combined with the Democrats to defeat the two regular Whig candidates. Although the victorious candidates claimed to be "independent Whigs," they subsequently voted with the Democrats to organize the house. Elsewhere in the northeast, where the residents stood to derive little direct benefit from the new central railroad, prorailroad Whigs were replaced by antirailroad Democrats in the normally Whig counties of Chowan and Perquimans. The greatest Whig losses occurred, however, in the piedmont —the center of support for the Danville connection. In Orange, Stokes, and Surry counties the Whigs lost four seats in 1850, while in Chatham County two prorailroad Whigs were replaced by a Democrat and an "independent" antirailroad Whig.[55]

To the jubilant Democrats the results of the state elections provided conclusive evidence that—in Holden's words—"North Carolina is at last completely and gloriously redeemed." The editor of the *Wilmington Journal* went so far as to claim that the election had proven "that North Carolina has all along been Democratic, without knowing it."[56] The Whigs, on the other hand, attributed their losses to Manly's unpopularity and to transitory local causes. The editor of the *Register* remarked that "it will not be denied that local issues unfortunately alienated much of the Whig support." According to the editor of the *Wilmington Commercial*: "Had there been any important question of national politics, in which the positions of the parties could have been identified, the democratic party would have been overwhelmed." Privately, however, the Whigs were less than optimistic about their chances of regaining control of the state. Congressman David Outlaw confided to his wife that his party would "have to struggle desperately to recover the ground which we have lost. It may be, we shall not be able to do so at all, as long as the local questions which divide the people remain unsettled."[57]

In retrospect, it is easy to conclude that the revival of state sectionalism not only cost the Whigs the governorship in 1850, but also consigned the party to a minority position for the remainder of the decade. From the perspective of 1850, however, it was by no means clear that the Democrats had replaced the Whigs as the majority party. The party had, indeed, ousted the unpopular Manly and captured control of the general assembly. But it remained to be seen whether the Democrats would be equally as successful in 1852 against a Whig candidate who did not have to bear the burden of Manly's unpopularity, and whether their legislative gains would be more than transitory. Much would depend upon the caliber of the new Democratic leadership and their adroitness in exploiting the sectional divisions among the Whigs while at the same time keeping their own sectional interests in harmony.

9 ✦ The Transit of Power:
North Carolina, 1850–1855

We have this State, and, by prudent management, we shall hold it almost indefinitely.—William W. Holden to Abraham W. Venable, 16 April 1851

Ascendancy is more easily lost than regained.—David Outlaw to Emily B. Outlaw, 7 August 1850

In 1850 the Democrats won control of the governorship and the two houses of the general assembly, thus ending more than a decade of Whig dominance (see table 9.1). Although party leaders no doubt rejoiced at their good fortune, they could not be confident that they had supplanted the Whigs as the majority party in North Carolina. The Democratic leaders undoubtedly remembered that their party had enjoyed even more substantial majorities during the legislative session of 1842–43, only to see those majorities disappear at the next election. No one could be certain that the Democratic triumph in 1850 would be any more enduring. To a large extent the success of the Democrats would depend upon the ability of Holden, Reid, and other party leaders to contain the sectional pressures within the new governing coalition.

As with the Whigs during the 1840s, the most troublesome state issue for the Democrats was the question of government aid to internal improvements. From its inception the Democratic party in the Old North State had been ambivalent about the propriety of state assistance to railroads and other transportation projects. During the 1830s many Democrats from the western counties and from urban constituencies in the east had joined the Whigs in support of a program of state investment in the Wilmington & Raleigh and other prospective railroads. However, when popular enthusiasm for internal improvements declined during the depression years of the late 1830s

Table 9.1   Party Strength in the North Carolina House of Commons,
1850–54

	Whig members				Democratic members			
	Coast	Pied-mont	Moun-tains	Total	Coast	Pied-mont	Moun-tains	Total
1850	22	23	10	55	36	24	5	65
1852	24	27	11	62	34	20	4	58
1854	19	23	13	55	39	22	4	65

Sources: Raleigh Standard, 28 August 1850, 25 August 1852, 23 August 1854.

and early 1840s, party leaders had tried to make political capital on the state's unsuccessful railroad ventures, and a majority of Democratic legislators had voted against measures to provide relief to the struggling railroads. At the same time, however, the party was unwilling to assume responsibility for the destruction of the railroad system, and Democrats always voted for the relief measures in sufficient numbers to secure their passage. In 1842, when the party enjoyed large majorities in both houses and could easily have defeated such measures, almost half of the Democratic commoners and almost one-third of the senators voted in favor of railroad relief.[1]

Throughout the 1840s the Democrats enjoyed the luxury of being able to revile the existing railroads without having to take a stand on state aid to new railroad projects. The controversy over the North Carolina Railroad bill in 1848 brought the latent divisions within the party out into the open. The bill was introduced into the legislature by William S. Ashe, a Democrat from New Hanover County, and it received the support of about one-third of the Democrats in the house of commons. The measure also benefited from the strong editorial endorsement of William W. Holden, who, despite his earlier hostility to the Raleigh & Gaston, now came out emphatically in favor of "a bold, a general, and a vigorous system of Internal Improvements."[2]

With its provision for a state subscription of $2 million, the North Carolina Railroad bill dwarfed all previous improvement measures. In many eastern counties leading men in both parties denounced the measure as a visionary scheme that would inevitably lead to high taxes and financial ruin. Antirailroad Democrats, who associated their party with a policy of opposition to all measures of state aid, were particularly critical of Holden's behavior. L. A. Gwyn, a former legislator from Caswell County, canceled his subscription to the *Standard* and denounced the North Carolina Railroad as a measure that had "done incalculable mischief in sundering the good feelings of Democrats in this region." Another correspondent of the *Standard* challenged the notion that "this doctrine of Internal Improvement by the State has always been a Democratic doctrine." The correspondent pointed out that the vast majority of Democrats had opposed relief for the railroads during the 1840s, whereas most of the Whigs had supported the relief bills. In his opinion, this was proof enough that "Internal Improvements, by the State, has not been a Democratic doctrine, but a Whig doctrine."[3]

Prorailroad Democrats denied that support for internal improvements was contrary to sound Democratic policy. Adopting an argument quite similar to the one that Thomas Loring had used a decade earlier, William W. Holden urged a policy of toleration and mutual forbearance on state issues. "It is enough that we agree as Democrats on the same broad, national principles," said Holden. "We cannot all think alike on matters of State policy, and it were idle to expect it. . . . They are questions . . . not *above* party but *beside* it—questions of State policy, which cannot be involved with our organization on national principles, without seriously disturbing if not entirely destroying that organization."[4]

Romulus M. Saunders, who had been a consistent supporter of state improvements throughout his long career, went even further by repudiating "this recent doctrine, that it is anti-democratic for the State to make Internal Improvements." Indeed, according to Saunders: "The cause of Internal Improvement has been at all times maintained by the Democratic party." Saunders acknowledged that there had been "party bickerings, and criminations and recriminations about relief bills for the [Raleigh &] Gaston Road." But he made a distinction between opposition to the Raleigh & Gaston, on the one hand, and a principled opposition to all state-supported internal improvements, on the other. The propriety of specific relief measures, argued Saunders, "had nothing to do with the question of the *power* of the Legislature, to make appropriations for Internal Improvements." In Saunders's opinion, the North Carolina Railroad was "a great State work on which all can unite, whether he be Whig or Democrat."[5]

Democratic wrangling over internal improvements peaked during the campaign of 1850. In many of the eastern counties candidates for the general assembly campaigned on a promise to prevent the construction of the newly chartered railroad. Other Democrats, like Holden and Saunders, were equally determined that the railroad should be built. In order for the party to present a united front during the campaign, it was essential that the gubernatorial standard-bearer be acceptable to both wings of the party. James C. Dobbin, a former congressman from Fayetteville, had been prominently mentioned for the nomination, but Dobbin was vulnerable on the railroad issue because he had voted not only for the North Carolina Railroad but for a host of other improvement measures during the session of 1848–49.[6]

From the viewpoint of William W. Holden, the logical choice was David S. Reid. Two years earlier Reid had run a strong campaign against Manly on the free-suffrage issue. Equally important, both wings of the party could find reason to support his candidacy. Reid made no secret of his opposition to the North Carolina Railroad, but now that the charter had been granted he had no desire to interfere with its construction. "Your election, under the circumstances, could not injure the Rail Road Democrats," Holden told Reid, "while it would give confidence to the anti-Rail Road Democrats, because they could trust you on the subject." Reid's renomination enabled the Democrats to avoid an open split over internal improvements in the gubernatorial election.[7]

Not all opponents of the North Carolina Railroad were as ready as Reid to accept the act of incorporation as a fait accompli. Indeed, during the session of 1850–51 antirailroad Democrats in the general assembly made a determined effort to reverse the decision of the previous legislature. Shortly after the general assembly convened, John V. Sherard, a Democrat from Wayne County, introduced a bill to repeal the act incorporating the North Carolina Railroad. Sherard's bill was quickly rejected by an overwhelming majority of 105 to 10. Even the opponents of the railroad proved unwilling to abrogate the state's "solemn contract" with the stockholders—a course of action that many regarded as a violation of the contract clause of the U.S. Constitution.[8] Later in the session Josiah Bridges of Franklin County introduced a milder resolution calling upon the stockholders to surrender their charter voluntarily. On the motion of James R. McLean, a Democrat from Surry County, Bridges's resolution was postponed indefinitely by a vote of 80 to 36.

The debate over the two antirailroad bills, along with the align-

Table 9.2   Vote in the House of Commons on Internal Improvements, 1850 (affirmative percentage by party and section)

	Whigs				Democrats			
	Coast	Pied-mont	Moun-tains	Total	Coast	Pied-mont	Moun-tains	Total
Postponement of Bridges bill	82	91	100	89	41	57	100	52
North Carolina & Tennessee Railroad	15	33	83	32	0	0	100	9
Appropriation for survey of western rail-road route	71	85	67	76	18	36	80	31

Sources: HJ, 1850–51, 621, 888, 961–62.

ment of votes on the Bridges bill, offers illuminating evidence about the sources of anti-improvement sentiment during the 1850s and the motives of the antirailroad legislators (see table 9.2).[9] The Whigs were almost unanimous in their opposition to a surrender of the charter. The Bridges bill received the support of only a handful of Whigs in the house of commons, although some eastern Whigs who voted against the bill admitted that they would have opposed the original charter if they had had an opportunity to vote on it in 1848.[10] On the other hand, almost half the Democratic legislators in the house of commons voted in favor of Bridges's motion. Eastern Democrats proved to be far more hostile to the railroad than westerners. Despite their support for the Danville connection in 1848, a majority of western Democrats were now determined that the North Carolina Railroad should be built.

The anti-improvement Democrats did not share a single viewpoint about the utility of railroads. Some hidebound conservatives like Curtis H. Brogden of Wayne County opposed all railroads and claimed that they inevitably brought ruin and distress upon those countries that had adopted them. But opposition to state support for internal improvements did not always mean hostility to the railroads themselves. Indeed, in his speech on behalf of his resolution for the surrender of the charter, Josiah Bridges took pains to emphasize that he was not opposed in principle to the notion of a state railroad system. Instead, he acknowledged that "there may be a time, and that time not far in the future, when it will be not only *expedient* but absolutely necessary to build the North Carolina Railroad." But Bridges argued that the construction of railroads was the responsibility of private enterprise, not the state government. "I am as much in favor of Internal Improvement as any man here," said Bridges, "provided the system be conducted by *individual* enterprise. But . . . when the people are to be taxed to accomplish any system the benefits of which are not, and cannot be *equally* distributed throughout the whole State, I feel bound to record my vote against it."[11]

By 1850 an overwhelming majority of Whig legislators and a much smaller majority of Democrats had gone on record in support of a statewide system of railroads. This bipartisan coalition managed to defeat efforts by Bridges and others to prevent construction of the North Carolina Railroad. Few legislators in either party, however, were willing to accede to demands for additional railroads to benefit the residents of the extreme east and the far west, and a measure to appropriate state funds to build a railroad through the mountains to Tennessee was defeated in the house of commons by an overwhelming majority of eighty-four to twenty. A bill to appropriate $12,000 for a survey of a western railroad did pass the lower house, but by a majority of only three votes. The vote on the survey bill clearly indicated that the Whigs were far more receptive to the idea of new improvements than were the Democrats (see table 9.2). Although he had vigorously supported the North Carolina Railroad, William W. Holden expressed the sentiments of those Democrats who were now urging a policy of caution and moderation. The editor reminded his readers that the North Carolina Railroad had already involved the state in a debt of over $3 million. "This, of itself, is considered by the people a heavy indebtedness; and we believe a large majority, of both parties, wish to see the present system fairly tested before other investments are made."[12]

At the same time that the issue of internal improvements was creating division and dissension within the Democratic party, the escalating controversy over constitutional reform was threatening the very existence of a statewide system of parties. The introduction of the free-suffrage issue in 1848 quickly led to demands for even more drastic reforms in the framework of government. Reform-minded westerners called for a variety of changes such as the abolition of property requirements for officeholding and the popular election of judges and other appointive officials. However, their principal demand was for a more equitable apportionment of seats in the state senate, where representation was based on wealth rather than population. The reformers claimed that it was unjust and antirepublican for one voter in a wealthy eastern county to have as much power as five voters in a poorer western county. According to one group of western legislators, the result of "this most odious anti-republican remnant of feudal aristocracy" had been the oppression and impoverishment of the western half of the state. "It is downright tyranny—tyranny in its most odious form. The few grinding into the dust the many, under the iron heel of power."[13]

Easterners responded to such arguments by claiming that wealth had just as much right to representation as numbers. If the residents of the eastern counties were deprived of their due weight in the legislature, they would no longer be able to protect themselves "against mad schemes of internal improvement, and other prodigal waste of public money." One eastern legislator bluntly told his western colleagues that his section intended to hold on to its power, regardless of what westerners might say about oppression or equal rights. "As long as the Eastern part of the State remains the tax-paying portion of the State, so long will the basis [of representation] stand as it is. That this tax paying section should surrender to the non-tax paying portion, the power of doing as they please . . . is flatly absurd. . . . The East never will think of changing the basis of representation. Never, never, never."[14]

The issue of constitutional reform divided both legislative parties into eastern and western blocs. The Whigs, however, proved much more vulnerable than their opponents to these sectional cross-pressures. Western Whigs constituted a majority both within their party and in most of the counties where reform sentiment was strongest. As a result, they were in a position to demand that their party take a positive stance on constitutional reform—a demand that the eastern Whigs strongly resisted. Reform-minded Democrats were in a much weaker position to make demands of their party. Although a few western Democrats like Samuel Flemming of Yancey County were in the vanguard of the reform movement, these legislators were a minority even within the party's western wing. Many western

Democrats represented staple-producing counties along the Virginia and South Carolina borders, and their constituents had nothing to gain from the adoption of the white basis of legislative apportionment. Because of the relatively weak position of the reformers within the party, Democratic leaders like Holden and Reid could afford to ignore reform demands with greater impunity than could their Whig counterparts.

Eastern and western Whigs found it impossible to unite on the substantive issues of constitutional reform. However, they discovered that it was much easier to achieve a unified stance in regard to the proper method for effecting constitutional amendments. The revised constitution of 1835 allowed for two possible methods for changing the instrument of government. The general assembly itself could amend the constitution by a vote of three-fifths of the total number of members in each house, provided that two-thirds of the members at the next session also agreed to the amendment. In addition, two-thirds of the members in each house could agree to call for a constitutional convention to consider revisions in the framework of government. In either case the proposed changes would not take effect until they were approved by the voters in a referendum.[15]

As early as the legislative session of 1848, it had become clear that western reformers, especially within the Whig party, supported the convention mode of amendment as the only practical means of effecting a radical overhaul in the framework of government. Eastern Whigs like Kenneth Rayner of Hertford County were also willing to vote in favor of a constitutional convention, provided that its powers be specifically limited so as to exclude consideration of the most radical western demand—a change in the basis of representation. In response to a Democratic bill providing for free suffrage by legislative enactment, Rayner introduced a substitute calling for a convention empowered to consider only the question of suffrage reform. If, as is likely, Rayner's principal motive was to provide the Whigs with a measure upon which both wings of the party could unite against the Democrats, then the ensuing vote proved him to be an astute political tactician. More than four-fifths of the Whig legislators in the house of commons voted in favor of Rayner's substitute, whereas all but two of the Democrats opposed it.[16]

By 1850 a majority of Whig editors had also come out in favor of the convention form of amendment. Undoubtedly these editors were mindful of how the Whig legislators during the previous session had been able to unite in support of Rayner's bill, despite their bitter arguments about the propriety of specific reform measures. By shifting the focus of debate from the substantive issue of constitutional reform to the proper method for effecting constitutional amendments, the party's chief editorial spokesmen were hoping to direct the explosive issue of constitutional reform into safer, partisan channels. The editors of the Democratic presses, meanwhile, were lining up against the idea of a convention and in favor of the legislative mode of amendment. Foremost among the proponents of the legislative method was William W. Holden of the *Raleigh Standard*, who warned that the agitation for a convention would exacerbate sectional difficulties between the east and the west without resolving any of the fundamental differences between them. According to Holden, the legislative method offered the people of North Carolina reform "without the agitation and expense incident to a Convention."[17]

At the same time that the editors of the partisan presses were defining the broad positions of their parties on the issue of constitutional reform, the members of the general assembly were grappling with specific reform measures. An analysis of the roll calls in the house of commons reveals the conflicting influences of party and section on the behavior of the legislators (see table 9.3). The ten Whigs and five Democrats who comprised the mountain delegation in the

Table 9.3 Vote in the House of Commons on Constitutional Reform, 1850 (affirmative percentage by party and section)

	Whigs				Democrats			
	Coast	Pied-mont	Moun-tains	Total	Coast	Pied-mont	Moun-tains	Total
Rayner bill	71	95	100	87	0	4	0	2
Hackney bill	57	95	100	81	9	21	80	19
Foster bill	33	100	100	73	0	8	80	10
First McLean bill	41	26	14	31	94	100	80	95
Second McLean bill	50	100	100	80	15	91	100	51

Sources: *HJ, 1850–51*, 731–33; *Raleigh Standard*, 22 January 1851; *Raleigh Register*, 22 January 1851.

lower house were almost unanimous in their support for a constitutional convention and for the white basis of representation. In this respect the mountain Democrats disagreed sharply with the position taken by Holden and other leading Democratic editors. Despite a consensus on the larger issues of constitutional reform, however, the mountain delegation split along party lines over their attitude toward free suffrage. Mountain Whigs were willing to support a change in the suffrage requirements, but only as one of many reforms to be considered by a convention. Mountain Democrats, on the other hand, were ready to vote for free suffrage by legislative enactment if they could not secure a convention bill.[18]

The twenty-three commoners who comprised the Whig delegation from the piedmont were only slightly less radical than the mountain delegation. Like the legislators from the far west, the vast majority of piedmont Whigs favored calling a convention and opposed free suffrage by legislative enactment. About one-fourth of the delegation, however, was prepared to support the legislative mode of amendment if free suffrage could not be achieved in any other way. The twenty-four Democratic commoners in the piedmont delegation, with only a few exceptions, loyally supported their party's proposal for free suffrage by legislative enactment. On the other hand, almost all of the piedmont Democrats were ready to defy their leaders and vote for a convention if a free-suffrage bill should fail to pass the general assembly. In this respect the western Democrats held the balance of power in the house of commons, and their willingness to support a convention under certain circumstances made the western Whigs even more determined to defeat free suffrage by legislative enactment.

Easterners in both parties staunchly opposed any change in the basis of representation that would reduce their power in the general assembly. With only a few exceptions, the thirty-six eastern Democrats in the house of commons supported free suffrage by legislative enactment. But they preferred to see suffrage reform defeated rather than risk calling a convention that might also consider more radical changes in the framework of government. The twenty-two Whigs who comprised their party's eastern delegation were divided over the merits of both free suffrage and a constitutional convention. Over a third of the eastern Whigs supported the Democrats' plan of amendment as the best means of staving off more radical efforts at constitutional reform. The other eastern Whigs were willing to support their party's call for a constitutional convention. However, only half of these proconvention Whigs were prepared to vote for an unlimited or "open" convention.

This complicated interplay of sectional and partisan interests made the success of all the proposed reform measures uncertain. Early in the session James R. McLean, the Democratic chairman of the House Committee on Constitutional Reform, reported a bill for free suffrage by legislative enactment and at the same time recommended against the various convention bills put forward by the western reformers. A few days later Kenneth Rayner reintroduced his substitute, which provided for a constitutional convention empowered to consider only free suffrage. Reformers in the house of commons subsequently offered numerous substitutes to both Rayner's and McLean's bills, but all of them, including the Rayner substitute itself, were rejected. The one that came closest to passage was a measure introduced by Daniel Hackney, a Whig from Chatham County. Hackney's bill provided for calling a constitutional convention empowered to consider free suffrage and the popular election of state judges, county justices of the peace, and other appointive officials—but not for a change in the basis of representation. The bill was defeated by a vote of fifty-four to sixty—twenty-six votes short of the two-thirds constitutional majority. After the house voted down Hackney's bill, it also disposed of a bill for an unlimited convention introduced by Whig Alfred G. Foster of Davidson County. Most of the support for the Hackney and Foster bills came from the western Whigs. Only a handful of Democrats outside the mountain delegation cast their votes in favor of a constitutional convention.

Up to this point the piedmont Democrats had loyally followed their party leaders and had voted against a majority of western Whigs. On 14 January 1851, the house finally passed McLean's bill by a vote of seventy-five to thirty-six.[19] When the bill was subsequently taken up by the senate, however, it fell one vote short of the constitutional majority.[20] Having failed to secure passage of free suffrage by legislative enactment, the western Democrats in the lower house were now ready to support the Whig plan for a constitutional convention. On 20 January McLean introduced a second bill providing for a referendum on a constitutional convention. The second McLean bill sailed through the house of commons by a vote of seventy-two to forty, with all but two of the western legislators in support.[21]

Throughout most of the session, party loyalty had taken precedence over sectional interest in determining the pattern of votes on reform measures. The failure of free suffrage in the senate dramatically transformed the issue of constitutional reform into a stark contest between east and west. Alarmed by the prospect of a convention bill passing the senate, a few eastern Whigs in the upper house were now ready to change their minds about free suffrage. On the same day that the referendum bill passed the lower house, William H. Washington, a Whig from Craven County, moved to reconsider the vote by which the upper house had rejected the free-suffrage amendment. Washington and three other Whigs who had voted against suffrage reform just four days earlier suddenly reversed their position, and the senate gave its approval to free suffrage.[22]

Reform-minded Whigs were unsparing in their denunciation of Washington and the other Whigs who had changed their votes on free suffrage. A correspondent of the *Asheville News* went so far as to call upon the people of the west to run a separate reform ticket during the next state elections. "The West need expect nothing," he lamented, "from the generosity of Eastern Whigs or Democrats, in effecting those Constitutional changes which she desires." With a view toward establishing a new party, the editor of the *News* suggested that a reform convention be held in Morganton during the second week of August. Reformers in many of the counties of the far west subsequently called public meetings to elect delegates to the Morganton convention. However, despite the commotion of the spring and early summer, the delegates never assembled.[23]

It was unfortunate for the reformers that the scheduled date of the Morganton convention coincided with a bitterly contested congressional election in the mountain district. Since 1848, when the general assembly had denied him a seat in the U.S. Senate, Congressman Thomas L. Clingman had been at odds with the leadership of the North Carolina Whig party. By 1851 Clingman and his allies, although nominally still Whigs, were cooperating with the Democrats of the mountain district in promoting the cause of southern rights, while those Whigs who remained loyal to the state party were rallying behind the leadership of Burgess S. Gaither, a former speaker of the state senate. The fierce contest between Clingman and Gaither for the congressional seat divided the forces of reform and prevented the two wings of the Whig party from keeping public attention focused on the Morganton convention. As one western reformer explained after the election, it had proven "impossible to bring the public mind to bear on more than one point at once."[24]

The failure of the Morganton convention did not deter the western Whigs from their determination to pressure their party into taking a stand in favor of an unrestricted convention. Eastern Whigs, on the other hand, predicted that the inclusion of a strong convention plank in the platform would mean disaster for the party in their part of the state.[25] The Whig state convention, which met in Raleigh on 26 April 1852, found itself confronted with the difficult task of devising a platform that would please, or at least not antagonize, both wings of the party. In deference to the easterners, the platform finally adopted by the party made no specific mention of the white basis of representation or, indeed, of any of the other constitutional amendments proposed by the reformers. It did, however, express a preference for the convention mode of amendment and, even more important, went on record "in favor of submitting it to the people, to say, whether such a Convention shall be called or not."[26]

The Whigs chose John Kerr of Caswell County as their gubernatorial candidate. In many respects Kerr seemed to be an ideal candidate. A westerner by birth and residence, Kerr was popular in that part of the state and had been endorsed for the nomination by public meetings in several of the western counties. At the same time, however, he came from a county with a large slave population, and eastern Whigs had good reason to believe that he would not take a radical position on the issue of reapportionment. Beginning his campaign in the extreme northeast, Kerr assured his audiences that he personally opposed a change in the basis of representation and "would give sanction to no measure, which would give the West the power to control the East, or the East power to control the West." While voicing his own opinion that the existing constitution was "as perfect as any that the wit of man has ever devised," the candidate dutifully endorsed his party's call for a referendum. "If it be well understood to be the opinion of the people of North Carolina, that the Constitution should be altered by a Convention," said Kerr, "that opinion should be concurred in."[27]

Instead of conciliating the two sections of the state, Kerr's position on constitutional reform frightened voters in the east and antagonized them in the west. The editors of the eastern Democratic presses warned their readers that the Whig candidate was a dangerous radical who would "betray *your* interests into the hands of the West." Although he might ostensibly support the existing basis of representation, Kerr was willing to acquiesce in a convention that would be controlled by western radicals whose avowed object was "to strike down the taxation basis in the Senate, and thus obtain full and unrestricted sway in the public councils."[28]

At the same time that eastern Democrats were denouncing Kerr for supporting a convention, the Clingman wing of the Whig party was assailing him for his opposition to a change in the basis of representation. Thomas W. Atkin of the *Asheville News*, who was one of the foremost editorial spokesmen for the western-rights movement, went so far as to withdraw his endorsement of Kerr. Clingman himself remained publicly silent but made no secret of his preference for Reid over Kerr.[29] The heated contests in the elections for the general assembly further weakened Kerr's position in the far west. In most counties Clingman supporters were challenging loyalist Whigs, and each side tried to outdo the other in its profession of support for western rights. As the attacks on Kerr became increasingly strident, even the loyalists felt compelled to put distance between themselves and their official standard-bearer.[30]

Assailed in the east as a radical and denounced in the west as an opponent of reform, Kerr ran poorly in both sections and lost the 1852 election to Governor Reid (see figure 9.1). The Whigs fared much better in the legislative elections, where their candidates could take differing, and even contradictory, positions on constitutional reform in their individual constituencies. The Whigs gained seven seats in the house of commons, an increase that enabled them to regain control of the lower house. In the state senate, on the other hand, the Democrats picked up one seat in a disputed election, a gain sufficient to give them a margin of six in the upper house and a majority of two on joint ballot.[31]

Reform-minded Whigs interpreted their party's victory in the lower house as evidence of a popular preference for the convention mode of amendment. It quickly became apparent, however, that many eastern legislators did not consider themselves bound by the referendum plank of their party's platform. Indeed, over half of the eastern Whigs in the house of commons joined the Democrats to defeat a referendum bill concerning the propriety of a convention intro-

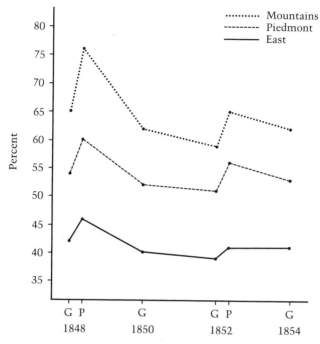

Figure 9.1 Whig Percentage of the Vote in North Carolina Gubernatorial and Presidential Elections, 1848–54. *Sources:* County voting returns, in Thomas E. Jeffrey, "The Second Party System in North Carolina," appendix A; and W. Dean Burnham, *Presidential Ballots*, pp. 646–68.

duced by James M. Leach of Davidson County (see table 9.4). After the defeat of the Leach bill, many western Whigs gave up their opposition to free suffrage by legislative enactment and joined the Democrats in pushing the suffrage amendment through the lower house. In the senate, on the other hand, the reformers remained more adamant in their opposition to free suffrage by legislative enactment. Altogether, thirty-three senators voted in favor of a free-suffrage amendment, but this was still one vote short of the two-thirds constitutional majority. Ironically, free suffrage had passed the Whig house only to fail in the Democratic senate. Equally ironic, most of the votes against free suffrage had come not from conservatives inimical to all constitutional changes but from reformers who believed that Reid's proposal did not go far enough.[32]

The proponents of internal improvements fared somewhat better

Table 9.4   Vote in the House of Commons on Constitutional Reform, 1852 (affirmative percentage by party and section)

	Whigs				Democrats			
	Coast	Pied-mont	Moun-tains	Total	Coast	Pied-mont	Moun-tains	Total
Leach referendum bill (5 November)	45	92	90	75	4	6	50	8
Free-suffrage bill (23 November)	58	50	50	53	100	100	100	100
Free-suffrage bill (8 December)	24	39	14	28	100	94	100	98
Leach referendum bill (23 December)	31	86	100	68	0	8	67	10

Sources: HJ, 1852, 146, 238, 335, 502.

during the session of 1852. Ever since the North Carolina Railroad had been chartered in 1848, residents of the extreme eastern and western counties had been agitating for an extension of the railroad to the seacoast and the mountains. Early in the session separate bills for the eastern and western extensions were introduced into the general assembly. Although a bill to provide a state subscription of $500,000 in the stock of the proposed Atlantic & North Carolina Railroad passed the house of commons by a margin of one vote (see table 9.5), both extension bills were defeated in the senate. Under the leadership of Democrat Romulus M. Saunders the proimprovement forces finally did secure passage of a bill that provided for the incorporation of companies for both extensions, along with a recommendation for a state subscription of two-thirds of the stock in each. In order to secure sufficient support for its passage, the bill's proponents agreed that the subscription would not be binding unless it was approved by the next legislature. The vote on the Saunders bill revealed that the Whigs remained much more sympathetic to the idea of state-supported improvements than did the Democrats. Two-thirds of the Whig commoners voted in favor of the measure, whereas an equal proportion of Democrats opposed it.[33]

The campaign of 1852 and the ensuing legislative session proved to be the high-water mark in the movement for a constitutional con-

Table 9.5   Vote in the House of Commons on Internal Improvements, 1852 (affirmative percentage by party and section)

	Whigs				Democrats			
	Coast	Pied-mont	Moun-tains	Total	Coast	Pied-mont	Moun-tains	Total
Atlantic & North Carolina Railroad	45	52	83	55	56	12	100	45
Saunders bill	56	57	100	65	29	27	100	35

Sources: HJ, 1852, 233, 440.

vention. By 1854 Whig leaders were taking measures to conciliate the eastern wing of the party even at the risk of antagonizing the western reformers. At the Whig state convention, which met at Raleigh on 21 February 1854, the party adopted a platform that assured easterners of its determination to "preserve the present basis of representation in the Legislature." The Whigs went on to endorse a constitutional convention, but one that would be clearly powerless to effect the principal reform demand.[34] With obvious satisfaction, William W. Holden remarked that the Whig platform "went just far enough . . . to excite well-founded suspicions in the Eastern Whig mind, but not far enough to secure the co-operation and support of the Western Whigs." Indeed, the western Whigs publicly denounced the platform as "ungenerous and ridiculous" and they privately urged Alfred Dockery, the party's gubernatorial candidate, to repudiate it and campaign instead on the white-basis issue.[35]

Like John Kerr, Alfred Dockery was a westerner who happened to live in a county with a large slave population. Unlike the previous Whig nominee, however, the rough-hewn Dockery was an experienced campaigner who had served in both the state legislature and the U.S. Congress. Fearing that the issue of constitutional reform would be "the rock upon which the Whig party would likely be split into a thousand atoms," Dockery decided to downplay the issue and instead try to unite his party behind a comprehensive program of internal improvements.[36] Dockery was largely successful in turning the issue from constitutional reform to internal improvements. The Whig candidate went beyond his party's platform, which had recommended an eastern and western extension of the North Carolina Railroad, and endorsed yet another railroad, which would run along the South Carolina border from Wilmington to the mountains. Capitalizing on the renewed public interest in land policy that had accompanied the debate over Henry Bennett's bill in Congress to distribute the public lands, Dockery and his supporters assured the voters that the Whig policy of distributing the public lands among the states would guarantee that "the system of improvement can be carried out without laying very heavy taxes upon the people."[37]

The Whig party entered the campaign of 1854 divided over the issue of constitutional reform but united in support of internal improvements. The Democrats found themselves in exactly the opposite position. By 1854 a large majority in the party was united in opposition to any constitutional changes besides free suffrage, and those Democrats who favored more radical revisions were unwilling to challenge their party on the issue.[38] On the other hand, eastern and western Democrats were sharply divided over the position that the party should take on the extension of the North Carolina Railroad. Former congressman Asa Biggs warned Governor Reid that "it is utterly impracticable to unite the party upon that issue," and he recommended that "nothing should be said about it in our Convention." An explicit endorsement of the extension, warned Biggs, "would greatly embarrass us in the East." At the same time, Democrats in the far west were advising Reid that a full Democratic turnout in their section depended upon the inclusion of a strong internal-improvements plank in the party platform. "The Democracy in the West are in fine spirits & confident of success if the Convention will only lay down some acceptable ground on the subject of Internal Improvements," one westerner informed Reid. "This question overrides every other in the counties west of Asheville, & no candidate who stands upon a platform worse in this respect than that of the Whigs can in my opinion pull the full strength of his party vote."[39]

The Democratic state convention, which met in Raleigh on 19 April 1854, adopted a platform designed to offer something to both wings of the party. In deference to the wishes of easterners, the party came out against a change in the basis of representation. In response to the pressure from its western wing, the convention explicitly endorsed a policy of state aid to internal improvements. However, unlike the Whig platform, which had spoken approvingly of the extension of the North Carolina Railroad, the Democratic resolutions were ambiguous and evasive. The convention resolved that "it would . . . be politic and proper for the legislature, from time to time, to extend such further aid in the completion of the works already undertaken, and the extension of the same, as a just regard for the . . . means and resources of the State will prudently allow." With some justification the Whigs claimed that the Democrats' resolutions were designed "to be read in every locality so as to catch the votes of that particular section."[40]

Throughout most of the 1840s the Democrats had pursued a strategy of remaining officially silent on the issue of state support to internal improvements, while at the same time nominating gubernatorial candidates with conspicuous links to the improvement cause. In 1854 the party reversed this strategy, adopted a proimprovement platform, and nominated Thomas Bragg of Northampton County, an easterner with no previous identification with the movement for state-financed railroads. In the conservative eastern counties the Democrats portrayed Bragg as an opponent of the extravagant projects supposedly endorsed by Dockery and the Whigs. The editor of the *Goldsboro Republican* assured his readers that Bragg opposed internal improvement "as the Whigs desire it to be carried out, by involving the state to any amount and taxing the people to meet the liabilities without regard to their will." While campaigning in the eastern counties, Bragg also took pains to present himself as a prudent and cautious man who would not rush headlong into extravagant programs of state development. At Edenton, for example, he promised his audience that he would go only "as far as the means and resources of the State would admit, so as not to incur a debt beyond the ability of the state to pay."[41]

In the counties of the far west, on the other hand, the Democrats tried hard to convince the voters that Bragg was a better railroad man than Dockery. Thomas W. Atkin, editor of the *Asheville News*, told his readers that the platform endorsed by the Democratic convention was "more comprehensive, stronger and better for the West than that of the Whig party," and he predicted that the Whig leaders would never support state aid wholeheartedly "for fear that their Eastern Whig brethren who are hostile to all works of Improvement, would bolt their nomination." At the same time that eastern Democrats were accusing Dockery of favoring extravagant plans of improvement, Atkin was describing the Whig candidate as a man who "stands alone as the enemy of the Rail Road interests of the State."[42]

It is unlikely that Atkin's accusations persuaded many voters who were not already predisposed to be convinced. During his long service in the general assembly Dockery had gone on record many times in favor of state assistance to internal improvements, whereas Bragg, as the Whigs repeatedly pointed out, was unable to cite one speech he had made, one letter he had written, one convention he had attended, or one dollar he had contributed toward the cause of state development. In the mountain district the Whigs made a vigorous effort to pin the anti-improvement label on Bragg. While campaigning in the west shortly before the August election, Dockery secured a letter from David A. Barnes, a Whig leader in Northampton County, affirming that Bragg had publicly taken ground in 1846 against the investment of public money in railroads. Dockery quoted this letter frequently and to great effect during his tour of the mountain counties. After the election, Marcus Erwin, who had temporarily taken over the editorship of the *Asheville News*, complained that Bragg would have carried the district handily "had it not been for the unscrupulous and unremitting efforts of our opponents to place him in an attitude of hostility to works of Internal Improvement."[43]

The gubernatorial election of 1854 was the closest such contest since Charles Manly had squeaked past David S. Reid in 1848. Dockery garnered 46,650 votes, the most ever received by a Whig gubernatorial candidate. The largest Whig gains were in the mountain region, where popular enthusiasm for internal improvements was strongest. Despite the opposition of Clingman, Erwin, Atkin, and other influential leaders who had renounced their Whig allegiance, Dockery won almost 750 more votes than Kerr had received in 1852, while Bragg garnered almost 400 fewer votes than Reid. Dockery also scored impressive gains in most of the counties along the South Carolina border, which stood to benefit from the proposed railroad from Wilmington to the mountains, and in the counties along the proposed route of the eastern extension of the North Carolina Railroad.[44]

Still, Dockery's total vote was 1,900 fewer than Bragg's. Unfortunately for the Whigs, Dockery's increases in the southern and extreme eastern and western counties were counterbalanced by Whig losses in seventeen counties along or near the Virginia border. These wealthy slaveholding counties stood to benefit little from the ambitious program of state development outlined by Dockery, yet the high value of their land and slaves guaranteed that they would have to pay a disproportionate share of the taxes that might be levied to finance this program. Dockery later claimed that he had "lost thousands of votes from the bold and fearless stand I took upon that question in the Eastern and middle counties." The internal-improvements issue probably contributed as well to the Whig loss of seven legislative seats in six counties along the Virginia border—a loss that gave the Democrats a comfortable majority of ten seats in the lower house.[45]

Although the Democrats had equivocated on the issue of internal improvements during the campaign, and had even used that issue against the Whigs in counties opposed to state aid, the party had officially gone on record in favor of a policy of governmental assistance. With considerable justification the editor of the *Raleigh Register* remarked after the election that "this contest has made everybody a friend to internal improvements in our good old State. It has been a struggle between the Gubernatorial candidates, to prove each the better friend to Railroads." However, it remained to be seen whether the Democrats in the general assembly would consider themselves bound by the promises made in their platform.[46]

By the end of the legislative session of 1854–55, not even the most ardent and uncompromising supporter of internal improvements could have been disappointed. In his inaugural address of 1 January 1855, Governor Bragg decisively threw his own influence behind the cause of state development and urged the legislators to approve both an eastern and a western extension of the North Carolina Railroad. The general assembly subsequently approved the subscription of $1 million in the stock of the Atlantic & North Carolina Railroad, which would run east from Goldsboro to Beaufort harbor on the Atlantic Ocean, and at the same time subscribed $4 million in the stock of the Western North Carolina Railroad, which was to run from the western terminus of the North Carolina Railroad at Salisbury to some point on the French Broad River beyond the Blue Ridge. The legislature also agreed to endorse the bonds of yet another railroad, which would traverse the South Carolina border between Wilmington and Charlotte.[47]

Analysis of the roll-call votes in the house of commons reveals

Table 9.6 Vote in the House of Commons on Internal Improvements, 1854 (affirmative percentage by party and section)

	Whigs				Democrats			
	Coast	Pied-mont	Moun-tains	Total	Coast	Pied-mont	Moun-tains	Total
Atlantic & North Carolina Railroad	94	96	83	92	78	47	100	69
Western North Carolina Railroad	53	100	100	84	45	44	100	48
Wilmington & Charlotte Railroad	83	71	100	82	36	25	67	34

Sources: HJ, 1854–55, 306, 410, 218.

that the Whigs consistently gave greater support to these railroad measures than did their opponents (see table 9.6). Large majorities in both parties voted in favor of the Atlantic railroad, but less than half the Democrats gave their approval to the western railroad. Moreover, two-thirds of the Democrats in the house of commons supported the unsuccessful attempt to strike out the endorsement of the bonds of the Wilmington railroad. Although the Democrats had promised the voters of North Carolina a judicious system of internal improvements, it was the Whigs who supplied most of the legislative muscle for its successful enactment.

The ambitious program of state development adopted by the legislature of 1854–55 necessitated a substantial increase in state taxes. Indeed, the Revenue Act of 1855 increased the tax burden of the people of North Carolina more than any other measure enacted before the Civil War. The tax on real estate, which had previously been six cents on every hundred dollars' worth of land, was doubled to twelve cents, and the poll tax was also doubled from twenty to forty cents per person. An income tax on the earnings of business and professional men, which had been enacted by the legislature in 1848, was also increased, and the number of exemptions was reduced, making a much larger number of people subject to the tax.[48]

Not all the Democrats were pleased by the administration's support for a policy of railroad building financed by increased taxes. Former congressman Abraham Rencher told Governor Bragg that the legislature had "pushed the system (if system it can be called) of Internal Improvements to great extremes. This must of necessity impose very heavy burthens upon the people and these burthens will fall mostly on sections receiving but little benefit from their expenditure. This will produce popular dissatisfaction and for this the Democratic party as a party must be held responsible." Shortly after the passage of the Revenue Act, George E. B. Singletary, a Democrat from Pitt County, introduced a resolution characterizing the measure as "an enormous and unjust burthen on the people of the State" and attributing it to the "reckless and unwise legislation on the subject of internal improvement." Although the house of commons tabled Singletary's resolution by a vote of seventy-seven to twenty-five, almost two-fifths of the Democrats in the lower house supported it.[49]

The same legislative session that witnessed the triumph of the railroad movement also saw the final defeat of the crusade for a constitutional convention. A coalition of Democrats and eastern Whigs handily defeated a Whig-sponsored bill for a referendum on a convention, and this time the reformers made no effort to block the passage of free suffrage. A Democrat-sponsored amendment sailed easily through both houses. Two years later the general assembly would again give its approval to the change in suffrage requirements, and the amendment would be ratified by a large popular majority in August 1857. The radical reformers within the Whig party would never again propound the convention issue in a state election.[50]

Ironically, the collapse of the convention movement can be attributed in no small part to the success of the railroad movement. Westerners had agitated for a convention primarily in order to change the basis of legislative apportionment, and they had sought a shift in the balance of power principally because of frustration at the unwillingness of easterners to vote for internal improvements. The legislative session of 1854–55 had demonstrated, however, that it was possible for westerners to secure their railroads and other improvements even under the existing system of representation. As a Whig correspondent of the *Greensboro Patriot* succinctly put it, "all has been accomplished which the west proposed to accomplish by a change of the basis."[51]

Surveying the political landscape from the perspective of 1855, an observer would be compelled to admit that the politics of the Old North State had undergone an important transformation in the five years since David S. Reid had defeated Charles Manly. Throughout the 1830s and 1840s the desire for intraparty harmony and for a clear definition of party lines had suggested a strategy of keeping the political focus on cohesive national issues and avoiding divisive questions of state policy. By the middle of the 1850s, however, the pressure of western reformers had resulted in an increasing amount of attention by both parties to state issues such as internal improvements and constitutional reform. This shift in emphasis was, in large part, responsible for the change in the balance of parties in the Old North State. Under the leadership of William W. Holden, the party's chief strategist, the Democrats attracted new voters in the east by capitalizing on popular suspicion of the radical tendencies of the western Whigs. At the same time the internecine warfare between the Clingman and anti-Clingman Whigs in the west contributed to the Democratic gains in that part of the state. Indeed, by 1854 Clingman and his chief political allies had formally abandoned their old party and joined the Democrats.

State issues thus played a paramount role in the transformation of North Carolina from a Whig to a Democratic state during the early 1850s. Many historians, however, have argued that the escalating sectional controversy over the status of slavery in the territories was an even more potent force behind the decline of the Whig party in the South after 1850. According to this interpretation, states'-rights Whigs in North Carolina and other southern states grew increasingly dissatisfied with the outspoken antislavery views of their northern Whig allies. The refusal of northern Whigs to support the Compromise of 1850, along with the widespread belief that Winfield Scott— the Whig presidential candidate in 1852—was controlled by the anticompromise wing of the party, contributed significantly to the Whig debacle in 1852 and to the collapse of the party soon thereafter. One historian has aptly summarized this viewpoint by characterizing the presidential election of 1852 as the "death knell of the Whig party in North Carolina."[52]

The importance of the slavery issue in North Carolina politics during this critical period cannot be denied. At the same time, however, the prevailing interpretation greatly exaggerates the influence of southern sectionalism on the decline of the Whig party. Indeed, there is evidence that the passage of Henry Clay's compromise measures in 1850 had a salutary effect on the fortunes of the Whig party in North Carolina. Party leaders did not hesitate to claim sole credit for the resolution of the sectional conflict, and the party held its own during the congressional elections of 1851, capturing six of the nine seats.[53] On the other hand, the presence of Winfield Scott at the head of the ticket in 1852 undoubtedly did put the Whigs at a disadvantage, despite the fact that North Carolina's own William A. Graham had been given the vice-presidential nomination. A Whig ticket headed by President Millard Fillmore would probably have carried the Old North State in 1852. Instead, Scott lost in North Carolina by a margin of 756 votes.[54]

The burden of Scott's unpopularity was a handicap for the Whigs, but not nearly as great a handicap as the deep divisions within the party over state issues. A comparison of Scott's vote in 1852 with the Whig vote for governor between 1848 and 1854 reveals that Old Fuss and Feathers did appreciably better in all sections of the state than any of the Whig gubernatorial standard-bearers (see figure 9.1). Indeed, only in the east in 1848 did the Whig percentage of the vote in a state election exceed Scott's percentage in the presidential election. Viewed in this light, the presidential election of 1852 was actually a high-water mark for the Whigs in North Carolina during the first half of the 1850s.

Despite their defeat in three successive state elections, the Whigs remained a viable opposition party in North Carolina during the early 1850s. Moreover, by 1854 the Whigs were even beginning to regain some of their strength. Dockery received 3,600 more votes than John Kerr had garnered in 1852, while Bragg improved on Governor Reid's showing by a paltry 6 votes. Pointing to the impressive Whig gains in the governor's election, the editor of the *Raleigh Register* interpreted the outcome as an indication of an important "change in the political barometers of both parties. . . . The democratic falls and the Whig rises, so that after all, this 'great democratic victory' is not such a great thing." The editor even predicted that the election of 1854 would go down in history as "the last democratic victory in North Carolina."[55]

This remark was more than just wishful thinking, for, now that they were confronted with the responsibility of governing, the Democrats were finding themselves increasingly bedeviled by the clashing sectional interests that had previously plagued the Whigs. As early as 1850, the railroad issue had threatened to divide the party into warring sectional factions, and five years later about half the party continued to be hostile toward measures of state assistance. By 1855 eastern Democrats like George E. B. Singletary were denouncing the high taxes and reckless expenditures that seemed to accompany their party's accession to power, and other conservatives like Abraham Rencher were warning of drastic political repercussions in the party's traditional eastern strongholds. From the viewpoint of the Whigs, the prospects for success in 1856 seemed promising. Yet even as the Whigs were celebrating their political resurgence in 1854, a new political force was already beginning to make its presence felt in the Old North State. By the congressional elections of 1855, the Whig organization was in shambles and the American party had emerged as the main opposition to the Democrats in North Carolina.

10 ✦ The Responsibility of Power: North Carolina, 1855–1860

It behooves the Democracy of the State to remember, that victory brings with it its duties and responsibilities as well as its rejoicing and rewards. . . . *We are in charge of the government in all its departments, and whatever the opposition may do or omit to do, the responsibility is upon us.* —*North Carolina Standard,* 3 November 1858

Every thing is going on here beautifully. . . . We have a cheering prospect of electing a Whig Governor.—George E. Badger to John J. Crittenden, 6 May 1860

In most of the states north of the Mason-Dixon line the midterm elections of 1853 and 1854 proved disastrous for the Whigs. In the traditional Whig strongholds of New England and the Middle Atlantic region, the Know-Nothing, or American party made impressive showings in the state and congressional elections and replaced the Whigs as the main opposition party. By 1854 the Whig party was also moribund in many parts of the South.[1] In North Carolina, on the other hand, the Whigs continued to be a viable political force. In 1853 the party won four of eight congressional seats.[2] A year later Alfred Dockery garnered almost half of the popular vote in the governor's election. Moreover, despite the Democrats' efforts to make political capital on the recently enacted Kansas-Nebraska Act, Dockery improved significantly over the showing of the previous Whig candidate in the slaveholding counties of the east as well as in the small-farm counties of the west. From the perspective of August 1854, few would have predicted that within six months the Know-Nothings would supplant the Whigs as the opposition party in the Old North State.[3]

Because their early activities were shrouded in secrecy, it is not possible to determine exactly when the Know-Nothings first appeared in North Carolina. There is no evidence of Know-Nothing activity prior to the state elections of 1854. By late summer, however, a few lodges had already been organized, and membership in the order grew rapidly during the fall and early winter. With their elaborate initiation ceremonies, passwords, grips, and secret oaths, the Know-Nothings initially bore a stronger resemblance to a fraternal organization than to a political party. Indeed, their first state constitution, which was adopted in January 1855, repeatedly referred to the organization as an "order" rather than a political party. Carefully avoiding the word "convention," the constitution established a series of state, district, and local "councils" to nominate candidates for governor, the U.S. Congress, and the state legislature. During the first months of its existence, Democrats and Whigs joined the order on the understanding that it was an organization unconnected with either of the traditional parties, whose object was "to check the emigration of persons of vicious and bad character from foreign countries, and to prevent the Church of Rome from interfering with elections."[4]

The Know-Nothing movement in North Carolina seems to have been initiated by obscure individuals with only tenuous connections to the two established parties. However, it was soon taken over by professional politicians and redirected into more conventional political channels. The first prominent North Carolinian to join the order was Kenneth Rayner, a former Whig legislator and congressman from Hertford County. During the early months of 1855 Rayner played an important role in lining up support for the new organization in the Albemarle Sound region. In the central counties near Raleigh, the principal organizer was Henry W. Miller, a longtime member of the Whig central committee.[5]

In some of the counties west of Raleigh, the Whig organization continued to function through the winter and early spring. In March the Whigs held meetings in Davidson, Forsyth, Rockingham, Stokes, and Surry counties and elected delegates to a district convention, which met in Winston on 11 April 1855 and nominated Richard C. Puryear as the Whig candidate for Congress. In the seven other congressional districts the Whigs did not attempt to make formal nominations. Instead, meetings of the "American party" assembled in May to nominate candidates in six of these districts, and by late June an American candidate was in the field to contest the seventh. By midsummer prominent western Whigs like John Baxter, David F. Cald-well, John A. Gilmer, Augustus S. Merrimon, and Henry K. Nash were actively campaigning on behalf of the American candidates.[6]

The Democrats were quick to denounce the American party as nothing more than Whiggery in disguise. According to the editor of the *Elizabeth City Democratic Pioneer:* "The foolish and unmeaning cry of danger from foreigners is but a scheme to rebuild the defunct Whig party, and to resuscitate, under a new name, what has been considered as worthless under an old."[7] In response to such accusations, the editors of the opposition presses retorted that the new party was composed of patriotic men from both of the old parties. And, indeed, the Americans could point to several well-known Democrats who had abandoned their party to join the movement. The most important of the Democratic defectors was James B. Shepard, a longtime member of the Democratic central committee. Shepard had been his party's candidate for governor in 1846, and for more than a decade he had unsuccessfully sought the congressional nomination in his heavily Democratic district. Frustrated ambition seems to have been the driving force behind Shepard's conversion to Know-Nothingism. Other ambitious Democrats like David Reid of Duplin, Samuel N. Stowe, and Thomas J. Latham also bolted their party and—like Shepard—accepted congressional nominations from the American party.[8]

The American party contained enough former Democrats to give credence to its claim that it was not simply the Whig party under a different name. On the other hand, the vast majority of the party's leaders undoubtedly did come from the ranks of the Whigs. While Democrats like Shepard and Reid supported the new party because of frustrated ambition, veteran Whigs like Rayner and Miller embraced it as the only practical alternative to the Democrats. For over two decades an association with a national party had been the lifeblood of politics in the Old North State. When the Whig organizations in the northern states began to crumble after the midterm elections of 1853 and 1854, the party lost its nationality. And just as the Federalist leaders of a previous generation had sought new political allies when their old party could no longer serve their ambitions, so too the Whig leaders endorsed Know-Nothingism in order to maintain their affiliation with a viable national party and to promote their own political fortunes.[9]

In North Carolina, as elsewhere in the nation, the Americans made a strenuous effort to dissociate themselves from both of the traditional parties. The party's official attitude was summarized in a platform that was adopted by the national council in June 1855 and subsequently endorsed in dozens of ratification meetings throughout North Carolina. According to its platform, the American party had "arisen upon the ruins, and in spite of the opposition, of the whig and democratic parties." It could not, therefore, "be held in any manner responsible for the obnoxious acts or violated pledges of either." The platform also expressed "hostility to the corrupt means by which the leaders of party have hitherto forced upon us our rulers and our political creeds," and it called for a return to "the purer days of the Republic" through the election of "men of higher qualifications, purer morals, and more unselfish patriotism."[10]

The American bill of complaint against organized political parties was similar in many respects to the antiparty sentiments that had been voiced by the anticaucus crusaders of the 1820s and 1830s and by insurgent Democrats and Whigs during the 1840s and 1850s. North Carolinians had never been totally comfortable with the disparities between the ideals of eighteenth-century republicanism and the realities of nineteenth-century party politics, and ambitious office seekers had never hesitated to capitalize on popular suspicion of organized parties in order to promote their own political careers. Yet the presence of so many seasoned political veterans within the ranks of the Americans belied their efforts to present their party as an organization dedicated to the purification of the political system. With some justification the Democrats characterized their opponents as a party that "preaches the doctrine of excluding from office old party hacks [but] seldom fails to bring them forward as candidates."[11]

Not all the Whig leaders in North Carolina were as eager as Rayner and Miller to embrace the American party. Some, like former senator George E. Badger, publicly endorsed the new party but privately admitted that they supported it only as the lesser of two evils. Others, like Edward J. Hale of the *Fayetteville Observer*, chastised the Americans for destroying the old Whig organization and for boasting that they had arisen upon the ruins of the two established parties.[12] Hale and Badger were both willing to give grudging support to the Americans, but there were other Whig leaders whose distaste for the party eventually drove them into the ranks of the Democrats. Perhaps the most prominent defector was John Kerr of Caswell County. Kerr had been the Whig standard-bearer in 1852, and a year later party leaders in his district had rewarded him with a seat in the U.S. Congress. Unlike many Whigs, Kerr refused to cast his lot with the Americans in 1855 and, instead, attempted to campaign once again as a Whig. The Americans subsequently nominated another Whig, Edwin G. Reade, who defeated Kerr in the general election. Soon thereafter the ex-congressman formally announced his support for the Democrats. Other prominent Whigs who bolted to the Democrats included Daniel M. Barringer, Paul C. Cameron, James W. Osborne, and Walter L. Steele.[13]

The congressional elections of 1855 offered the first test of strength for the American party in North Carolina. In an effort to win over Democratic voters, the Americans nominated ex-Democrats to contest the districts that had been traditionally dominated by that party. Ironically, despite the American claim that the new party was unrelated to either of the established organizations, the persistence of traditional party alignments proved to be the most salient feature of the elections. All three of the districts carried by the Americans had previously been controlled by the Whigs, and the party failed to make significant inroads in the four Democratic districts. In the mountain district Thomas L. Clingman campaigned for the first time as a Democrat, and he easily outdistanced Leander B. Carmichael, his American opponent. Outside of Clingman's district, however, the balance of parties in 1855 was almost identical to what it had been in the gubernatorial election of 1854.[14]

The outcome of the congressional elections revealed the potential strength of the American party in North Carolina and offered its leaders hope of wresting power from the Democrats in the upcoming state and national elections. In October 1855 an American convention met in Raleigh and adopted a series of resolutions that officially transformed the order into an organized political party. The resolutions abolished all the ceremonies, passwords, secrets, and other appurtenances of a fraternal order and affirmed "that we do constitute ourselves into a publicly organized party . . . [and] do challenge our opponents to the public discussion of our principles." The meeting officially embraced the convention system as a legitimate mechanism for selecting candidates and recommended that a state convention be held in Greensboro to name a candidate for governor.[15]

On 10 April 1856 230 delegates from forty-six counties assembled in Greensboro and nominated the veteran Whig leader John A. Gilmer as their candidate to oppose Governor Bragg. Recognizing the debilitating effect that state issues had exercised on the Whig party during the 1850s, the Americans adopted a strategy of ignoring divisive state issues like constitutional reform and concentrated instead on the threat that Catholics and foreigners supposedly presented to the American way of life. Thus, the party's platform promised to avoid the "vexed State questions, made up by former political organizations" and to eschew "sectional issues in the State as well as in the Union." Despite previous efforts by the Americans to put distance between themselves and the old Whig organization, the convention unabashedly appointed an executive committee composed almost entirely of veteran Whig leaders. Whatever the initial intentions of its founders, by 1856 the American party in North Carolina was little more than a surrogate for the Whig party.[16]

The Americans quickly discovered that their standard-bearer was no more immune to the deleterious effect of state sectionalism than his Whig predecessors had been. In the eastern counties the Democrats did not hesitate to make an issue of Gilmer's long record in support of internal improvements and constitutional reform. As evidence of Gilmer's "partiality for the West and opposition to the East," the editor of the *Democratic Pioneer* pointed out that the American standard-bearer had voted for a constitutional convention during the previous legislative session, that he favored the white basis of legislative apportionment, and that he proposed to distribute the public school fund according to the same principle. The editor of the *New Bern Journal* characterized Gilmer as a reckless demagogue, who would "go . . . in with a perfect rush on the subject of Internal Improvements," unlike Governor Bragg, "who seeks not to increase your already burdensome taxation."[17]

At the same time that eastern Democrats were lambasting Gilmer for his dangerous views on internal improvements and constitutional reform, western Democrats like Thomas W. Atkin of the *Asheville News* were denouncing "the great apostle of the White Basis" for surrendering his egalitarian principles for a chance at the governor's chair. Atkin also condemned the "non-commitalism of the [American] Convention . . . on the subject of Internal Improvement," while claiming that Bragg "favored, openly and boldly, whatever appropriations were necessary to complete the Central Road and to extend it East and West." Although the improvement legislation enacted by the legislature of 1854–55 had resulted from a bipartisan effort, western Democrats were not averse to assigning full credit to their own party. "A Democratic Governor and a Democratic Legislature have brought our Rail Roads to the foot of the Blue Ridge," boasted Atkin. "If Bragg is elected, and a Democratic Legislature to act with him, that Legislature will provide for crossing the Blue Ridge."[18]

Bragg easily won the governor's election, capturing over 56 percent of the vote. Not since Edward B. Dudley had trounced John Branch almost twenty years earlier had the winning candidate received so large a percentage. A major factor behind Bragg's strong showing was his party's ability to attract new and previously uncommitted voters. Since 1848 the percentage of voters participating in state elections had been steadily rising. Between 1854 and 1856 it increased from 77 percent of the total electorate to 80 percent. Altogether, over seven thousand new voters cast their ballots in the governor's election in 1856. The Democrats benefited from this increase far more than the Americans. East of the mountains, Gilmer received approximately the same number of votes that Dockery had won in 1854, whereas Bragg received almost six thousand more votes than he had garnered two years earlier (see figure 10.1).[19]

Bragg's gains in the coastal and piedmont counties were impressive enough, but they paled in comparison to his stunning triumph in the mountain region. The Democratic vote in the far west increased by more than 60 percent from the previous election, while the opposition vote dropped by almost 18 percent. For the first time the Democrats had actually carried the mountain district in a state election. The outcome of the legislative elections paralleled that of the governor's contest (see figure 10.2 and figure 10.3). The Democrats gained fifteen seats in the house of commons and three in the state senate, giving them a comfortable majority of fifty-six seats on joint ballot (see table 10.1). Again, the most impressive gains were in the mountain region. In 1854 the Democrats had held only four of the seventeen seats in the mountain delegation to the house of commons. In 1856 they gained seven additional seats, which gave them a lopsided majority of eleven to six (see figure 10.4).

State issues undoubtedly played an important role in affecting the outcome of both the gubernatorial and the legislative elections.

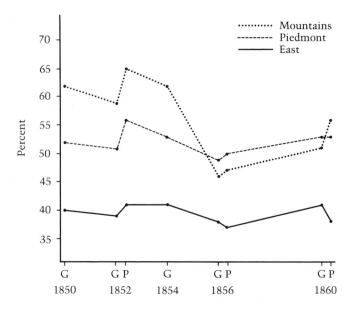

Figure 10.1 Whig/American Percentage of the Vote in North Carolina Gubernatorial and Presidential Elections, 1850–60. *Sources:* County voting returns, in Thomas E. Jeffrey, "The Second Party System in North Carolina," appendix A; and W. Dean Burnham, *Presidential Ballots*, pp. 646–68.

According to the editor of the *Wilmington Herald:* "*National* politics had but a small agency in controlling the election. . . . The issues principally involved had reference to our State affairs, and as such had their due weight." The editor of the *Kinston American Advocate* agreed that the Democrats had succeeded in diverting "the public mind from these [national] issues to some local matters in various

Table 10.1 Party Strength in the North Carolina House of Commons, 1856–60

| | Whig/American members | | | | Democratic members | | | |
	Coast	Pied-mont	Moun-tains	Total	Coast	Pied-mont	Moun-tains	Total
1856	14	20	6	40	44	25	11	80
1858	15	19	5	39	43	26	12	81
1860	19	25	12	56	39	20	5	64

Sources: Raleigh Standard, 3 September 1856, 25 August 1858, 15 August 1860.

sections." The editor claimed that "in the East Mr. Gilmer was represented as a White basis man—desiring to change the present basis of representation. In the West, he was charged with being untrue to the West; and . . . thousands in each section were induced to vote for Gov. Bragg."[20]

On the other hand, state issues by themselves cannot explain why the opposition losses were so staggering, especially in the mountain region. With the advantage of hindsight, it can be said that the American strategists blundered badly when they self-consciously dissociated themselves from the old Whig organization. Especially was this true in Clingman's congressional district in the far west. Since 1852 Clingman and his allies had been working hard to transfer the congressman's personal popularity into votes for Democratic candidates. Yet despite Clingman's own lopsided majorities in the congressional elections, the vast majority of Whig voters had remained loyal

Figure 10.2   Party Affiliation in the North Carolina House of Commons, 1850–60. *Source:* Thomas E. Jeffrey, "Internal Improvements and Political Parties in Antebellum North Carolina," table 1.

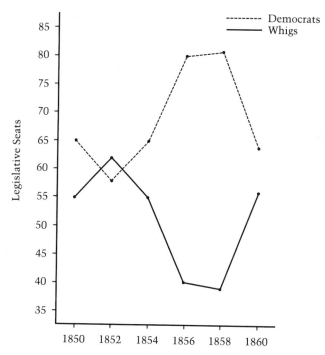

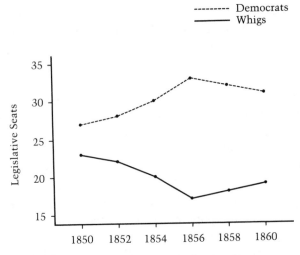

Figure 10.3 Party Affiliation in the North Carolina Senate, 1850–60. *Sources: Raleigh Standard*, 28 August 1850, 25 August 1852, 23 August 1854, 3 September 1856, 25 August 1858, 15 August 1860.

to their party. As late as 1854, 62 percent of the voters in the mountain region had cast their ballots for the Whig gubernatorial candidate. Shortly before that election, one Clingman supporter had accurately predicted that "there are many warm Clingman men in the District who will not go for an out & out Democrat yet, though if all things work right for a space they will."[21]

By playing down their association with old-line Whiggery, the Americans gave Clingman a powerful weapon to use against them in the west. The congressman told his constituents that the Whig party was dead and that the Americans were in no way related to it. According to Clingman: "The members of the old Whig party . . . are, of course, not under the slightest obligation to go for the nominee of the Know-Nothing convention, because that convention denounced both the Whig and Democratic parties as corrupt and proclaimed that it had 'arisen on the ruins of both and in spite of their opposition.'" A loyal Whig could thus support the Democratic nominee "with propriety, and without any loss of self-respect." Without the formidable name of "Whig" on their banner, the Americans in the mountain district proved no match against a popular Democratic congressman and a party that had gone on record in support of state development.[22]

The presidential election of 1856 revealed other forces working against the Americans besides the divisive state issues of internal improvements and constitutional reform. The split within the national American party over the issue of slavery in the territories, together with the rapid rise of the Republican party in the northern states, lent credence to the Democrats' claim that they alone were strong enough to protect the South against the forces of abolitionism. Several prominent Whigs, most notably former congressman Daniel M. Barringer, publicly embraced the Democratic party because of this consideration. Three months after the state elections, James Buchanan, the

Figure 10.4 Whig/American Strength in the North Carolina House of Commons, 1850–60. *Source:* Thomas E. Jeffrey, "Internal Improvements and Political Parties in Antebellum North Carolina," table 1.

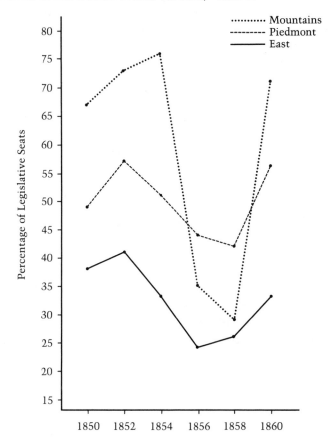

Democratic presidential candidate, handily defeated Millard Fillmore, his American opponent, by a margin of over eleven thousand votes. In the east Buchanan improved slightly over Bragg's vote in the August election, while Fillmore did marginally better than Gilmer in the piedmont and mountain regions. Overall, Buchanan's 56.6 percent of the vote was almost identical to Bragg's 56.2 percent.[23]

Despite their overwhelming victory in the state and national elections, the Democrats were soon to discover that the task of governing North Carolina would not be an easy one. The most vexatious problem continued to be the issue of state aid to internal improvements. In many of the eastern counties party leaders were calling for a moratorium on state spending, at least until North Carolina could construct and pay for its existing railroads. At the same time other elements within the party were agitating for additional improvement measures. In the far west supporters of the Western North Carolina Railroad were demanding the modification of the so-called "section feature" of its charter, which stipulated that construction had to be entirely completed on one section before the state could provide money for work on another section farther west. In the counties near the South Carolina border, the promoters of the Wilmington & Charlotte Railroad were requesting modifications in its charter in order to extend the road into eastern Tennessee. At the other end of the state, supporters of the Atlantic & North Carolina Railroad, confronted by escalating expenses, were asking for an additional loan of $400,000.

There were also demands for new improvements to benefit those counties that would not be served by these railroads. The residents of the upper Cape Fear were requesting an appropriation of $600,000 to build a railroad from Fayetteville to the potentially rich coalfields of Chatham County. Another prospective railroad from Cheraw, South Carolina, to the coalfields was being promoted by legislators from some of the counties west of Fayetteville. Legislators from the lower Cape Fear, also anxious to tap the wealth of the coalfields, were sponsoring an appropriation of $300,000 to aid the Cape Fear and Deep River Navigation Company, a corporation in which the state had already invested several thousand dollars. In the counties along the Virginia border there was renewed interest in a railroad link to Danville—the so-called Danville connection. Unfortunately for their promoters, most of these new projects were opposed not only by conservatives worried about the increasing state debt but also by proimprovement legislators with vested interests in the existing projects.[24]

Perhaps not surprising, it was the railroad with the fewest enemies that enjoyed the greatest measure of success in the North Carolina General Assembly of 1856–57. Although conservatives claimed that the $400,000 loan to the Atlantic & North Carolina Railroad would further drain an already "crippled and empty treasury," the bill passed the house of commons by a nine-vote majority (see table 10.2). The friends of the Western North Carolina Railroad were not as fortunate. By a vote of sixty-six to forty-one the house of commons decisively rejected a motion to remove the section feature from its charter. The lower house did agree to a compromise bill providing for the extension of the first section as far west as Morganton, but even this measure was approved by only a two-vote margin. The promoters of the western extension took some comfort, however, in the overwhelming defeat of the bill to extend the Wilmington & Charlotte Railroad into Tennessee. Had both extensions been al-

Table 10.2 Vote in the House of Commons on Internal Improvements, 1856 (affirmative percentage by party and section)

	Americans				Democrats			
	Coast	Pied- mont	Moun- tains	Total	Coast	Pied- mont	Moun- tains	Total
Atlantic & North Carolina Railroad	75	67	100	74	54	35	40	46
Western North Carolina Railroad	42	83	100	72	14	12	78	21
Cheraw & Coal- fields Railroad	71	83	100	81	43	92	100	69
Rockingham & Coalfields Railroad	83	100	80	91	50	71	100	67
Fayetteville & Coalfields Railroad	29	88	80	63	18	52	100	41
Cape Fear & Deep River	100	25	100	57	48	65	29	52

Sources: HJ, 1856–57, 394, 403–4, 411–12, 284, 268, 483.

lowed, the two railroads would have been direct competitors for the trade of the mountain region.[25]

The Cape Fear interests received even less satisfaction than the proponents of the western railroad. The friends of the Fayetteville & Coalfields Railroad successfully defeated an effort in the house of commons to extend its proposed route eastward from Fayetteville to Beaufort harbor, but the Beaufort interests retaliated by voting en masse against the subscription bill. The bill to improve the Deep River passed the senate toward the end of the session, but in the lower house the bill's opponents managed to prevent a final vote on the measure. Equally galling to the Cape Fear interests, the general assembly approved a charter for the Cheraw & Coalfields Railroad, a project that its opponents claimed would divert the trade of the southern counties from Wilmington to Cheraw and Charleston and thus deal "a death blow to the Wilmington and Charlotte Road."[26]

The friends of the Danville connection also found their schemes rebuffed by the general assembly. A bill to charter a railroad between Danville and Greensboro was defeated in the senate by a large majority and never even came to a vote in the lower house. Another effort to charter a railroad from Greensboro to the coalfields on the Dan River in Rockingham County passed the house of commons by a comfortable majority, but only after being amended to provide that it would not run nearer than nineteen miles to Danville. The railroad's enemies in the senate subsequently succeeded in preventing the upper house from voting on the bill.[27]

An analysis of the vote in the house of commons on these measures reveals that the Americans, like their Whig predecessors, were far more sympathetic to internal improvements than were the Democrats (see table 10.2). While a majority of American legislators voted in favor of the Atlantic, Western, and Fayetteville bills, a majority of Democrats opposed them. Neither party, however, voted as a monolithic unit on internal improvement measures, and clashing sectional interests continued to affect the pattern of voting behavior. The sectional divisions within the Democratic party were far more pronounced than those within the opposition. A majority of American legislators from the coastal, piedmont, and mountain delegations voted together on three of the six roll calls presented in table 10.2. The three Democratic delegations, on the other hand, failed to vote together even once.

After the adjournment of the general assembly, William W. Holden conceded that many regions in the state "have been disappointed . . . by the failure of cherished schemes" of internal improvement. The editor expressed his own belief that "much more would doubtless have been accomplished, if the majority of members . . . had been more easy in their minds in relation to the State's financial condition." Despite Holden's efforts to put the best possible light on the situation, important elements in the governing coalition were bitterly disappointed by their party's inability to promote their interests effectively. The editor of the *Wilmington Journal* denounced the legislators for neglecting the interests of the Cape Fear, while at the same time chartering a railroad that would draw the trade of the state to South Carolina. With dripping sarcasm the editor suggested that "if the Legislators think this is good and right for the State . . . to cut her own throat . . . they ought to be willing to have it tried on themselves personally." The Raleigh correspondent of the *Asheville News* was equally caustic in his assessment of the general assembly. In his opinion, "much has been said, little done, and that little not for the West. . . . The counties West of the Blue Ridge have been 'slaughtered,' their just and reasonable expectations thwarted, and their members . . . 'go home, emphatically, with their fingers in their mouths!'"[28]

In response to this criticism, Holden appealed to his fellow Democrats not to blame their party for the shortcomings of the general assembly. Both parties, he claimed, were internally divided over state issues, and neither should be held responsible for the conduct of its individual members. "There are Democrats," said Holden, "who are for internal improvements by the State, and Democrats opposed to improvements by the State; and the Whigs and 'Americans' are divided in the same way. . . . No one party can be justly held responsible, *as a party*, for the failure or the success of particular schemes. . . . Let us hear no more, therefore, of the stale and unfounded charge that a *Democratic* Legislature refused to redeem its pledges."[29]

To the opposition editors this disclaimer of responsibility was absurd. With their overwhelming majorities the Democrats had the power to legislate as they wished, and it was ridiculous to argue that the party should not be held accountable for the actions of its members. According to the editor of the *Fayetteville Observer*: "The Democrats had the Legislature by an unprecedented majority. They are very willing to take the credit of any real or supposed good law passed; they should assume the responsibility for all. If they are unwilling to bear the responsibility of power, let them give place to those who have more courage." The editor of the *Greensboro Patriot* expressed his opinion that, despite the efforts of Holden and other party leaders to abjure responsibility, "the people will hold the Democracy of the last Legislature responsible, for although they were very weak intellectually—yet they had the physical power to do whatever they saw fit, and they will be held to a strict account."[30]

From the viewpoint of the opposition, the willingness of the Democratic legislators to vote for additional increases in the land and poll taxes only added insult to injury. That the state was desperately in need of revenue was a fact that no knowledgeable person could gainsay. Yet the Americans denied that the Democratic solution—a 25 percent increase in the tax rates—was the only feasible alternative. Indeed, the vast majority of Americans in the house of commons cast their votes against the Revenue Act of 1857. At the same time all but a handful of the opposition legislators supported a substitute, introduced by James M. Leach of Davidson County, that would have significantly reduced the tax on land and polls (see table 10.3).

Opposition spokesmen claimed that the Revenue Act placed a disproportionate burden on the ordinary citizen while allowing the wealthier elements to escape their share of taxes. According to M. S. Sherwood, the editor of the *Greensboro Patriot*: "It has become the established rule of our legislators to raise the necessary funds, by oppressing the poor men of the country . . . while the wealthy and overgrown corporations are constantly increasing in wealth, and yet pay little or no taxes." The most offensive of these "overgrown corpora-

Table 10.3 Vote in the House of Commons on Revenue Measures, 1856 (affirmative percentage by party and section)

	Americans				Democrats			
	Coast	Pied-mont	Moun-tains	Total	Coast	Pied-mont	Moun-tains	Total
Revenue Act	31	5	0	13	100	96	56	93
Leach's amendment	86	89	100	89	6	36	70	25

Sources: HJ, 1856–57, 392, 379–80.

Table 10.4 Vote in the House of Commons on Banking Measures, 1856 (affirmative percentage by party and section)

	Americans				Democrats			
	Coast	Pied- mont	Moun- tains	Total	Coast	Pied- mont	Moun- tains	Total
Bank of North Carolina	63	6	0	20	86	81	78	83
Scott's "bonus" bill	33	100	100	75	17	29	64	29
People's Bank	79	89	100	87	3	4	60	12

Sources: HJ, 1856–57, 300, 301–2, 350–51.

tions," in the eyes of Sherwood, was the state bank, whose stock-holders received annual dividends of 10 percent—money that was actually another indirect tax upon the people. In language reminiscent of that used by the Democrats during the bank wars of the early 1840s, Sherwood warned that "the stockholders of the State Bank and other similar corporations are growing rich at the expense of the people, and . . . a monied power, to which all other powers are becoming subject, is fast growing up in this State. . . . The few are becoming immensely rich, and at the same time bear little or no part of the burdens of the State, while the masses are growing poorer every day, and as they become poorer their taxes are constantly increased."[31]

The editor of the Patriot was not alone in his hostility toward the state bank. Opposition legislators in the general assembly demonstrated a similar attitude when they voted overwhelmingly against a renewal of the bank's charter (see table 10.4). Three-fourths of the American legislators in the house of commons also gave their support to a bill introduced by Levi M. Scott of Guilford County, which would have required the bank to pay a bonus of $50,000 "upon the principle that those who received all the profits and made all the money, should at least bear a portion of the taxes." Ironically, the Democrats, who a decade earlier had characterized the bank as a "manufactory of rogues and swindlers," now found themselves defending it as a "long tried, well managed, useful, and necessary institution."[32]

At the same time that the Americans were denouncing the Democrats for discriminating against ordinary farmers and laborers in favor of wealthy corporations, they were also condemning the party for giving away North Carolina's share of the public domain, "making rich and prosperous other sections, while . . . [our] own are getting daily poorer."[33] The policy of distributing federal land revenue among the states had been a cardinal principle of the Whig party since 1834. Although the American platform of 1856 had officially opposed the squandering of the public lands for the benefit of "foreign paupers and convicts," the party had not emphasized the land issue during the campaigns of 1855 and 1856. By 1857, however, the pressing need for additional sources of revenue had led opposition leaders to take a more favorable view of the political potential of the distribution issue. According to the editor of the *Register*, land policy was the issue on which the Democrats were most vulnerable. "The people of North Carolina are heavily taxed by the Democracy, and have *not got used to it*," he exclaimed. "Let this distribution question be put before the people by strong, clear-headed men on the stump, and our life for it, it will drive [the] opposition . . . to the wall."[34]

The propriety of distributing public land sale proceeds (or even the lands themselves) among the states thus became the principal campaign issue in the congressional contest of 1857. During the previous congressional campaign the Americans had tried hard to dissociate themselves from the Whig party and its policies. By 1857, however, opposition leaders were appealing openly to old-line Whig voters by calling themselves "American Whigs." The Democrats reacted to the new strategy with a mixture of amusement and disdain. The editor of the *Asheville News* expressed doubt that the prospects of the opposition "will be bettered by adding 'Whig,' after the foul treatment that venerable and once respected party cognomon [*sic*] has received at their hands. . . . It looks, at all events, a good deal like murdering a man and then canonizing him."[35]

The results of the congressional elections proved disastrous for the Americans. The party lost two of the three districts it had won in 1855 and captured the third by an unimpressive 54 percent of the vote. In the five other districts the Americans did not even field a candidate. A comparison between the vote in 1857 and the previous congressional election reveals that the Americans lost almost one thousand votes in the three districts they contested, while the Democrats gained over three thousand votes. The demise of the national

American party following the adjournment of its national council in June 1857 undoubtedly demoralized the opposition leaders and contributed to the disastrous showing of the North Carolina party a few months later. The elections demonstrated once again that a link with a viable national party was an important prerequisite of success for a state party in North Carolina.[36]

Almost as soon as the congressional elections were over, opposition leaders began debating the course they should pursue in the next state campaign. One faction, whose most vocal proponent was John W. Syme, the new editor of the *Raleigh Register*, argued that the American Whigs were too weak to field a gubernatorial candidate of their own and recommended that the party support a Democrat who favored the distribution of the public lands.[37] The other faction, which was spearheaded by the editors of the *Greensboro Patriot* and the *Elizabeth City Sentinel*, urged the opposition leaders to nominate one of their own as standard-bearer. Even if the American Whigs went down to defeat, said the editor of the *Sentinel*, it was better for the party to stand by its own principles than to desert its flag for a "one principle candidate" with no affinity to the party except on the single issue of land policy.[38]

Despite vociferous demands for a state nominating convention to select an opposition candidate for governor, no convention was ever called. The logical person to issue the call was Henry W. Miller, the chairman of the American party's central committee. But Miller remained silent until 11 March 1858, when he announced that his authority as chairman had ceased with the presidential election of 1856. Two weeks later Miller interjected yet more confusion into the opposition ranks by bolting to the Democrats. Despite Miller's defection, opposition leaders probably still would have called for a state convention had they been able to find a prominent politician willing to accept its nomination. Their inability to find a candidate willing to canvass the state and risk almost certain defeat guaranteed that the governor's election would be contested between opposing factions within the majority party.[39]

The introduction of Henry Bennett's land bill into the U.S. Congress in 1853 had reopened the latent divisions within the Democratic party over the issue of land policy. Bennett's bill provided for the distribution of the public lands (rather than the proceeds from their sale) between the new and old states in a ratio of two to one, an arrangement that would have given North Carolina approximately 1.6 million acres of public lands. Only six southern Democrats voted for the measure, one of them Congressman Abraham W. Venable of North Carolina. Venable's support for distribution incurred the enmity of William W. Holden, who subsequently managed to prevent his reelection in 1853. With considerable justification Venable and his supporters blamed Holden and the Raleigh Clique for his defeat. The split between the friends of Venable and Holden widened in 1855, after a district convention passed over the former congressman in favor of George W. Thompson, a Holden ally. According to one Venable supporter who had attended the convention, the delegates had acted "to please Holden" and to prevent a nomination that would have been construed as "a victory over the Raleigh clique."[40]

Holden's decision to seek the Democratic gubernatorial nomination in 1858 galvanized the dissidents within the party in an effort "to redeem the state from the Raleigh bondage."[41] Indeed, the Democratic insurgency was as much a protest against the alleged power of the Raleigh Clique as it was an effort to promote the distribution of public lands. The insurgents had no intention of submitting their claims to the decision of the Democratic state convention. Venable and his principal ally, former congressman Archibald H. Arrington, had both suffered defeat in nominating conventions controlled by their political enemies, and they undoubtedly believed that they would be outmaneuvered by a skillful political manipulator like Holden in any convention fight. Although Venable seemed the logical choice as the distribution candidate for governor, he was in poor health and chose to wage a less demanding campaign for a seat in the general assembly. After much informal consultation the distribution leaders finally settled on Duncan K. McRae, a former legislator from Cumberland County. On 26 April 1858 McRae formally announced himself as a candidate for governor "without restraint by any dictation of caucus."[42]

Contrary to the expectations of the distributionists, the Democratic state convention, which met at Charlotte on 14 April 1858, did not tender the gubernatorial nomination to Holden. During his long tenure as editor of the *Raleigh Standard*, Holden had acquired numerous enemies within the Democratic party, and by early spring of 1858 Judge John W. Ellis of Rowan County had emerged as the editor's principal rival for the nomination. In an effort to appear above the battle, Holden refrained from using his own newspaper to promote his cause, but the intemperate attacks against Ellis in other pro-Holden presses (allegedly written by Frank I. Wilson, the associate editor of the *Standard*) antagonized Ellis's supporters without adding appreciably to Holden's strength. Both candidates carried their fight to the floor of the state convention, which gave the nomination to Ellis.[43]

The choice of a gubernatorial candidate was not the only difficulty confronting the delegates to the Charlotte convention. With the state already deeply in debt, eastern Democrats wanted assurance that their party contemplated no new measures of internal improvement that would lead to further increases in taxes. At the same time, proponents of the Western North Carolina Railroad and other improvement projects were demanding a commitment from the party to provide additional assistance in the construction or completion of these works. Two weeks before the convention outgoing Governor Thomas Bragg expressed his opinion that the controversy over a gubernatorial candidate "will all blow over after the Convention, if they do not fall out about the *platform*. There will be more difficulty about that, than there will be about the Candidate. There will be extremes for & agt. Internal Improvement & unless there shall be some middle ground assumed upon which all can stand, we shall probably have some trouble." The platform finally adopted by the convention adroitly finessed the issue of internal improvements by explicitly endorsing "the works of internal improvement already begun, and the construction of such others as may be deemed expedient," while stipulating that state aid should extend only so far "as the credit of the State, and the means of her citizens may permit, without injuriously affecting the one or imposing too onerous burdens on the other."[44]

It was no surprise that McRae denounced the Democratic platform as *"purposely constructed to be* equivocal," and he promised that *"my* language shall be used to *express* and not to *hide* my opinions." McRae's own position on internal improvements, however, was no less ambiguous than that of his opponents. The candidate declared himself "an advocate of the completion of our present system, and of extending aid to other more important works now slighted or neglected." At the same time he claimed to be "opposed to any increase of the State debt, or any addition to her liability for works of internal improvement." In the conservative eastern counties McRae emphasized the burdens imposed on the people by the heavy state debt, while in the western counties he promised support for the coalfields railroad, the Danville connection, and the removal of the section feature from the charter of the Western North Carolina Railroad. The editor of the *Wilmington Journal* sarcastically remarked that McRae seemed to be "two gentlemen in one. His Eastern face is to decry debt and taxes, never to sanction any additional appropriations for any work in progress or to be begun. His Western face is to tell the people of the West that he goes for giving them all they ask, and, that in fact, he is a better Railman than Judge Ellis."[45]

Despite their lack of consensus over the issue of additional state aid to internal improvements, McRae's supporters could agree that the taxes on land and polls had risen beyond the capacity of ordinary people to pay and that the public lands could provide a more equitable source of revenue. According to the editor of the *Salisbury Watchman*: "The *great* question to be decided . . . is high or low taxes. If you want high taxes for 30 or 40 years, vote for Ellis. . . . If you want low taxes, and our rights in the public lands, then vote for McRae." In a similar vein, the editor of the *Louisburg American Eagle* reminded his readers that "your taxes are much higher than ever before . . . and you know that the locofoco [Democratic] party imposed this high tax upon us. . . . This being the state of things then, and the rulers of the locofoco party having brought them about, we ask, is it not high time that they were dethroned, and good men put at the head of the affairs of State?" During their years out of power the Democrats had been bitter in their denunciation of the rather modest state debt incurred by the Whig administrations. Ironically, they now found themselves in the awkward position of having to defend large deficits and unpopular taxes.[46]

Unfortunately for the opposition, however, McRae was far from the ideal candidate to lead a crusade against the ruinous policies of the Democratic administration. McRae's decision to campaign as "a states-right democrat of the strictest school" and to support the national administration of James Buchanan limited his appeal among the Whig and American leaders. Although John W. Syme of the *Register* worked aggressively on his behalf, many of the other opposition papers remained neutral and refused to give him their editorial support. Instead of promoting McRae's cause, the endorsement of the *Register* probably gave credence to Democratic charges that the distribution candidate was nothing more than a stalking horse for the Whigs and Americans.[47]

Unable to secure the full support of the American Whigs or to make significant inroads into the Democratic vote, McRae lost the election by more than 16,000 votes. Ellis received over 58 percent of the vote, the largest percentage for a gubernatorial candidate since Dudley had vanquished Branch twenty years earlier. Yet even the Democrats acknowledged that Ellis's impressive showing could be attributed primarily "to McRae's weakness, and not to our strength as brought into the field." Despite his increased majority, Ellis received over 1,000 fewer votes than did Thomas Bragg in 1856—the first time since 1846 that a Democratic candidate for governor had failed to win as many votes as his predecessor. Although 80 percent of the electorate had participated in the previous state election, turnout in 1858 fell to 72 percent—the lowest percentage in a gubernatorial election since 1842. According to the Democratic editor of the *Elizabeth City Democratic Pioneer*, the result might have been quite different, "had the 'American' party been fully organized, and its strength concentrated upon one of its own party. As a body, they could not, and did not, vote for Mr. McRae. Had they done so . . . there is no telling what we might have experienced."[48]

The apathy among the opposition voters in the gubernatorial election also had its impact on the legislative elections (see figure 10.2 and figure 10.3). As in 1856, the Democrats won a majority of fifty-six seats. Despite their preponderance of legislative seats, party leaders had good reason to believe that the upcoming session would not be a harmonious one. Conservative easterners expected their party to oppose the passage of new internal-improvement projects that might add to the state debt. At the same time Democrats in the far west were again agitating for the removal of the section feature from the charter of the Western North Carolina Railroad. Both Ellis and Holden had vigorously supported a liberalization of the charter during the campaign, and the party's platform had also held out hope to the railroad's supporters.

The removal of the section feature would have involved no additional state assistance beyond the $4 million committed in 1854. But it would have enabled construction to proceed simultaneously along the entire length of the proposed route and would thus have entailed a much more rapid expenditure of state funds. Unfortunately for the railroad's proponents, a majority of the legislators were in no mood to sanction additional expenditures at a time when it was unclear whether the state would be able to pay for its existing works of improvement. The house of commons decisively voted down a bill to liberalize the charter that was introduced by Whig Tod R. Caldwell of Burke County. Another bill, sponsored by Democrat Stephen E. Williams of Caswell County, was subsequently defeated by an even greater majority.[49]

Although a majority of legislators in both parties had voted against the two measures, Democrats in the far west were quick to denounce their own party as the main obstacle to the western extension. According to Thomas Atkin of the *Asheville News*: "The short comings of the Legislature cannot be saddled on the opposition . . . because there is a Democratic majority of 52 [*sic*] in the body, and they have the power to do justice to the West, in spite of the factious opposition, and for a failure to do so, they will be held to a strict accountability." Another Democratic critic warned his fellow partisans that the action of the legislature had created "a fatal danger . . . to the ascendency of the Democratic party of North Carolina" and had "put a powerful weapon into the hands of our opponents, with which . . . they will cut our throats at the next State elections."[50]

The defeat of the western extension bill was particularly galling to the mountain Democrats because the general assembly accompanied it with yet another round of tax increases. At the beginning of the session, outgoing Governor Thomas Bragg had informed the legislators that the state debt had grown to almost $7 million and that the treasury would need more than $1 million in additional revenue over the next two years to meet its obligations. In response to Bragg's request, the general assembly passed a new revenue bill, which raised the land tax by 33 percent and the poll tax by 60 percent. As in the previous session, all but a handful of opposition legislators voted against the revenue bill. More ominous for the future of the Democratic party, half of the mountain Democrats in the house of commons also cast their votes against the measure (see table 10.5). Many western Democrats obviously agreed with Thomas Atkin that the people of the mountain counties should not "submit to additional taxation, after their claims have been spurned, and they treated with contempt."[51]

Opponents of the revenue bill were especially critical of the failure of the legislature to tax slave property according to its market value. The amended constitution of 1835 provided that all slaves between the ages of twelve and fifty and all free males between twenty-one and forty-five must be subject to a uniform poll tax. This provision allowed slaves under twelve and over fifty to escape taxation altogether. It also meant that any increase in the tax on slaves would have to be accompanied by an identical increase in the tax on whites. Until the mid-1850s there had been few complaints about the manner in which slave property was taxed. However, as the successive Democratic administrations drastically raised the rate of taxation in order to finance internal improvements, reformers began demanding that the constitution be amended so that slaves could be taxed ad valorem.

During the session of 1858–59, proponents of ad valorem could be found among legislators in both parties. However, the most conspicuous advocates of equal taxation were William W. Holden and his allies in the Wake County delegation. Early in the session Moses Bledsoe, the Democratic senator from Wake, introduced a series of resolutions endorsing the principle of ad valorem taxation and denouncing "any system of revenue, imposing upon any class of citizens or property, more than their equitable share of the burdens of government."[52] Similar resolutions were introduced into the house of commons by George H. Faribault, another Democrat from Wake County. Perhaps because Bledsoe and Faribault were Democrats and close political allies of Holden, the Whigs were initially reluctant to lend their support to the ad valorem resolutions. Early in January 1859 two-thirds of the opposition members in the house of commons joined a majority of the Democrats in voting to table the Faribault resolutions (see table 10.5). Later that month, however, William H. A. Speer, a Whig from Yadkin County, introduced a set of resolutions almost identical to the ones offered by Faribault. This time over four-fifths of the Whigs in the house of commons supported the ad valorem resolutions, whereas the proportion of Democrats voting in the affirmative dropped to 27 percent. Altogether, three-fourths of the Whigs and two-fifths of the Democrats voted for one or both of the ad valorem resolutions.

Although a large majority of Whigs and a substantial minority of Democrats were willing to endorse the abstract principle of ad valorem taxation, a much smaller number of legislators proved ready to support a constitutional amendment subjecting slave property to the same tax rate as real estate. Early in the session Bledsoe had introduced a bill into the senate providing that "all the colored inhabitants of this State shall be subject to such capitation or other tax as the General Assembly may impose."[53] Late in January, after a debate that occupied the attention of the upper house for more than a week, the senate rejected Bledsoe's amendment by a vote of thirty-one to ten. Most of the support for the amendment came from the Whigs. Indeed, aside from Bledsoe himself, only one other Democrat voted in favor of the amendment, while almost half the Whigs supported it.[54]

Despite the appearance of unanimity, one important element within the Democratic coalition dissented from the party's opposition to ad valorem. Both of the Democratic senators from the mountain district supported a bill introduced by Whig Ralph Gorrell of Guilford County, which provided for calling a constitutional convention in order to consider ad valorem taxation and other reforms.[55] In the house of commons, where the counties of the far west had a much larger number of legislative seats, the extent of support for ad valorem among mountain Democrats was even more evident. Early in February the lower house rejected an amendment introduced by Speer that was almost identical in language to the Bledsoe amendment. All but one of the Democrats from the coastal and piedmont counties voted against the Speer amendment, but eight of the nine mountain Democrats recorded their votes in its favor. About half of the Whigs also supported the bill, with most of the Whig opposition coming from the party's eastern delegation (see table 10.5).

If Holden and Bledsoe hoped that "equal taxation" would serve as a rallying cry for the Democrats in the same manner as "equal suffrage" had done a decade earlier, the legislative session of 1858–59 certainly blasted these hopes. Instead of uniting the party behind the banner of constitutional reform, the ad valorem issue divided the Democrats along sectional lines. Eastern and western Whigs also disagreed over the merits of ad valorem, but they were united in the belief that Democratic fiscal policy was unjust and discriminatory, and that some alternative source of revenue was necessary. Thus the Whigs had voted almost unanimously against the revenue bill in the general assembly. Mountain Democrats, on the other hand, were gradually becoming estranged from their party on a number of issues—the western extension, the revenue bill, and ad valorem taxation. Nor was the Democratic position in the eastern counties totally

Table 10.5 Vote in the House of Commons on Revenue Measures, 1858 (affirmative percentage by party and section)

	Whig/Americans				Democrats			
	Coast	Pied-mont	Moun-tains	Total	Coast	Pied-mont	Moun-tains	Total
Revenue bill	17	0	20	9	86	95	50	83
Faribault reso-lutions	9	46	50	32	24	41	80	38
Speer resolu-tions	64	93	100	83	24	20	50	27
Speer amend-ment	25	73	100	56	0	5	89	16

Sources: *Charlotte Western Democrat*, 8 February 1859; *HJ, 1858–59*, 263–64, 408–9, 529–30.

secure. Eastern Democrats certainly were not pleased by the steadily increasing taxes that seemed to accompany their party's accession to power. As the decade of the fifties drew to a close, the Democratic party in North Carolina was finding itself increasingly burdened by the responsibilities of power.

While Democratic spokesmen were either denouncing the conduct of their party in the general assembly or apologizing for it, the Whigs were looking toward the future with renewed optimism. Early in the session the opposition leaders had decided to dissociate themselves completely from the defunct American party and to revive the Whig organization. The legislators appointed an executive committee to meet in Raleigh in September 1859 in order to fix the time and place for a Whig state convention. Many leaders of the old Whig party, including former governor William A. Graham and former congressmen Alfred Dockery, Richard Spaight Donnell, and Kenneth Rayner, served as members of the committee.[56]

At the same time that the Whigs were organizing at the state level, party leaders were also preparing for the summer congressional elections. Early in March 1859 the *Edenton Express* issued a call for a Whig district convention at Gatesville to select a candidate to oppose Congressman Henry M. Shaw. During the spring and summer Whig conventions assembled in other counties and districts throughout the state, and by August there were Whig candidates in five of the eight congressional districts.[57] The outcome of the elections revealed that the Whigs had once again become a force to be reckoned with in North Carolina. Two years earlier the opposition party had captured only one of the eight congressional seats. In 1859 they won four of the five seats that they contested, defeating two Democratic incumbents in the process. According to the editor of the *Fayetteville Observer*, the elections provided conclusive evidence that "the corruptions and extravagance of the democracy are telling upon the public mind, not, perhaps, with the whirlwind force of 1840, but with such effect as to foreshadow a similar downfall of the corrupt party."[58]

As this remark indicates, the Whigs made a major issue of the allegedly extravagant expenditures and corrupt conduct of the Buchanan administration. These charges were extensively documented in a pamphlet entitled *What It Costs to Be Governed*, which the Whigs distributed widely not only in North Carolina but in Virginia and Tennessee as well.[59] There were many Democratic editors, however, who agreed with the *Democratic Pioneer* that "the 'high taxes,' as they are termed by the Opposition . . . have been principally instrumental in producing the disastrous result." The Democratic editor of the *New Bern Progress* criticized his party for its failure to convince the voters of the necessity for the steadily increasing state taxes. "The cry of taxation—high taxes—is a powerful argument on the stump," the editor acknowledged. "We care not what party is in power, if taxes are to be increased they will soon find that the people must be prepared for the change before it is made, or they will soon be out of power."[60]

The congressional elections suggested the potential effectiveness of the tax issue for the Whigs. Yet opposition leaders admitted that an increase in state revenue was necessary in order to finance the debt and to pay for new projects of internal improvement. If the tax burden was to be lowered, other sources of revenue would have to be found. As the state elections of 1860 approached, many Whigs, particularly in the west, demanded that their party come out unequivocally in support of ad valorem taxation. As one western Whig put it: "The friends of reform . . . must in the proposed [Whig state] Convention, take a *bold, determined, and unflinching* stand in behalf of that reform. It must be distinctly understood, that the incorporation of reform policy into any platform of principles, is a *sine qua non*, if the friends of this policy are expected to aid in any canvass."[61]

While western Whigs were demanding that ad valorem be incorporated into the party platform, eastern Whigs remained distinctly cool toward the idea. During the legislative session of 1858–59 a majority of easterners in the party had voted against the reform bills offered by the various proponents of ad valorem. Yet eastern Whigs were not oblivious to the potential popularity of the issue among the nonslaveholders who comprised a majority of their constituents. Indeed, even some of the Democrats reluctantly acknowledged the widespread appeal of the "equal taxation" issue. While personally against ad valorem, the editor of the *New Bern Progress* admitted that he "should not like to oppose it before the people of Craven [County] as a candidate for their suffrages. The masses who were urged to support free suffrage as conferring additional privileges on them will not be able to understand readily how they should oppose an extension of the principle in the adoption of *ad valorem* taxation."[62]

The Whig state convention, which met in Raleigh on 22 February 1860, was the largest such gathering in the party's history. Leading Whigs like George E. Badger, William A. Graham, and Charles Manly, who had been absent from politics since the demise of the national party, played an active role in the proceedings of the convention. Lavish praise for Henry Clay and "our old Whig flag" filled the convention hall, and prominent party leaders like Badger proudly informed their listeners that "I have always been a Whig, a national Whig, a Clay Whig, and my conscience has never smote me for acting under its flag." The platform adopted by the convention condemned the extravagance of the Democrats, denounced their efforts to control elections through the corrupting power of patronage, and decried their attempts to place "unusual and dangerous powers in the hands of the executive." Perhaps in deference to their allies in other states, who were organizing for the presidential election under the banner of the Constitutional Union party, the old-line Whigs in North Carolina officially adopted the name "Opposition party" instead of opting for the cognomen "Whig." Yet, unlike the Americans, who had self-consciously played down their connections with Whiggery, the Opposition party in 1860 warmly embraced the principles of that party and proudly boasted of its Whig pedigree.[63]

Indeed, the Opposition platform of 1860 bore a striking resemblance to the ones that Whig gubernatorial candidates had stood upon during the party's heyday in the forties. After articulating the principles of orthodox Whiggery, however, the platform went on to resolve that "whereas great inequality exists in the present mode of taxation . . . we recommend a Convention of the people of the State . . . for the purpose of so modifying the Constitution that every species of property may be taxed according to its value." In order to conciliate the party's eastern wing, which was still lukewarm toward the idea of ad valorem, the convention nominated John Pool, a popular legislator from the Albemarle region, as its candidate for governor. This was the first time that a resident of the extreme east had been chosen to carry the Whig standard.[64]

The Democrats, meanwhile, were experiencing more serious divisions over the ad valorem issue. During the session of 1858–59, most Democrats from the far west had eagerly embraced the idea, while party members from the eastern counties had been almost uniformly hostile. Unlike most easterners, however, William W. Holden and his allies in the Raleigh Democratic organization had taken a leading role in promoting ad valorem. Holden's interest in tax reform continued after the adjournment of the general assembly. In October 1859 Frank I. Wilson, the associate editor of the *Standard*, and Quentin Busbee, another Holden ally, were the driving force behind the formation of the Wake County Working-Men's Association, an organization devoted exclusively to the reformation of the revenue laws. Although Holden did not take an active part in the activities of the association, he served as a publisher for its addresses and proceedings, and he defended the organization against charges by other Democratic presses that it was fomenting class divisions and weakening the institution of slavery.[65]

While personally sympathetic to ad valorem, Holden recognized that a majority of leading Democrats opposed the idea, and he urged his party not to make it a formal issue in the state campaign. The editor advocated a strategy of ignoring divisive state issues like tax reform and concentrating, instead, on the threat presented by the Republican party in the North. "No party in this or in any other State . . . has ever been a unit on State affairs," the editor reminded his readers shortly after the Democratic state convention. "The black Republican pressure upon us from without will grow stronger and stronger, leaving us no time to dispute about State issues among our-selves. . . . Shall we divide here at home on State issues, and thus incur defeat at the hands of our enemies?" Despite Holden's efforts to focus the campaign on cohesive national issues, the Democratic state convention confronted the taxation issue head-on by adopting a plat-form denouncing ad valorem as "premature, impolitic, dangerous, and unjust."[66]

In his speech accepting his party's nomination, Governor Ellis introduced an argument against ad valorem that the Democrats would make repeatedly throughout the campaign. In deference to the sensibilities of the party's eastern wing, the Whigs had refrained from using the word "slaves" in their ad valorem plank and instead had advocated that "every species of property" be taxed according to its value. Ellis cleverly twisted the meaning of this phrase and cited it as evidence that the Whigs favored a lowering of taxes on luxury items and an imposition of new levies on previously untaxed items such as farming tools, household furniture, crops, and livestock. According to Ellis, such a "rigid, unbending and uniform rule of *ad valorems* [would] . . . send the tax-gatherer into every house, with inquisitorial powers, exacting with a relentless hand, a tax upon every species of property great and small . . . making no discrimination between nec-essaries and luxuries—those things that are essential to the support of life and such as lead to vice and idleness."[67]

The Whigs denied that ad valorem would increase the tax burden of the poor. They pointed out that the state constitution already gave the legislature the power to tax all kinds of property, except slaves, at value. The Whigs claimed that they were not advocating new objects of taxation but were merely proposing "the right to equalize taxation between lands and negroes." Despite the Whig denials, the Demo-crats continued to insist that their opponents planned to lay a tax on "every thing from a tract of land to a tin cup." By the end of the campaign the Whigs acknowledged that their party had made a se-rious mistake in not simply calling for the taxation of slaves to the same degree as land.[68]

In the counties of the far west, the issue of internal improve-ments played as important a role in the election as did the question of tax reform. Governor Ellis had a well-deserved reputation as a sup-porter of western development, and two years earlier he had cam-paigned aggressively for the removal of the section feature from the charter of the western railroad. With considerable justification the Democrats portrayed Ellis as one who "has always stood by Western interests and uniformly voted for Western appropriations." Pool's record on internal improvements was more spotty. Although not an adamant opponent of state-supported railroads, Pool had voted in the general assembly of 1856–57 against the removal of the section feature—an action that did nothing to endear him to the people of the far west.[69]

Ellis and other proimprovement Democrats used the same tactics against Pool that Dockery and the Whigs had employed against Thomas Bragg six years earlier. The governor characterized his opponent as "a gentleman who has voted against every Railroad . . . now in course of construction, and who never voted for, talked for, or worked for, any Railroad that ever has been built in North Carolina, or in my opinion, that ever will be built." As evidence of Pool's opposition to railroads, the Democrats circulated a letter written by J. Parker Jordan, who had run unsuccessfully for the state senate against Pool in 1856. According to Jordan, Pool had "declared time and again on the stump that he would never support, if elected, any measure which in its nature would benefit the mountain region of this State."[70]

On 2 August 1860 almost 113,000 North Carolinians went to the polls to cast their votes for governor. More than four-fifths of the eligible voters participated in the election—a proportion that previously had been exceeded only during the "log cabin campaign" of 1840. Pool's total fell about 6,000 short of Ellis's, but he received more votes than any Whig gubernatorial candidate had ever won before. The Whig gains in the legislative elections were even more impressive. In 1858 the Democrats had enjoyed a comfortable majority of fifty-six seats on joint ballot. In 1860 their majority was reduced to twenty (see figure 10.2 and figure 10.3).[71]

According to William W. Holden, the outcome of the election of 1860, with the Democrats winning 52.8 percent of the votes, "probably exhibits the strength of parties more accurately than any that has occurred since 1850."[72] Compared to their dismal showing in the state elections of 1856 and 1858, when the Democrats had won 56.2 and 58.5 percent of the vote, the opposition gains in 1860 were nothing short of astounding. However, a comparison of the vote in the governor's election of 1860 with the vote in 1850 reveals that the

Democrats were actually in a somewhat stronger position at the end of the decade than they had been at its beginning when they won only 51.6 percent of the vote. Similarly, the Democrats controlled the general assembly in 1860 by a slightly larger margin than they had enjoyed in 1850 (see figure 10.4).

After reaching a peak in 1856, however, Democratic strength had been steadily subsiding in all sections of the state. Indeed, by 1860 the Democratic percentage of the vote in many coastal and piedmont counties had dropped below the party's percentage in the 1850 governor's election (see map 4). On the other hand, their proportion of the vote in the mountain counties was eleven percentage points above their showing a decade earlier (see figure 10.1). Just as the mountain region had been the key to the successive string of Whig victories during the 1840s, so too it was a major factor behind the Democratic successes of the 1850s. As the editor of the *Greensboro Patriot* put it: "It was the large majorities which used to roll down from the mountains, that enabled the Whigs to carry the State so triumphantly in 40, 42, 44, and 46, and it was not until this section of the State became estranged from the Whig party, that democracy gained the ascendant."[73]

By 1860, however, there were ominous signs that another political revolution was brewing in the mountain region. The Democratic administrations of the 1850s had proven little more successful in satisfying the improvement demands of the far west than had the Whig regimes of the 1840s. Although the Western North Carolina Railroad had been chartered with a generous infusion of state aid, the Democratic general assembly had repeatedly refused to expedite construction by removing the section feature, despite the entreaties of Ellis, Holden, and other friends of western development. At the same time the legislature had steadily increased the tax on land and polls, while refusing to tax the slaves of the eastern planters according to their market value.

The ad valorem campaign of 1860 also put the mountain Democrats on the defensive. Pool's record of hostility to the western railroad and his ambiguous record on tax reform undoubtedly limited the Whig gains in the governor's election. Still, Pool won 1,600 more votes in the mountain region than Gilmer had received in 1856, whereas Ellis garnered 200 fewer votes than Bragg had won four years earlier. In the legislative elections, the signs of a shift in the balance

Map 4   Change in the Democratic Vote, 1850–60

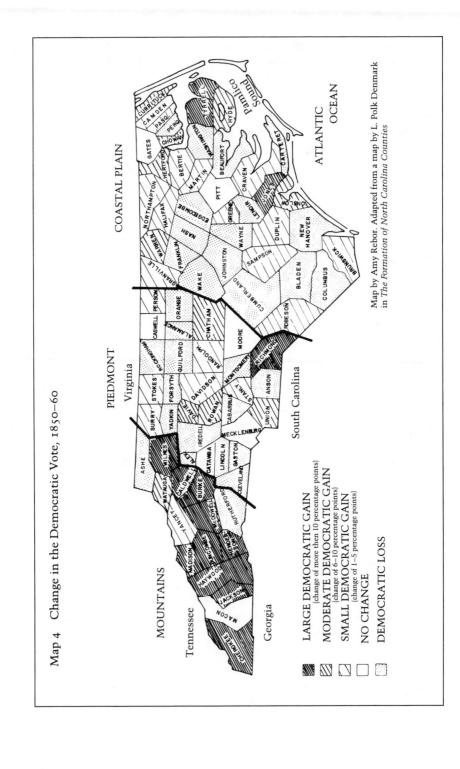

Map by Amy Rebor. Adapted from a map by L. Polk Denmark
in *The Formation of North Carolina Counties*

LARGE DEMOCRATIC GAIN
(change of more then 10 percentage points)

MODERATE DEMOCRATIC GAIN
(change of 6–10 percentage points)

SMALL DEMOCRATIC GAIN
(change of 1–5 percentage points)

NO CHANGE

DEMOCRATIC LOSS

of parties were even more ominous. In 1858 the Democrats had controlled twelve of the seventeen seats in the mountain delegation to the house of commons. In 1860 they lost eight of these seats and gained only one that had previously been held by the Whigs.[74]

As the decade of the 1850s drew to a close, the party system in the Old North State remained highly competitive, and the parties themselves were once again almost evenly balanced. The vitality of the party system on the eve of the Civil War can be attributed in large part to the predominance of state issues in the partisan debate. Throughout the latter half of the 1850s opposition leaders in North Carolina took the Democrats to task for plunging the state deeply into debt and for adopting revenue measures that discriminated against ordinary taxpayers in favor of the wealthy. Internal improvements also played an important role in state elections during the late 1850s, despite the lack of intraparty consensus on this issue. Overall, the Democrats probably exploited the improvements issue more effectively than their opponents. In the eastern counties the Democrats continued to portray themselves as the enemies of the spending policies traditionally favored by their opponents. In the west, on the other hand, party leaders took full credit for the improvement measures enacted by the general assembly and argued that their standard-bearers were better improvement men than the candidates put forward by the opposition.

Partisan divisions over state issues were also reflected in the alignment of votes in the North Carolina General Assembly. Legislators from the two parties divided over banking policy in 1856, over the revenue bills in 1856 and 1858, and—to a somewhat lesser extent—over ad valorem taxation in 1858. As in previous years, both legislative parties were internally divided over the issue of state support for internal improvements. As late as 1856, however, Whig and American legislators were considerably more sympathetic to improvement measures than were the Democrats.

State issues thus played an important role in shaping the contours of the partisan debate in North Carolina during the late 1850s. This interpretation of party politics conflicts sharply with the "consensus" interpretation that has been propounded in several recent studies of the second American party system. One historian, for example, has argued that, "by 1855, North Carolina's parties had helped shape a consensus on issues ranging from social and economic policy making to constitutional revision. . . . Most of the outstanding issues had been settled. . . . [and] the interparty differences of the mid-1840s became the interparty consensus of the mid-1850s."[75] Whatever its validity for other states, the consensus interpretation distorts the character of party politics in the Old North State during the late 1850s. North Carolina elections were not placid affairs devoid of conflict over substantive state issues, nor were the sessions of the general assembly consentaneous love feasts, where legislators deliberated state policy within a framework of mutual agreement about important state issues.

Partisan conflict over state issues was not the only factor contributing to the vitality of the party system during the late 1850s. The long-standing sectional divisions between eastern and western North Carolina also kept the system competitive by making the Democratic majority a precarious one. Once they were confronted with the responsibilities of governing, the Democratic party found it increasingly difficult to adopt policies that would satisfy both its eastern and western wings. By the end of the decade this intraparty conflict had resulted in a significant erosion of voter support in all sections of the state. The Democrats managed to retain their majority status until the start of the Civil War, but they never occupied the commanding position that the Democrats had assumed in many southern states by the late 1850s.

For their part, the Whigs in North Carolina were justifiably optimistic about the prospects ahead. Despite their failure to capture either the governorship or the general assembly in 1860, the party had made impressive gains and the momentum seemed to be shifting in their direction. The editor of the *Iredell Express* claimed that the state elections of 1860 had "brought the foe within shooting distance," and he confidently predicted victory in 1862.[76] During the summer of 1860, as party leaders turned their attention from state politics to the upcoming presidential election, few could have foreseen that the crisis of the Union would soon create a new set of issues that would prove even more effective in driving the Democrats from power.

11 ✦ The Politics of Union: North Carolina and the "Irrepressible Conflict"

The Democracy themselves, are constantly keeping the slavery question "in the ring." Whenever they are in danger of losing office, the South is in danger of losing *cuffee.—Raleigh Register*, 11 April 1860

The Democracy are now engaged in playing the old game of crying out that the Union is in peril.—*Raleigh Register*, 30 March 1859

As elsewhere throughout the South, the issues of slavery, southern rights, and Union played an important role in shaping the style and substance of the political debate in North Carolina. One scholar has accurately pointed out that both parties in the Old North State "were pro-slavery to the core. Each longed to win the distinction of being the better slaveholder's party."[1] Ironically, this broad consensus did not prevent politicians from exploiting slavery-related issues for partisan advantage. Each party tried to associate the other with abolitionism and to persuade the electorate that it alone was capable of protecting slavery and defending southern rights.

Like most southerners, the majority of North Carolinians hoped to preserve the institution of slavery within the Union. Until 1860 no prominent member of either North Carolina party was prepared to advocate a policy of disunion. And just as Democrats and Whigs both attempted to exploit the slavery issue for partisan advantage, each party also tried at various times between 1836 and 1860 to wrap itself in the mantle of the Union and to convince the voters that the leaders of the opposition were reckless demagogues whose policies would destroy God's best hope for mankind. During the 1830s it was the Democrats who exploited the Union issue most effectively. The debate over the Compromise of 1850 marked a turning point, however, as the Whigs co-opted the Union issue and the Democrats adopted the mantle of southern rights. By 1861 most Democratic leaders in the Old North State were prepared to follow the lower South out of the Union.

When organized parties emerged during the early 1830s, slavery already played an integral role in the economy and society of North Carolina. In 1830 slaves comprised about one-third of the population, a proportion that would change very little during the next three decades. About two-thirds of the slaves lived in the coastal plain, where they made up almost 45 percent of the population. On the other hand, less than 4 percent lived in the mountain counties, and they comprised only 10 percent of the population in that region. In the piedmont there were large concentrations of slaves in several counties bordering Virginia and South Carolina, but in the remainder of the region the proportion of slaves was only slightly higher than in the mountain counties.[2]

Historians of North Carolina's antebellum parties have frequently claimed that the dichotomy between eastern plantation counties and western small-farm counties was also reflected in political divisions between Democrats and Whigs. According to one scholar: "The strong slaveholding counties were [generally] Democratic, while the Whig strongholds were confined primarily to the counties where the slave population was relatively small. The average Whig, therefore, was less interested in the maintenance of the institution than the average Democrat."[3] Despite its superficial plausibility, this interpretation exaggerates the extent to which the slaveholding counties identified with the Democratic party, and it underestimates the importance of slavery in the small-farm regions of the west.

Certainly there is some evidence to support the traditional view that the Democrats were strongest in the counties with the greatest number of slaves. Throughout the antebellum period the Democrats polled commanding majorities in most of the plantation counties in the middle east and along the Virginia border in the piedmont. Overall, the proportion of the Democratic vote in the eastern counties ranged from a low of 54 percent in the gubernatorial election of 1840 to a high of 62 percent in 1856. These figures also reveal, however, that the Whigs comprised a substantial minority in the slaveholding east. Indeed, in the Albemarle Sound region and in many of the counties that had earlier been dominated by the Federalists, the Whigs were consistently in the majority. Without the support of its eastern wing, the Whig party would never have been a formidable contender in North Carolina politics.[4]

The traditional argument that the Whigs were the dominant party in most of the small-farm counties of the west is substantially correct, at least for the period prior to 1856. In the gubernatorial election of 1850, for example, the Whigs carried twenty-two of the thirty-three counties where the white population was equal to or greater than the statewide average. By the mid-1850s, however, the strength of the Democratic party had increased substantially in many of the low-slaveholding counties of the far west. Thus, in the governor's election of 1856 the Democrats polled majorities in twenty-four of the forty counties where the white population was greater than the statewide average.[5]

Even in those counties where slaves constituted a relatively small proportion of the population, the institution had a political impact far greater than the numbers themselves might suggest. Although the vast majority of families in the piedmont and mountain regions did not own slaves, many of the political elite were slaveholders and had, therefore, a vested interest in the protection and perpetuation of slavery. Western legislators repeatedly made the point that their devotion to the South's peculiar institution was second to no one's. According to one group of westerners, the number of slaves residing within each of the two sections was less important than the number of slaveholders. "Hence it is in Western North Carolina we are more interested in the preservation of slave property; because, although we may have fewer slaves, we have more *slave owners*; and, of course, a greater number of persons to watch over any aggressions upon it." The fact that western slave owners had fewer holdings than their eastern counterparts in no way diminished their determination to protect their property from outside interference.[6]

Recent studies of politics in the antebellum South have emphasized the extent to which ordinary voters, as well as the slaveholding elite, had a stake in the preservation of slavery. Although the majority of southerners lacked a tangible economic interest in slavery, the idea of a free, biracial society was a concept totally beyond their understanding. The subordination of the black race was viewed as a necessary prerequisite to the maintenance of racial purity and equality among the white race, and white southerners unquestioningly assumed that slavery was the only viable means of racial control. In the minds of most southerners, the alternative to slavery was racial chaos, and any effort to challenge the legitimacy of the institution was beyond the bounds of permissible discussion. As one group of North Carolina legislators put it: "Upon the subject of the Abolition of Slavery we have but one opinion, and will not permit ourselves to entertain or debate it; and any effort to provoke discussion will be instantly met with the most decisive reprobation."[7]

Antebellum North Carolinians may have accepted slavery as an indisputable fact of southern life, but they also venerated the Union as the source of their liberty, prosperity, and happiness. "In North Carolina, I know of but one feeling, a feeling of the deepest horror, at the very thought of a dissolution of the Union," one Tarheel politician wrote Senator Willie P. Mangum in the midst of the nullification controversy. When South Carolina threatened the stability of the Union by nullifying the tariff, political leaders throughout the Old North State organized public meetings to proclaim their devotion to the "blessed Union" and to affirm their belief that "any act or circumstance calculated to dissolve or even to impair that Union would be the greatest of all calamities." North Carolinians applauded Andrew Jackson for his forthright defense of the Union, even though some of them chided him for his eagerness to coerce the nullifiers.[8]

Most North Carolinians assumed that slavery could be protected and southern rights preserved within the framework of the Union. Until the secession crisis both parties asserted that the values of Union and southern rights were mutually compatible. Yet, in their efforts to direct popular sentiment into partisan channels and to stake out opposing positions on all the important issues of the day, the leaders of the two parties frequently differed over which of these two values they chose to emphasize. During the early years of the second party system it was the Whigs who seized upon the issue of southern rights and the Democrats who most often tried to portray themselves as the defenders of the Union.

In 1836 southern Whigs enjoyed the luxury of running a presidential candidate who was not on the ballot in any of the northern states. Party leaders could thus tailor their campaign to an exclusively southern constituency. North Carolina Whigs lauded their own candidate, Hugh Lawson White, as a man "who is identified with us in interest," while denouncing his opponent, Martin Van Buren, as "a

Northern man in soul, in principle and in action, with no one feeling of sympathy or of interest for the South."9 While the Whigs were' appealing to the sectional prejudices of the North Carolina voters, the Democrats attacked their opponents for "laboring . . . to create a feeling of hostility against the North among the people of the South." The party's official address quickly passed over economic issues like the Bank of the United States and focused instead on the dangers of mixing slavery with party politics. If pursued to its logical culmination, the Democrats warned, such a course would result in the creation of two sectional parties and, ultimately, the destruction of the Union. Party leaders urged the voters to resist the sectional blandishments of the opposition by showing them "that your love of country is not confined to any section but extends to all the United States."10

Although North Carolina Democrats had lost the state elections just three months earlier, they won the presidential election of 1836 by a comfortable majority. Whether the Democratic victory represented a triumph of the politics of Union over the politics of slavery is a question that cannot be answered definitively. During the campaign the Democrats had practiced their own version of the politics of slavery by denouncing William Henry Harrison, the candidate of the northern Whigs, for his alleged antislavery views and by portraying White as nothing more than a stalking horse for Harrison. At the very least the election of 1836 revealed that political success did not invariably go to the party taking the most militant prosouthern stance.

Four years later both parties resurrected all the charges against Van Buren and Harrison that had been made during the previous campaign. Noticeably absent from the campaign of 1840 was the broad unionist appeal that had characterized the rhetoric of the Democrats four years earlier. Instead, the Democrats vied with the Whigs in trying to prove that their party was sounder on the issue of southern rights. The substitution of Harrison for White as the Whig standard-bearer and the unwillingness of the Democrats to alienate the nullifiers who had recently followed Calhoun into their party undoubtedly dictated this change in strategy. Whether the Democrats erred in abandoning the unionist strategy that had served them so well during the previous campaign is another one of those questions that historians can only speculate upon. It seems unlikely, however, that any Democratic strategy could have prevented the Whig landslide in 1840. The election was not a referendum on southern rights or the

Union but rather on the condition of the economy, and a majority of North Carolina voters accepted the Whig argument that the economic policies of the Jackson and Van Buren administrations were responsible for the financial panic of 1837 and the depression that followed.[11]

During the campaign of 1844 the issues of southern rights and Union again played an important role in the party debate. Following the lead of President Tyler and Secretary of State Calhoun, the Democrats argued that the acquisition of Texas was a matter of vital interest to the South. According to the Democrats, an independent Texas dominated by Britain would certainly abolish slavery, and an abolitionized Texas would just as assuredly present a threat to the institution in the American Southwest. North Carolina Whigs, on the other hand, took their cue from Henry Clay's "Raleigh letter," in which the Whig presidential candidate spoke out against the immediate annexation of Texas on the grounds that it would involve the nation in a war with Mexico and would endanger the integrity of the Union. The Whigs did not rule out the eventual acquisition of Texas, but they warned that premature annexation would lead to a breach between the North and the South and a dissolution of the Union.[12]

The Whigs denounced the Democrats for their apparent unconcern about this threat, and even accused them of conspiring with South Carolina disunionists in a deliberate attempt to force the South out of the Union. Despite their enthusiasm for immediate annexation, the Democrats took pains to rebut the Whig accusation that the demand for Texas was a disunionist plot. Thus William W. Holden retorted that he would prefer to see "Texas . . . smitten by the hand of Providence into a barren and neglected desert" than to countenance any policy that would lead to the destruction of the Union. While denying that annexation posed a threat to the Union, the Democratic central committee made its priorities quite clear to the voters: "The UNION AND TEXAS—TEXAS AND THE UNION—but . . . the Union, TEXAS OR NO TEXAS."[13]

Despite the supercharged rhetoric, there is little evidence that the issues of Texas, slavery, and disunion had a significant impact on the 1844 state or national elections in North Carolina. Instead, the high correlation between the popular vote for president in 1844 and the vote for governor two years earlier suggests that Tarheel voters loyally supported their respective parties, regardless of their own opinions about the propriety of annexation. Certainly neither party attributed the Whig victory in North Carolina to the Texas issue.[14]

The decisive American victory over Mexico in 1848 and the acquisition of a vast expanse of territory in the Southwest added a new dimension to the politics of slavery. The introduction of the Wilmot Proviso, which prohibited the entrance of slaves into any territory that might be obtained from Mexico, sparked a bitter controversy between the North and the South over the status of slavery in the territories. Before the Compromise of 1850 put a temporary end to the controversy, many southern leaders, particularly in the Deep South, had expressed their opinion that disunion would be preferable to continuance in a Union that stigmatized them and their way of life. As David M. Potter cogently observed, "the idea of secession as a possible recourse first won widespread acceptance in the South during the prolonged deadlock of 1846–1850."[15]

It is unclear whether ordinary North Carolinians ever accepted the notion that the issue of slavery in the territories was a matter of vital concern to them. Astute political observers like William H. Haywood, Jr., and Asa Biggs privately expressed their doubts. In May 1849 Haywood told Martin Van Buren that "there is less sensibility in the South about the question than her politicians pretend there is. . . . I have no doubt myself that the People care very little (if let alone) whether Slavery goes to California or not." Biggs went even further, suggesting to President Polk that the majority of North Carolinians actually opposed the expansion of slavery. "*Even* in eastern North Carolina," said Biggs, "a large vote could now be obtained for the Proviso, if the movement were headed by *one* influential man."[16]

Of course, no influential politician in the state chose to endorse the restriction of slavery in the territories. Instead, both parties tried to capitalize on the issue by denouncing their opponents as "Wilmot Provisoists." The Whigs probably got the better of the exchange, especially after the Democratic national convention nominated Lewis Cass for the presidency in June 1848. According to the Whigs, Cass's residence in "the hot-bed of abolitionism in the Northwest" made him an unreliable defender of slavery. "We may say most unequivocally," declared the editor of the *Register*, "that Lewis Cass . . . is *against the South, and with the Abolition factionalists of the North,* on the great question of slavery." In his well-publicized "Nicholson letter," Cass had affirmed the right of the territories to decide for themselves about the status of slavery. But the Whigs dismissed Cass's doctrine of "popular sovereignty" as nothing more than empty campaign rhetoric. "When the hour of trial comes," the *Register* predicted, "he will desert the South, and join league with the Abolitionists and Anti-Slavery Provisoists of the North!"[17]

While southern Democrats pinned their hopes for success on a policy statement that could be construed in different ways in each section, the Whigs sidestepped the territorial issue and rallied behind a presidential candidate who was at once a military hero, a southerner, and a slaveholder—Zachary Taylor. For the first time since 1836 a northern Democrat opposed a southern Whig in a presidential election. And once again the Whigs affirmed that their candidate's southernism was sufficient in itself to make him a more trustworthy defender of slavery than his northern opponent. According to the editor of the *Register*, it was "safer to trust Gen. Taylor, a Southern man and a Slaveholder, than Gen. Cass, who, until he felt he might possibly need the help of Southern voters, was an acknowledged opponent of their institutions."[18]

Taylor carried the Old North State by a majority of 8,500 votes, and the Democrats were quick to attribute the result to their opponents' exploitation of the sectional issue. Shortly after the election, Holden told his readers that "it is with pain that we confess the mortifying fact, that in this State we have lost hundreds of votes, solely on the ground that Gen. Cass was a Northern and Gen. Taylor a Southern man! . . . This . . . is one of the main causes of our defeat in the State." Certainly there was some truth in this assessment. Cass received almost 6,500 fewer votes than David S. Reid had won three months earlier in the governor's election, and 3,000 fewer votes than Polk had garnered in the previous presidential election. Taylor, on the other hand, polled only 500 more votes than Henry Clay had four years earlier. Democratic indifference toward Cass seems to have been the primary factor behind the impressive Whig showing in 1848.[19]

The election of Taylor did nothing to resolve the fundamental differences between the North and the South over the issue of slavery in the territories. Instead, the territorial issue dominated the deliberations of the second session of the Thirtieth Congress, which convened a month after the presidential election. In the face of northern efforts to exclude slavery from the territories and to outlaw the slave trade in the District of Columbia, John C. Calhoun tried to unify southerners of all political persuasions in defense of southern rights. Calhoun's plan was to issue a militant proslavery address listing his section's grievances and calling for a southern convention. The convention would then present an ultimatum to the North. Calhoun's efforts foundered on the rocks of partisanship. In North Carolina, as elsewhere throughout the South, the Whigs were adamantly opposed to Calhoun's strategy, and the Democrats themselves were unable to present a united front. The eight Whigs in the North Carolina congressional delegation boycotted the southern caucus and refused to sign the southern address. Moreover, only one of the state's Democratic congressmen attended the meeting, although two of its three Democratic members eventually signed the address.[20]

The southern address received little notice in the political meetings that assembled throughout the state during the spring of 1849 to choose candidates for Congress. In at least two districts, however, the Democrats did make the protection of southern rights a major campaign issue. The Whigs, for their part, reaffirmed their own devotion to the constitutional rights of the South. The outcome of the elections suggest that most North Carolinians did not perceive any significant difference between the two parties over this issue. The Whigs carried all six of the districts that they had won in 1847, while the Democrats were successful in only three districts. It is difficult to disagree with the assessment that "the result was determined by the strength of the two parties and not by the attitude of the candidates on the issues of slavery and disunion."[21]

Until late in 1849 southern Whigs had been confident that the Taylor administration would propose an acceptable solution to the problem of slavery in the territories. Instead, Taylor's plan to confer immediate statehood on California and New Mexico incurred the opposition not only of the southern Democrats but of many southern Whigs as well.[22] In the face of Taylor's intransigence, southern Whigs in Congress came forward with their own answer to the sectional crisis. In January 1850 Henry Clay introduced a series of resolutions designed to serve as the basis for a comprehensive settlement of all the points at issue between the two sections. Clay's resolutions provided for (1) the admission of California into the Union as a free state; (2) the organization of the remainder of the Mexican Cession into territories without restrictions on slavery; (3) the cession by Texas of most of the disputed border territory to New Mexico in return for federal assumption of its outstanding debts; (4) the passage of a more effective fugitive slave law; and (5) the abolition of the slave trade (but not slavery) in the District of Columbia.[23]

An analysis of the speeches and votes by the North Carolina delegation to the Thirty-first Congress reveals the extent to which Clay's compromise proposals became a source of interparty conflict in the Old North State. The two North Carolina Democrats who formally addressed the House of Representatives—Abraham Venable and John R. J. Daniel—announced their opposition to the very idea of compromise. In their view the North was the sole aggressor. As the injured party, the South could compromise nothing but its honor and its rights. Despairing of the possibility of protecting southern rights within the Union, the two congressmen spoke frequently about the possibility and even desirability of disunion. According to Venable: "Attachment to the Union is now but little more than a sentiment . . . rapidly yielding to another sentiment . . . a determination to redress our wrongs, whatever may be the consequence. . . . We are rapidly approaching the conviction, that in feeling and in interest we are not one people." The congressman stopped short of advocating immediate secession, but he did not hesitate to express his belief that "disunion is better than emancipation."[24]

The two Whigs who addressed the House of Representatives took opposing positions on the compromise issue. Like Venable and Daniel, Edward Stanly represented a district that was an integral part of the plantation region of North Carolina. In 1850 slaves comprised over two-fifths of its population, a proportion considerably above the average for the state as a whole. Three of its counties ranked among the top four North Carolina counties in average farm value. Thomas L. Clingman, on the other hand, came from the district with the smallest proportion of slaves in North Carolina. The plantation system was nonexistent in the mountain region, only one in ten families held black property, and large slaveholders were rare.[25] Logically, one might have expected Stanly to be one of "the most ultra-Southern of the North Carolina delegation" and Clingman to be "the most liberal member . . . from North Carolina," the member most "lightly attached to the institution of slavery."[26] Instead, it was Stanly who counseled for conciliation and moderation on the floor of the House of Representatives and Clingman who took an "ultra-Southern" position.

Indeed, Clingman's speech consisted of a blistering attack on northern politicians and newspaper editors who, he claimed, had poisoned the minds of northerners against the South and its institutions. After arguing at length that the South would be better off economically outside the Union, Clingman demanded that a fair share of the territories be allotted to his section. "We do not love you, people of the North, well enough to become your *slaves*. . . . Do us justice, and we continue to stand with you; attempt to trample on us, and we part company."[27]

Stanly, on the other hand, denied Clingman's contention that most northerners were fundamentally hostile to southern institutions. While denouncing northern fanatics for their meddlesome insults to southern sensibilities, Stanly reserved most of his fire for the southern Democrats, who, he claimed, were cynically exploiting the slavery issue "to build up the party whom the people hurled from power in November, 1848." Although he acknowledged that the South had legitimate grievances, Stanly did not believe that they were of sufficient magnitude to justify disunion. "This Union cannot be, shall not be destroyed," he proclaimed. "Those whom God hath joined together, no man or set of men can put asunder."[28]

Although the five other members of the North Carolina delegation in the House of Representatives did not express their opinions in formal speeches, the general attitude of the delegation toward the compromise proposals can be ascertained by their votes on the various bills that came before the House in September 1850 (see table 11.1). They voted unanimously in favor of the fugitive slave bill and the organization of the territory of Utah, and, except for Stanly, they all opposed the bill to abolish the slave trade in the District of Columbia. All three North Carolina Democrats and four of the Whigs voted against the California statehood bill, while Stanly and Joseph P. Caldwell supported the measure. On the organization of New Mexico and the boundary settlement with Texas (combined as one bill in the House), the North Carolina delegation divided along party lines. The Democrats unanimously opposed the bill; the Whigs, except for Clingman, solidly supported it.

In one sense the alignment of votes seems to indicate that the similarities in outlook among North Carolina's congressmen out-

Table 11.1 Vote of the North Carolina Delegation on Clay's Compromise Measures

District	Congressman	Slave percent-age in district	Texas/ New Mexico	Cali-fornia	Utah	Fugi-tive slave law	Abolish slave trade
First	Clingman (W)	14.2	N	N	NV	Y	N
Second	Caldwell (W)	17.8	Y	Y	Y	Y	N
Third	Deberry (W)	32.3	Y	N	Y	Y	N
Fourth	Shepperd (W)	19.0	Y	N	Y	Y	NV
Fifth	Venable (D)	39.2	N	N	NV	Y	N
Sixth	Daniel (D)	46.0	N	N	Y	Y	NV
Seventh	Ashe (D)	40.0	N[a]	N	Y	Y	N
Eighth	Stanly (W)	41.0	Y	Y	Y	Y	Y[b]
Ninth	Outlaw (W)	45.0	Y	N	Y	Y	N

[a]Ashe did not vote on the New Mexico bill when it came before the House on 6 September 1850. However, on 9 September he asked the consent of the House to record his vote in the negative.

[b]Stanly did not vote on the restriction of the slave trade, but he was paired with a congressman who opposed the measure.

Sources: Roll-call votes from Holman Hamilton, *Prologue to Conflict*, appendix C. The percentage of slaves in each congressional district was calculated from data in J. D. B. De Bow, *Statistical View of the United States* (Washington, D.C., 1854), 278–89. For congressional districts, see David L. Corbitt, "Congressional Districts of North Carolina, 1789–1934," *NCHR* 12 (1935): 173–88.

weighed their differences, since a majority of members in both parties favored the fugitive slave and Utah bills and opposed the California and slave trade bills. On the other hand, an argument can be made that the passage of the Texas–New Mexico bill—the first of Clay's proposals to be voted on by the House—was the key to the success of the entire compromise package. Had the extremists in the North and South succeeded in defeating that measure, southern moderates like Stanly and Caldwell probably would not have voted for California statehood. In that case California would have been admitted to the Union by a purely sectional vote, New Mexico would have remained unorganized, and the situation on the Texas border would have continued to be explosive. Such a state of affairs would have strengthened the hand of the radicals in the South and might have dealt a fatal blow to the chances for a peaceful resolution of the sectional conflict.

No one can predict with certainty how North Carolina's congressmen would have voted had they been forced to accept or reject the compromise as a single package. Undoubtedly the Democrats would have found Clay's compromise distasteful under any circumstances. There is reason to believe, however, that the desire of the Whigs for a peaceful adjustment of the sectional differences would, on balance, have outweighed their misgivings about California statehood and the abolition of the slave trade in the District of Columbia. Certainly, a majority of the Whig presses in North Carolina supported the compromise and rejoiced after its passage by Congress, while Democratic newspapers like the *Raleigh Standard* opposed the key compromise proposals and regarded their passage as a defeat for the South. This difference in perspective was aptly summarized by William W. Holden in 1851: "A large portion of the Democratic party . . . regarded these measures as aggressive and unjust; but [after their passage] they announced it at once as their purpose to acquiesce in these measures for the sake of the Union. . . . The Whigs, on the contrary, gave their sanction to these measures and declared them in their opinion, to be just, fair, and worthy of general approbation."[29]

The acrimonious debate over Clay's compromise proposals had thus put the North Carolina Democratic party firmly in the southern-rights camp. As recently as 1848, the Whigs had managed to outmaneuver the opposition on this issue by capitalizing on the southernism of Zachary Taylor. The controversy over the compromise offered the Democrats an opportunity to reaffirm their commitment to southern rights and to create an image of their opponents as cowardly submissionists who were willing to sacrifice the interests of their own section in the name of compromise and moderation. Democratic leaders could thus regard the outcome of the controversy of 1849–50 as a strategic victory for their party, despite their tactical defeat on the compromise itself. According to Holden, the debate over the status of slavery in the territories had strengthened the Democratic party in North Carolina because "we have gained and will gain, in the long run, by our Southern Rights, or rather *State's* Rights position, which grew out of it."[30]

The controversy over the Compromise of 1850 also signaled the conversion of Thomas L. Clingman to the cause of southern rights—an event that would have dire consequences for the Whig party in North Carolina. By his vigorous denunciations of northern aggression and his demand for immediate satisfaction of southern grievances as the price for continuance in the Union, Clingman had clearly placed himself on the Democratic side of the southern-rights issue and had commenced an odyssey that would lead him into the Democratic party. Clingman owned no slaves himself, and the vast majority of his constituents were also nonslaveholders. Contemporary observers and historians alike have debated the motives behind Clingman's astounding metamorphosis from a moderate Whig to a radical southern-rights Democrat. Some have argued that Clingman's long-standing desire for a seat in the U.S. Senate was the main factor behind his political transformation. As one Whig editor put it: "His particular ambition is to be elected to the Senate of the U. States by the aid of the Democratic party. . . . [This desire] furnishes a ready clue to the intricacies of his present position." According to this interpretation, Clingman's Whig constituents in the mountain district supported him in spite of, rather than because of, his position on southern rights.[31]

Other historians have attributed Clingman's alienation from the Whig party to his dissatisfaction with the outspoken antislavery views of the northern Whigs. After it became apparent to him that the northern wing of the party was committed to the Wilmot Proviso and to the abolition of slavery in the District of Columbia, Clingman found his allegiance to the Whig party increasingly difficult to reconcile with his loyalty to the South. According to this interpretation, Clingman never doubted that his "strong prosouth message [would] strike . . . a responsive chord among North Carolina's mountain electorate." Although few voters in the far west owned slaves themselves, the residents of this region were as "sensitized to the threat of northern interference and aggression" as were voters in other parts of the state. By adroitly linking the issue of southern rights in the nation with the movement for western rights in his home state, Clingman successfully cultivated the image of a crusader battling against the "abuses inflicted on his constituents from government powers in both Raleigh and Washington."[32]

A substantial number of voters in the mountain district were receptive to Clingman's southern-rights message. Although a majority of his support after 1850 probably came from Democrats, a considerable number of mountain Whigs remained loyal to Clingman throughout the 1850s. It is unlikely that these Whigs would have continued to vote for Clingman if his position on southern rights had been repugnant to them. Mountain Whigs were not indifferent to the defense of southern rights, but their attitudes do not explain why Clingman felt obliged to take a more radical position than did eastern Whigs—like Edward Stanly—who had a more tangible interest in protecting slavery against northern aggression. It is unlikely that Clingman's abrupt change in course was dictated by constituent pressure. Nor is it probable that his defection to the Democrats was primarily a result of his disillusionment at the behavior of northern Whigs. Even in the plantation counties of the east, the vast majority of North Carolina Whigs considered the northern Democrats to be even more unreliable defenders of slavery than the northern Whigs, and they regarded the southern Democrats as irresponsible agitators whose ambition for office had brought the nation to the brink of disunion. It seems likely, therefore, that Clingman's contemporaries were correct in their assessment that political expediency was the main factor behind his conversion to the cause of southern rights.

The congressional elections of 1851 offered both parties an opportunity to test the political effectiveness of their respective positions on the Compromise of 1850. The Democratic candidates roundly denounced the compromise measures as a surrender of southern rights in the territories and warned that further aggressions on the part of the North would inevitably drive the South to resistance. While defending the right of an aggrieved state to secede from the Union, the Democrats denied that they favored the immediate exercise of that right. Instead, they claimed that the best way to preserve the Union was to elect leaders who were determined to maintain the rights of the South. A victory for the Whigs, on the other hand, would serve to encourage northern aggression because the antislavery forces would interpret it as evidence that the people of North Carolina were willing to submit tamely to any violation of their rights.[33]

At the same time that the Democrats were characterizing their opponents as submissionists, the Whigs were portraying themselves as the defenders of the Union and were accusing their rivals of secretly plotting its destruction. According to the Whigs, North Carolina had every reason to be satisfied with the present condition of affairs. The Wilmot Proviso had been decisively rejected and a more effective fugitive slave law had been enacted. "In short," claimed the editor of the *Register*, "we have a new lease on slavery, and that species of property is more secure than it has been for twenty-five years, if there can only be a subsidence of agitation and an acquiescence in the measures of Compromise!" Yet the Democrats were recklessly agitating the slavery question, exaggerating the wrongs inflicted upon the South, and openly advocating the doctrine of state secession. The inevitable effect of this agitation, the Whigs predicted, would be "to exasperate the people, and to alienate their attachment to the Union."[34]

The Whigs were especially optimistic about their prospects in the mountain district. Although Clingman was nominally still a Whig, his factional enemies were confident that his outspoken defense of southern rights and his thinly veiled threats of secession had made him extremely vulnerable to a challenge by a strong unionist Whig. The candidate of the anti-Clingman Whigs was Burgess S. Gaither, a former speaker of the state senate. Gaither enjoyed the support of the influential *Raleigh Register*, as well as the endorsement of western newspapers like the *Carolina Watchman* and the *Highland Messenger*.[35] Throughout the campaign Gaither vigorously assailed Clingman's votes against the compromise measures and repeatedly accused his opponent of being a secessionist. Although Clingman remained firm in his opposition to the compromise, Gaither's persistent questioning of his opponent's unionism forced the congressman to retreat from the violent rhetoric he had uttered on the floor of Congress and to deny being an advocate of the right of secession. Indeed, according to one anti-Clingman Whig, Clingman even claimed to be "a stronger Union man than Gaither."[36]

Despite the incumbent's belated efforts to wrap himself in the mantle of the Union, about half the Whigs voted for Gaither. But a solid Democratic vote, combined with a substantial proportion of the Whig vote, enabled Clingman to carry his district by a margin of two to one. After the election, the editor of the *Register* attributed Clingman's success to his clever manipulation of the Union issue. "Had our friends been able to make the issue [of Union] in this District . . . there would have been no doubt . . . of Col Gaither's election. [But] Clingman . . . has invariably denied that he was an advocate of the right of *secession*!"[37]

While the Whigs had considered Clingman to be the most vulnerable anticompromise incumbent, the Democrats were particularly sanguine about their chances of capturing Edward Stanly's district. Two years earlier Stanly had carried his district by a majority of only forty-seven votes; and there was every reason for the Democrats to believe that his vote in favor of the admission of California and his acknowledged opposition to the slave trade in the District of Columbia would alienate enough voters to turn the tide in their favor.[38] Thomas Ruffin, the Democratic candidate, attacked Stanly's votes on the compromise and described its provisions as "a series of acts more or less aggressive upon the rights of the South." Holden enthusiastically joined the attack, characterizing the Whig incumbent as "an apologist for Northern aggression." If Stanly were reelected, said Holden, the result would be regarded in the North as "a triumph of Freesoilism in the midst of a slaveholding people." To the delight of the Democrats, Stanly made no apologies for his behavior during the previous session of Congress. He described his controversial vote on California statehood as "one of the proudest acts of his life," and he refused to recant his statement that slavery was a necessary evil rather than a blessing. The congressman denied that a state had a constitutional right to secede from the Union, and he forthrightly expressed his belief in the power of the federal government to coerce a seceding state into submission. According to the Democrats, Stanly even promised to "send a fleet to South Carolina, if she seceded."[39]

If ever there was a southern politician vulnerable to the politics of slavery, that politician was Edward Stanly. Yet, to the surprise of the Democrats and probably many Whigs as well, the voters of the eighth district returned the embattled incumbent to Congress by an increased majority. The secret of Stanly's success lay in his unswerving unionism. Throughout the campaign he had wrapped himself in the mantle of the Union and had denounced Ruffin as "an avowed, open, and strong secessionist." By rejecting the politics of slavery and appealing instead to the unionist sensibilities of his constituents, Stanly succeeded in retaining the support of the Whig voters of his district. After the election, the congressman characterized his victory as "much greater than a mere party triumph. It is a victory of the friends of the Union. It has proved that the people of this district condemn those who advocate even the 'abstract right of secession.'"[40]

Despite the heated debates over the Compromise of 1850, the political complexion of the North Carolina congressional delegation in 1851 remained exactly as it had been two years earlier. The Whigs captured six districts, including Clingman's, while the Democrats won only three. According to the editor of the *Raleigh Star*, the outcome could be attributed primarily "to the strength of the Whig party, and not to the state of public opinion on any collateral question growing out of the contest between the North and the South. . . . Though the issues of *Union or disunion, secession or anti-secession*, were raised and urged with great vehemence in the campaign, it could not have been a test vote on either." On the other hand, the editor of the *Register* announced that the results of the election offered proof that "North Carolina stands by the Compromise and the Union."[41]

Both of these interpretations were substantially correct. Despite the claims by the Democrats that Clay's compromise measures constituted a betrayal of southern rights, voters in the Whig plantation districts joined their fellow Whigs in the small-farm counties in returning the supporters of compromise to Congress. By the same token, the three districts controlled by the Democrats also reelected their incumbents, despite efforts by the Whigs to make an issue of their votes against the compromise. In this respect, party loyalty proved to be the controlling force affecting the outcome of the election. At the same time, however, it is unlikely that the Whigs could have maintained their standing among the voters had not their appeals to unionism and their defense of the compromise struck a responsive chord among their constituents. In this sense the congressional elections of 1851 represented a triumph of the politics of Union over the politics of slavery.

The results of the elections convinced the Democrats of the futility of campaigning against the Compromise of 1850. It also drove home the danger of taking too advanced a position on the southern-rights issue. In their state and national platforms of 1852 the Democrats affirmed their willingness to abide by the compromise as a final settlement of the sectional differences. With the two parties in agreement about the finality of the compromise, the presidential election in North Carolina revolved around the timeworn question of which of the two candidates held the sounder views on slavery.[42]

Winfield Scott, the Whig presidential candidate, was not popular among many of the leaders in the North Carolina party. He was suspected of being under the control of William H. Seward and other northern antislavery Whigs, and his reluctance to endorse the compromise served only to reinforce these suspicions. The Democrats did everything in their power to capitalize upon this disaffection, warning that "a vote for Scott in '52 is a vote for Seward in '56." Democratic hopes for a victory in the presidential election were also bolstered by the defection of Clingman, who publicly endorsed Franklin Pierce one month before the election.[43]

On the other hand, Pierce was hardly the ideal candidate to galvanize the North Carolina electorate. Despite the efforts of his party to depict the New Hampshire congressman as a northern man with southern principles, Pierce was roundly and repeatedly denounced by the Whigs as a Free-Soiler. The Whig case against Pierce was aptly summarized by a correspondent of the *Register*, who characterized the Democratic candidate as a man "steeped and baptised in fanatical abolitionism—a regular preacher of the Higher Law, who hates Southern institutions." Compared to Pierce, said the correspondent, the Whig candidate "is absolutely invulnerable. . . . Scott is emphatically the Southern candidate, and as such will be sustained by the Southern people."[44]

Pierce managed to edge Scott in North Carolina by about 700 votes—the first time since 1836 that a Democratic presidential candidate had carried the state. The most salient feature of the election of 1852, however, was the dramatic decline in the Democratic vote during the short interval between the August state elections and the November presidential election. Although Scott received 4,000 fewer votes than John Kerr, the Whig candidate for governor, Pierce polled almost 9,000 fewer votes than the victorious Governor Reid. The disparity between the outcome of the two elections reveals that state issues had a greater impact on the declining fortunes of the Whig party in North Carolina during the early 1850s than did issues relating to slavery and southern rights.[45]

Undoubtedly most Whig leaders in North Carolina would have preferred Millard Fillmore as their presidential standard-bearer in 1852. Yet, ironically, the Whigs fared much better in 1852 with the unpopular Scott than they did four years later, when Fillmore headed the opposition ticket as the candidate of the American party. Democrat James Buchanan carried the Old North State handily in 1856, winning 8,500 more votes than Pierce had received in 1852. At the same time Fillmore won 2,000 fewer votes than Scott. The success of the Democrats in the presidential election of 1856 was due mainly to their ability to convince a majority of the voters that they were the party better able to preserve the Union.[46]

The rise of the avowedly antisouthern Republican party added a new and ominous dimension to the presidential campaign of 1856 in North Carolina. The leaders of both parties agreed that the election of John C. Frémont would be a blow to southern institutions and a threat to the Union. Instead of crusading on the southern-rights issue, however, the Democrats waged their campaign on the premise that Buchanan was the only truly national candidate. Fillmore had no chance of winning more than a handful of electoral votes, they argued, because most of the northern Whig vote would inevitably go to Frémont. According to Holden, the outcome of the election would determine "whether the Union shall be perpetuated . . . [or] snapped asunder." A vote for Fillmore would merely dissipate the strength of the unionists, whereas a large vote for Buchanan would ensure the defeat of the Republicans and the preservation of the Union.[47]

This argument received important support from some old-line Whigs like Daniel M. Barringer and James Osborne, who publicly endorsed Buchanan on the grounds that the Democrats were now the only truly national party.[48] For their part, the supporters of Fillmore denied that their candidate had no chance of winning, denounced Buchanan as the candidate of the southern extremists, and argued that "the Fillmore and Donelson ticket is the only ticket for the lovers of the Union to rally upon." After the election, however, opposition leaders acknowledged that thousands of voters "who honestly preferred Mr. Fillmore to all others, were . . . frightened from his support and induced to go for Mr. Buchanan" because of "the cry that 'Fillmore stood no chance!'"[49]

The Democrats could rejoice that their candidate had been victorious both in North Carolina and in the nation, but their enthusiasm was dampened by the realization that Frémont had outpolled Buchanan in most of the northern states. Nor were the opposition leaders, who earlier had boasted of Fillmore's strength among the conservative elements in the North, overjoyed to learn about their candidate's poor showing in the Whig constituencies north of the Mason-Dixon line. Although Edward J. Hale of the *Fayetteville Observer* could find "much consolation in the defeat of the purely sectional candidate," he was not optimistic about the future. The power of the antislavery forces "has increased too rapidly during the last four years to justify a hope of its decrease during the next four," said Hale. "It is a revolution that will not go backwards. . . . The election of Buchanan will be but a postponement for four years of the sectional triumph. Already are they marshalling their forces . . . for the campaign of 1860."[50]

As the presidential election of 1860 approached and the prospect of a Republican victory loomed nearer, the leaders of the North Carolina parties presented the voters with two contrasting plans of action. Urging moderation and forbearance, the Whigs argued that the rights of the South "can be better effected within the Union than by its destruction." The party also put itself on record as opposing secession, even if a Republican should be elected. "We do not acquiesce," said the Whigs, "in the necessity for a dissolution of the Union as a remedy for grievances now existing, or that in our belief are likely to occur." Rallying behind the candidacy of John Bell and the banner of the Constitutional Union party, the Whigs denounced John C. Breckinridge, the presidential candidate of the southern Democrats, as a tool of the disunionists. "Whether Breckinridge may or may not be a Disunionist," one widely circulated Whig pamphlet warned the voters, "it is certain that every vote for him will HELP THE CAUSE OF DISUNION, and EVERY DISUNIONIST IN NORTH CAROLINA OR ELSEWHERE IS WARMLY SUPPORTING HIM."[51]

The Democrats affirmed their belief that "the people of this State will resist aggression upon their Constitutional rights whenever the emergency arises." Unlike the Whigs, the party failed to reassure the voters that a Republican victory would not be grounds for disunion. At the same time, however, the Democrats carefully refrained from making any public statements that would give credence to the charge that a vote for Breckinridge was a vote for disunion. Although a promise to take drastic action in the event of Lincoln's election might well have fired up the radical prosouthern elements within the party, it might also have driven more moderate Democrats to vote for Stephen A. Douglas, whose supporters were running a separate electoral ticket in North Carolina. From the viewpoint of the Democratic leadership, it seemed the better strategy to wait until after the election to discuss the proper course of action should the Republicans be victorious.[52]

The election of 1860 resulted in a narrow victory for the Breckinridge ticket in North Carolina. The Democratic candidate polled 50.5 percent of the statewide vote, compared to 46.7 percent for Bell and

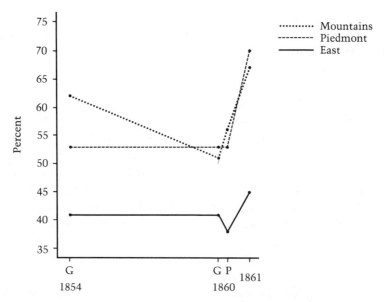

Figure 11.1 Whig/Unionist Percentage of the Vote in North Carolina Elections, 1854–61. *Sources:* County voting returns in Thomas E. Jeffrey, "The Second Party System in North Carolina," appendix A; and W. Dean Burnham, *Presidential Ballots,* pp. 646–68. For the Union vote in 1861 see note 74.

only 2.8 percent for Douglas. In general, the distribution of votes was along traditional party lines. Breckinridge carried forty-two of the forty-seven counties that had given majorities to Governor Ellis in the August state elections, whereas Bell won thirty-six of the thirty-nine counties in which Pool had polled a majority. On the other hand, the issues of Union and southern rights did have some impact on the results. In the mountain counties, where pro-Union sentiment was strong, the percentage of the anti-Democratic vote increased from 51 percent in the gubernatorial election to 56 percent in the presidential contest. In the plantation-oriented east, however, the opposition vote dropped from 41 percent to 38 percent (see figure 11.1).[53]

Once they became convinced that South Carolina and the other cotton states would leave the Union, Democratic leaders in North Carolina moved quickly to prepare the people of their own state for secession. In his message to the general assembly on 20 November 1860, Governor Ellis expressed his opinion that "hostility to African slavery is deeply fixed in the minds of the northern people" and that "there exists but little ground upon which to rest a hope that our rights will be secured to us by the general government administered at their hands." Ellis recommended that the legislature appoint delegates to consult with the other southern states and that a state convention be called to consider North Carolina's relationship to the Union. The governor stopped short of openly advocating disunion, but secessionists within his party applauded him for his "patriotic and bold stand."[54]

Democrats like Ellis were determined to take North Carolina out of the Union before the hysteria and confusion surrounding Lincoln's election had a chance to subside. "No time is to be lost," one secessionist counseled the governor in November. "We must throw ourselves upon the tide which is *now* in our favor, and strike at once for a Southern Confederacy."[55] One of the first priorities of the radicals was to establish a newspaper in Raleigh that would advocate the cause of secession. In late November they selected John Spelman, an editor from Ellis's home town of Salisbury, to edit a new organ called the *State Journal*. In constant communication with the radicals in South Carolina, Governor Ellis coordinated the distribution and circulation of secessionist propaganda. The radicals also adopted the strategy of organizing public meetings to create the impression of a grass-roots movement on behalf of state action. During late November and early December secession meetings were held in at least twenty-five North Carolina counties.[56]

Considering their relatively moderate position during the presidential campaign, it is remarkable how quickly Ellis and the other leaders of the North Carolina Democratic party rallied behind the secession banner in the first weeks after Lincoln's election. Opponents of radical action accused the Democrats of having intentionally deceived the voters by preaching moderation while, at the same time, plotting disunion.[57] The possibility that party leaders deliberately concealed their real intentions in order to win unionist Democrats over to the Breckinridge ticket in 1860 is an explanation that cannot be conclusively ruled out.

It is not necessary, however, to condemn the Democrats as hypocrites in order to explain their behavior. Until November neither the election of Lincoln nor the secession of the cotton states was a foregone conclusion. During the campaign southern Democrats could honestly believe that a strong showing for Breckinridge was the best means of preventing a crisis of the Union. If Breckinridge carried the South and Lincoln failed to sweep the North, the election would go into the House of Representatives, where Breckinridge might have a chance for success. Certainly the Democrats had nothing to gain by calling attention to the fact that, under certain circumstances, they might favor disunion.[58]

Once it became apparent that South Carolina and the rest of the lower South would form a separate confederacy, Democratic leaders in the Old North State found themselves in a quite different situation. For years these leaders had controlled the federal government because of the dominant position of the South within the national Democratic party. Now they faced the prospect of being consigned to a permanent minority, not only within the Union but also within the Democratic party itself. For ambitious politicians inured to holding the reins of power, the future must have looked grim indeed. On the other hand, if North Carolina joined a southern confederacy, these Democratic leaders could continue to play a dominant role in government and to enjoy the perquisites of power. With some justification the opponents of secession remarked that "the lust for office under new forms has much to do in exciting and pushing forward the disunion movement."[59]

The Whigs viewed the political landscape from a much different perspective. Unlike the Democrats, they had long been accustomed to living under a national government controlled by their political enemies. Moreover, they were well aware that the leaders of the Republican party, as well as most of its rank and file, had been Whigs until the upheavals of the mid-1850s had broken up that party. Although they might deplore the antisouthernism of the Republican party, at least some North Carolina Whigs envisioned the possibility of establishing a new party composed of southern Whigs and conservative northern Republicans—a party in which they might become a dominant element. On the other hand, the Whig leaders had no hope of exercising a controlling influence in shaping the policies of a southern confederacy that was certain to be dominated by their Democratic enemies.[60]

One scholar has argued recently that, throughout the South, the Democratic party was the indispensable vehicle for effecting secession during the winter of 1860–61. Through their control of the party organization and their appeals to the partisan loyalties of their constituents, the secessionists, in effect, delivered the Democratic electorate into the disunion camp.[61] The evidence for North Carolina lends strong support to this argument. In the elections to the state convention in February 1861, secessionist candidates won majorities in most of the counties carried by Breckinridge, including some counties where slaves comprised only a small proportion of the population. At times the unionists begrudgingly acknowledged the power of the Democratic organization. Shortly before the convention election, a unionist in Burke predicted that the people in his small-farm county would give a large antisecession vote "if they were permitted to go to the polls and vote their own sentiments without interference on the part of leaders." Unfortunately, he added, "we have . . . many active, unscrupulous, men amongst the democratic leaders, who are all secessionists, and who will resort to any means, no matter how base, to carry their point." Because of the strength of the Democratic organization in Burke, the secessionist candidate was elected to the convention.[62]

If the Democratic party was the driving force behind the secession impulse in North Carolina, the strength of the Whig organization proved to be the main bulwark against disunion. Despite the defection of a few local leaders, especially in the counties along the South Carolina border, the majority of Whig leaders campaigned actively against secession. Although there is no reason to question the sincerity of their devotion to the Union, it is unlikely that the Whigs were oblivious to the political implications of the Union issue. Since the 1830s both North Carolina parties had attempted at various times to win votes by wrapping themselves in the mantle of the Union. In the recent presidential campaign the Whigs had repeatedly accused their opponents of being secessionists, and the behavior of Ellis and the other Democratic leaders in the weeks immediately after the election seemed to confirm these accusations. From the viewpoint of the Whigs, an aggressive appeal to the unionist sensibilities of the North Carolina electorate offered a promising road to a political comeback. There was more than a grain of truth in the *Western Democrat*'s observation that the opposition was trying "to get into office by huzzaing for the Union."[63]

Although Whig leaders like George E. Badger, John M. Morehead, William A. Graham, Zebulon B. Vance, and Jonathan Worth all played active roles in promoting the cause of unionism in North

Carolina, they received important editorial support from an unlikely Democratic ally. For almost twenty years, William W. Holden had been one of the strongest proponents of southern rights in the state. Time and again he had criticized the Whigs for tamely submitting to northern aggression, while extolling his own party for its devotion to southern rights. Holden seemed the logical person to lead the secession movement in North Carolina. Yet, as the majority of Democratic leaders moved toward disunion in the weeks following the presidential election, Holden set his course in exactly the opposite direction.

Historians have often speculated about the factors behind Holden's sudden conversion to unionism in 1860. His disappointment at his failure to win high political office, his growing belief that the people of North Carolina were opposed to secession, and his hostility toward the "slaveholding oligarchy" that supposedly controlled the Democratic party have all been offered as possible explanations for his behavior.[64] A survey of the evidence suggests, however, that the principal factor behind Holden's dramatic political turnabout was his steadfast commitment to the idea of party organization.

Throughout his career as editor of the *Raleigh Standard*, Holden vigorously extolled the virtues of organization, regularity, and party discipline. In Holden's view, it was the duty of every Democrat to support the regular nominee of the party, regardless of his own personal preference. Those who refused to do so were "disorganizers" who justly deserved to be consigned to political oblivion. "Let us insist from the outset on the most rigid organization," Holden proclaimed in 1858. "Let the Democratic people on all occasions compel aspirants for office to subordinate their own wishes and their own hopes to a wholesome and unbending party organization; for . . . if any favor is shown to self seekers and disorganizers, we may expect defeat—and what is more to be deplored, we will deserve it."[65]

Unlike John C. Calhoun, William L. Yancey, and other militant proponents of southern rights, Holden did not view parties as obstacles in the path of a united South. Indeed, for Holden, the preservation of the rights of the South depended on the maintenance of a national Democratic organization. The quadrennial national convention served as the means of ensuring harmony among the party's northern and southern wings, and it was the duty of every Democrat to rally behind the nominee and platform of his party. If the Democrats were to serve as the institutional bulwark against abolitionism, it was also important that the party adopt a platform upon which both northerners and southerners could stand. As one of North Carolina's delegates to the Democratic national convention in 1860, Holden stubbornly resisted efforts by Yancey and other radicals to commit the party to the support of a congressional slave code for the territories. Nor was the editor prepared to bolt the convention should Stephen A. Douglas win the nomination. Although he had assailed Douglas bitterly in 1858 for opposing the admission of Kansas as a slave state, Holden was quite willing to campaign for the Little Giant or, indeed, for any other candidate that the party might nominate. "It is worse than idle," he said, "to go into Conventions, to participate in their deliberations, and then refuse to support the nominees."[66]

Committed as he was to the doctrine of party regularity, Holden had nothing but scorn for the delegates from the lower South who bolted the Charleston convention in April. He believed that Yancey and other radicals had deliberately sought to break up the national party organization because it stood in the way of their disunion plans.[67] While denouncing Yancey and the other bolters, Holden praised those southerners who, like himself, had remained in the convention "and thus preserved the party from utter disorganization."[68] When the national convention reassembled in Baltimore and the delegates from the South again walked out, he was one of the few southerners to remain. Holden did not vote for Douglas in the convention, but after its adjournment he announced his editorial support for "the regular nominee of the national Democracy" in preference to the "irregular ticket" of Breckinridge and Lane. "We now stand," he told his readers, "upon our rights—upon regularity, upon organization and nationality."[69]

Democratic presses throughout North Carolina denounced Holden's decision to remain in the Baltimore convention and to defend its nominee. By standing firmly behind his party's national organization, Holden found himself, ironically, at odds with his own state organization. Moreover, by promoting a separate Douglas ticket against the wishes of a majority of Democratic leaders in his state, the editor had, in effect, become a "disorganizer" himself. In view of his long-standing belief in the importance of party regularity, Holden could not have felt completely comfortable in his endorsement of Douglas. After it became apparent that North Carolina's Democratic electors intended to support the Breckinridge ticket, he reluctantly went along with his party and unsuccessfully tried to prevent the formation of a separate Douglas ticket.[70]

Despite Holden's belated support for Breckinridge, Governor Ellis and the other Democratic leaders never forgave him for his refusal to join the seceders at Baltimore or for his lukewarm support for their ticket thereafter. When the general assembly convened three weeks after the presidential election, the Democratic caucus voted to punish Holden by depriving him of his lucrative position as public printer. The loss of the printership signaled the end of Holden's influence within the party, and it provided the formal occasion for his break with the Democratic leadership. The editor denounced the caucus decision as evidence that control of the party had been "usurped by ambitious and designing men, who . . . will commit this State to revolution, anarchy, and civil war." In the weeks that followed, Holden lashed out continuously against Ellis and the "disunion clique" with a fury that he had previously reserved for the Whigs. At the same time he denied that he had gone over to the opposition. "So far from wishing to put the Democratic party down," said Holden, "we are laboring to preserve it *by keeping it clear of the taint of disunion.*" Although Holden forswore any intention of abandoning his party, his adamant opposition to Ellis and the other secessionist Democrats drove him inexorably into the opposition camp.[71]

As elsewhere in the South, the secessionists in North Carolina hoped to accomplish their goal through the agency of a state convention. Ellis recommended such a convention in his November message to the legislature, and on 12 December 1860 a joint committee on federal relations submitted a bill providing for the election of delegates. The Democrats controlled a majority of legislative seats, but a state convention required the approval of two-thirds of the entire membership. This meant that a substantial amount of Whig support would be necessary in order to secure passage of the convention bill. The Democrats found some unexpected allies in a group of western Whigs who hoped to secure a convention in order to effect ad valorem taxation and other reforms in the state constitution. Some Whigs also hoped that a state convention under their control might take some action to reconcile the estranged states of the lower South. Proconvention Whigs insisted, however, that any action taken by the convention should be submitted to the people for approval. The bill that finally passed the legislature on 29 January 1861 went even further by stipulating that the electorate should have an opportunity to vote for or against a convention at the same time that they were electing delegates. The convention bill passed the house of commons by a vote of eighty-six to twenty-seven, with the support of all the Democrats and about half the Whigs.[72]

On 28 February 1861 the people of North Carolina voted against the proposed state convention by a margin of 47,338 to 46,671. Although the majority against the convention was razor thin, the voters decisively rejected secession by electing an overwhelming number of unionist delegates. Estimates differed, but Holden's tally of eighty-three unionists and thirty-seven secessionists was probably not far from the mark. The secessionists did best in those counties that the Democrats had carried in 1860. Indeed, all but five of the thirty-three counties electing secessionist delegates had given majorities to Breckinridge three months earlier. On the other hand, many North Carolina Democrats rejected secession in 1861. Unionist candidates won majorities in nineteen Breckinridge counties, as well as in thirty-six Bell counties. Overall, the convention election constituted a dramatic rebuke to secession and to the Democratic leadership who championed the cause of disunion.[73]

To what extent was the outcome of the election affected by the traditional animosity between the plantation-oriented east and the small-farm west? An analysis of the geographical distribution of the vote for convention delegates confirms the commonsense notion that unionist sentiment was considerably more prevalent in the western counties than in the slaveholding east, a majority of whose voters endorsed secession (see figure 11.1).[74] However, a comparison of the convention vote in 1861 with the gubernatorial and presidential vote in 1860 reveals that even in the east the unionist vote was substantially larger than the Whig vote. This suggests that the number of eastern Whigs who defected to the secessionists was considerably smaller than the number of eastern Democrats who sided with the Union. The surge in the unionist vote in the piedmont and mountain regions was even more impressive. Except in a few counties near the South Carolina border, the unionists prevailed everywhere in the west. Sectionalism seems to have been a factor contributing to the size of the unionist victory in western North Carolina, but it did not help the secessionists appreciably in the east.[75]

The strength of unionism in North Carolina and the other states of the upper South stands in sharp contrast to the overwhelming force of the secessionist impulse in the lower South. Several recent studies of antebellum politics have attributed this dichotomy to the persistence of two-party competition in the upper South and the absence of interparty conflict in the lower South. According to this argument, the voters in states like North Carolina "had learned that, although a party may be out of power, with effort it could regain power; so for them Lincoln's election was but a temporary setback, something that could be rectified four years hence. In states of the lower South without party systems, the people could see nothing but Republican victories in the foreseeable future. Nothing in their immediate experience suggested that the Republicans might be driven from power at some future date." The persistence of partisanship thus instilled a popular faith in the efficacy of traditional party politics to resolve the sectional crisis, whereas the absence of partisanship paved the way for popular acquiescence in more radical solutions.[76]

Despite its superficial plausibility, there are some serious problems with this interpretation. Some states simply do not fit the model. For example, Louisiana, which had a strong two-party system until the end of the antebellum era, opted—like all the other states of the Deep South—for secession. On the other hand, Arkansas, which never had a competitive party system, followed the pattern of the rest of the upper South by voting against disunion. One might argue, therefore, that the states in the lower South reacted in the same way toward Lincoln's election regardless of the degree of interparty competition within them, and so did the states in the upper South.

Equally important in the case of North Carolina, a faith in the effectiveness of the traditional party system was not shared by Whigs and Democrats in equal numbers. Less than 5 percent of the North Carolina Whigs voted against the Union in 1861, compared to almost 70 percent of the Democrats. It was not the persistence of partisan competition in itself, but rather the strength of the Whig organization that accounts for the triumph of unionism in North Carolina in 1861.[77]

On the other hand, a sizable minority of Democrats did desert their party to join forces with the Whigs against secession. As the congressional elections of 1861 approached, a fundamental realignment of parties seemed to be in the making. On 22 March delegates from twenty-five counties assembled in Goldsboro to form a Southern Rights party. In attendance were three of the state's Democratic congressmen, as well as numerous other party luminaries. At the same time the unionists were taking steps to perfect their own organization. Astute observers like William W. Holden sensed that the end of an era was approaching. On 13 April the editor remarked that "Democratic principles and Whig principles will always exist, but the parties that were once organized on those principles have perished. . . . Two new parties have since been formed—one . . . being for disunion, and the latter opposed to it. The issue, therefore, *now* is *Union* or *Disunion*."[78]

Whether the unionist coalition of 1860–61 would have been any more enduring than the Union parties that sprang up in several states of the Deep South during the crisis of 1850–51 is a question that can never be answered conclusively. In Alabama, Georgia, and Mississippi the Union parties of the early 1850s splintered into their original discordant elements almost as soon as the crisis had ended. A decade later, however, the crisis of the Union was not resolved peacefully. Indeed, on the same day that Holden proclaimed the advent of a new party system in the Old North State, the federal garrison at Fort Sumter surrendered to the army of the Confederate States of America. Two days later, on 15 April 1861, Secretary of War Simon Cameron cabled Governor Ellis requesting troops to put down the rebellion.[79] Finally confronted with the reality of civil war, unionists and southern-rights men alike opted to side with the other states of the South and to resist the northern invaders. On 20 May 1861 a convention met in Raleigh and unanimously voted to sever North Carolina's connection with the Union.

But even as the people of North Carolina girded for war, the animosities between the original secessionists and the erstwhile unionists continued to linger beneath the surface. By the summer of 1861 unionists were already voicing their displeasure at the "proscriptive, unscrupulous & corrupt policy of the dominant party" and were predicting that "when the people begin to *feel* the evils which await us," they would overthrow the party that had brought the South to the edge of the abyss.[80] The day of reckoning was not long in coming. In 1862 a coalition of Whigs and unionist Democrats, under the banner of the newly organized Conservative party, soundly defeated the secessionists in the state elections and elected former Whig congressman Zebulon B. Vance to the governorship. The state elections of 1862 thus "represented a dramatic popular repudiation of the Democratic leadership that had controlled the state for more than a decade."[81]

The political upheavals of the Civil War brought an end to the second party system in North Carolina. The war ended the political careers of most of the Democratic leaders who had championed secession in 1860–61, and it vindicated the position of the unionists, who had predicted all along that secession meant war. For many years after the war, old-line Whigs like William A. Graham, John Pool, and Zebulon B. Vance, along with Union Democrats like William W. Holden, Robert P. Dick, and Thomas Settle, Jr., would dominate the politics of the Old North State. But the new party system that emerged after 1865 bore only a passing resemblance to the one that had prevailed during the antebellum years. Not even the most astute political observer in 1860 would have predicted that within a decade Vance, Graham, and many other Whig leaders would become dominant figures in the North Carolina Democratic party. Nor could anyone possibly have imagined that William W. Holden—that dauntless defender of Democracy, slavery, and southern rights—would find himself in the same political bed with Thaddeus Stevens, Charles Sumner, and the other "Black Republicans" whom he had denounced so vigorously during the antebellum years.

During the years before the Civil War, most of the laws that affected
the everyday lives of the American people were enacted by the state
and local governments, not by the national government in Washington. Indeed, apart from the presence of the local postmaster and, in
some areas, the customs official or land agent, the influence of the
federal government on the ordinary citizen was almost nonexistent.
Like government itself, the parties also functioned concurrently at
the national, state, and local levels. Most government activity was
centered around the state legislatures, the county courts, and the
various other institutions of local government, yet the choicest and
most lucrative patronage plums were distributed by the federal government in Washington. Hence, control of Congress and the presidency became an overriding consideration in the minds of those who
chose to make a career of politics.

Indeed, an emphasis on national politics and an association with
a national party system were prerequisites for the viability of state
parties in North Carolina. After the Federalist party gave up the contest for the presidency and ceased to be a national organization, party
leaders in the Old North State abandoned the Federalist label and
formed a new political coalition with dissident Republicans that later
evolved into the Whig party. When that party, in turn, lost its nationality during the mid-1850s, Whig leaders forged a new alliance
with the short-lived American party. By the end of the decade, the
Whigs in North Carolina and other southern states had regrouped nationally under the banner of the Constitutional Union party and were
contesting the various state elections once again as Whigs.

A national party system by definition requires national issues to
link the various state organizations to each other and to the national
party in Washington. Thus, from the end of the American Revolution
until the beginning of the Civil War, national politics provided the

leaders of the two competing state parties with a sense of identity and enabled them to establish a clear definition of party lines. During the Federalist era foreign policy was the main bone of contention between the parties. A generation later the controversial policies of the Jackson administration formed the pivot on which the electoral battles of the second party system turned. By the end of the antebellum era national economic issues like the tariff and national bank had been overshadowed by the even more momentous question of Union or disunion.

National politics dominated the rhetoric of the state parties not only in presidential and congressional campaigns but even in gubernatorial and legislative elections. Yet national politics had only limited influence on the voters' choice of parties. In North Carolina Democrats and Whigs built much of their popular support on local rivalries and group identities that antedated the emergence of parties as national institutions. Long-standing community conflicts, many of them dating back to the upheavals of the American Revolution, played a significant role in conditioning the pattern of partisan loyalties at the grass-roots level. However, national politics did have some impact on voter behavior, especially when the parties were able to make clear connections between national issues and local concerns. Thus, the Whigs attracted many voters to their party during the 1830s by linking their national program on land policy to the widely felt need for public financing of internal improvements.

Once a voter had chosen a party, he usually supported it loyally from one election to the next. The strong positive correlation between the distribution of the popular vote in each pair of elections between 1840 and 1860 attests to the strength and durability of party loyalties.[1] Not all the voters, however, were irrevocably committed to a political party. As the editor of the *Asheville News* remarked in 1860: "Out of one hundred thousand voters . . . there are always several thousands who are indifferent on the subject of politics, or who make up their minds as to their course only on the day of the election." Because of the close balance of parties during most of the 1840s and 1850s, these swing voters had an impact on elections far out of proportion to their actual numbers.[2]

Unlike today's voters, most North Carolinians did not have access to nonpartisan or independent sources of information about national politics. They knew only what their local leaders or newspaper editors told them. As a result, ordinary voters often allowed their leaders considerable latitude in determining the lines of interparty conflict. During the period between 1836 and 1846, for example, the Whig party in North Carolina moved from an avowedly states'-rights position on the slavery and tariff issues to a more nationalistic stance, without an appreciable loss of popular support.

Critics occasionally complained that the electorate relied unthinkingly on their leaders for opinions about national politics. In 1846 the editor of the *Mecklenburg Jeffersonian* provided an excellent description of the tension that invariably existed between the republican ideal of an independent electorate and the reality of partisan politics. The editor complained that "too much heed is paid to *party leaders*, and too strict an obedience paid to *party drill* to admit of a calm view on the part of voters, of the true principles at stake in our party contests. One will say—'I am a Democrat: my party is for such a measure, and I go for it.' Another says 'I am a whig; my party is for this measure, and I go [for] it, too, without a why or wherefore,' not stopping to inquire—Is the measure right or wrong, or is it my duty as a patriot, to go for or against it, in my honest endeavors to advance the honor and interest of my State?"[3] Despite these occasional expressions of misgiving, partisanship exercised a predominant influence on the way most antebellum North Carolinians perceived national politics. As a result of this "partisan imperative," leaders and followers alike "acted less and less as individuals and more and more as parts of a well-defined, collective group with conscious and well-understood ideas and outlooks."[4]

The two state parties emphasized national politics during the 1830s and 1840s not because the voters demanded that they do so, but because national politics provided the state parties with issues over which they could agree to disagree. Studies of congressional voting behavior by Joel H. Silbey and Thomas B. Alexander have graphically revealed the binding power of national issues, especially those relating to banking, land, and tariff policies.[5] Similarly, an examination of roll-call votes in the North Carolina General Assembly offers evidence that resolutions about the independent treasury, tariff and land policies, the veto power of the president, the annexation of Texas, the Mexican War, and other issues of national politics invariably generated a high degree of intraparty cohesion and inevitably resulted in a clear definition of party lines.[6]

State issues, on the other hand, often produced division instead of cohesion within the legislative parties. Bills relating to constitutional reform, internal improvements, the distribution of the public school fund, and the creation of new counties divided the legislators within both parties into eastern and western blocs. The two parties did not hold identical or indistinguishable views about state issues. By analyzing partisan alignments in the general assembly, it is possible to point out "central tendencies" within each party over many of these issues. Yet it is important not to confuse central tendencies with official party positions. That a majority of Democratic legislators consistently voted against state aid to railroads, the creation of new counties, and a more equitable distribution of the public school fund is striking testimony to the power and influence of the party's eastern wing, but it does not necessarily mean that the Democrats *as a party* officially opposed these measures or that Democrats and Whigs offered clear-cut alternatives to the voters.

Indeed, there is abundant evidence that party leaders stubbornly resisted efforts to turn state issues into tests of party orthodoxy. In 1852, for example, Seaton Gales of the *Raleigh Register* reminded his readers why "differences of opinion on matters of State policy have heretofore been tolerated in the Whig Party." "In times past," said Gales, "it was never customary to demand . . . 'you must say *yea* or *nay* on the Penitentiary question—the Internal Improvement question—the school question—the tax bill question'—or any other measure of State policy. The reason is apparent. No Party can exist, for a twelve month, which acts on such a principle. If such an intolerant doctrine were adopted, in reference to matters of mere State policy, a Party, founded as the Whig Party is, on great and fundamental principles, connected with the National Government, and its policy, would soon degenerate into a *State* party, and as soon thereafter become a mere *sectional party in the State*."[7]

Despite his differences with Gales over specific policy issues, William W. Holden was in complete agreement about the importance of national politics. "We cannot all think alike on State affairs, and it were idle to expect it," Holden counseled his fellow Democrats. "Let us, therefore, while we differ in these minor matters, agree to unite upon great [national] issues." Even in regard to a state issue as important to him as free suffrage, Holden was willing to tolerate differences of opinion within his party. Thus the editor told Weldon N. Edwards, an ardent opponent of suffrage reform, that "I shall hail your election with as much gratification as if you were the strongest Equal Suffrage man in the State. It is no test of Democracy. We can agree to disagree about it." On the other hand, Holden was unsparing in his denunciations of fellow partisans, like William H. Haywood, Jr., and Abraham W. Venable, who deviated from the party's official positions on tariff and land policy.[8]

Although leaders like Holden and Gales urged a policy of toleration and forbearance within their own party, they did not hesitate to use state issues against their opponents whenever they thought they could win votes by doing so. One of the remarkable features of the second party system was the ability of party leaders to agitate state issues, despite the absence of sharp party differences over them. During the mid-1830s the Whigs appealed to a popular desire for public schools and improved transportation facilities by promising the voters that their policies would produce these benefits without an increase in state taxes. Whig spokesmen also claimed that the Democrats were opposed to schools and internal improvements. Despite the Whig accusations, there is no evidence that the parties offered the voters of North Carolina a clear choice between positive and negative state government. There were many leading Democrats who aggressively championed state development, but they were unable to devise an attractive alternative to the Whig plan of financing schools, railroads, and other improvements with federal land revenue. Simply put, the Whigs outpromised the Democrats, and this strategy enabled them to become the majority party as early as 1836.

Once confronted with the responsibility of governing, the Whigs found it difficult to develop policies that would satisfy both sectional wings of the party. The onset of the depression and the failure of Congress to enact a distribution bill compounded the problems of the governing party. The Democrats were quick to exploit these difficulties for partisan advantage. During most of the 1840s North Carolina Democrats tried to make political capital on the issues of state banking and railroad relief. However, party leaders abandoned their attacks against banks and railroads once they realized that their efforts were proving counterproductive. Not until they advocated free suffrage in 1848 did the Democrats find a state issue with enduring popular appeal.

Some historians have interpreted the antibank and antirailroad campaigns of the 1840s as evidence that the Democrats opposed the idea of a market economy. "If Whigs expected good things to come from the market economy," one scholar has recently argued, "Democrats feared it. Instead of viewing banks, railroads, and corporations as the bases of liberation, they saw them as hazards to freedom."[9] Certainly there is evidence that many ordinary North Carolinians deeply distrusted banks, railroads, and other concentrations of wealth and power. However, opposition to these institutions is not prima facie evidence of hostility to the market economy. The issue of state assistance to internal improvements best illustrates the distinction. Unlike Alabama, where opposition to internal improvements was strongest among small farmers living on the fringes of the market economy, anti-improvement sentiment in North Carolina was most prevalent in the plantation counties of the middle east, which even before the 1830s were intimately involved in the market economy.[10] By 1840 the residents of these counties also enjoyed railroad connections with markets in Norfolk, Petersburg, Richmond, and Wilmington. A majority of voters in these wealthy counties were unwilling to pay higher taxes in order to construct railroads in remote parts of the west. Easterners thus tended to oppose internal improvements because they were already part of the market economy, whereas westerners tended to favor them because they wanted to share in the benefits of that economy.

When generalizing about party attitudes toward banks and railroads, it is important to make a distinction between the parties as formal institutions, on the one hand, and the rank-and-file voters who supported those parties, on the other.[11] At the leadership level the Democratic attitude toward banks and railroads during the 1840s can best be characterized as a love-hate relationship. Urban-oriented party leaders like Romulus M. Saunders, Louis D. Henry, James B. Shepard, and Robert Strange were intimately associated with these institutions as directors, stockholders, and promoters, and the Whigs never hesitated to remind the voters of this connection. Moreover, even though Democratic leaders roundly denounced banks and railroads for their alleged misdeeds, they made no serious effort to discipline them. In 1842 the Democrats could easily have slain the "monster bank" by accepting the surrender of its charter, and they could have destroyed the railroad system by refusing to vote for the necessary relief measures. But the destruction of these institutions would have brought untold economic hardship upon the state and, equally important, would have ended their potential as campaign issues. The Democrats preferred to keep the banks and railroads alive in order to crusade against them another day.

To argue that the Democrats opportunistically used these issues to win votes is not to say that politics in the Old North State was entirely devoid of ideological content. On the contrary, antebellum North Carolinians viewed the battles of the second party system within the context of eighteenth-century republican ideology. Fundamentally antipower in character, republican ideology produced a widespread distrust of authority and a suspicion of all concentrations of political and economic power, whether in the form of a caucus, a bank, a railroad, or an organized political party. Neither party in North Carolina enjoyed a monopoly on antibank and antirailroad rhetoric. When the Democrats accused their opponents of supporting irresponsible banking practices and extravagant railroad expenditures, the Whigs often replied in kind by denouncing the "pet banks," by characterizing the independent treasury as a "government bank," and by pointing to the extravagant policies supposedly endorsed by prorailroad Democrats.

Yet a close examination of party rhetoric reveals the existence of subtle differences in the manner in which the parties exploited these issues. During the 1840s, for example, the Whigs always directed their antibank rhetoric toward distant institutions in other states. Unlike the Democrats, they never attacked the policies of their own state bank, and they rarely indulged in blanket condemnation of the banking system. The Whigs also consistently defended the economic importance of paper money, while Democrats frequently took a hard-money stance. Similarly, despite their criticisms of the "extravagant" and "visionary" programs of certain proimprovement Democrats, the Whigs never attacked the concept of state-supported internal improvements and rarely criticized specific improvement projects. Democrats, on the other hand, appealed blatantly to anti-improvement sentiment by attacking the Whig policy of support for the Raleigh & Gaston Railroad and by condemning the extravagant debts supposedly incurred by the Whig administrations.

During the 1840s it was the Democrats who took the initiative in crusading against banks and railroads, as well as against the high taxes and burdensome debts for which those institutions were supposedly responsible. By the end of the antebellum era, however, the positions of the two parties had changed dramatically. In 1856 a majority of Whig and American legislators voted against the revenue bill and the recharter of the state bank, and, at the same time, launched an all-out attack against the management of the North Carolina Railroad. The Democrats, meanwhile, found themselves in the awkward position of supporting and defending the tax increases, the bank recharter, and the policies of the North Carolina Railroad.[12]

One historian has recently remarked that "by the mid-1850s Democrats [in North Carolina] increasingly came to accept Whig premises and policies."[13] By the same token, one might conclude that the Whigs increasingly embraced Democratic ideas and practices. Yet the behavior of the two parties can be explained without resorting to the dubious argument that each abandoned its own principles and co-opted those of the opposition. Much of the party maneuvering on state issues during the 1840s and 1850s was not a product of ideology but, instead, was a function of which party happened to be in control of the state government. As the in-party during the 1840s, the Whigs were vulnerable to popular dissatisfaction with the slow pace of economic recovery, the growing state debt, the inability of the banks to resume specie payments, and the failure of the railroads to yield an immediate profit. As the out-party, the Democrats naturally tried to capitalize on these issues to unseat their opponents. During the 1850s, on the other hand, it was the Democrats who were saddled with the responsibility of power, a position that made them increasingly vulnerable to Whig charges of extravagance, mismanagement, and burdensome taxation.

The parties were able to exploit state issues, despite their lack of internal consensus, because local leaders within each party could take differing, and sometimes even contradictory, positions on these issues in their individual county constituencies. Michael F. Holt's recent study of antebellum parties has demonstrated brilliantly how the northern and southern wings of the two national parties were able to exploit the issues of slavery and territorial expansion at the state level, despite the absence of intraparty consensus at the national level. "Because both parties functioned at different levels, politicians had the luxury of saying different things in different parts of the country. They could define for home audiences lines of interparty conflict that did not necessarily apply to the country as a whole."[14] A similar comment can be made about the manner in which the parties in North Carolina handled divisive state issues. In both cases, however, the party system could work smoothly only so long as local activists refrained from trying to impose their views on the entire party.

At both the national and state levels the second party system was vulnerable to what Holt has aptly called the "politics of impatience."[15] Impatient with the temporizing policies of the northern Democrats on the territorial issue, southern Democrats during the 1850s tried to make their own position a test of party orthodoxy, first by demanding that their party support the Kansas-Nebraska Act, then by insisting that Kansas be admitted as a slave state under the Lecompton Constitution, and, finally, by demanding a federal slave code for the territories. The inevitable result of these escalating demands was the disruption of the national Democratic party. In many of the northern states the politics of impatience took the form of ethnocultural conflict. Dissatisfied with the inability of the traditional parties to address important state issues like nativism and prohibition, thousands of voters in these states bolted the Whigs and Democrats and joined the Republican or American parties, which took a forthright stand on these issues.

The party system in North Carolina was equally vulnerable to the politics of impatience, especially in regard to the sectionally explosive issue of constitutional reform. The introduction of the free-suffrage issue in 1848 threw the question of constitutional reform back into the political arena after an absence of more than a decade, and reignited the sectional controversy between the plantation counties of the east and the small-farm counties of the west. Not satisfied with David S. Reid's rather modest proposal for a change in the suffrage requirements, western activists within the Whig party began pressuring their leaders to take a clear-cut position on a range of reform issues; most important, a change in the basis of legislative apportionment. The increase in sectional consciousness during the 1850s also led western Democrats to exert pressure on their own party to abandon its traditional reticence on internal improvements and come out unequivocally in favor of a policy of state assistance.

That these pressures did not shatter the second party system in North Carolina is a tribute to the political dexterity of the party leaders and their adroitness in redirecting sectional issues into safer, partisan channels. Whig leaders attempted to contain the pressure for constitutional reform by shifting the debate from the substantive points at issue to the procedural question of whether the legislature or a convention was the proper agency for making constitutional changes. Although this strategy did not forestall the erosion of their power, it did enable the Whigs to prevent the disintegration of their party. By the same token, the Democrats contained the pressure for internal improvements by adopting platforms that emphasized both fiscal responsibility and support for a "judicious system" of state development. This formula enabled party leaders in each section to interpret the platform in a manner consistent with the interests of their constituents. In addition, the chartering of the Western North Carolina Railroad in 1854 satisfied the most pressing western improvement demand and, at the same time, helped defuse the movement for a radical change in the distribution of power between the two sections.

At the end of the antebellum era the second party system in North Carolina was every bit as vigorous as it had been during its heyday in the 1840s. Although the Democrats replaced the Whigs as the majority party early in the 1850s, by the end of the decade there were signs that the political momentum was again shifting to the Whigs. The high rate of voter turnout also indicated the strength and durability of the party system. During the 1850s the proportion of the electorate voting in state elections steadily increased. In the state elections of 1860, 82 percent of the eligible voters went to the polls— the highest percentage in twenty years.[16]

The vitality of the second party system in North Carolina on the eve of the Civil War stands in sharp contrast to its moribund condition in the North and in the lower South. A study of politics in one state alone cannot provide all the answers to the complex question of why the system broke down in some states but not in others. Yet an examination of the North Carolina experience does provide insight into some of the factors behind the decline of the second American party system and offers an opportunity to test some well-known hypotheses about the political crisis of the 1850s.

Michael F. Holt has recently attributed the disintegration of the second party system to a crisis of popular confidence arising out of the growing congruence between the parties on almost all the national issues that had formed the cutting edge of party competition during the 1830s and 1840s. When the national issues that had imparted a sense of identity and distinctiveness to the parties during Andrew Jackson's time no longer seemed to matter, party lines began to blur and voter loyalty to the old organizations eroded.[17]

Holt has made a persuasive argument, but his interpretation does not adequately explain why some states, like North Carolina, remained immune to the disruptive effects of the crisis of confidence.[18] Nor has Holt proven conclusively that banking, currency, and tariff issues ceased to have meaning to antebellum voters. During the 1850s new issues entered the political arena and, for a time, overshadowed the older issues in the rhetoric of the parties. But, as Joel H. Silbey cautions, "that does not necessarily mean that the earlier issues were dead or even less important to very many people."[19] Finally, Holt's argument fails to take full account of the fact that the stability of the system depended primarily on popular perceptions of party differences. The parties could very well have seemed different to the voters, regardless of whether they really offered clear-cut policy alternatives to them.[20]

In the arena of party politics, images are often just as important as issues. In the Old North State the perennial debates over national politics enabled the leaders of the state parties to construct images of themselves as the defenders of republican virtue and to conjure up visions of their opponents as the enemies of republican government. Both parties characterized the electoral battles of the day as momentous struggles for the survival of the republic, and each claimed that the preservation of liberty and equality depended upon the defeat of the opposition. Political scientists have pointed out that organized parties—in contrast to transient factions—tend to develop such contrasting perspectives. Once they are created, these positive and negative images can assume a life of their own, independent of the specific issues that initially spawned them. Indeed, as one scholar has remarked, they can act as powerful influences on party stability and cohesion "even in periods of party fatigue or comparatively empty politics-as-usual, when sentiments become increasingly vague, detached from immediately relevant issues, or flaccid. Even in such epochs, party loyalties and symbolism remain among the most tenacious of the ties that bind."[21]

The images that the parties created of themselves and of their opponents persisted in North Carolina long after issues such as the national bank, the independent treasury, and the tariff had lost their predominant position in the rhetoric of the parties. Even after 1850 the Whigs continued to warn the voters that the Democrats were plotting to corrupt elections, to augment the power of the president, and to create a clique of public pensioners dependent on the executive rather than the people for their livelihood. At the same time the Democrats continued to refer to their opponents as a "body of anti-quated politicians and office seekers" and to denounce their policies as "unconstitutional, anti-democratic, and impolitic."[22]

In making his case for a crisis of confidence in the existing party system, Holt has placed considerable emphasis on the growth of anti-party rhetoric during the 1850s. Yet the intensification of antiparty rhetoric in North Carolina and in other states during this decade may have been more a symptom than a cause of the decline of the second party system. Certainly the prevalence of antiparty rhetoric among the leaders of the American party in North Carolina is not, by itself, evidence of a widespread crisis of confidence in the party system. Seasoned politicians used such rhetoric to justify the existence of the American party, to persuade the electorate to abandon long-established voting habits, and to broaden their base of popular support. North Carolinians had always been uncomfortable with the contradictions between the ideals of eighteenth-century republican ideology and the realities of nineteenth-century party politics, and ever since the crusade against the congressional caucus during the 1820s, ambitious politicians there had persistently tried to exploit this ambivalence for their own advantage.

The vitality of the second party system in North Carolina at the end of the antebellum period was, in large part, the result of its immunity to the deleterious effects of ethnocultural conflict and the controversy over slavery—the two forces that undermined the system in the North and in the lower South. While the rapid influx of foreigners was exacerbating long-standing cultural antagonisms between immigrants and native Americans in the northern communities during the 1850s and impelling many voters to desert their traditional parties, few of these newcomers chose to settle in North Carolina or, for that matter, in any other southern state. Recent studies of the second party system in the South suggest that Americans below the Potomac paid little attention to the ethnocultural issues that divided the northern electorate into warring political subcultures.[23]

The sudden but temporary collapse of the North Carolina Whig party in 1855 did not result from ethnocultural pressures on the party system from within the state. Rather, it was a by-product of the demise of the Whigs as a national party. In their efforts to maintain a connection with a national organization, opposition leaders in North Carolina abandoned the Whig label and allied themselves with the burgeoning American party. Yet Know-Nothingism in North Carolina was, as its enemies always claimed it to be, little more than Whiggery in disguise. As soon as it became obvious that the Americans were no longer a viable national party, opposition leaders shed their disguises and again began calling themselves Whigs.

The party system in the Old North State proved equally impervious to the baneful effects of the escalating controversy over slavery. Historians have often attributed the short life span of the second party system to the inability of a nationally based party system to deal effectively with the sectionally divisive issues of slavery and territorial expansion.[24] Recent studies have confirmed this view by demonstrating the deleterious effect that the growth in sectional consciousness had on the Whig party in the lower South during the 1850s. The refusal of President Taylor to repudiate the Wilmot Proviso, the unwillingness of antislavery northern Whigs to endorse the Compromise of 1850, the widespread perception that Whig presidential candidate Winfield Scott was controlled by the northern antislavery forces, and the steadfast opposition of the northern Whigs to the Kansas-Nebraska Act all contributed to drive voters in the lower South out of the Whig party during the 1850s.[25]

Despite their commitment to the preservation of slavery, the people of the Old North State were more concerned about preserving the integrity of the Union than they were about upholding the rights of the South in the territories. By taking an uncompromising position in support of the preservation of the Union and branding their opponents with the secessionist label, North Carolina Whigs managed to retain the loyalty of their supporters, despite Democratic charges of "submissionism." Until the crisis of 1860–61, the controversy over slavery seems to have had little impact on the overall balance of parties in North Carolina.[26]

The Achilles' heel of the second party system in North Carolina, and in many other states as well, proved to be the inability of the two parties to take clear-cut positions on state issues that mattered at least as much to the voters as the national issues and presidential contests that occupied the attention of their leaders. The local issues that engaged the interest of antebellum voters varied considerably from one part of the country to another. Yet in states as different in their political, economic, and social complexion as North Carolina and Massachusetts, popular dissatisfaction with the ineffectiveness of the party system at the state level contributed in no small part to the transformation of politics during the 1850s.

Ronald P. Formisano's recent study of party politics in antebellum Massachusetts cogently underscores this point. In Massachusetts, as in North Carolina, "both local and state leaders preferred to focus on 'great national questions' such as the tariff, a national bank, the subtreasury, and the currency." At the same time party leaders "eschewed or equivocated on . . . moral issues, such as temperance . . . and they avoided a frank and open discussion of a good many economic and social matters directly affecting the lives of Massachusetts citizens." Parties could not take clear-cut positions on state issues because these issues "cut unpredictably across party lines." Popular frustration with the temporizing policies of the traditional parties reached a boiling point during the 1850s, and "populist movements arose to force politicians to confront such issues." "What followed," concludes Formisano, "was a populist revolt of unprecedented proportions, a movement whose lowest common denominator was nominally nativism and anti-Catholicism, but which included temperance, antislavery, and other dissident elements gathered into one great rejection of party politicians and established party organizations."[27]

The most important state issues in North Carolina did not revolve around ethnocultural matters. Instead, they centered on the long-standing sectional rivalries between the plantation counties of the east and the small-farm counties of the west. The constitutional amendments adopted in 1835 temporarily alleviated sectional antagonisms and made it possible to construct a statewide system of parties. But the revival of sectionalism after 1848 posed as much of a threat to the existence of the system in North Carolina as the intensification of ethnocultural conflict did to the parties in the North. Indeed, during the early 1850s many western reformers called for the creation of a state party that would be independent of both national parties, and there was talk in the far west of nominating an independent candidate for governor in 1852.

Despite the commotion, nothing became of these schemes. Part of the reason was that reform sentiment in North Carolina was too narrowly confined to the counties of the far west to have a chance of becoming the basis for a new majority coalition. Unlike their counterparts in the northern communities, reformers in the Old North State reached the conclusion that the best method of achieving their goals was to force concessions from the existing parties. Equally important, the bitter controversy between the Clingman and anti-Clingman factions in the mountain district divided the forces of reform, militated against the creation of a unified state reform party, and served to reinforce existing party divisions. Finally, as mentioned earlier, party leaders proved particularly adept at developing strategies to direct sectionally explosive issues into safer, partisan channels.

Richard P. McCormick has observed that the parties that developed in the United States during the 1830s were able to "perform a variety of functions, and meet a number of obvious needs." But "they were incapable of performing the one function most commonly associated with the idea of party. They could not govern." Other astute observers of antebellum politics have reached the same conclusion. After carefully evaluating the evidence, Edward Pessen has concluded that "for all their unique styles of operation" the two parties "were alike great vote-getting machines, 'primarily concerned . . . not with framing issues and drawing up distinctive programs, but in trying to discover some way of bringing together . . . as large a proportion of the voters as possible.'"28

The evidence for North Carolina tends to support this argument. During the antebellum period political parties there proved much more adept at competing for power than at exercising that power effectively in the management of government. Indeed, one can argue that the fierce conflict between the two parties had very little relationship to the policies that were actually enacted by the state government. Even though the majority of Whig legislators favored banks and railroads, only two banks were chartered and only a few miles of railroad lines were constructed while the Whigs were in power. The Democrats, on the other hand, were supposedly hostile to banks and railroads, yet during their decade in power seventeen additional banks were chartered and railroad mileage increased from 154 miles to 937 miles.[29] The conclusion seems inescapable that the two ante-bellum parties failed to offer their constituents genuine policy alter-natives on issues like internal improvements and state banking.

At the same time, however, political parties were not irrelevant fixtures on the political landscape of antebellum North Carolina. A case can be made, for example, that the rapid growth in partisanship during the early 1830s contributed to the success of the constitu-tional reform movement in 1835. Whigs and Democrats both realized that it was in their mutual interest to resolve this issue in order to unite their eastern and western wings behind the national programs of the two parties, and a bipartisan coalition of legislative leaders suc-ceeded in marshaling a sufficient number of eastern legislators to se-cure passage of a convention bill. Twenty years later the intense com-petition between Democrats and Whigs for the loyalty of the voters in the mountain region led both parties to endorse officially the concept of state-supported internal improvements. The passage of the West-ern North Carolina Railroad Act during the legislative session of 1854–55 was a logical outcome of this interparty competition.[30]

A strong argument can also be made that the "partisan impera-tive" played a predominant role in conditioning popular reaction to the secession crisis. In North Carolina, as elsewhere throughout the South, the Democratic party was the driving force behind the seces-sionist impulse. At the same time the strength of the Whig organiza-tion proved a powerful bulwark against radical action. Throughout the antebellum era the politics of slavery had invariably succumbed to the politics of Union whenever the voters were offered a clear-cut choice between the two. The crisis of 1860–61 was no exception. Capitalizing on the unionist proclivities of the voters, the Whigs, along with some unionist Democrats, soundly defeated their oppo-nents in the election of delegates to a state convention. By the spring of 1861 a realignment of parties around the issues of Union and dis-union seemed inevitable. Lincoln's response to the Confederate at-tack on Fort Sumter temporarily united the two groups in a common determination to resist northern aggression. But the upheavals of the Civil War ultimately discredited the policies of the Democrats and vindicated those of the Whigs, and it would be the Whigs whom the people of North Carolina would ultimately entrust with the responsi-bility for leading them out of the Civil War and into the New South.[31]

Appendix: Classification of Federalist and Republican Counties

The problem of identifying Federalist and Republican counties is an extremely difficult one. Only fragmentary returns from congressional and presidential elections survive for the period prior to 1824. There was no statewide race for governor until 1836, and successful candidates in legislative elections were usually not identified by their party affiliation until 1834.

James H. Broussard has recently attempted to rank the counties in North Carolina according to Federalist strength (see the map in *The Southern Federalists, 1800–1816* [Baton Rouge: Louisiana State University Press, 1978], 407). Broussard's classification system is based on a close analysis of all the extant congressional and presidential returns in the North Carolina Division of Archives and History (Compiled Election Returns, Miscellaneous Collections), along with the small number of party-line roll calls in the general assembly. The problem with Broussard's system is that it arbitrarily divides the counties into four quartiles. Those counties comprising his first quartile were undoubtedly Federalist in political orientation, and the counties in the lowest two quartiles were indisputably Republican. However, because there were more Republican than Federalist counties in the state as a whole, not all of the counties in the second quartile can be classified as Federalist.

In attempting to determine the party preferences of the North Carolina counties, I also looked at all the extant presidential and congressional election returns. I supplemented this information with an analysis of the vote in the North Carolina House of Commons of 1815 on two important roll calls that divided the legislators strictly according to party: Bedford Brown's resolution praising the conduct of President James Madison during the war with Britain and the bill to choose presidential electors on a general ticket (*House of Commons Journal, 1815*, 46, 53).

All the counties in Broussard's first quartile, as well as an additional six in the second quartile, have been classified as Federalist in this study (see map 1). Craven County presents a special problem. I have classified it as a Federalist county in my analysis of presidential and gubernatorial elections (tables 1.2, 3.1, 3.2, and 3.3) because the strength of the party in New Bern was generally sufficient to give the Federalists a majority in the county as a whole. On the other hand, in my analysis of votes in the house of commons (tables 1.1 and 1.3), I have classified Craven as a Republican county because New Bern, which was one of seven boroughs allowed to elect its own commoner, did not participate in the election of the two commoners who represented the remainder of the county. In addition to New Bern, the following boroughs were classified as Federalist: Edenton, Fayetteville, Salisbury, and Wilmington. The boroughs of Halifax and Hillsborough were classified as Republican.

Counties created between 1815 and 1840 have been assigned the same political affiliation as their parent county. These are: Davidson (Federalist, created in 1822 from Rowan); Macon (Republican, created in 1828 from Buncombe); Yancey (Republican, created in 1833 from Burke and Buncombe); Davie (Federalist, created in 1836 from Rowan); and Cherokee (Republican, created in 1839 from Macon).

This classification system cannot be regarded as definitive. One problem with an "either-or" system is that it cannot account for change over time. For example, Lincoln County, which was strongly Federalist during the 1790s, seems to have been much less so by the 1810s. There are so few returns available for some counties that it is risky to make any judgment about party affiliation. In a few counties the party balance was so close that it is difficult to assign majority status to either party. These caveats should not obscure the fact that most North Carolina counties can, with a reasonable degree of confidence, be classified as Federalist or Republican. Even if a few of the more doubtful counties were reclassified, the changes would not significantly affect my generalizations about the continuities between the grass-roots divisions of the Federalist era and those of the second party system. Indeed, if the two most doubtful counties—Lincoln and Stokes—were reclassified as Republican, the relationship between Federalist and Whig counties demonstrated in the tables in chapter 3 would appear even stronger.

Notes

Abbreviations

HJ   *Journal of the House of Commons of North Carolina*
JAH   *Journal of American History*
JSH   *Journal of Southern History*
NCDAH   North Carolina Department of Archives and History, Division of Cultural
        Resources, Raleigh, North Carolina
NCHR   *North Carolina Historical Review*
SHC   Southern Historical Collection, University of North Carolina, Chapel Hill,
        North Carolina
SJ   *Journal of the Senate of North Carolina*

Introduction

1. For surveys of the recent literature, see Ronald P. Formisano, "Toward a Reorientation of Jacksonian Politics: A Review of the Literature, 1959–1975," *JAH* 63 (1976): 42–65; and Richard L. McCormick, "Ethno-Cultural Interpretations of Nineteenth-Century American Voting Behavior," *Political Science Quarterly* 89 (1974): 351–77.

2. Daniel Feller, *The Public Lands in Jacksonian Politics* (Madison: University of Wisconsin Press, 1984), xvi.

3. Harry L. Watson, *Jacksonian Politics and Community Conflict: The Emergence of the Second Party System in Cumberland County, North Carolina* (Baton Rouge: Louisiana State University Press, 1981). Watson has ably demonstrated how politics in Cumberland County was conditioned by the rivalry between Fayetteville and the rural hinterland. Yet Fayetteville was one of only four North Carolina towns with a population greater than 5,000 and one of only fifteen with a population greater than 1,000. Hershal L. Macon, "A Fiscal History of North Carolina, 1776–1860" (Ph.D. diss., University of North Carolina at Chapel Hill, 1932), 300; Guion Griffis Johnson, *Ante-Bellum North Carolina: A Social History* (Chapel Hill: University of North Carolina Press, 1937), 114–15.

4. Marc W. Kruman, *Parties and Politics in North Carolina* (Baton Rouge: Louisiana State University Press, 1983), 55.

5. See, for example, Lee Benson, *The Concept of Jacksonian Democracy: New York as a Test Case* (Princeton: Princeton University Press, 1961), 86–109; and Herbert Ershkowitz and William G. Shade, "Consensus or Conflict? Political Behavior in the State Legislatures during the Jacksonian Era," *JAH* 58 (1971): 591–

621. For North Carolina, see Kruman, *Parties and Politics in North Carolina*, 55–63.

6. Marvin Meyers, *The Jacksonian Persuasion: Politics and Belief* (New York: Vintage Books, 1960), 13.

7. These two viewpoints are not necessarily incompatible. See, for example, Watson, *Jacksonian Politics and Community Conflict*.

8. In his study of politics in Cumberland County, Watson concludes that the Whigs were strongest among the merchants and planters in Fayetteville and in the wealthiest, most commercially oriented parts of the rural hinterland, whereas the Democrats were strongest among small farmers in the poorer, more remote sandhills precincts (*Jacksonian Politics and Community Conflict*, 212–13, 245, 278–80). However valid Watson's conclusions may be for Cumberland County, they do not apply to North Carolina as a whole. As the data in this study reveal, the Democrats were the majority party in most of the commercially oriented plantation counties of eastern North Carolina, whereas the Whigs were strongest in the poorer, more remote, and less-developed counties of the mountain region and the extreme northeast. Even in Cumberland County, according to Watson, "political preference was not strictly a matter of economic self-interest" (ibid., 141).

9. Kruman's study, for example, ignores the first party system entirely and mentions the election of 1824 only in passing (*Parties and Politics in North Carolina*, 18). William S. Hoffmann, *Andrew Jackson and North Carolina Politics* (Chapel Hill: University of North Carolina Press, 1958), a detailed account of party formation in North Carolina before 1836, also disregards earlier partisan competition between Federalists and Republicans and devotes a scant five pages to the election of 1824.

10. The reference to "remarkable staying powers" is from Richard P. McCormick, *The Second American Party System: Party Formation in the Jacksonian Era* (Chapel Hill: University of North Carolina Press, 1966), 200. See also David H. Fischer, *The Revolution of American Conservatism: The Federalist Party in the Era of Jeffersonian Democracy* (New York: Harper and Row, 1965), 213n.

11. For an excellent introduction to the concept of republican ideology, see Robert E. Shalhope, "Toward A Republican Synthesis: The Emergence of an Understanding of Republicanism in American Historiography," *William and Mary Quarterly*, 3d ser., 29 (1972): 49–80.

12. One recent study that does relate the development of party structures to the persistence of antiparty ideology is Richard P. McCormick, *The Presidential Game: The Origins of American Presidential Politics* (New York: Oxford University Press, 1982). See, for example, pp. 6–8, 142–43, 235.

13. The following historiographical discussion is a summary of the argument in Thomas E. Jeffrey, "The Progressive Paradigm of Antebellum North Carolina Politics," *Carolina Comments* 30 (1982): 66–75.

14. The quotations are from Hugh T. Lefler and Albert R. Newsome, *North Carolina: The History of a Southern State*, 2d ed. (Chapel Hill: University of North Carolina Press, 1963), 368, 356, 358, 359.

15. John S. Bassett, "Suffrage in the State of North Carolina (1776–1861)," in *Annual*

Report of the American Historical Association for the Year 1895 (Washington: Government Printing Office, 1896), 271–85.

16. J. G. de Roulhac Hamilton, *Party Politics in North Carolina, 1835–1860* (Durham: Seeman Printery, 1916), 109, 77, 121.

17. Clarence C. Norton, *The Democratic Party in Ante-Bellum North Carolina, 1835–1861* (Chapel Hill: University of North Carolina Press, 1930), 166.

18. Herbert D. Pegg, *The Whig Party in North Carolina* (Chapel Hill: Colonial Press, 1968), 50, 170 (originally written in 1932 as a Ph.D. dissertation).

19. Edgar E. Folk, "W. W. Holden and the *North Carolina Standard*, 1843–1848: A Study in Political Journalism," *NCHR* 19 (1942): 22–47; Horace W. Raper, *William W. Holden: North Carolina's Political Enigma* (Chapel Hill: University of North Carolina Press, 1985). The quotation is from Folk, "W. W. Holden and the *North Carolina Standard*," 26.

20. Paul A. Reid, *Gubernatorial Campaigns and Administrations of David S. Reid, 1848–1854* (Cullowhee: Western Carolina College Press, 1953); Lindley S. Butler, "David S. Reid, 1813–1850: The Making of a Governor," *Journal of Rockingham County History and Genealogy* 4 (1979): 1–21. The quotation is from Butler, "David S. Reid," 20.

21. Max R. Williams, "William A. Graham: North Carolina Whig Party Leader, 1804–1849" (Ph.D. diss., University of North Carolina at Chapel Hill, 1965), 252, 257.

22. Kruman, *Parties and Politics in North Carolina*, 102.

23. Lefler and Newsome, *North Carolina*, 355.

24. Ralph A. Wooster, *Politicians, Planters, and Plain Folk: Courthouse and Statehouse in the Upper South, 1850–1860* (Knoxville: University of Tennessee Press, 1975), 118–27.

25. Pegg, *Whig Party in North Carolina*, 89.

1. Origins of Political Conflict

1. Quoted in A. Roger Ekirch, *"Poor Carolina": Politics and Society in Colonial North Carolina, 1729–1776* (Chapel Hill: University of North Carolina Press, 1981), 28n.

2. Robert D. W. Connor, *Race Elements in the White Population of North Carolina* (Raleigh: College, 1920), 39.

3. Quoted in Hugh T. Lefler and William S. Powell, *Colonial North Carolina: A History* (New York: Scribner, 1973), 124.

4. The Regulator movement has been the subject of much historiographical controversy. Emphasizing the sectional aspect of the conflict, A. Roger Ekirch has presented a persuasive analysis of the movement as a challenge to the right of the North Carolina provincial elite to govern (*"Poor Carolina,"* 161–202). Ekirch's most persistent critic has been Marvin L. Michael Kay, who has characterized the Regulators as "class-conscious white farmers in the west who attempted to democratize local government." See Kay, "The North Carolina Regulation, 1766–1776: A Class Conflict," in Alfred F. Young, ed., *The American Revolution: Explorations in the History of American Radicalism* (Dekalb: Northern

Illinois University Press, 1976), 73. For a summary of these and other interpretations, see Alan D. Watson, "The Regulation: Society in Upheaval," in Lindley S. Butler and Alan D. Watson, eds., *The North Carolina Experience: An Interpretive and Documentary History* (Chapel Hill: University of North Carolina Press, 1984).

5. Ekirch, *"Poor Carolina,"* 203–11; Robert O. DeMond, *The Loyalists in North Carolina during the Revolution* (Durham: Duke University Press, 1940), 34–61; Leonard L. Richards, "John Adams and the Moderate Federalists: The Cape Fear Valley as a Test Case," *NCHR* 43 (1966): 18–21. Although the vast majority of Highland Scots were indisputably loyal to Britain during the Revolution, historians have disagreed about Regulator affinities. After surveying the evidence, Alan D. Watson has concluded that "the majority of former Regulators [probably] remained neutral . . . perhaps because the westerners saw little future in a government dominated by an eastern elite, whether British or Whig" ("The Regulation," 109–10). For a similar assessment, see Kay, "The North Carolina Regulation," 103–7.

6. Ronald Hoffman has aptly characterized the Revolution in the Carolinas as "total civil war. . . . Murder and banditry, brutal intimidation, and retaliation became a way of life. . . . The struggle proceeded in scores of unrecorded skirmishes." See Hoffman, "The 'Disaffected' in the Revolutionary South," in Young, ed., *The American Revolution*, 293. For a vivid description of the atrocities inflicted upon the North Carolina Loyalists, see DeMond, *Loyalists*, 118–23.

7. Quoted in Hoffman, "The 'Disaffected' in the Revolutionary South," 294–95.

8. Carole W. Troxler has concluded that "in general the overriding issues appear to have been local, and some of them were of a family or personal nature." See Troxler, *The Loyalist Experience in North Carolina* (Raleigh: North Carolina Division of Archives and History, 1976), 57. Jeffrey J. Crow contends that "the conflicts between . . . whig and tory often reflected deep-seated class tensions." According to Crow, loyalism in North Carolina was primarily a lower-class resistance movement directed against "an aggressive Revolutionary government that was dominated by and conducted in the interests of an upper class consisting of planters, merchants, and lawyers." Crow also emphasizes that "discontent with the Whigs' policies . . . extended far beyond the Regulator and Highland Scots' communities." See Crow, "Liberty Men and Loyalists: Disorder and Disaffection in the North Carolina Backcountry," in Ronald Hoffman, Thad W. Tate, and Peter J. Albert, eds., *An Uncivil War: The Southern Backcountry during the American Revolution* (Charlottesville: University Press of Virginia, 1985), 127, 137.

9. William H. Nelson, *The American Tory* (Oxford: Clarendon Press, 1961), 91. See also Troxler, *Loyalist Experience*, 2.

10. Crow, "Liberty Men and Loyalists," 145.

11. Norman K. Risjord, *Chesapeake Politics, 1781–1800* (New York: Columbia University Press, 1978), 92–95, 127–29, 196–201; Delbert H. Gilpatrick, *Jeffersonian Democracy in North Carolina, 1789–1816* (New York: Columbia University Press, 1931), 28–29; DeMond, *Loyalists*, 159–69; Mary C. Wyche, "The

Tory War in North Carolina" (Master's thesis, University of North Carolina at Chapel Hill, 1941), 151–58; and Henry G. Wagstaff, *Federalism in North Carolina* (Chapel Hill: University Press, 1910), 9.

12. Risjord, *Chesapeake Politics*, 130–32, 157–59, 317–18, 337–41, 357–58; Gilpatrick, *Jeffersonian Democracy*, 29–35, 38–42.

13. Gilbert L. Lycan, "Alexander Hamilton and the North Carolina Federalists," *NCHR* 25 (1948), 449–56; James H. Broussard, *The Southern Federalists, 1800–1816* (Baton Rouge: Louisiana State University Press, 1978), 10–11; Gilpatrick, *Jeffersonian Democracy*, 42–47; Risjord, *Chesapeake Politics*, 450, 512.

14. Jerald A. Combs, *The Jay Treaty: Political Battleground of the Founding Fathers* (Berkeley: University of California Press, 1970), 150–63.

15. Gilpatrick, *Jeffersonian Democracy*, 67–71; Richards, "Adams and the Moderate Federalists," 24–25; Risjord, *Chesapeake Politics*, 461–62, 537. For the impact of the Jay Treaty on national party development, see Joseph Charles, *The Origins of the American Party System* (Williamsburg: Institute of Early American History and Culture, 1956; reprint, New York: Harper, 1961), 93–95, 108–11, 116–18, 122; and William Nisbet Chambers, *Political Parties in a New Nation: The American Experience, 1776–1809* (New York: Oxford University Press, 1963), 77–80, 85–91. For an account of how the Federalists capitalized on the fear of war to mobilize public opinion behind the Jay Treaty, see Combs, *Jay Treaty*, 179–84.

16. Gilpatrick, *Jeffersonian Democracy*, 86–100; Broussard, *Southern Federalists*, 14, 20–21, 30, 86, 215. The Federalists came within fourteen votes of winning a fifth electoral district.

17. Ibid., 22, 54, 67, 380–83.

18. Nineteen of the thirty-one strongest Republican counties were on, or within a few miles of, the Virginia border. Only three were in the southern part of the state. See the map in Broussard, *Southern Federalists*, 407. For Federalist use of the subservience-to-Virginia theme, see Gilpatrick, *Jeffersonian Democracy*, 72–73, 229–30; and Risjord, *Chesapeake Politics*, 512.

19. Delbert H. Gilpatrick, "North Carolina Congressional Elections, 1803–1810," *NCHR* 10 (1933); Gilpatrick, *Jeffersonian Democracy*, 91–99, 199–204. A complete set of extant returns for presidential and congressional elections between 1790 and 1835 can be found in Compiled Election Returns, Miscellaneous Collections, NCDAH.

20. DeMond, *Loyalists*, 57–59, 103, 138–40; Richards, "Adams and the Moderate Federalists," 20; James S. Brawley, *The Rowan Story: A Narrative History of Rowan County, 1753–1953* (Salisbury: Rowan Printing, 1953), 65–73; Alonzo T. Dill, "Eighteenth Century New Bern: A History of the Town and Craven County, 1700–1800," *NCHR* 23 (1946): 357–59; Samuel A. Ashe, *History of North Carolina*, 2 vols. (Greensboro: C. L. Van Noppen, 1908–25), 1:686–89, 721; Wyche, "Tory War," 99.

21. Ashe, *History of North Carolina*, 2:2.

22. Broussard, *Southern Federalists*, 178, 226–34, 292–303; Gilpatrick, *Jeffersonian Democracy*, 152–53.

23. The percentage of Federalist seats in the house of commons dropped from 43 percent in 1800 to a mere 25 percent in 1805 (Broussard, *Southern Federalists,* 295).

24. See, for example, the remarks of the *Wilmington Gazette,* quoted in Broussard, *Southern Federalists,* 103.

25. For the campaign of 1808, see Broussard, *Southern Federalists,* 97–109; and Gilpatrick, *Jeffersonian Democracy,* 166–67.

26. Broussard, *Southern Federalists,* 150; Gilpatrick, *Jeffersonian Democracy,* 199–204.

27. Gilpatrick, *Jeffersonian Democracy,* 206–8.

28. Broussard, *Southern Federalists,* 172–77; Gilpatrick, *Jeffersonian Democracy,* 220–23.

29. Broussard has made a persuasive argument that the Federalist party in the South disbanded "by the voluntary decision of its leaders" (*Southern Federalists,* 177–79).

30. Charles S. Sydnor, "The One-Party Period of American History," *American Historical Review* 51 (1946): 439.

31. Shaw Livermore, *The Twilight of Federalism: The Disintegration of the Federalist Party, 1815–1830* (Princeton: Princeton University Press, 1962; reprint, New York: Gordian Press, 1972), 69–131, 266–70; Richard P. McCormick, *The Presidential Game: The Origins of American Presidential Politics* (New York: Oxford University Press, 1982), 81; David H. Fischer, *The Revolution of American Conservatism: The Federalist Party in the Era of Jeffersonian Democracy* (New York: Harper and Row, 1965), 80–81.

32. Nathaniel Macon to Bartlett Yancy, 12 December 1823, in Kemp P. Battle, ed., *Letters of Nathaniel Macon to John R. Eaton and Bartlett Yancey* (Chapel Hill: University Press, 1900), 69; Romulus M. Saunders to Yancy, 30 December 1821, in Albert R. Newsome, ed., "Letters of Romulus M. Saunders to Bartlett Yancy, 1821–1828," *NCHR* 8 (1931): 430; Lewis Williams to Thomas Ruffin, 22 December 1821, in J. G. de Roulhac Hamilton, ed., *The Papers of Thomas Ruffin,* 4 vols. (Raleigh: Edwards and Broughton, 1918–20), 1:258. The quotation is from the speech of Thomas W. Blackledge, in Albert R. Newsome, ed., "Debate on the Fisher Resolutions," *NCHR* 4 (1927): 455. The standard study of the campaign of 1824 is Albert R. Newsome, *The Presidential Election of 1824 in North Carolina* (Chapel Hill: University of North Carolina Press, 1939). For the Crawford campaign and the sources of his support in North Carolina, see pp. 43–46, 102–22.

33. Romulus M. Saunders to Thomas Ruffin, 5 February 1824, in Hamilton, *Ruffin Papers,* 1:289. According to Congressman Willie P. Mangum, Calhoun "has taken the principles of the old Federalists but press[es] their principles much further . . . on the subjects of internal improvements etc., and especially in a latitudinous construction of the constitution generally" (Mangum to Ruffin, 20 January 1824, ibid., 287).

34. Newsome, *Election of 1824,* 47–53, 59, 123–29; John C. Calhoun to Ninian Edwards, 23 September 1823, in Clyde N. Wilson and W. Edwin Hemphill, eds., *The Papers of John C. Calhoun,* 17 vols. to date (Columbia: University of South Carolina Press, 1959–), 8:281.

35. Originally published in pamphlet form, the debates are reprinted in their entirety in Newsome, "Fisher Resolutions."

36. Speech of Augustine H. Shepperd; speech of John Stanly, in Newsome, "Fisher Resolutions," 458, 215.

37. Speech of Thomas W. Blackledge, ibid., 456, 445, 454.

38. For Federalist antipathy to caucuses, see Broussard, *Southern Federalists*, 177, 302; and Gilpatrick, *Jeffersonian Democracy*, 163–64. See also the communication from "AB," in *Raleigh Minerva*, 24 May 1816.

39. Noble E. Cunningham, *The Jeffersonian Republicans: The Formation of Party Organization, 1789–1801* (Chapel Hill: University of North Carolina Press, 1957), 164–66; McCormick, *Presidential Game*, 63–64, 81–82; Noble E. Cunningham, *The Jeffersonian Republicans in Power: Party Operations, 1801–1809* (Chapel Hill: University of North Carolina Press, 1963), 107–8.

40. James S. Chase, *Emergence of the Presidential Nominating Convention, 1789–1832* (Urbana: University of Illinois Press, 1973), 23. See also McCormick, *Presidential Game*, 90–92; and Cunningham, *Jeffersonian Republicans in Power*, 113–20.

41. McCormick, *Presidential Game*, 96–97.

42. Ibid., 92–94.

43. Ibid., 97–99. For the reference to a "coalition" of Federalists and dissident Republicans, see ibid., 99.

44. Livermore, *Twilight of Federalism*, 88–95. See also Richard H. Brown, "The Missouri Crisis, Slavery, and the Politics of Jacksonianism," *Atlantic Quarterly* 65 (1966): 57–61.

45. Speech of Thomas W. Blackledge; speech of John Stanly, in Newsome, "Fisher Resolutions," 453–54, 222. For evidence that Calhoun and his leading supporters were consciously trying to construct an alliance of Federalists and dissident Republicans, see Livermore, *Twilight of Federalism*, 151–54.

46. Of the legislators supporting the anticaucus resolutions, 72 percent represented Federalist constituencies and only 28 percent represented Republican constituencies. On the other hand, 83 percent of the legislators opposing Fisher's resolutions came from Republican constituencies.

47. Newsome, *Election of 1824*, 73–77, 84–87.

48. William B. Lewis to William Polk, 15 March 1824, William Polk Papers, NCDAH; William S. Hoffmann, *Andrew Jackson and North Carolina Politics* (Chapel Hill: University of North Carolina Press, 1958), 2–3; Newsome, *Election of 1824*, 87n, 91–92, 138. For evidence of widespread Federalist support for Jackson throughout the country, see Livermore, *Twilight of Federalism*, 223–41.

49. Archibald D. Murphey to William Polk, 27 February, 21 March 1824, in William H. Hoyt, ed., *The Papers of Archibald D. Murphey*, 2 vols. (Raleigh: E. M. Uzzell, 1914), 1:291–93, 294–95; Henry Potter to Polk, 22 October 1824, Polk Papers; Newsome, *Election of 1824*, 96–100.

50. *Salisbury Western Carolinian*, 2 November 1824; *Raleigh Star*, 5 November 1824; *Fayetteville Observer*, 14 October 1824. Although John Quincy Adams did not lack his share of supporters in the state, they did not try to set up a separate

electoral ticket. Henry Clay, the other presidential candidate, seems to have had no significant support in North Carolina in 1824.

51. Speech of Thomas W. Blackledge, in Newsome, "Fisher Resolutions," 455; *To the Freemen of North Carolina* (n.p., 1824), 6; circular by Alfred M. Gatlin, 30 April 1824, in Noble E. Cunningham, ed., *Circular Letters of Congressmen to Their Constituents, 1789–1829*, 3 vols. (Chapel Hill: University of North Carolina Press, 1978), 3:1206.

52. Quoted in Newsome, *Election of 1824*, 104. The *Register* itself was quoting from an address to the people of South Carolina.

53. In this study the "east" or "coastal plain" is considered to comprise those counties lying east of the western boundaries of Granville, Wake, Harnett, Cumberland, and Robeson counties. This includes the subregions designated as the "Albemarle region" (or "northeast," or "extreme east") and the "middle east." The terms "mountain region," "extreme west," and "far west" are used to designate those counties lying west of the western boundaries of Surry, Yadkin, Alexander, Catawba, and Cleveland counties. The term "piedmont" refers to those counties lying between the coastal plain and the mountain region. The term "west" is used to designate the piedmont and mountain region considered in unison.

54. Crawford polled over 75 percent of the vote in Bladen, Caswell, Chatham, Granville, Person, Randolph, and Warren counties. He polled between 60 and 75 percent of the vote in Ashe, Brunswick, Guilford, Halifax, Nash, and Northampton counties. Only Guilford was a Federalist county. Guilford had a large Quaker population and its majority for Crawford was more a protest against Jackson, the military candidate, than an endorsement of Crawford's conservative Republicanism (Newsome, *Election of 1824*, 159). The People's ticket polled over 75 percent of the vote in the following Federalist counties: Anson, Cabarrus, Carteret, Cumberland, Davidson, Greene, Montgomery, and Rowan. The Republican counties that gave over 75 percent to the People's ticket were: Buncombe, Burke, Haywood, and Rutherford in the mountain region; and Currituck, Gates, Hertford, Hyde, Pasquotank, and Tyrrell in the Albemarle Sound region (see the map in Newsome, *Election of 1824*, 163).

55. Prior to 1824 no resident of the mountain region had ever sat in the governor's chair, and only one—Montford Stokes of Wilkes—had been elected to the U.S. Senate. With the exception of David Stone of Bertie, no politician from the Albemarle region had ever been governor or senator. It is interesting that Bertie was the westernmost county in the Albemarle region and Wilkes was the easternmost county in the mountain region. Bertie was also one of the two Albemarle counties that supported Crawford in 1824. Crawford won 48 percent of the vote in Wilkes, although he won only 25 percent in the mountain region as a whole.

56. Newsome, *Election of 1824*, 14, 17–21, 37.

57. Ibid., 17–21, 132–33, 137. In 1823, while Calhoun was still in the presidential race, his North Carolina supporters had praised him for his efforts to "bind the Republic together, with a perfect system of roads and canals." See *An Address to the Citizens of North-Carolina on the Subject of the Presidential Election* (n.p., 1823), 13.

58. Thomas Jefferson Green to William Polk, 2 February 1824, Polk Papers; Robert Williamson to Bartlett Yancy, 26 July 1824, in J. G. de Roulhac Hamilton and Henry M. Wagstaff, eds., *Letters to Bartlett Yancy* (Chapel Hill: University Press, 1911), 46; Priestly H. Mangum to Willie P. Mangum, 15 April 1824, in Henry T. Shanks, ed., *The Papers of Willie Person Mangum*, 5 vols. (Raleigh: State Department of Archives and History, 1950–56), 1:134. An excellent discussion of the sources of Jackson's popular appeal can be found in John W. Ward, *Andrew Jackson: Symbol for an Age* (New York: Oxford University Press, 1955).

59. For voter turnout, see J. R. Pole, "Election Statistics in North Carolina, to 1861," *JSH* 24 (1958): 227. The vast majority of Adams supporters who participated in the election seem to have voted for the People's ticket, and in some counties most of the votes for that ticket were cast by Adams men (Newsome, *Election of 1824*, 158–59).

60. Robert Remini, *Andrew Jackson and the Course of American Freedom, 1822–1832* (New York: Harper and Row, 1981), 77.

61. John H. Eaton to William Polk, 17 March 1824, Polk Papers. The Calhoun campaign of 1823 and early 1824 had a similar antiauthoritarian thrust. The South Carolinian characterized the contest as "a struggle between the people and . . . what are called the leading politicians." Calhoun to Charles Fisher, 2 December 1823, in Albert R. Newsome, ed., "Correspondence of John C. Calhoun, George McDuffie and Charles Fisher, Relating to the Presidential Campaign of 1824," *NCHR* 7 (1930): 483.

62. Most historians who have commented upon the matter have argued that state sectionalism was the principal factor. "When the East turned to Jackson in 1828 in opposition to Adams, the West . . . allied itself with the new Whig party." J. Carlyle Sitterson, *The Secession Movement in North Carolina* (Chapel Hill: University of North Carolina Press, 1939), 31. See also J. G. de Roulhac Hamilton, *Party Politics in North Carolina, 1835–1860* (Durham: Seeman Printery, 1916), 34; and Clarence C. Norton, *The Democratic Party in Ante-Bellum North Carolina, 1835–1861* (Chapel Hill: University of North Carolina Press, 1930), 44, 47. This explanation fails to recognize the multisectional character of both North Carolina parties. Marc W. Kruman's recent study ignores the estrangement of the original Jackson men, noting only that "Jackson drove hordes of Democrats into the opposition" by ordering the removal of the federal deposits from the Bank of the United States. See Kruman, *Parties and Politics in North Carolina, 1836–1865* (Baton Rouge: Louisiana State University Press, 1983), 19.

63. Remini, *Jackson and the Course of American Freedom*, 86–111.

64. Bartlett Yancy to Willie P. Mangum, 25 January 1826, in Shanks, *Mangum Papers*, 1:240.

65. Nathaniel Macon to Bartlett Yancy, 8 December 1825, in Battle, *Letters of Macon to Eaton and Yancey*, 76.

66. Willie P. Mangum to Charity A. Mangum, 8 April 1826, in Shanks, *Mangum Papers*, 1:268. For evidence that a concern about slavery was an important factor behind Republican hostility toward Adams, see Brown, "Missouri Crisis," 66–68; and William J. Cooper, *The South and the Politics of Slavery, 1828–1856* (Baton Rouge: Louisiana State University Press, 1978), 7–9.

Notes to Pages 34–37

67. Daniel M. McFarland, "Rip Van Winkle: Political Evolution in North Carolina, 1815–1835" (Ph.D. diss., University of Pennsylvania, 1954), 224–25; John Niven, *Martin Van Buren: The Romantic Age of American Politics* (New York: Oxford University Press, 1983), 179–80, 183–84; Hoffmann, *Jackson and North Carolina*, 12–13.

68. Hoffmann, *Jackson and North Carolina*, 17–18.

69. The chairman of the central Jackson committee was William Polk, the ex-Federalist who had served as Old Hickory's campaign manager in 1824. Other committee members with Federalist backgrounds included George E. Badger, Polk's son-in-law and a future U.S. senator; John L. Taylor, the chief justice of the state supreme court; Charles Manly, a young Raleigh lawyer who would later become governor; and George W. Haywood, the son of the veteran state treasurer. The names of the fourteen committee members appear in the *New Bern Carolina Sentinel*, 12 January 1828.

70. *New Bern Spectator*, 11 October, 8 November 1828. For a general account of the campaign of 1828, see Robert V. Remini, *The Election of Andrew Jackson* (Philadelphia: Lippincott, 1963), especially pp. 101–19, 151–63. For North Carolina, see Hoffmann, *Jackson and North Carolina*, 19–21.

71. Voting returns by county can be found in *Raleigh Register*, 5 December 1828. Adams carried Brunswick, Guilford, Iredell, Randolph, Beaufort, Carteret, Jones, and Pitt counties. The first four counties had given majorities to Crawford in 1824, which suggests that the Adams men in those counties either sat out that election or—unlike their counterparts in most North Carolina counties—actually voted for Crawford.

72. According to Shaw Livermore, Jackson appointed more Federalists to important offices than all his Republican predecessors combined (*Twilight of Federalism*, 241).

73. John H. Wheeler, *Historical Sketches of North Carolina*, 2 vols. in 1 (Philadelphia: Lippincott, 1851), 2:94–96; Newsome, *Election of 1824*, 67; Hoffmann, *Jackson and North Carolina*, 17, 27–28; McFarland, "Rip Van Winkle," 154–55, 219–20, 251–52.

74. James Iredell, Jr., to Willie P. Mangum, 4 February 1832, in Shanks, *Mangum Papers*, 1:471–73.

75. For evidence that Van Buren did not manipulate Jackson into dissolving the cabinet, see Remini, *Jackson and the Course of American Freedom*, 300–314. The reference to the "master stroke" was by Isaac Hill and can be found in ibid., 317. For an analysis of the rift between Jackson and Calhoun, see Richard B. Latner, *The Presidency of Andrew Jackson: White House Politics, 1829–1837* (Athens: University of Georgia Press, 1979), 58–85, 140–45; and William W. Freehling, *Prelude to Civil War: The Nullification Controversy in South Carolina, 1816–1836* (New York: Harper and Row, 1966), 187–92.

76. Communication from Branch, in *New Bern Spectator*, 21 May 1831; Branch to *Roanoke Advocate*, and to the citizens of Bertie County, in *Tarborough Press*, 13 September 1831. See also William S. Hoffmann, "John Branch and the Origins of the Whig Party in North Carolina," *NCHR* 35 (1958).

77. *Salisbury Western Carolinian*, 7 May 1832.

78. See, for example, *Fayetteville North Carolina Journal*, 27 June, 4, 18, 25 July 1832.

79. *Raleigh Star*, in *Fayetteville Observer*, 7 August 1832; *Salisbury Western Carolinian*, 4, 18 June 1832. For the Barbour movement, see Cooper, *South and the Politics of Slavery*, 17–22.

80. *Fayetteville Observer*, 13 November 1832; Hoffmann, *Jackson and North Carolina*, 56. For voter participation, see Pole, "Election Statistics in North Carolina," 227. The question of whether Barbour really did withdraw from the vice presidential race became a matter of controversy in North Carolina after the election. A few weeks before the election Barbour had written a public letter to his supporters in Virginia expressing his fear that the divisions within the Jackson ranks might throw the election in his home state to Clay, and urging his followers to vote for the Jackson–Van Buren ticket nominated by the state legislature. The context of Barbour's letter suggests that he hoped that a strong showing for the Jackson–Barbour ticket in North Carolina and other southern states would lead the Virginia electors to abandon Van Buren and vote for him. But the Van Buren newspapers in North Carolina quickly cited the letter as evidence that Barbour had, in fact, withdrawn from the race. Moreover, the editor of the *Raleigh Star*, a leading Barbour supporter, placed a similar construction on the letter and issued an extra edition announcing that the candidate had withdrawn. After the election, Edward J. Hale of the *Fayetteville Observer* bitterly complained that the Barbour leaders in North Carolina had "weakened, divided, [and] destroyed their own party" (*Fayetteville Observer*, 13 November 1832). A detailed discussion of the controversy surrounding Barbour's letter can be found in ibid., 6 November 1832.

81. Latner, *Presidency of Andrew Jackson*, 86. See also Remini, *Jackson and the Course of American Freedom*, 315–30.

82. *Raleigh Star*, 9 October 1834; *Salisbury Western Carolinian*, 26 April 1834.

83. The antinullification resolutions passed the house of commons by a vote of 98 to 22 and the senate by 49 to 9 (McFarland, "Rip Van Winkle," 352–53, 368–70). Interestingly, pronullification sentiment in North Carolina did not center in the plantation counties of the middle east but rather in the central piedmont and Albemarle Sound regions—areas where Calhoun had been popular since 1824. William S. Hoffmann claims that Tarheel nullifiers were motivated less by ideology than by loyalty to Calhoun (*Jackson and North Carolina*, 68).

84. Elizabeth S. Hoyt, "Reactions in North Carolina to Jackson's Banking Policy, 1829–1832," *NCHR* 25 (1948). For a discussion of state banking during the 1820s, see chapter 5 in this volume.

85. Abraham Rencher, *To the Freemen of the Tenth Congressional District of North Carolina* (Washington, D.C., 1835), 6.

86. Address of the New Hanover County Republicans, in *Raleigh Register*, 5 October 1832; *Raleigh Star*, 8 May 1834.

87. Rencher, *To the Freemen*, 7.

88. *Raleigh Star*, 20 March 1834; Willie P. Mangum to Duncan Cameron, 7 February 1834, in Shanks, *Mangum Papers*, 2:73; Herbert D. Pegg, *The Whig Party in North Carolina* (Chapel Hill: Colonial Press, 1968), 10. Although he had sup-

ported Crawford in 1824, Mangum's perception of the political crisis of the early 1830s was identical to that of the original Jackson men. Mangum claimed that he and his political friends "had been compelled to take position agt. the administration" because of "the selfishness, the ambition & the intrigues of Mr. Van Buren." Mangum to John Bell, 15 June 1835, in Shanks, *Mangum Papers*, 2:349.

89. Edward B. Dudley to Willie P. Mangum, 23 March 1834, in Shanks, *Mangum Papers*, 2:127; Spencer O'Brien to Mangum, 17 February 1834, ibid., 2:86.

90. See, for example, *Salisbury Western Carolinian*, 4 February 1833. For the origins of the name "Whig," see E. Malcolm Carroll, *Origins of the Whig Party* (Durham: Duke University Press, 1925), 123–24.

91. Compare the resolutions adopted by the pro- and anti-Jackson meetings in Fayetteville, in *North Carolina Journal*, 19 June 1834; and *Raleigh Register*, 1 July 1834.

92. *Fayetteville Observer*, 2 September 1834.

93. For conflicting estimates of the strength of the two parties, see *Salisbury Western Carolinian*, 30 August 1834; *Raleigh Star*, 4 September 1834 (extract from *Salisbury Carolina Watchman*), 11 September 1834 (extracts from *Milton Spectator* and *Warrenton Reporter*); and *Fayetteville Observer*, 9 September 1834 (extract from *Wilmington People's Press*).

94. Hoffmann, *Jackson and North Carolina*, 77–79.

95. See the resolutions from Chowan County, Fayetteville, and Washington, N.C., in Shanks, *Mangum Papers*, 2:290–91, 299–300, 333–34. For invitations to dinners and other public celebrations, see ibid., 319–22, 326–32, 334–37, 340–41, 347–48, 355–56, 359–61.

96. *Raleigh Register*, 1 September 1835; McFarland, "Rip Van Winkle," 448–55.

97. Richard P. McCormick, *The Second American Party System: Party Formation in the Jacksonian Era* (Chapel Hill: University of North Carolina Press, 1966), 250–54, 340; Cooper, *South and the Politics of Slavery*, 15–16, 52–58; Kruman, *Parties and Politics in North Carolina*, 20. The so-called McCormick thesis has been challenged by Burton W. Folsom, who attributes the rise of the Whig party to "Jackson's failure to placate personally or ideologically an influential coterie of Southern leaders." See "Party Formation and Development in Jacksonian America: The Old South," *Journal of American Studies* 7 (1973): 229.

98. Pole, "Election Statistics in North Carolina," 227–28.

99. Hoffmann, *Jackson and North Carolina*, 29–30, 43.

100. Burton served as governor from 1824 until 1827; Swain, from 1832 until 1835. On the other hand, support for Jackson seems to have been a necessary prerequisite for elevation to the U.S. Senate. An examination of campaign literature for the period 1824–33 in the pamphlet and broadside collections of the University of North Carolina and Duke University suggests that national issues did not play a significant role in legislative elections, although many legislative candidates apparently found it to their advantage to express general support for Andrew Jackson. For a good discussion of shifting factions within the North Carolina General Assembly, see Hoffmann, *Jackson and North Carolina*, 26–36.

101. The quotation is from Robert V. Remini, *Andrew Jackson and the Course of American Democracy, 1833–1845* (New York: Harper and Row, 1984), 151.

102. *Raleigh North Carolina Standard*, in *Fayetteville North Carolina Journal*, 29 July 1835; *Raleigh Register*, 6 August 1824.

2 Sectionalism and Party Formation

1. J. R. Pole, "Election Statistics in North Carolina, to 1861," *JSH* 24 (1958): 227.
2. Speech of Augustine H. Shepperd, in Albert R. Newsome, ed., "Debate on the Fisher Resolutions," *NCHR* 4 (1927): 457.
3. Harold J. Counihan, "North Carolina 1815–1836: State and Local Perspectives on the Age of Jackson" (Ph.D. diss., University of North Carolina at Chapel Hill, 1971), 4, 51n, 170; Thomas E. Jeffrey, "The Second Party System in North Carolina, 1836–1860" (Ph.D. diss., Catholic University of America, 1976), 85–93.
4. Hershal L. Macon, "A Fiscal History of North Carolina, 1776–1860" (Ph.D. diss., University of North Carolina at Chapel Hill, 1932), 181–97; Counihan, "North Carolina 1815–1836," 94–103.
5. The North Carolina Constitution of 1776, along with the amendments adopted in 1835, can be found in Francis N. Thorpe, *The Federal and State Constitutions, Colonial Charters, and Other Organic Laws*, 7 vols. (Washington, D.C.: Government Printing Office, 1909), 5:2787–99.
6. After comparing the number of voters in gubernatorial elections (after 1835) with those in state senatorial elections, Richard P. McCormick concluded that "nearly one-half of those who went to the polls to vote for governor were unable to vote for state senators because they lacked the requisite fifty-acre freehold." McCormick, "Suffrage Classes and Party Alignments: A Study in Voter Behavior," *Mississippi Valley Historical Review* 46 (1959): 408.
7. Counihan, "North Carolina 1815–1836," 10–11.
8. William S. Hoffmann, *Andrew Jackson and North Carolina Politics* (Chapel Hill: University of North Carolina Press, 1958), 26–36; Counihan, "North Carolina 1815–1836," 83–88.
9. Counihan, "North Carolina 1815–1836," 97–99, 105–13; Thomas E. Jeffrey, "Internal Improvements and Political Parties in Antebellum North Carolina, 1836–1860," *NCHR* 55 (1978): 113–16.
10. Counihan, "North Carolina 1815–1836," 111–12, 128–29.
11. Ibid., 131–32 (note); Daniel M. McFarland, "Rip Van Winkle: Political Evolution in North Carolina, 1815–1835" (Ph.D. diss., University of Pennsylvania, 1954), 60–61.
12. James H. Broussard, *The Southern Federalists 1800–1816* (Baton Rouge: Louisiana State University Press, 1978), 226–28.
13. McFarland, "Rip Van Winkle," 60–61, 79–80, 97–98, 115–16, 124–25.
14. *Salisbury Western Carolinian*, 13 June 1820, 21 August, 2 October, 1821.
15. Quoted in ibid., 8 October 1822.
16. *Proceedings of the Friends of Convention at a Meeting Held in Raleigh December, 1822* (Raleigh, 1822), 3.
17. *To the Freemen of Orange County* (n.p., 1823), 4, 6.

18. *Journal of a Convention Assembled at the City of Raleigh on the 10th of November, 1823* (Raleigh: J. Gales and Son, 1823); *The Proposed New Constitution of the State of North Carolina* (Raleigh: J. Gales and Son, 1823); Counihan, "North Carolina 1815–1836," 132–34.

19. McFarland, "Rip Van Winkle," 151–52.

20. *Salisbury Western Carolinian*, 25 May 1825.

21. Years later, Fisher himself observed how national politics had inhibited the formation of sectional parties in North Carolina. "The peculiar situation in which the Southern States stand to the rest of this Confederacy, will always make [state] sectional parties give way to the stronger excitements which grow out of the action of the Federal Government. In other words, local parties will always be merged into the great political parties of the country. Federal politics, like Aaron's serpent, will swallow up the rest. . . . Heretofore, that has been the case in North Carolina." In *Proceedings and Debates of the Convention of North-Carolina Called to Amend the Constitution of the State* (Raleigh: Joseph Gales and Son, 1836), 117–18.

22. McFarland, "Rip Van Winkle," 329–31; Counihan, "North Carolina 1815–1836," 90.

23. McFarland, "Rip Van Winkle," 345–46; Counihan, "North Carolina 1815–1836," 91–92.

24. Speech of William L. Long; speech of John R. J. Daniel, in *Debate in the Legislature of North-Carolina on a Proposed Appropriation for Re-building the Capitol and on the Convention Question* (Raleigh: J. Gales and Son, 1832), 25–26, 54–55.

25. McFarland, "Rip Van Winkle," 366–67; Counihan, "North Carolina 1815–1836," 135–36.

26. William H. Haywood, Jr., to Martin Van Buren, April 1833; Haywood to Van Buren, 10 January 1833, in Elizabeth G. McPherson, ed., "Unpublished Letters from North Carolinians to Van Buren," *NCHR* 15 (1938): 59, 57–58.

27. Van Buren's reply to Haywood is summarized in McFarland, "Rip Van Winkle," 392.

28. McFarland, "Rip Van Winkle," 404–5; Counihan, "North Carolina 1815–1836," 135–36.

29. For the members of the executive committee, see J. G. de Roulhac Hamilton and Max R. Williams, eds., *The Papers of William Alexander Graham*, 7 vols. to date (Raleigh: Division of Archives and History, 1957–), 1:303. William R. Hargrove was a local leader from Granville County who served one term in the house of commons in 1833. John H. Wheeler, *Historical Sketches of North Carolina*, 2 vols. in 1 (Philadelphia: Lippincott, 1851), 2:166.

30. *Raleigh North Carolina Constitutionalist*, 25 June 1833; *Raleigh Register*, 14 January 1834. See also the extracts from other eastern newspapers in *Register*, 4, 25 February, 25 March 1834.

31. Hoffmann, *Jackson and North Carolina*, 81–85.

32. McFarland, "Rip Van Winkle," 377–88; Counihan, "North Carolina 1815–1836," 65–69, 121–24, 137.

33. McFarland, "Rip Van Winkle," 399–400; Counihan, "North Carolina 1815–1836," 127–28.
34. Extracts from the *Journal, Examiner,* and *Free Press* appear in *Raleigh Register,* 4 February 1834. Numerous other extracts from both eastern and western newspapers appear in this issue.
35. *Salisbury Western Carolinian,* in *Raleigh Register,* 4 February 1834.
36. Hoffmann, *Jackson and North Carolina,* 82–83.
37. *Salisbury Carolina Watchman,* in *Raleigh Register,* 29 July 1834.
38. William H. Haywood, Jr., *To the People of Wake County* (Raleigh, 1834).
39. William H. Haywood, Jr., to William A. Graham, 17 January 1834, in Hamilton and Williams, *Graham Papers,* 1:282–83; *Raleigh Register,* 29 July, 12 August 1834.
40. McFarland, "Rip Van Winkle," 432–34; Counihan, "North Carolina 1815–1836," 138–41; Hoffmann, *Jackson and North Carolina,* 84–85.
41. *Proceedings and Debates of the Convention of North-Carolina,* 117–18.
42. Harold J. Counihan, "The North Carolina Constitutional Convention of 1835: A Study in Jacksonian Democracy," *NCHR* 46 (1969): 336–37.
43. Ibid.
44. Ibid., 337–40.
45. Ibid., 341–60.
46. Ibid., 355–56; remarks of Emanuel Shober, in *Proceedings and Debates of the Convention of North-Carolina,* 346. William B. Meares, who introduced the motion requiring the approval of two-thirds of the legislators for the calling of a convention, admitted that his purpose was to protect the east from further changes in the basis of legislative apportionment (*Proceedings and Debates of the Convention of North-Carolina,* 371). The convention approved Meares's amendment by a vote of 90 to 29 (ibid., 373).
47. Counihan, "Constitutional Convention," 361.
48. Max R. Williams, "Reemergence of the Two-Party System," in Lindley S. Butler and Alan D. Watson, eds., *The North Carolina Experience: An Interpretive and Documentary History* (Chapel Hill: University of North Carolina Press, 1984), 248; Herbert D. Pegg, *The Whig Party in North Carolina* (Chapel Hill: Colonial Press, 1968), 18. See also Max R. Williams, "The Foundations of the Whig Party in North Carolina: A Synthesis and a Modest Proposal," *NCHR* 47 (1970): 124; J. G. de Roulhac Hamilton, *Party Politics in North Carolina, 1835–1860* (Durham: Seeman Printery, 1916), 33–34; and Clarence C. Norton, *The Democratic Party in Ante-Bellum North Carolina, 1835–1861* (Chapel Hill: University of North Carolina Press, 1930), 43–44. Marc W. Kruman's recent study does not challenge this interpretation. See *Parties and Politics in North Carolina, 1836–1865* (Baton Rouge: Louisiana State University Press, 1983), 10–14.
49. Norton, *Democratic Party in Ante-Bellum North Carolina,* 44; Pegg, *Whig Party in North Carolina,* 17; Counihan, "Convention of 1835," 338n. In the house of commons, 30 of the 65 Democrats voted in favor of the convention bill, compared to 36 of the 63 Whigs.
50. In Lincoln, Mecklenburg, Chatham, Orange, Stokes, and Surry counties, the

number of seats allotted in the house of commons increased from 13 to 20. In the Whig counties of Anson, Cabarrus, Davidson, Guilford, Iredell, Montgomery, Moore, Randolph, Rowan, and Richmond, on the other hand, the number increased from 21 to only 22. In the eight mountain counties, the number of seats in the house of commons actually dropped from 16 to 14. The eastern counties lost heavily as a result of the change in the basis of representation. In the nineteen counties that usually gave majorities to the Whigs, the number of legislative seats dropped from 41 to 28. In nineteen other counties, which were usually carried by the Democrats, the number dropped from 40 to 31. For the partisan affiliation of the North Carolina counties between 1836 and 1850, see the map in chapter 6.

51. William Gaston to Robert H. G. Moore, 16 August 1835, Matthias Evans Manly Papers, SHC. See also Gaston's remarks in the Convention of 1835 (*Proceedings and Debates of the Convention of North-Carolina*, 336–39).

52. *Raleigh Register*, 24 January 1849. For a brilliant analysis of how local animosities shaped the pattern of party alignment in one North Carolina county, see Harry L. Watson, *Jacksonian Politics and Community Conflict: The Emergence of the Second American Party System in Cumberland County, North Carolina* (Baton Rouge: Louisiana State University Press, 1981).

3 Whiggery Triumphant

1. J. R. Pole, "Election Statistics in North Carolina, to 1861," *JSH* 24 (1958): 227–28.

2. Charles Fisher, *To the Freemen of Rowan County* (n.p., 1833).

3. Circular of Lewis Williams, in *Raleigh Register*, 10 March 1835; speech of Frederick Norcom, ibid., 8 March 1835.

4. *Raleigh Register*, 12 March 1833. For the development of public land policy as a political issue during the 1830s, see Daniel Feller, *The Public Lands in Jacksonian Politics* (Madison: University of Wisconsin Press, 1984), especially pages 143–88.

5. Circular of Lewis Williams; circular of William J. Alexander, in *Raleigh Register*, 10 March 1835.

6. Circular of Lewis Williams, ibid.; *Raleigh Register*, 5 July, 8 March 1836.

7. *Raleigh North Carolina Constitutionalist*, 2 April 1833; circular of Thomas Hall, in *Tarborough Press*, 4 July 1835.

8. Abraham Rencher, *To the Freemen of the Tenth Congressional District of North Carolina* (Washington, D.C., 1835), 10–11; Rencher, *To the People of the Tenth Congressional District of North Carolina* (Washington, D.C., 1837), 3.

9. William S. Hoffmann, *Andrew Jackson and North Carolina Politics* (Chapel Hill: University of North Carolina Press, 1958), 92–95; Herbert D. Pegg, *The Whig Party in North Carolina* (Chapel Hill: Colonial Press, 1968), 14–15.

10. *Raleigh Register*, 5 July, 7 June 1836; Pegg, *Whig Party in North Carolina*, 78–79. For a breakdown of the vote on Clay's land bill, see *Raleigh Register*, 14 June 1836.

11. Bedford Brown to Martin Van Buren, 11 October 1836, in Elizabeth G. McPherson, ed., "Unpublished Letters from North Carolinians to Van Buren," *NCHR* 15 (1938): 69; Pegg, *Whig Party in North Carolina*, 68.

12. Pegg, *Whig Party in North Carolina*, 67–68. Voting returns by county for the gubernatorial election of 1836 can be found in Thomas E. Jeffrey, "The Second Party System in North Carolina, 1836–1860" (Ph.D. diss., Catholic University of America, 1976), appendix A; and in Robert D. W. Connor, comp., *A Manual of North Carolina* (Raleigh: North Carolina Historical Commission, 1913), 993–94. According to Connor, Dudley received 33,993 votes, compared to 29,950 votes for Spaight.

13. Dudley polled over 75 percent of the vote in Anson, Beaufort, Davidson, Iredell, Montgomery, Richmond, and Rowan (Federalist); in Camden, Perquimans, Tyrrell, and Washington (Albemarle); in Wilkes (mountains); and in Randolph (central piedmont). Spaight received over 75 percent of the vote in Edgecombe, Nash, New Hanover, Warren, and Wayne (middle east); in Caswell (northern piedmont); in Currituck (Albemarle); and in Haywood and Yancey (mountains). Jeffrey, "Second Party System in North Carolina," appendix B.

14. *Fayetteville Observer*, 25 August 1836; *Greensboro Patriot*, in *Raleigh Register*, 13 September 1836; *Raleigh North Carolina Standard*, 15 September 1836.

15. Voting returns by county for the presidential election of 1836 can be found in W. Dean Burnham, *Presidential Ballots, 1836–1892* (Baltimore: Johns Hopkins University Press, 1955), 646–68. According to Burnham, Van Buren received 26,810 votes, and White 23,643 votes. For voter participation, see Pole, "Election Statistics in North Carolina," 227.

16. *Fayetteville Observer*, in *New Bern Spectator*, 12 August 1836; *New Bern Carolina Sentinel*, 7 September 1836; Hoffmann, *Jackson and North Carolina*, 96; Feller, *Public Lands in Jacksonian Politics*, 182–83; Hershal L. Macon, "A Fiscal History of North Carolina, 1776–1860" (Ph.D. diss., University of North Carolina at Chapel Hill, 1932), 348, 370.

17. *New Bern Carolina Sentinel*, 7 September 1836.

18. Communication from "Halifax," in *Raleigh Register*, 2 September 1834; *New Bern Carolina Sentinel*, 7 September 1836.

19. *New Bern Carolina Sentinel*, 7 September 1836.

20. *Raleigh North Carolina Standard*, 23 June, 14 July 1836; Jeffrey, "Second Party System in North Carolina," 247.

21. In 1836 Spaight carried the Federalist counties of Craven, Greene, Johnston, and Pitt. This accounts for his relatively strong showing among the Federalist counties in table 3.1. The Democrats lost all four of these counties in 1838, and they lost all but Johnston in 1840.

22. Thomas E. Jeffrey, "Internal Improvements and Political Parties in Antebellum North Carolina, 1836–1860," *NCHR* 55 (1978): 119–20.

23. Bedford Brown to Martin Van Buren, 11 October 1836, in McPherson, "Letters to Van Buren," 69.

24. Dudley's letter was published in *Raleigh Register*, 23 February 1836.

25. Report and Resolutions, Orange County Whig Meeting, 24 February 1836, in J. G. de Roulhac Hamilton and Max R. Williams, eds., *The Papers of William*

Alexander Graham, 7 vols. to date (Raleigh: Division of Archives and History, 1957–), 1:413.

26. For a vivid description of the "great fear" in North Carolina, see Daniel M. McFarland, "Rip Van Winkle: Political Evolution in North Carolina, 1815–1835" (Ph.D. diss., University of Pennsylvania, 1954), 331–40.

27. Pegg, *Whig Party in North Carolina,* 89–90.

28. *Raleigh Register,* 5 April 1836; Pegg, *Whig Party in North Carolina,* 90.

29. For partisan exploitation of the slavery issue during the campaign of 1836, see William J. Cooper, *The South and the Politics of Slavery, 1828–1856* (Baton Rouge: Louisiana State University Press, 1978), 74–97.

30. *Raleigh North Carolina Standard,* 16 June 1836.

31. National Republican [Democratic] Party, *An Address to the Freemen of North Carolina* (Raleigh, 1836), 7; communication from "Vindex," in *Raleigh North Carolina Standard,* 23 June 1836.

32. *Hillsborough Recorder* (extract), 14 July 1837, in Hamilton and Williams, *Graham Papers,* 2:516; "To the Freemen of Wake County," *Raleigh Register* extra, 5 August 1837; Pegg, *Whig Party in North Carolina,* 95.

33. *Raleigh North Carolina Standard,* 23 August 1837. The reference to "pecuniary distress" is from the *New Bern Carolina Sentinel,* quoted in the same issue of the *Standard.*

34. *Raleigh North Carolina Standard,* 7, 14 February 1838.

35. Communications from "A Republican," in *Tarborough Press,* 17 February, 10 March 1838. For Loring's reply, see *Raleigh North Carolina Standard,* 21 February, 14 March 1838.

36. *Raleigh Register,* 16 July 1838; Clarence C. Norton, *The Democratic Party in Ante-Bellum North Carolina, 1835–1861* (Chapel Hill: University of North Carolina Press, 1930), 92–96.

37. *Salisbury Western Carolinian,* in *Raleigh North Carolina Standard,* 5 September 1838; Jeffrey, "Second Party System in North Carolina," 271–72.

38. Jeffrey, "Second Party System in North Carolina," appendix A. Voting returns by county for the gubernatorial election of 1838 can also be found in Connor, *Manual of North Carolina,* 993–94. According to Connor, Dudley received 34,329 votes, compared to 20,153 votes for Branch. For the total number of eligible voters in 1836 and 1838, see Pole, "Election Statistics in North Carolina," 227–28.

39. For the Cherokee removal issue in 1838, see Jeffrey, "Second Party System in North Carolina," 247–48.

40. *Raleigh North Carolina Standard,* 21 August 1839. The Democratic resurgence can be attributed, at least in part, to the economic recovery of 1838–39. Prices rose steadily throughout 1838, and in August the three banks of North Carolina joined others throughout the nation in resuming specie payments. See Peter Temin, *The Jacksonian Economy* (New York: Norton, 1969), 148–51; Brantson B. Holder, "The Three Banks of the State of North Carolina, 1810–1872" (Ph.D. diss., University of North Carolina at Chapel Hill, 1937), 332–35. On the other hand, the Democratic gains in 1839 are not as impressive as they at first appear. The party gained one seat because of the defection of Charles Shepard, who was first elected to Congress in 1837 with Whig support. In the Ninth District,

Augustine H. Shepperd, the six-term Whig incumbent, was defeated by only forty-seven votes. Charles Fisher, the other new congressman claimed by the Democrats, had denied during the campaign that he favored Van Buren or the independent treasury. After the election, however, Fisher did declare himself a Democrat. See Pegg, *Whig Party in North Carolina*, 96; Charles Fisher, *To the Freemen of the Tenth Congressional District* (n.p., 1839), 3; *Raleigh North Carolina Standard*, 12 August 1840.

41. Cooper, *South and the Politics of Slavery*, 103, 114–15; John Niven, *Martin Van Buren: The Romantic Age of American Politics* (New York: Oxford University Press, 1983), 454–55, 460–61; Pegg, *Whig Party in North Carolina*, 87–88, 96. Contrary to the assertions of many historians, Calhoun did not immediately rejoin the Democratic party after his endorsement of the independent treasury in 1837.

42. Temin, *Jacksonian Economy*, 148, 153–55; Holder, "The Three Banks of the State of North Carolina," 332–35; Charles S. Sydnor, *The Development of Southern Sectionalism, 1819–1848* (Baton Rouge: Louisiana State University Press, 1948), 262–64.

43. See, especially, Temin, *Jacksonian Economy*.

44. Resolution of the Cumberland County Whigs, quoted in Harry L. Watson, *Jacksonian Politics and Community Conflict: The Emergence of the Second American Party System in Cumberland County, North Carolina* (Baton Rouge: Louisiana State University Press, 1981), 261. See also the Whig resolutions in *Raleigh Register*, 17 April, 1 May 1840.

45. James Graham to William A. Graham, 19 March 1840, in Hamilton and Williams, *Graham Papers*, 2:77.

46. For an exhaustive discussion of Van Buren and the independent treasury, see Major L. Wilson, *The Presidency of Martin Van Buren* (Lawrence: University Press of Kansas, 1984), 61–146.

47. George E. Badger, *Speech Delivered at the Great Whig Meeting in the County of Granville* (n.p., 1840), 4–5.

48. James B. Shepard, *Speech Delivered at the Great Republican Meeting in the County of Granville* (Raleigh, 1840), 19.

49. *Raleigh Register*, 28 January 1839.

50. Pegg, *Whig Party in North Carolina*, 97–98; Cooper, *South and the Politics of Slavery*, 125–28; William R. Brock, *Parties and Political Conscience: American Dilemmas, 1840–1850* (Millwood, N.Y.: KTO Press, 1979), 73.

51. Badger, *Speech at Granville*, 6; N.C. Whig Central Committee, *Address to the People of North Carolina* (n.p., 1840), 25; Cooper, *South and the Politics of Slavery*, 135–36, 141–45.

52. N.C. Whig Central Committee, *Address*, 15–16; *Raleigh Register*, 21 February 1840.

53. N.C. Democratic Executive Committee, *Address . . . to the Freemen and Voters of North Carolina* (n.p., 1840), 4, 8–9. The evidence for North Carolina does not support Cooper's argument that "the politics of slavery dwarfed all economic issues" during the campaign of 1840 (*South and the Politics of Slavery*, 132).

54. *Fayetteville North Carolinian*, 15 August 1840.

55. *Fayetteville Observer*, 2 September 1840; Pegg, *Whig Party in North Carolina*, 70–73.

56. *Raleigh Register*, 21 August 1840. Voting returns by county for the gubernatorial election of 1840 can be found in Jeffrey, "Second Party System in North Carolina," appendix A; and in Connor, *Manual of North Carolina*, 993–94. According to Connor, Morehead received 44,484 votes, compared to 35,903 votes for Saunders. For the legislative elections, see Pegg, *Whig Party in North Carolina*, 74.

57. *Salisbury Western Carolinian*, 7 August 1840; *Fayetteville North Carolinian*, 29 August 1840. Between 1838 and 1840 the Whig vote for governor increased by 61 percentage points in Macon, 29 points in Haywood, and 22 points in Yancey (Jeffrey, "Second Party System in North Carolina," appendix B).

58. In Charles Fisher's congressional district, the Democratic vote for governor increased between 1836 and 1840 by 33 percentage points in Rowan, 20 points in Davidson, and 11 points in Randolph. In newly created Davie County, which had voted with Rowan in 1836, the Democratic vote increased by 26 percentage points between 1838 and 1840. In the east the Democratic vote increased by 21 percentage points in Northampton, 18 points in Granville, 12 points in Washington, and 11 points in Perquimans (Jeffrey, "Second Party System in North Carolina," appendix B).

59. Voting returns by county for the presidential election of 1840 can be found in Burnham, *Presidential Ballots*, 646–68. According to Burnham, Harrison received 45,705 votes, and Van Buren 33,781 votes. For voter participation and the number of eligible voters, see Pole, "Election Statistics in North Carolina," 227–28.

60. Richard P. McCormick, *The Second American Party System: Party Formation in the Jacksonian Era* (Chapel Hill: University of North Carolina Press, 1966), 208, 349–50.

61. This, of course, is the thesis of Cooper, *South and the Politics of Slavery*.

4 Cliques, Caucuses, and Conventions

1. For an interpretation of Whig antipartyism that emphasizes the influence of evangelical Protestantism, see Ronald P. Formisano, "Political Character, Antipartyism and the Second Party System," *American Quarterly* 21 (1969).

2. Resolutions of Davidson County Whigs, in *Raleigh Register*, 21 April 1835; resolutions of Rowan County Whigs, ibid., 2 June 1835.

3. Communication from "W.C.," in *Raleigh Register*, 24 March 1835. Morehead is quoted in ibid., 12 April 1836.

4. Resolutions of Nash County Democrats, in *Raleigh North Carolina Standard*, 27 March 1835.

5. *Raleigh North Carolina Standard*, 24 December 1835.

6. After the election of 1836, Henry Clay wrote Hugh Lawson White that "the condition of the opposition . . . at the last election was unfortunate. No mode was devised and none seemed practicable to present a single candidate in opposition." Horace Greeley agreed that Van Buren "might have been beaten *by season-*

able concert and effort." Quoted in Joel H. Silbey, "Election of 1836," in Arthur M. Schlesinger and Fred L. Israel, eds., *History of American Presidential Elections, 1789–1968*, 4 vols. (New York: Chelsea House, 1971), 1:600. For a persuasive argument that the decision to run three Whig candidates in 1836 was not the result of a prearranged strategy, see Richard P. McCormick, "Was There a 'Whig Strategy' in 1836?" *Journal of the Early Republic* 4 (1984). McCormick points out that "talk of 'throwing the election into the House' represented not party strategy, but a scare tactic that originated with and was exploited by the Democrats" (70).

7. Henry Clay to Willie P. Mangum, 31 May 1838, in Henry T. Shanks, ed., *The Papers of Willie Person Mangum*, 5 vols. (Raleigh: State Department of Archives and History, 1950–56), 2:525. As early as August 1837, Clay was urging the Whigs to hold a national convention (McCormick, "Was There a 'Whig Strategy,'" 70n).

8. *Raleigh Register*, 11 June 1838.

9. Communication from "No Change-About," in *Salisbury Western Carolinian*, 29 November 1839; James W. Bryan to William A. Graham, 3 January 1839, in J. G. de Roulhac Hamilton and Max R. Williams, eds., *The Papers of William Alexander Graham*, 7 vols. to date (Raleigh: Division of Archives and History, 1957–), 2:30; Herbert D. Pegg, *The Whig Party in North Carolina* (Chapel Hill: Colonial Press, 1968), 97–98; William N. Chambers, "Election of 1840," in Arthur M. Schlesinger and Fred L. Israel, eds., *History of American Presidential Elections, 1789–1968*, 4 vols. (New York: Chelsea House, 1971), 1:662–65.

10. *Raleigh North Carolina Standard*, 10 March 1836; Luther N. Byrd, "The Life and Public Service of Edward Bishop Dudley, 1789–1855" (Master's thesis, University of North Carolina at Chapel Hill, 1949), 47.

11. *Raleigh North Carolina Standard*, 10 March 1836; Byrd, "Life and Public Service of Dudley," 46. For evidence that Dudley had been chosen as the Whig candidate several weeks in advance of his official nomination, see Weston R. Gales to Willie P. Mangum, 22 January 1836, in Shanks, *Mangum Papers*, 2:380–81; communication from Thomas G. Polk, 18 January 1836, in *Raleigh Register*, 2 February 1836.

12. *Fayetteville North Carolina Journal*, in *Tarborough Press*, 22 September 1838.

13. The resolutions of the Democrats can be found in *Raleigh North Carolina Standard*, 23 October 1839. A copy of the Whig resolutions, in the handwriting of William A. Graham, can be found in Hamilton and Williams, *Graham Papers*, 2:36–37.

14. *Raleigh Register*, 16 November 1839; *Raleigh North Carolina Standard*, 15 January 1840; Thomas E. Jeffrey, "The Second Party System in North Carolina, 1836–1860" (Ph.D. diss., Catholic University of America, 1976), 144–45.

15. *Salisbury Western Carolinian*, 24 April 1840; *Salisbury Carolina Watchman*, 17 January 1840. For evidence that both Morehead and Saunders had been chosen as candidates well in advance of their official nominations, see James W. Bryan to William A. Graham, 3 January 1839, in Hamilton and Williams, *Graham Papers*, 2:30; and Romulus M. Saunders to Weldon N. Edwards, 23 December 1839, Katherine P. Conway Collection, NCDAH.

16. George C. Mendenhall to William A. Graham, 12 January 1843, in Hamilton and Williams, *Graham Papers*, 2:412–13; John H. Bryan to James W. Bryan, 9 December 1843, Bryan Family Papers, SHC; William A. Graham to James W. Bryan, 11 January 1848, in Hamilton and Williams, *Graham Papers*, 3:213; Charles Manly to Samuel F. Patterson, 26 February 1854, Jones and Patterson Family Papers, SHC.

17. J. Julius Wherden to David S. Reid, 8 January 1846, David S. Reid Papers, NCDAH; Clarence C. Norton, *The Democratic Party in Ante-Bellum North Carolina, 1835–1861* (Chapel Hill: University of North Carolina Press, 1930), 225–32.

18. *Raleigh North Carolina Standard*, 13 February 1850; *Wilmington Journal*, in *North Carolina Standard*, 15 October 1845.

19. For Democratic conventions in the Wilmington, Fayetteville, and Edenton districts, see *Fayetteville North Carolina Journal*, 25 March, 29 April 1835; and *Raleigh North Carolina Standard*, 15, 22, 29 May 1835. For Whig conventions in the Charlotte and Tarboro districts, see *North Carolina Standard*, 26 June 1835; and William S. Hoffmann, *Andrew Jackson and North Carolina Politics* (Chapel Hill: University of North Carolina Press, 1958), 93.

20. Extract from *Washington North State Whig*, 17 April 1845, in *Fair Play* (n.p., 1845); Thomas Sparrow to [unknown], 13 February 1845, Thomas Sparrow Papers, SHC; Norton, *Democratic Party in Ante-Bellum North Carolina*, 144–45.

21. Henry I. Toole, *To the Voters of Johnston, Wake, Franklin, Warren, Halifax, Nash, and Edgecombe* (n.p., 1847).

22. Ibid.

23. *Wilmington Journal*, 30 July 1852.

24. In 1853 the bitter factional quarrels among the Democrats in the Raleigh district made it impossible to hold a nominating convention. Abraham W. Venable, the Democratic incumbent, announced himself as a candidate, but anti-Venable Democrats brought out A. M. Lewis. Whig candidate Sion H. Rogers won the election because of the divided Democratic vote (Norton, *Democratic Party in Ante-Bellum North Carolina*, 239–41).

25. *Salisbury Western Carolinian*, 31 May 1839.

26. Richard L. Zuber, *Jonathan Worth: A Biography of a Southern Unionist* (Chapel Hill: University of North Carolina Press, 1965), 60–64; Marc W. Kruman, *Parties and Politics in North Carolina, 1836–1865* (Baton Rouge: Louisiana State University Press, 1983), 39; Jeffrey, "Second Party System in North Carolina," 132–34.

27. Jeffrey, "Second Party System in North Carolina," 205–6. In each of the four gubernatorial elections during the period 1840–1846, about half of the counties favored the winning candidate by majorities of 66 percent or more. In only a fourth of the counties was the winning majority less than 58 percent (ibid., appendix B).

28. *Greensboro Patriot*, 11 July 1856; *Wadesboro North Carolina Argus*, 12 July 1860.

29. *Wilmington Journal*, 30 July 1858; J. J. Martin to Jesse Waugh, 28 February 1858, Jones-Patterson Papers.

30. *Wadesboro North Carolina Argus,* 24, 31 May, 5 July 1860.

31. Communication from "Many Democrats," in *Wilmington Commercial,* 23 July 1852. Larkins's appeal to the voters of New Hanover to assert their independence from their party leaders did not prove sufficient to overcome the sanction of the convention nomination. His opponent, James Kerr, won the election by a comfortable margin of 305 to 226 (*Wilmington Journal,* 13 August 1852).

32. *Salem People's Press,* 20 August 1858.

33. *Tarboro Southerner,* 7 August 1852; *Winston Western Sentinel,* in *Salem People's Press,* 20 August 1858; *Washington North State Whig,* 27 July 1842.

34. *Raleigh North Carolina Standard,* 18 February 1836.

35. Jeffrey, "Second Party System in North Carolina," 134–41.

36. *Wilmington Journal,* 19 May 1848.

37. Pegg, *Whig Party in North Carolina,* 40–41; Norton, *Democratic Party in Ante-Bellum North Carolina,* 35–36; Kruman, *Parties and Politics in North Carolina,* 35–36; Jeffrey, "Second Party System in North Carolina," 122–23.

38. Until 1816 there were no statewide elections in North Carolina (even the presidential electors were elected by districts), and neither party established a state committee system. The first central committees were established in 1824 to direct the presidential campaign. The nascent parties also set up committees for the campaigns of 1828 and 1832, but these organizations seem to have functioned on an ad hoc basis. Prior to 1835 there is no evidence of a central committee acting as an executive committee between campaigns. See Noble E. Cunningham, *The Jeffersonian Republicans in Power: Party Operations, 1801–1809* (Chapel Hill: University of North Carolina Press, 1963), 187–89, 201–2; Jeffrey, "Second Party System in North Carolina," 26, 43, 45–46.

39. Gales, Haywood, and Manly also served as members of the committee in 1836. Bryan, Gales, Manly, and Miller were members in 1844. John H. Bryan was a former congressman from New Bern who moved to Raleigh in 1828 to practice law. George W. Haywood, the son of veteran treasurer John Haywood and the cousin of Democratic Senator William H. Haywood, Jr., was a Raleigh lawyer and unsuccessful candidate for Congress. Henry W. Miller, a native of Virginia who settled in Raleigh after graduating from the University of North Carolina, was a distinguished lawyer with a widespread reputation as an eloquent public speaker. Other members of the central committee during these years included: Charles L. Hinton, the state treasurer from 1838 until 1850; Richard Hines, a former congressman from Edgecombe County; and George E. Badger, a native of New Bern, who served as U.S. senator from 1846 until 1854. For the composition of the Whig committees of 1836 and 1840, see *Raleigh Register,* 29 December 1835, 20 March 1840; for 1844, see the "Confidential Letter" [1844], in the John Herritage Bryan Papers, NCDAH. For brief biographical sketches, see William S. Powell, ed., *Dictionary of North Carolina Biography,* 2 vols. to date (Chapel Hill: University of North Carolina Press, 1979–), 1:79–80 (Badger), 118 (Battle), 255–56 (Bryan); Hamilton and Williams, *Graham Papers,* 1:497n (Hinton); 2:63n (Haywood), 69n (Miller), 447n (Hines); Pegg, *Whig Party in North Carolina,* 126n (Manly); and John H. Wheeler, *Historical Sketches of North Carolina,* 2 vols. in 1 (Philadelphia: Lippincott, 1851), 2:86 (McQueen).

40. For the composition of the Democratic central committees, see Raleigh *North Carolina Standard*, 6 October 1836; and N.C. Democratic Executive Committee, *Address . . . to the Freemen and Voters of North Carolina* (n.p., 1840). For brief biographical sketches, see Samuel A. Ashe, *Biographical History of North Carolina from Colonial Times to the Present*, 8 vols. (Greensboro: C. L. Van Noppen, 1905–17), 6:296–303 (Haywood); J. G. de Roulhac Hamilton, *Party Politics in North Carolina, 1835–1860* (Durham: Seeman Printery, 1916), 81 (Henry), 106 (Shepard); Norton, *Democratic Party in Ante-Bellum North Carolina*, 14–17 (Loring).

41. For Holden's early career, see Horace W. Raper, *William W. Holden: North Carolina's Political Enigma* (Chapel Hill: University of North Carolina Press, 1985), 3–10; and William C. Harris, *William Woods Holden: Firebrand of North Carolina Politics* (Baton Rouge: Louisiana State University Press, 1987), 8–15.

42. Communication from "A Republican," in *Tarborough Press*, 17 February 1838.

43. Calvin Graves to David S. Reid, 15 January 1846, Reid Papers; *Charlotte Journal*, 16 January 1846. Caldwell's letter of declination was published in *Raleigh North Carolina Standard*, 28 January 1846.

44. *Lincoln Courier*, in *Raleigh Register*, 17 April 1846; *Raleigh North Carolina Standard*, 11, 18 March 1846; Walter Leak to *Fayetteville Observer*, in *Raleigh Register*, 31 March 1846.

45. *Raleigh Register*, 20 March 1846. For extracts from Democratic newspapers and county meetings, see ibid., 17 April, 8, 15, 22 May 1846.

46. Thomas D. S. McDowell to James I. McKay, 23 July 1846, C. B. Heller Collection, NCDAH. For Leak's withdrawal, see *Raleigh North Carolina Standard*, 20 May 1846.

47. Graham received almost 1,000 more votes than he had won in 1844, while Shepard polled 3,700 fewer votes than Michael Hoke, Graham's earlier opponent. After the election, the editor of the *Wilmington Journal* claimed that "we are beaten by the lukewarm, indifferent and disaffected portions of our party, and to no other cause can our defeat be attributed." Quoted in *Raleigh North Carolina Standard*, 19 August 1846. The vote by county for the gubernatorial elections of 1844 and 1846 can be found in Jeffrey, "Second Party System in North Carolina," appendix A; and in Robert D. W. Connor, comp., *A Manual of North Carolina* (Raleigh: North Carolina Historical Commission, 1913), 995–96.

48. William A. Graham to James W. Bryan, 11 January 1848, in Hamilton and Williams, *Graham Papers*, 3:212–13; *Washington North State Whig*, in *Raleigh North Carolina Standard*, 8 March 1848; communication from "A Whig of 1840," in *Charlotte Hornet's Nest*, 2 February 1850.

49. William D. Valentine Diary, 7 March 1848, SHC; *Washington North State Whig*, in *Raleigh North Carolina Standard*, 8 March 1848.

50. *Raleigh North Carolina Standard*, 1 March 1848; William W. Holden to Abraham W. Venable, 12 March 1848, Abraham Watkins Venable Papers, SHC.

51. For the influence of the Raleigh Clique issue on the campaign of 1848, see Thomas E. Jeffrey, "'Free Suffrage' Revisited: Party Politics and Constitutional Reform in Antebellum North Carolina," *NCHR* 59 (1982): 36. For the election of 1850, see chapter 8 in this volume.

52. Cunningham, *Jeffersonian Republicans in Power*, 187–89, 200–202; James H. Broussard, *The Southern Federalists, 1800–1816* (Baton Rouge: Louisiana State University Press, 1978), 268, 302.

53. Brian G. Walton, "Elections to the United States Senate in North Carolina, 1835–1861," *NCHR* 53 (1976): 170, 174–75.

54. Romulus M. Saunders, *An Address . . . to the People of North Carolina* (Washington, D.C., 1843), 3, 5.

55. Walton, "Elections to the United States Senate in North Carolina," 179–80, 185–87; Jeffrey, "Second Party System in North Carolina," 217–21, 223.

56. William B. Shepard to Ebenezer Pettigrew, 28 September 1840, Pettigrew Family Papers, SHC; William A. Graham to James W. Bryan, 18 November 1840, in Hamilton and Williams, *Graham Papers*, 2:119.

57. Speech of William B. Shepard, in *Raleigh North Carolina Standard*, 6 January 1841.

58. Speech of Thomas L. Clingman, in *Raleigh Register*, 1 January 1841.

59. For an interpretation of Clingman's career that places primary emphasis on his political ambition, see Thomas E. Jeffrey, "'Thunder from the Mountains': Thomas Lanier Clingman and the End of Whig Supremacy in North Carolina," *NCHR* 56 (1979). Marc W. Kruman and John C. Inscoe have recently challenged this interpretation. See Kruman, "Thomas L. Clingman and the Whig Party: A Reconsideration," *NCHR* 64 (1987); and Inscoe, "Thomas Clingman, Mountain Whiggery, and the Southern Cause," *Civil War History* 33 (1987). For an assessment of the evidence, see chapter 11 in this volume.

60. Thomas L. Clingman, *Address of T. L. Clingman on the Recent Senatorial Election* (Washington, D.C.: J. and G. S. Gideon, 1849), 10, 12.

61. *Raleigh Register*, 24 January 1849.

62. Ronald P. Formisano has been the most outspoken critic of the notion that party organization contributed significantly to the mobilization of the antebellum electorate. See, for example, "Deferential-Participant Politics: The Early Republic's Political Culture, 1789–1840," *American Political Science Review* 68 (1974): 483; and *The Transformation of Political Culture: Massachusetts Parties, 1790s-1840s* (New York: Oxford University Press, 1983), 125, 312.

63. Max R. Williams, "Reemergence of the Two-Party System," in Lindley S. Butler and Alan D. Watson, eds., *The North Carolina Experience: An Interpretive and Documentary History* (Chapel Hill: University of North Carolina Press, 1984), 251; Pegg, *Whig Party in North Carolina*, 34, 43; Hamilton, *Party Politics in North Carolina*, 63, 77–78. On the other hand, Norton argues that the successive Democratic defeats "were due not to any insufficiency in the machinery, but to the ineffectual uses of such machinery. The Whigs had practically the same machinery, but, before 1850, used it with greater effectiveness" (*Democratic Party in Ante-Bellum North Carolina*, 40).

64. For the contrasting viewpoints of the two parties, see *Raleigh North Carolina Standard*, 6 October 1836, 17 August 1842; and *Raleigh Register*, 18 October 1836.

65. Formisano, "Deferential-Participant Politics," 474.

66. The most eloquent exponent of the electoral machine concept is Richard P. Mc-

Cormick. See, for example, *The Second American Party System: Party Forma-tion in the Jacksonian Era* (Chapel Hill: University of North Carolina Press, 1966), 4, 354–55.

67. The reference to parties as "great hoaxes" is by Edward Pessen, quoted in Joel H. Silbey, *The Partisan Imperative: The Dynamics of American Politics before the Civil War* (New York: Oxford University Press, 1985), 58.

68. Silbey, *Partisan Imperative*, 64.

5 Ideology and Political Culture

1. Charles S. Sydnor, *The Development of Southern Sectionalism, 1819–1848* (Baton Rouge: Louisiana State University Press, 1948), 319, 317.

2. Charles G. Sellers, "Who Were the Southern Whigs?" *American Historical Review* 59 (1954): 346.

3. William R. Brock, *Parties and Political Conscience: American Dilemmas, 1840–1850* (Millwood, N.Y.: KTO Press, 1979), 24. See also Lee Benson, *The Concept of Jacksonian Democracy: New York as a Test Case* (Princeton: Princeton University Press, 1961); Joel H. Silbey, *The Shrine of Party: Congressional Voting Behavior, 1841–1852* (Pittsburgh: University of Pittsburgh Press, 1967); James R. Sharp, *The Jacksonians versus the Banks: Politics in the States after the Panic of 1837* (New York: Columbia University Press, 1970); Michael F. Holt, *The Political Crisis of the 1850s* (New York: Wiley, 1978); and Herbert Ershkowitz and William G. Shade, "Consensus or Conflict? Political Behavior in the State Legislatures during the Jacksonian Era," *JAH* 58 (1971). For North Carolina, see Harry L. Watson, *Jacksonian Politics and Community Conflict: The Emergence of the Second Party System in Cumberland County, North Carolina* (Baton Rouge: Louisiana State University Press, 1981); and Marc W. Kruman, *Parties and Politics in North Carolina, 1836–1865* (Baton Rouge: Louisiana State University Press, 1983).

4. Recent studies that have emphasized the importance of republican ideology include Robert E. Shalhope, "Thomas Jefferson's Republicanism and Antebellum Southern Thought," *JSH* 42 (1976); Richard B. Latner, *The Presidency of Andrew Jackson: White House Politics, 1829–1837* (Athens: University of Georgia Press, 1979); and Holt, *Political Crisis of the 1850s.*

5. *Charlotte Miners' and Farmers' Journal,* in *Raleigh Register,* 2 September 1834.

6. Charles Fisher, *To the Freemen of the Tenth Congressional District* (n.p., 1839), 4; Henry I. Toole, *To the Voters of Johnston, Wake, Franklin, Warren, Halifax, Nash, and Edgecombe* (n.p., 1847).

7. *New Bern Spectator,* 11 August 1837; communication from John McLeod, in *Raleigh Register,* 8 September 1835.

8. Jesse A. Bynum, *An Address to the Reflecting Men of Northampton County, North Carolina* (n.p., 1836), 13.

9. *Raleigh Register,* 30 December 1834; communication from "A Republican," in *Tarborough Press,* 24 March 1838.

10. James Graham, *Circular to the People of the Twelfth Congressional District in North Carolina* (n.p., 1843), 14, 4.

11. *Raleigh Register*, 27 July 1839.

12. Charles Shepard, *To the Freemen of the Fourth Congressional District of North Carolina* (Washington, D.C.: Jos. Etter, 1838), 6; *Hillsborough Recorder*, 28 October 1836.

13. Herbert D. Pegg, *The Whig Party in North Carolina* (Chapel Hill: Colonial Press, 1968), 79; Peter Temin, *The Jacksonian Economy* (New York: Norton, 1969), 168.

14. N.C. Whig Central Committee, *Address to the People of North Carolina* (n.p., 1840), 9–10.

15. The Democratic platform for 1842 can be found in *Raleigh North Carolina Standard*, 19 January 1842.

16. Clarence C. Norton, *The Democratic Party in Ante-Bellum North Carolina, 1835–1861* (Chapel Hill: University of North Carolina Press, 1930), 101–2.

17. For an extended discussion of alignments within the North Carolina General Assembly on internal improvements, see Thomas E. Jeffrey, "Internal Improvements and Political Parties in Antebellum North Carolina, 1836–1860," *NCHR* 55 (1978); and chapters 8–10 in this volume. In this study I have used the term "anti-improvement" to characterize an attitude of opposition to the use of state funds for constructing railroads and other transportation facilities. However, an opposition to state-funded improvements did not necessarily signify hostility to the improvements themselves. On this point, see the evidence presented in chapter 9 in this volume.

18. Jeffrey, "Internal Improvements and Political Parties," 119–20.

19. Ibid., 120.

20. *Raleigh North Carolina Constitutionalist*, 23 July 1833; *Proceedings of the Internal Improvement Convention Held in the City of Raleigh, November, 1833* (Raleigh: Joseph Gales and Son, 1834), 16.

21. See, for example, Kruman, *Parties and Politics in North Carolina*, 22–24. For an extended discussion of the Raleigh & Gaston issue, see also chapter 7 in this volume.

22. *Raleigh North Carolina Standard*, 18 September 1844; *Fayetteville North Carolinian*, 7 September 1844. William C. Harris points out that as early as 1844, Holden "was willing, at least in principle, to support aid to any railroad in which the state owned stock and shared in the management and profits." See Harris, *William Woods Holden: Firebrand of North Carolina Politics* (Baton Rouge: Louisiana State University Press, 1987), 31.

23. *Raleigh North Carolina Standard*, 28 August 1844. For examples of partisan use by the Whigs of the internal improvements issue, see Jeffrey, "Internal Improvements and Political Parties," 129–35; and chapter 7 in this volume.

24. Pegg, *Whig Party in North Carolina*, 57; Norton, *Democratic Party in Ante-Bellum North Carolina*, 49. See also Max R. Williams, "Reemergence of the Two-Party System," in Lindley S. Butler and Alan D. Watson, eds., *The North Carolina Experience: An Interpretive and Documentary History* (Chapel Hill:

University of North Carolina Press, 1984), 246; and Kruman, *Parties and Politics in North Carolina*, 59.

25. Pegg, *Whig Party in North Carolina*, 59–60. The first school bill passed the state senate by a vote of 43 to 4, with three Whigs and one Democrat voting in the negative. A second bill, which was designed to reconcile differences between the senate bill and one that had been approved by the house, sailed through the house of commons without opposition and passed the state senate with only two Whigs and one Democrat voting in the negative (ibid., 59). The law provided that funds to support the school system would come from the Literary Fund, which had recently been replenished by federal revenues secured through the Deposit Act (ibid., 51–52, 58).

26. *New Bern Spectator*, quoted in Pegg, *Whig Party in North Carolina*, 60.

27. *Raleigh North Carolina Standard*, 21 August 1839.

28. For the vote on the penitentiary bill, see *HJ, 1840–41*, 638–39. The other roll calls cited in this paragraph are from table 11 in Kruman, *Parties and Politics in North Carolina*, 61. One of the weaknesses in Kruman's approach to roll-call analysis is his failure to use cross-tabulations to measure the influence of state sectionalism on legislative voting behavior.

29. For roll calls on these measures, see table 11 in Kruman, *Parties and Politics in North Carolina*, 61. Kruman presents no evidence that issues like the penitentiary and the school for the deaf and dumb were actually topics of partisan discussion. Indeed, his argument represents one species of the "voting bloc fallacy," by which legislative voting blocs are automatically equated with organized parties. For evidence that the penitentiary was not a partisan issue, see Pegg, *Whig Party in North Carolina*, 110. See also note 65, below.

30. David L. Swain, *Governor Swain's Inaugural Address* (n.p., 1834), 3; Abraham Rencher, *To the Freemen of the Tenth Congressional District of North Carolina* (Washington, D.C., 1835), 13.

31. Robert V. Remini, *Andrew Jackson and the Bank War* (New York: Norton, 1967), 47. See also Thomas Brown, "Southern Whigs and the Politics of Statesmanship, 1833–1841," *JSH* 46 (1980): 361–62; and Latner, *Presidency of Andrew Jackson*, 32–33.

32. *Raleigh Register*, 19 July 1844, 23 January 1846, 11 October 1836.

33. Edward B. Dudley to William A. Graham, 10 July 1841, in J. G. de Roulhac Hamilton and Max R. Williams, eds., *The Papers of William Alexander Graham*, 7 vols. to date (Raleigh: Division of Archives and History, 1957–), 2:212.

34. Brantson B. Holder, "The Three Banks of the State of North Carolina, 1810–1872" (Ph.D. diss., University of North Carolina at Chapel Hill, 1937), 75–114; Hershal L. Macon, "A Fiscal History of North Carolina, 1776–1860" (Ph.D. diss., University of North Carolina at Chapel Hill, 1932), 174–75; Sydnor, *Development of Southern Sectionalism*, 104–18.

35. Quoted in Albert R. Newsome, *The Presidential Election of 1824 in North Carolina* (Chapel Hill: University of North Carolina Press, 1939), 29.

36. Communication from "Leonidas" to *Raleigh Minerva*, quoted in Newsome, *Election of 1824*, 28n.

37. Holder, "Three Banks of North Carolina," 229–67; Daniel M. McFarland, "Rip

Van Winkle: Political Evolution in North Carolina, 1815–1835" (Ph.D. diss., University of Pennsylvania, 1954), 238–41, 254–60.

38. James Iredell, Jr., to Willie P. Mangum, 4 February 1832, in Henry T. Shanks, ed., *The Papers of Willie Person Mangum,* 5 vols. (Raleigh: State Department of Archives and History, 1950–56), 1:472; William H. Haywood, Jr., to James K. Polk, 17 February 1831, in Elizabeth G. McPherson, ed., "Unpublished Letters from North Carolinians to Polk," *NCHR* 16 (1939): 66; Elizabeth S. Hoyt, "Reactions in North Carolina to Jackson's Banking Policy, 1829–1832," *NCHR* 25 (1948).

39. *Raleigh North Carolina Constitutionalist,* 24 September 1833. Both of North Carolina's U.S. senators and nine of its thirteen congressmen voted against the recharter bill (Pegg, *Whig Party in North Carolina,* 8).

40. *Correspondence between Louis D. Henry . . . and the Committee Appointed to Inform Him of His Nomination as the Democratic Candidate for the Office of Governor of the State of North Carolina* (Fayetteville, 1842), 5; William H. Haywood, Jr., *To the Freemen of Wake County* (Raleigh: P. White, 1835), 19.

41. George E. Badger, *Speech Delivered at the Great Whig Meeting in the County of Granville* (n.p., 1840), 9.

42. Pegg, *Whig Party in North Carolina,* 133–34.

43. Ibid., 135. The Whig platform for 1844 can be found in *Raleigh Register,* 12 December 1843.

44. *Raleigh Register,* 30 January 1846; A. W. Mebane, *Address to the People of Northampton, Martin, Hertford, and Bertie* (n.p., 1840), 11.

45. Communication from "W.B.G.," in *Tarborough Press,* 17 August 1839.

46. N.C. Democratic Executive Committee, *Address . . . to the Freemen and Voters of North Carolina* (n.p., 1840), 2–3, 9; James C. Curtis, *The Fox at Bay: Martin Van Buren and the Presidency* (Lexington: University Press of Kentucky, 1970), 147.

47. Communication from "Nathan," in *Raleigh Register,* 17 July 1840; communication from "Romeo," in *Raleigh North Carolina Standard,* 8 April 1840; communication from "A Planter," ibid., 21 February 1844.

48. Thomas E. Jeffrey, "National Issues, Local Interests, and the Transformation of Antebellum North Carolina Politics," *JSH* 50 (1984): 53–54. Compare with Ershkowitz and Shade, "Consensus or Conflict," 597.

49. James B. Shepard, *Speech Delivered at the Great Republican Meeting in the County of Granville* (Raleigh, 1840), 3.

50. *HJ,* 1840–41, 645.

51. Marvin Meyers, *The Jacksonian Persuasion: Politics and Belief* (New York: Vintage Books, 1960), vii, 13. For the symbolic importance of the banking issue, see also Sharp, *Jacksonians versus the Banks,* 3–24.

52. *Raleigh Register,* 19 July 1844; Pegg, *Whig Party in North Carolina,* 4.

53. Shepard, *Speech at Granville,* 30; Badger, *Speech at Granville,* 9.

54. Pegg, *Whig Party in North Carolina,* 128–29; Glyndon G. Van Deusen, *The Jacksonian Era, 1828–1848* (New York: Harper, 1959), 164–66.

55. The Democratic platform for 1844 can be found in *Raleigh North Carolina Standard,* 20 December 1843.

56. Speeches of William A. Graham, in *Raleigh Register*, 29 December 1843, 31 May 1844.

57. *Raleigh North Carolina Standard*, 10, 17 July 1844.

58. Pegg, *Whig Party in North Carolina*, 129–31; Van Deusen, *Jacksonian Era*, 196, 200–204; Silbey, *Shrine of Party*, 71–72.

59. Pegg, *Whig Party in North Carolina*, 131–33.

60. Norton, *Democratic Party in Ante-Bellum North Carolina*, 59–61; Pegg, *Whig Party in North Carolina*, 80–81, 184–85.

61. For the attitudes of North Carolina congressmen toward internal improvements, see the scalograms in Silbey, *Shrine of Party*, appendix 2.

62. Speech of William B. Shepard, in *Raleigh Register*, 5 January 1841. For Whig support in the general assembly for the Nags Head inlet, see Jeffrey, "Internal Improvements and Political Parties," 152–53.

63. Thomas H. Hall, *Circular to the Freemen of the 3rd. Congressional District of N.C.* (Tarboro: Free Press, 1831), 2–6; Pegg, *Whig Party in North Carolina*, 75–76.

64. For one example of how Democrats used the term "strong and splendid Government," see the communication from James B. Shepard, in *Raleigh North Carolina Standard*, 28 February 1844.

65. The penitentiary bill passed the general assembly in 1844 with almost no opposition. The referendum was held in August 1846. Complete returns were probably never published, but the citizens in twenty-one widely scattered counties rejected the measure by a vote of 21,086 to 5,316 (Pegg, *Whig Party in North Carolina*, 110). According to Pegg, Whig editors "scarcely mentioned" the penitentiary issue during the months preceding the referendum "on the alleged ground that the question should be kept out of politics." Indeed, "each political party occupied a neutral position on the penitentiary, and left it entirely to the tender mercies of a conservative electorate" (ibid.).

6 *Social Bases of Party Allegiance*

1. Arthur C. Cole, *The Whig Party in the South* (Washington: American Historical Association, 1913), 71–72.

2. J. Mills Thornton, *Politics and Power in a Slave Society: Alabama, 1800–1860* (Baton Rouge: Louisiana State University Press, 1978), 40–58; Harry L. Watson, *Jacksonian Politics and Community Conflict: The Emergence of the Second American Party System in Cumberland County, North Carolina* (Baton Rouge: Louisiana State University Press, 1981), 212–13, 245, 278–80.

3. Ronald P. Formisano, *The Birth of Mass Political Parties: Michigan, 1827–1861* (Princeton: Princeton University Press, 1971), 10–14, 55; Paul Kleppner, *The Third Electoral System, 1853–1892: Parties, Voters, and Political Cultures* (Chapel Hill: University of North Carolina Press, 1979), 7–15.

4. On North Carolina's reputation for backwardness, see Richard N. Current, "Tarheels and Badgers: A Comparative History of Their Reputations," *JSH* 42 (1976): 5–6. For illiteracy in North Carolina, see William S. Powell, *North Carolina: A*

Bicentennial History (New York: Norton, 1977), 104. Olmsted is quoted in Current, "Tarheels and Badgers," 5. Murphey characterized the people of the Old North State as "lazy, sickly, poor, dirty, and ignorant." Quoted in Guion G. Johnson, *Ante-Bellum North Carolina: A Social History* (Chapel Hill: University of North Carolina Press, 1937), 41.

5. See, for example, Edward B. Dudley to Willie P. Mangum, 23 March 1834, in Henry T. Shanks, ed., *The Papers of Willie Person Mangum*, 5 vols. (Raleigh: State Department of Archives and History, 1950–56), 2:127; *Raleigh Register*, 6 August 1824; Thomas Jefferson Green to William Polk, 2 February 1824, William Polk Papers, NCDAH; Mat M. Moore to Mangum, 17 April 1834, in Shanks, *Mangum Papers*, 2:147.

6. *Fayetteville North Carolina Journal*, 25 July 1832; James Graham to William A. Graham, 19 January 1834, in J. G. de Roulhac Hamilton and Max R. Williams, eds., *The Papers of William Alexander Graham*, 7 vols. to date (Raleigh: Division of Archives and History, 1957–), 1:284.

7. James Graham, *Circular to the People of the Twelfth Congressional District in North Carolina* (n.p., 1843), 11; John Bragg to Willie P. Mangum, 4 March 1832, in Shanks, *Mangum Papers*, 1:505.

8. *Raleigh Register*, 19 August 1842; James Graham to William A. Graham, 19 March 1840, in Hamilton and Williams, *Graham Papers*, 2:78.

9. William D. Amis to Willie P. Mangum, 24 June 1834, in Shanks, *Mangum Papers*, 2:172. Because Amis's list was prepared at a time when party lines were still fluid, it probably represented a majority of the local elite of Northampton County. These individuals comprised about 7 percent of the Northampton voters who participated in the governor's election of 1836. For voting returns by county, see Thomas E. Jeffrey, "The Second Party System in North Carolina, 1836–1860" (Ph.D. diss., Catholic University of America, 1976), appendix A.

10. At the same time that James Graham was advising his brother, William, to court the influential men, he was also telling him that "much may be done by appealing to the pride of people to *act* for themselves, and not permit any would-be leader to *dictate* to them" (James Graham to William A. Graham, 19 March 1840, in Hamilton and Williams, *Graham Papers*, 2:78).

11. *Washington* (N.C.) *Republican*, in *Tarborough Press*, 8 May 1841; Lewis H. Marsteller to David S. Reid, 15 January 1854, Governor's Papers, NCDAH.

12. Watson, *Jacksonian Politics and Community Conflict*, 234–35; Ralph Wooster, *Politicians, Planters, and Plain Folk: Courthouse and Statehouse in the Upper South, 1850–1860* (Knoxville: University of Tennessee Press, 1975), 49; Herbert D. Pegg, *The Whig Party in North Carolina* (Chapel Hill: Colonial Press, 1968), 24.

13. Voting returns for the following counties and towns were examined: Beaufort County (Washington), in *Washington North State Whig*, 1 August 1844; Carteret County (Beaufort), ibid., 14 August 1850; Chowan County (Edenton), in *Elizabeth City Democratic Pioneer*, 17 August 1852; Craven County (New Bern), in *New Bern Republican*, 9 August 1848; Cumberland County (Fayetteville), in *Fayetteville Observer*, 19 August 1840; Edgecombe County (Tarboro), in *Tarborough Press*, 1 August 1840; Lenoir County (Kinston), in *New Bern Republi-*

can, 7 August 1850; Mecklenburg County (Charlotte), in *Charlotte Journal*, 11 August 1842; New Hanover County (Wilmington), in *Wilmington Journal*, 9 August 1850; Pasquotank County (Elizabeth City), in *Elizabeth City Democratic Pioneer*, 10 August 1852; Rowan County (Salisbury), in *Salisbury Carolina Watchman*, 12 August 1844; Wake County (Raleigh), in *Raleigh North Carolina Standard*, 9 August 1848. In all of the counties except Beaufort, Pasquotank, and Rowan, the Whigs' percentage of the town vote exceeded their percentage of the rural vote. The Whigs managed to carry only six of the twelve urban precincts, but this does not necessarily mean that a majority of town dwellers in the other six counties preferred the Democrats. North Carolinians were not required by law to vote in their home districts, and many country residents apparently traveled to the county seat to cast their ballots. As one contemporary pointed out: "At an election in town, where the country people can vote, the result is no evidence of the sentiment of the town." In *Proceedings and Debates of the Convention of North-Carolina Called to Amend the Constitution of the State* (Raleigh: Joseph Gales and Son, 1836), 206. See also Watson, *Jacksonian Politics and Community Conflict*, 312–13.

14. Hershal L. Macon, "A Fiscal History of North Carolina, 1776–1860" (Ph.D. diss., University of North Carolina at Chapel Hill, 1932), 301.

15. Edward B. Dudley to William A. Graham, 10 July 1841, in Hamilton and Williams, *Graham Papers*, 2:212.

16. The editor of the *Register* characterized the deposits issue as "a matter which the people can understand, and reason about, as well as the politicians—the main facts on both sides of the question are indisputable—the propriety, therefore, of the measure, is the matter presented for their judgment" (*Raleigh Register*, 15 April 1834).

17. During the 1830s and 1840s the Whigs were the majority party in fifteen of the twenty-three Federalist counties. In three additional counties—Johnston, Robeson, and Stokes—they were strong enough occasionally to win majorities in the governor's election and to elect Whig legislators to the general assembly. In the Federalist counties of Cumberland, Martin, Onslow, Wayne, and Lincoln, on the other hand, the Whigs were clearly in the minority, although the party did manage to carry all but Lincoln in at least one gubernatorial election during the period 1836–50.

18. *Salisbury Carolina Watchman*, 24 August 1844; *Raleigh Register*, 30 August 1844.

19. Communication from James B. Shepard, in *Raleigh North Carolina Standard*, 28 February 1844.

20. *Raleigh North Carolina Standard*, 13 October 1836.

21. James Graham to William A. Graham, 8 April 1840, in Hamilton and Williams, *Graham Papers*, 2:84.

22. *Raleigh Register*, 30 August 1844. The Locofocos were members of the radical wing of the Democratic party in New York. They supposedly acquired their nickname when they used "locofoco" matches to light candles at a meeting after their conservative opponents had turned off the gaslights. Throughout the antebellum years Whigs in all parts of the nation frequently referred to the Demo-

crats as "Locofocos" to imply that they were dangerous radicals. Edmund Rucker was an obscure Tennessean who gained notoriety at the Democratic National Convention of 1835. To the profound embarrassment of President Jackson, no delegate from his home state showed up in Baltimore to attend the convention. Rucker, who happened to be in the city at the time, was enlisted as a delegate and subsequently delivered all of Tennessee's convention votes to Martin Van Buren. According to Robert V. Remini, "It was an exceedingly stupid thing to do, for it provided the opposition press with ammunition to taunt Democrats over their 'Ruckerized Office-Holder's Convention.'" See Remini, *Andrew Jackson and the Course of American Democracy, 1833–1845* (New York: Harper and Row, 1984), 255.

23. *Fayetteville North Carolinian*, in *Raleigh North Carolina Standard*, 23 February 1842.

24. *Hillsborough Recorder*, in *Fayetteville Observer*, 16 March 1842; communication from "A Farmer," in *Raleigh Register*, 26 April 1842.

25. *Raleigh Register*, 3 May 1844.

26. Resolutions of Lincoln County Democrats, in *Raleigh North Carolina Standard*, 22 April 1840.

27. Communication from "Grandson of a Whig" to *Greensboro Patriot*, in *Raleigh Register*, 3 July 1840.

28. Communication from "A," in *Greensboro Patriot*, 31 May 1851.

29. *Raleigh Register*, 28 June 1844; Charles G. Sellers, *James K. Polk, Jacksonian, 1795–1843* (Princeton: Princeton University Press, 1957), 14–16.

30. See, for example, "Vindication of Ezekiel Polk," by U.S. Senator William H. Haywood, Jr., in *Raleigh North Carolina Standard*, 18 September 1844.

31. For Democratic accusations against John Davidson, maternal grandfather of William A. Graham, see *Raleigh North Carolina Standard*, 17 July 1844. The Whig accusations against Michael Quickel, grandfather of Michael Hoke, are rebutted in ibid., 24 July 1844.

32. In 1850 Lenoir ranked second among seventy-nine North Carolina counties both in average value of farmland and in average acreage. Greene ranked tenth and twelfth, respectively, in these categories (Jeffrey, "Second Party System in North Carolina," appendixes G, H). In the North Carolina General Assembly of 1838–39, the Whig commoner from Greene voted against measures to provide state support to the Raleigh & Gaston and Fayetteville & Western railroads, as well as against a resolution supporting the inlet at Nags Head (*HJ, 1838–39*, 501, 509–10, 520, 525–28).

33. John Washington, "Lenoir County," in Albert R. Newsome, ed., "Twelve North Carolina Counties," *NCHR* 6 (1929): 182; Bill Sharpe, *A New Geography of North Carolina*, 4 vols. (Raleigh: Sharpe, 1954–65), 3:1382–84; William S. Powell, *Annals of Progress: The Story of Lenoir County and Kinston, North Carolina* (Raleigh: State Department of Archives and History, 1963), 31–34. For congressional elections, see Compiled Election Returns, Miscellaneous Collections, NCDAH.

34. LeGette Blythe and Charles R. Brockmann, *Hornet's Nest: The Story of Charlotte and Mecklenburg County* (Charlotte: McNally, 1961), 21–23; Rufus Bar-

ringer, "Early German Settlers in Eastern Cabarrus County," in John H. Wheeler, ed., *Reminiscences and Memoirs of North Carolina and Eminent North Carolinians* (Columbus, Ohio: Columbus Printing Works, 1884; reprint, Baltimore: Genealogical Publishing, 1966), xlvi. For Cornwallis's characterization of Mecklenburg, see Samuel A. Ashe, *History of North Carolina*, 2 vols. (Greensboro: C. L. Van Noppen, 1908–25), 1:636. For the address of the German Loyalists, see Josiah Martin to the earl of Dartmouth, 28 August 1775, in William L. Saunders, ed., *The Colonial Records of North Carolina*, 10 vols. (Raleigh: State Printer, 1886–90), 10:231. For the congressional election of 1813, see Compiled Election Returns.

35. The most conspicuous exception to this generalization is Cumberland County. Like most counties where Toryism flourished, Cumberland was strong in its support for the Federalist party and for the People's party during the 1820s. However, Cumberland was one of the few Federalist counties that remained loyal to the Jackson party after 1834. In this respect, as in so many others, Cumberland was a most untypical North Carolina county. For an explanation relating Cumberland's untypical political behavior to chronic infighting within the local Federalist party, see Jeffrey, "Second Party System in North Carolina," 28.

36. James W. Wall, *History of Davie County in the Forks of the Yadkin* (Mocksville: Davie County Historical Publishing Association, 1969), 22–24, 56–71. For the gubernatorial election of 1842, see *Salisbury Carolina Watchman*, 21 August 1842.

37. Manly W. Wellman, *The County of Warren, North Carolina, 1586–1917* (Chapel Hill: University of North Carolina Press, 1959), 42.

38. Bartlett Yancy, "Caswell County," in Newsome, "Twelve North Carolina Counties," *NCHR* 5 (1928): 422, 427. For Yancy's remark about "Spumy Irishmen," see Sharpe, *New Geography of North Carolina*, 4:1752. On the absence of Loyalist resistance in Caswell, see also Jeffrey J. Crow, "Liberty Men and Loyalists: Disorder and Disaffection in the North Carolina Backcountry," in Ronald Hoffman, Thad W. Tate, and Peter J. Albert, eds., *An Uncivil War: The Southern Backcountry during the American Revolution* (Charlottesville: University Press of Virginia, 1985), 133.

39. According to one estimate, North Carolinians of English stock comprised only 45 percent of the colony's white population in 1760. Robert D. W. Connor, *Race Elements in the White Population of North Carolina* (Raleigh: College, 1920), 18. For the attitude of the Scotch-Irish toward the Revolution, see ibid., 89; Chalmers G. Davidson, *Piedmont Partisan: The Life and Times of Brigadier-General William Lee Davidson* (Davidson: Davidson College Press, 1951), 29, 75; and Alexander J. McKelway, *The Scotch-Irish of North Carolina* (Raleigh: W. S. Sherman, 1905), 18. For the Germans, see Connor, *Race Elements*, 111; Ruth Blackwelder, "The Attitude of the North Carolina Moravians toward the American Revolution," *NCHR* 9 (1932); and Davidson, *Piedmont Partisan*, 60. For the Highland Scots, see Connor, *Race Elements*, 61–68; James C. MacRae, *The Highland-Scotch Settlement in North Carolina* (Raleigh: E. M. Uzzell, 1905), 15; and the sources cited in chapter 1, note 5, in this volume. For the

Quakers, see Dorothy Gilbert Thorne, "North Carolina Friends and the Revolution," *NCHR* 38 (1961). James Broussard has pointed out that in North Carolina there was a "clear and well-marked preference of ethnic minorities for the Federalist cause. . . . The average Federalist county in that state had twice as many Scots, Scotch-Irish, Irish, and Germans as the typical Republican county. . . . Very possibly the Tory connection explains much of this sharp division between ethnic groups." In *The Southern Federalists, 1800–1816* (Baton Rouge: Louisiana State University Press, 1978), 399–400.

40. Marc W. Kruman, *Parties and Politics in North Carolina, 1836–1865* (Baton Rouge: Louisiana State University Press, 1983), 15.
41. MacRae, *Highland-Scotch Settlement in North Carolina*, 20.
42. Jordan K. Rouse, *North Carolina Picadillo* (Salisbury: Rowan Business Forms, 1966), 46; Carl Hammer, *Rhinelanders on the Yadkin: The Story of the Pennsylvania Germans in Rowan and Cabarrus Counties, North Carolina*, 2d rev. ed. (Salisbury, N.C.: Rowan, 1943; reprint, Salisbury, 1965), 97. As late as the 1830s, latent antagonisms between the Germans and the Scotch-Irish sometimes surfaced in political debates. During the Convention of 1835, for example, one delegate vehemently objected to a proposal to combine the counties of Moore and Montgomery into a single senatorial district. "Montgomery and Cabarrus were properly united in a district," he said, "it was Dutch [German] to Dutch. But if Moore and Montgomery were united, it would be Dutch to Scotch" (*Proceedings and Debates of the Convention of North-Carolina*, 343).
43. Broussard, *Southern Federalists*, 399.
44. Ronald P. Formisano, *The Transformation of Political Culture: Massachusetts Parties, 1790s-1840s* (New York: Oxford University Press, 1983), 6–7.

7 National Issues and Local Interests

1. Because of the Democratic gerrymander of 1842, the Whig majorities in the general assembly were not paralleled by majorities within the North Carolina congressional delegation. In 1843 the Whigs won only four of the nine congressional districts, and in 1845 they won only three districts. After the Whig-dominated general assembly redistricted the state in 1846, however, the Whigs carried six of the nine districts in every congressional election from 1847 until 1851. See Herbert D. Pegg, *The Whig Party in North Carolina* (Chapel Hill: Colonial Press, 1968), 149, 152–53, 202–3.
2. The Whig percentage of the vote for each county in each of the thirteen gubernatorial elections between 1836 and 1860 can be found in Thomas E. Jeffrey, "The Second Party System in North Carolina, 1836–1860" (Ph.D. diss., Catholic University of America, 1976), appendix B. For the results of the legislative elections of 1840 and 1844, see *Fayetteville Observer*, 26 August 1840, 21 August 1844.
3. For the results of the legislative elections of 1842 and 1846, see *Raleigh North Carolina Standard*, 14 September 1842, 9 September 1846.
4. *Hillsborough Recorder*, 13 August 1840; *Raleigh Register*, 23 August 1836.

5. W. P. Richards, *To the Freemen of Davidson County* (n.p., 1846); communications from "A Whig," in *Hillsborough Recorder*, 14 March, 4 April 1844.

6. J. G. de Roulhac Hamilton, in Hamilton and Max R. Williams, eds., *The Papers of William Alexander Graham*, 7 vols. to date (Raleigh: Division of Archives and History, 1957–), 2:456n.

7. Charles Fisher to Michael Hoke, 10 February 1842, Robert Frederick Hoke Papers, SHC.

8. Alexander McRae and Griffith J. McRee, *To the Freemen of New Hanover County* (Wilmington, 1844); Richards, *To the Freemen*.

9. William H. Thomas, *To the People of the Senatorial District Embracing the Counties of Haywood, Macon, and Cherokee, North Carolina* (n.p., 1846).

10. *Fayetteville Observer*, 17 August 1842; speech of Tod R. Caldwell, ibid., 22 February 1843; William S. Powell, ed., *Dictionary of North Carolina Biography*, 2 vols. to date (Chapel Hill: University of North Carolina Press, 1979–), 1:71–72.

11. William A. Jeffreys to William W. Holden, 3 August 1844, William Andrew Jeffreys and Family Papers, NCDAH.

12. William E. Mills to William A. Graham, 30 May 1844, in Hamilton and Williams, *Graham Papers*, 2:503; John W. Hampton to David S. Reid, 27 August 1844, David S. Reid Papers, NCDAH. A detailed analysis of county division as a campaign issue can be found in Thomas E. Jeffrey, "County Division: A Forgotten Issue in Antebellum North Carolina Politics, Part II," *NCHR* 65 (1988).

13. William A. Jeffreys to William W. Holden, 3 August 1844, Jeffreys Papers.

14. *Raleigh North Carolina Standard*, 6 June 1838; *Raleigh Register*, 20 May 1842.

15. *Raleigh Register*, 23 August 1836.

16. *Raleigh Register*, 9 August 1842; *Fayetteville Observer*, 17 August 1842.

17. See, for example, *Raleigh North Carolina Constitutionalist*, 12 February 1833; *Fayetteville North Carolina Journal*, in *Raleigh Register*, 4 February 1834.

18. Speech of William H. Haywood, Jr., November 1839, in *Tarborough Press*, 20 June 1840.

19. North Carolina. General Assembly. *Report of the Joint Select Committee on the Suspension of Specie Payments by the Banks* (n.p., 1841), 4.

20. *Washington* (N.C.) *Republican*, in *Tarborough Press*, 20 February 1841.

21. *Correspondence between Louis D. Henry . . . and the Committee Appointed to Inform Him of His Nomination as the Democratic Candidate for the Office of Governor of the State of North Carolina* (Fayetteville, 1842), 2, 8; *Charlotte Mecklenburg Jeffersonian*, 1 February 1842.

22. Priestly H. Mangum to William A. Graham, 12 May 1842, in Hamilton and Williams, *Graham Papers*, 2:308.

23. *Raleigh Register*, 8, 18 February 1842; *Fayetteville Observer*, 2 March 1842.

24. *Fayetteville Observer*, 16 February, 16 March, 1 June 1842; *Fayetteville Observer*, in *Raleigh Register*, 14 June 1842.

25. *SJ, 1842–43,* 271–72; *HJ, 1842–43,* 976.

26. McRae and McRee, *To the Freemen*. For the vote on Jones's resolution, see *HJ, 1842–43,* 750–51; for the senate substitute, see *SJ, 1842–43,* 268–69. For a lengthy analysis of the partisan maneuvering in the legislature of 1842–43 from a Whig point of view, see [Bartholomew F. Moore], *To the Freemen of North*

Carolina (n.p., 1843), 9–15. This address can also be found in *Raleigh Register*, 19 July 1844.

27. *Charlotte Mecklenburg Jeffersonian*, 10 January 1843.
28. *Raleigh Register*, 6 January 1843. Between 1838 and 1845 the state bank generally paid 6¼ percent per annum in dividends. In 1841 North Carolina derived $63,914 of its income from bank stock dividends, compared to $87,162 from taxes. Total revenue for 1841 amounted to $191,213. See Hershal L. Macon, "A Fiscal History of North Carolina, 1776–1860" (Ph.D. diss., University of North Carolina at Chapel Hill, 1932), 370, 372, 376.
29. *Raleigh Register*, 3 January 1843. For the votes in the house of commons on the bill to establish an investigating committee, see *HJ*, *1842–43*, 694, 709.
30. Richard D. Spaight, Jr., to Weldon N. Edwards, 8 December 1842, Katherine P. Conway Collection, NCDAH; *Fayetteville North Carolinian*, 10 August 1844.
31. *Raleigh North Carolina Standard*, 11 January 1843.
32. Ibid., 11 January, 15 February 1843. For Democratic criticism of Loring, see *Charlotte Mecklenburg Jeffersonian* and *Washington Republican*, in *Raleigh North Carolina Standard*, 25 January, 22 February 1843; and *Mecklenburg Jeffersonian*, 14, 21 February 1843. The prospectus for the *Independent* can be found in *North Carolina Standard*, 7 June 1843. For Loring's endorsement of Clay and Graham, see *Raleigh Register*, 25 June 1844.
33. Raleigh *North Carolina Standard*, 11, 18 January 1843.
34. Thomas E. Jeffrey, "Internal Improvements and Political Parties in Antebellum North Carolina, 1836–1860," *NCHR* 55 (1978): 123–24, 128, 152–53.
35. Henry's position on the Raleigh & Gaston was thoroughly discussed in a communication from "Cumberland," in *Raleigh North Carolina Standard*, 6 July 1842. It is possible that Henry himself may have been the author of the "Cumberland" letter, although there is no conclusive proof. The reference to "gambling debts" can be found in the communication from "One of the People" to *Raleigh Register*, in *Washington North State Whig*, 25 May 1842.
36. *Raleigh North Carolina Standard*, 25 March, 30 December 1840; 11 May, 22 June 1842.
37. Communication from "One of the People" to *Raleigh Register*, in *Washington North State Whig*, 25 May 1842.
38. *Wilmington Chronicle* and *Fayetteville Observer*, in *Charlotte Journal*, 9, 16 June 1842.
39. *Fayetteville Observer*, 17 August 1842; John M. Morehead to James Wyche, 20 September 1842, Governor's Letter Books, NCDAH.
40. Jeffrey, "Internal Improvements and Political Parties," 132; Macon, "Fiscal History," 347, 370.
41. *Raleigh North Carolina Standard*, 24 July 1844. While enthusiastically joining in the Democratic assault on the Raleigh & Gaston, Holden carefully avoided attacking the state bank. In 1843 Duncan Cameron, the president of the state bank, had loaned Holden $2,000 of the $2,500 that he used to purchase the *Standard* from Thomas Loring. See William C. Harris, *William Woods Holden: Firebrand of North Carolina Politics* (Baton Rouge: Louisiana State University Press, 1987), 14–15.

42. Jeffrey, "Internal Improvements and Political Parties," 132–33.

43. *Raleigh Register*, 7 June 1844.

44. Ibid., 9 August 1844; Pegg, *Whig Party in North Carolina*, 121–23.

45. *Raleigh North Carolina Standard*, 10 April, 19 June 1844; Marc W. Kruman, *Parties and Politics in North Carolina, 1836–1865* (Baton Rouge: Louisiana State University Press, 1983), 108–12; George H. Gibson, "Opinion in North Carolina Regarding the Acquisition of Texas and Cuba, 1835–1855," *NCHR* 37 (1960): 8–10.

46. Quoted in Max R. Williams, "William A. Graham and the Election of 1844: A Study in North Carolina Politics," *NCHR* 45 (1968): 41.

47. Communication from "A Freeman," in *Raleigh Register*, 19 July 1844.

48. *Raleigh North Carolina Standard*, 28 August 1844.

49. Ibid., 14 January 1846.

50. Pegg, *Whig Party in North Carolina*, 144–47. Polk is quoted in ibid., 144.

51. Quoted in ibid., 147.

52. Michael F. Holt, *The Political Crisis of the 1850s* (New York: Wiley, 1978), 39–66.

53. For the Whig and Democratic platforms for 1848, see *Raleigh Register*, 1 March 1848, and *Raleigh North Carolina Standard*, 19 April 1848.

54. Charles L. Hinton to Samuel F. Patterson, 10 July 1846, Jones and Patterson Family Papers, SHC.

55. Jeffrey, "Internal Improvements and Political Parties," 133–34; Cecil K. Brown, *A State Movement in Railroad Development: The Story of North Carolina's First Effort to Establish an East and West Trunk Line Railroad* (Chapel Hill: University of North Carolina Press, 1928), 50–54.

56. Richards, *To the Freemen; Raleigh North Carolina Standard*, 8, 15, 22, 29 April, 10 June, 8 July 1846.

57. *Raleigh Register*, 22 May 1846.

58. Ibid., 3 July 1846.

59. Ibid. Graham's remarks are paraphrased in *Raleigh North Carolina Standard*, 27 May 1846.

60. *Raleigh North Carolina Standard*, 27 May 1846; communication from "Paul Pry," in *Raleigh Register*, 12 June 1846.

61. *Raleigh Register*, 21 August 1846.

62. *Raleigh North Carolina Standard*, 12 August 1846.

63. Ibid., 8 November 1848.

64. Kruman, *Parties and Politics in North Carolina*, 22, 75, 85.

8 *Democracy Triumphant*

1. The percentages in table 8.1 and in the other tables in this chapter indicate the proportion of legislators voting on the affirmative side of each issue (in favor of state aid to railroads, new counties, etc.). However, the percentages do not invariably indicate "yea" votes, because many of the roll calls involved a motion to table or strike out a particular measure. Legislators who supported the measure would naturally vote "nay" on such a motion.

2. Thomas E. Jeffrey, "Internal Improvements and Political Parties in Antebellum North Carolina, 1836–1860," *NCHR* 55 (1978): 121–24; Cecil K. Brown, *A State Movement in Railroad Development: The Story of North Carolina's First Effort to Establish an East and West Trunk Line Railroad* (Chapel Hill: University of North Carolina Press, 1928), 31–40, 45–49.

3. Jeffrey, "Internal Improvements and Political Parties," 118, 121–25.

4. Ibid., 136–38.

5. Ibid., 124–25.

6. Ibid., 125.

7. Speech of William B. Shepard, in *Raleigh North Carolina Standard*, 6 January 1841; Herbert D. Pegg, *The Whig Party in North Carolina* (Chapel Hill: Colonial Press, 1968), 56; Jeffrey, "Internal Improvements and Political Parties," 128–29.

8. Speech of Thomas L. Clingman, in *Raleigh Register*, 1 January 1841.

9. Ora Blackmun, *Western North Carolina: Its Mountains and Its People to 1880* (Boone: Appalachian Consortium Press, 1977), 315–17.

10. The evidence in table 8.5 corroborates the argument that party-line voting on internal improvement measures increased substantially during the legislative sessions of 1844–45 and 1846–47.

11. Edgar W. Knight, *Public School Education in North Carolina* (Boston: Houghton Mifflin, 1916), 140–44, 147–50; Pegg, *Whig Party in North Carolina*, 59–61.

12. Speech of Leander B. Carmichael, in *Raleigh Register*, 31 January 1849.

13. Message of Charles Manly, in *Raleigh Register*, 27 November 1850.

14. In 1844, for example, 96 percent of the senate Whigs supported a bill to create a superintendent of public schools, compared to only 4 percent of the Democrats. Four years later, a similar bill attracted the support of 91 percent of the Whigs but only 14 percent of the Democrats. See Marc W. Kruman, *Parties and Politics in North Carolina, 1836–1865* (Baton Rouge: Louisiana State University Press, 1983), 61.

15. *HJ, 1850–51*, 641, 650–51. Only nine of the twenty-nine Whigs favoring the white basis supported Wiley's unamended bill, compared to seventeen of the twenty-four federal-basis Whigs.

16. Eighteen of the twenty-one Whig votes against the superintendent bill in the house of commons were cast by westerners. Overall, 66 percent of the house Whigs supported the bill, compared to 49 percent of the Democrats (*HJ, 1852*, 203). For the role of Cuningham in promoting support for school reform among the Democrats, see Thomas E. Jeffrey, "'Our Remarkable Friendship': The Secret Collaboration of Calvin H. Wiley and John W. Cuningham," *NCHR*, forthcoming.

17. Speech of Robert G. A. Love, in *Raleigh Register*, 28 February 1849.

18. Ibid. Although the general assembly did not create new counties as quickly as westerners might have desired, that body was not entirely oblivious to the needs of the west. During the period 1836–61 the legislature created twenty-four new counties, all but two of them in the west. By contrast, it created only five counties during the period 1801–35. See David L. Corbitt, *The Formation of the North Carolina Counties, 1663–1943* (Raleigh: State Department of Archives and History, 1950). For an analysis of county division as a public policy issue, see

Thomas E. Jeffrey, "County Division: A Forgotten Issue in Antebellum North Carolina Politics, Part I," *NCHR* 65 (1988).

19. Rufus Barringer, *History of the North Carolina Railroad* (Raleigh: News and Observer Press, 1894), 12.

20. Speech of John W. Ellis, 26 December 1844, in Noble J. Tolbert, ed., *The Papers of John Willis Ellis*, 2 vols. (Raleigh: State Department of Archives and History, 1964), 1:17.

21. *Raleigh North Carolina Standard*, 29 July 1840; *Salisbury Western Carolinian*, 7 August 1840; *Fayetteville North Carolinian*, 29 August 1840. The Democrats could at least take comfort in the belief that the impact of Morehead's sectional appeal would be transitory. Halfway through his second term one western Democrat told Morehead that the next election would reveal "the greate efect [*sic*] that your personal popularity had on this community. . . . Your side of politics has not got another John M. Morehead to plead their cause" (J. R. Love to Morehead, 22 November 1843, Governor's Papers, NCDAH).

22. Bayles M. Edney to William A. Graham, 13 May 1844, in J. G. de Roulhac Hamilton and Max R. Williams, eds., *The Papers of William Alexander Graham*, 7 vols. to date (Raleigh: Division of Archives and History, 1957–), 2:498–99.

23. A copy of *Plain Thoughts* can be found in Hamilton and Williams, *Graham Papers*, 2:503–6. For the role of Haywood and Holden in writing and circulating this tract, see *Raleigh Register*, 12 July 1844; and *Fayetteville Observer*, 11 September 1844.

24. *Plain Thoughts*, in Hamilton and Williams, *Graham Papers*, 2:506.

25. *Hillsborough Recorder*, in *Raleigh North Carolina Standard*, 11 September 1844. See also *Fayetteville Observer*, 14 August 1844. The Whig percentage of the vote for each county in each of the gubernatorial elections between 1836 and 1860 can be found in Thomas E. Jeffrey, "The Second Party System in North Carolina, 1836–1860" (Ph.D. diss., Catholic University of America, 1976), appendix B.

26. Voting returns by county for the gubernatorial election of 1844 can be found in Jeffrey, "Second Party System in North Carolina," appendix A; and in Robert D. W. Connor, comp., *A Manual of North Carolina* (Raleigh: North Carolina Historical Commission, 1913), 995–96. For the presidential election, see W. Dean Burnham, *Presidential Ballots, 1836–1892* (Baltimore: Johns Hopkins University Press, 1955), 646–68.

27. J. Julius Wherden to David S. Reid, 8 January 1846; Calvin Graves to Reid, 15 January 1846, David S. Reid Papers, NCDAH; *Raleigh North Carolina Standard*, 28 January 1846; Clarence C. Norton, *The Democratic Party in Ante-Bellum North Carolina, 1835–1861* (Chapel Hill: University of North Carolina Press, 1930), 150–51.

28. *Raleigh Register*, 14 April 1846. Shepard's reference to Graham as an "advocate of Western improvements and interests" can be found in an extract from the *Elizabeth City Old North State* in the same issue of the *Register*. The Democratic percentage of the vote increased from 1844 in only ten counties, nine of them in the east (Jeffrey, "Second Party System in North Carolina," appendix B).

29. William K. Boyd, ed., *Memoirs of W. W. Holden* (Durham: Seeman Printery, 1911), 3–4.

30. Holden's version of these events can be found in Boyd, *Memoirs of Holden*, 4–5. For Reid's version, see his circular, 28 June 1850, in *Raleigh North Carolina Standard*, 6 July 1850.

31. Boyd, *Memoirs of Holden*, 5–6; Thomas E. Jeffrey, "'Free Suffrage' Revisited: Party Politics and Constitutional Reform in Antebellum North Carolina," *NCHR* 59 (1982): 26.

32. Jeffrey, "'Free Suffrage' Revisited," 30–31.

33. *Greensboro Patriot*, 27 May 1848; *Raleigh Register*, 28 June 1848.

34. Communication from Everard Hall, in *Raleigh Register*, 26 July 1848; William A. Graham to *Newbernian*, 13 July 1848, in Hamilton and Williams, *Graham Papers*, 3:233. Graham's letter was published in *Newbernian*, 18 July 1848.

35. William A. Graham to *Newbernian*, 13 July 1848, in Hamilton and Williams, *Graham Papers*, 3:235; communication from "Davie," in *Raleigh Register*, 21 June 1848.

36. For the impact of free suffrage on the election of 1848, see Jeffrey, "'Free Suffrage' Revisited," 33–37. Voting returns for the gubernatorial election of 1848 can be found in Jeffrey, "Second Party System in North Carolina," appendix A; and in Connor, *Manual of North Carolina*, 995–96. For the presidential election, see Burnham, *Presidential Ballots*, 646–68.

37. Thomas L. Clingman to Willie P. Mangum, 1 September 1848, in Henry T. Shanks, ed., *The Papers of Willie Person Mangum*, 5 vols. (Raleigh: State Department of Archives and History, 1950–56), 5:109–10; *Asheville Highland Messenger*, 27 July 1848; *Greensboro Patriot*, 12 August 1848; *Salisbury Carolina Watchman*, 24 August 1848.

38. Proceedings of Buncombe County Whigs, in *Salisbury Carolina Watchman*, 30 May 1850.

39. *New Bern Republican*, 3 July 1850.

40. Whig platform, in *Raleigh Register*, 19 June 1850.

41. Communication from "A," in *Elizabeth City Old North State*, 18 May 1850. For newspaper endorsements of eastern Whigs for governor, see *Raleigh Register*, 23 January, 24 April 1850; *Old North State*, 20 April 1850; and *Raleigh North Carolina Standard*, 29 June 1850. For proceedings of county nominating conventions, see *Old North State*, 18 May, 1 June 1850; *Fayetteville Observer*, 28 May 1850; *Raleigh Register*, 12 June 1850; and *Washington North State Whig*, 19 June 1850.

42. Manly was endorsed by local conventions in the eastern counties of Halifax, Northampton, Hyde, Franklin, Johnston, Bertie, Brunswick, Granville, Onslow, Sampson, Wayne, Greene, Carteret, and Jones (*Fayetteville Observer*, 5, 19 March, 9, 16, 30 April, 21, 28 May, 4 June 1850).

43. *Greensboro Patriot*, 29 June 1850.

44. William W. Holden to David S. Reid, 7 July 1850, Reid Papers; Jeffrey, "'Free Suffrage' Revisited," 38–39.

45. *Raleigh North Carolina Standard*, 17 July 1850.

46. *Raleigh Register*, 17 July 1850; Jeffrey, "'Free Suffrage' Revisited," 41, 44.

47. *Raleigh North Carolina Standard*, 31 July 1850.

48. William W. Holden to David S. Reid, 7 July 1850, Reid Papers.

49. *Raleigh North Carolina Standard*, 20 July, 26 June 1850. The Whigs, of course, denied that Manly owed his nomination to Raleigh influence. See, for example, the communication from "A Whig of the Centre," in *Raleigh Register*, 27 February 1850.

50. Jeffrey, "Second Party System in North Carolina," appendix B; Jeffrey, "'Free Suffrage' Revisited," 43–45. In 1850 Halifax and Northampton ranked second and seventh among all North Carolina counties in percentage of slave population (Jeffrey, "Second Party System in North Carolina," appendix C).

51. *Rutherfordton Mountain Banner*, 25 June 1850; Jeffrey, "Second Party System in North Carolina," appendix B.

52. For the impact of the railroad issue, see Jeffrey, "Internal Improvements and Political Parties," 141–42. Despite repeated Whig denials, many historians have erroneously claimed that Governor Manly actually did come out in favor of a change in the basis of representation. See, for example, Max R. Williams, "Reemergence of the Two-Party System," in Lindley S. Butler and Alan D. Watson, eds., *The North Carolina Experience: An Interpretive and Documentary History* (Chapel Hill: University of North Carolina Press, 1984), 248–49; and William C. Harris, *William Woods Holden: Firebrand of North Carolina Politics* (Baton Rouge: Louisiana State University Press, 1987), 35.

53. Jeffrey, "Internal Improvements and Political Parties," 140.

54. Ibid., 138–40, 152. The story of the Danville connection and the North Carolina Railroad has been told many times. Most accounts are based on Rufus Barringer's *History of the North Carolina Railroad*. Barringer was a Whig member of the house of commons from Cabarrus County and an active participant in the events he described.

55. *Halifax Roanoke Republican*, in *Tarborough Press*, 17 August 1850; *Raleigh North Carolina Standard*, 7, 14 August 1850; Maurice Q. Waddell to William A. Graham, 4 August 1850, in Hamilton and Williams, *Graham Papers*, 3:342–43.

56. *Raleigh North Carolina Standard*, 7 August 1850; *Wilmington Journal*, 14 August 1850.

57. *Raleigh Register*, 11 September 1850; *Wilmington Commercial*, 16 August 1850; David Outlaw to Emily B. Outlaw, 7 August 1850, David Outlaw Letters, SHC.

9 *Transit of Power*

1. In the North Carolina General Assembly of 1842–43, 43 percent of the Democratic commoners and 29 percent of the senators voted in favor of railroad relief, although only 14 percent of the commoners and 11 percent of the senators had supported relief measures two years earlier. See Marc W. Kruman, *Parties and Politics in North Carolina, 1836–1865* (Baton Rouge: Louisiana State University Press, 1983), 58.

2. *Raleigh North Carolina Standard*, 13 December 1848, reprinted in Lindley S.

Butler and Alan D. Watson, eds., *The North Carolina Experience: An Interpretive and Documentary History* (Chapel Hill: University of North Carolina Press, 1984), 258.

3. Communication from L. A. Gwyn, 29 April 1850, in *Raleigh North Carolina Standard*, 15 May 1850; communication from W. Heartsfield, 23 May 1850, ibid., 29 May 1850.

4. *Raleigh North Carolina Standard*, 13 February 1850.

5. Speech of Romulus M. Saunders, 7 May 1850, in *Raleigh North Carolina Standard*, 29 May 1850.

6. For Dobbin's candidacy, see James Fulton to John W. Ellis, 25 June 1849, in Noble J. Tolbert, ed., *The Papers of John Willis Ellis*, 2 vols. (Raleigh: State Department of Archives and History, 1964), 1:87; J. G. de Roulhac Hamilton, *Party Politics in North Carolina, 1835–1860* (Durham: Seeman Printery, 1916), 140.

7. William W. Holden to David S. Reid, 1 June 1850, David S. Reid Papers, NCDAH.

8. *HJ, 1850–51*, 522. For a summary of the legislative debate on Sherard's bill, see *Raleigh Register*, 3 December 1850, and *Raleigh North Carolina Standard*, 4 December 1850.

9. The percentages in table 9.2 and the other tables indicate the proportion of legislators voting on the affirmative side of each issue. However, they do not invariably indicate "yea" votes because some of the roll calls involved motions to table, strike out, or postpone.

10. Speech of David Barnes; speech of Patrick H. Winston, in *Raleigh Register*, 3 December 1850.

11. Speech of Curtis H. Brogden, in *Raleigh North Carolina Standard*, 4 December 1850; speech of Josiah Bridges, ibid., 1 January 1851.

12. *Raleigh North Carolina Standard*, 12 February 1851.

13. "An Address to the People of North Carolina on the Subject of Constitutional Reform," in *Raleigh Register*, 5 February 1851.

14. William B. Shepard, *Speech of the Hon. William B. Shepard* (n.p., 1851), 3; speech of Patrick H. Winston, in *Raleigh Register*, 15 January 1851.

15. Francis N. Thorpe, *The Federal and State Constitutions, Colonial Charters, and Other Organic Laws*, 7 vols. (Washington, D.C.: Government Printing Office, 1909), 5:2798.

16. *HJ, 1848–49*, 655. Although they would undoubtedly have preferred an unlimited convention, Whig reformers supported the Rayner bill in order to forestall the passage of free suffrage by legislative amendment. Many reformers apparently believed that if a free-suffrage amendment passed the legislature, "the Eastern men, who wanted that and no more, would not help us get a Convention." Communication from "Western Reserve" to *Asheville Highland Messenger*, in *Raleigh North Carolina Standard*, 12 February 1851.

17. *Raleigh North Carolina Standard*, 11 December 1850. For an analysis of the arguments for and against a convention, see Thomas E. Jeffrey, "Beyond 'Free Suffrage': North Carolina Parties and the Convention Movement of the 1850s," *NCHR* 62 (1985): 397–400.

18. Only one mountain Democrat, William W. Avery of Burke County, supported

the position of the party leadership on the convention and white-basis issues. But even Avery expressed a willingness to support an open and unrestricted convention if free suffrage by legislative enactment was defeated. See *Speech of William W. Avery, Esq. of Burke upon the Subject of Constitutional Reform, Delivered in the House of Commons of North Carolina, on the 18th of December 1850* (n.p., n.d.), 8.

19. Most of the Whig support for the free-suffrage amendment came from conservative easterners who opposed a convention. Only two of the nine eastern Whigs who supported free suffrage had voted earlier in favor of Rayner's convention bill. On the other hand, all thirteen eastern Whigs who voted against free suffrage had voted in favor of Rayner's bill. The only eastern legislators who voted against both free suffrage and the Rayner bill were Democrats Isaac B. Kelly of Duplin and William Eaton, Jr., of Warren.

20. Twenty-nine senators, all but three of whom were Democrats, voted in favor of the free-suffrage amendment. At this point Weldon N. Edwards, a Democrat and inveterate foe of free suffrage, could have saved the bill by casting an affirmative vote. But Edwards, who as speaker of the senate normally did not vote, declined to exercise his prerogative, and the measure, shy one vote, went down to defeat. Historians have often commented upon Edwards's role in the defeat of free suffrage during the legislative session of 1852 but, curiously, no one has recognized the part he played in frustrating reform efforts two years earlier. A breakdown by party of the vote in the senate can be found in [Calvin H. Wiley, ed.], *The Constitution of North Carolina . . . Together with an Account and Explanation of the Questions of Constitutional Reform Now Agitating the People of the State* ([Raleigh]: N.C. Institution for the Deaf and Dumb and the Blind, 1851), 53.

21. In introducing his referendum bill, McLean reminded his colleagues that he had previously been "the ardent and devoted friend of Free Suffrage by legislative enactment." The legislative method had failed, however, and "the only practicable way of obtaining free suffrage, and other constitutional reforms, was by an open convention." He had accordingly introduced his bill "as an entering wedge to effect that purpose" (*Raleigh Register*, 22 January 1851).

22. For a breakdown by party of the vote in the senate, see [Wiley], *Constitution of North Carolina*, 54–56. The evidence does not support the claim of some historians that conservative Whigs supported a convention as a means of defeating free suffrage. Indeed, exactly the opposite seems to have been the case. Conservative Whigs like William H. Washington were willing to swallow their distaste for free suffrage in order to stave off a convention that might enact more radical reforms.

23. Communication from "C" [Thomas L. Clingman?], in *Asheville News*, 9 January 1851; Jeffrey, "Beyond 'Free Suffrage,'" 405–6.

24. Nicholas W. Woodfin to David F. Caldwell, 11 October 1851, David Franklin Caldwell Papers, SHC. Clingman easily defeated Gaither by a margin of two to one (see chapter 11 in this volume).

25. The editor of the *Elizabeth City Old North State* bluntly told the reformers that "the question of an open Convention had better be dropped if they desire the

success of the Whig party in the coming election" (quoted in *Greensboro Patriot*, 14 February 1852).

26. Whig platform, in *Raleigh Register*, 5 May 1852.

27. Speech of John Kerr in Edenton (extract from *Edenton Albemarle Bulletin*), in *Raleigh Register*, 2 June 1852; speech of John Kerr in Raleigh, in *Raleigh Register*, 9 June 1852.

28. *Elizabeth City Democratic Pioneer*, in *Elizabeth City Old North State*, 26 June 1852.

29. For the position of the *Asheville News*, see *Greensboro Patriot*, 17 July 1852; for Clingman's views, see Clingman to James F. E. Hardy, 18 July 1852, Clingman and Puryear Family Papers, SHC.

30. Calvin Graves to Thomas Settle, 10 July 1852, Thomas Settle Papers (Group 1), SHC; Settle to David S. Reid, 16 July 1852, Reid Papers.

31. Reid received 48,567 votes, compared to 43,003 for Kerr. Robert D. W. Connor, comp., *A Manual of North Carolina* (Raleigh: North Carolina Historical Commission, 1913), 997–98. In the senatorial district of Currituck and Camden, both Democrats and Whigs claimed victory. The Democrat-controlled senate subsequently awarded the seat to Henry M. Shaw, the Democratic candidate. *Raleigh North Carolina Standard*, 25 August 1852; *Raleigh Register*, 12 January 1853.

32. For a breakdown of the vote on free suffrage in the senate, see *Raleigh North Carolina Standard*, 15 December 1852. All ten of the western Whigs in the senate voted against free suffrage, as did five of the eleven eastern Whigs. On the same day that the senate rejected the free-suffrage amendment, the Democrats introduced a new bill in the house of commons. On 8 December, however, their bill fell nine votes short of the required three-fifths majority. Five eastern Whigs and three western Whigs who had supported the first free-suffrage bill subsequently reversed their position on the second bill (see table 9.4).

33. Cecil K. Brown, *A State Movement in Railroad Development: The Story of North Carolina's First Effort to Establish an East and West Trunk Line Railroad* (Chapel Hill: University of North Carolina Press, 1928), 97–99; Thomas E. Jeffrey, "Internal Improvements and Political Parties in Antebellum North Carolina, 1836–1860," *NCHR* 55 (1978): 142–43.

34. Whig platform, in *Raleigh Register*, 1 March 1854.

35. *Raleigh North Carolina Standard*, 19 April 1854; *Greensboro Patriot*, 18 March 1854.

36. Alfred Dockery to David F. Caldwell, 10 March 1854, Caldwell Papers.

37. *Raleigh Star*, in *Greensboro Patriot*, 15 April 1854; Jeffrey, "Internal Improvements and Political Parties," 145–46.

38. Thomas W. Atkin, the editor of the *Asheville News*, admitted that he personally remained "a White Basis man, up to the hub" and that he disapproved of the official Democratic position on that issue. But, according to Atkin, the Democrats at least were honest in their opposition to a change in the basis, in contrast to the Whigs, who were taking one position in the east and a contradictory stance in the west. "On this subject," said Atkin, "the Democratic party has at least been consistent—and in so far as men prefer *honesty* to *dishonesty*, and

consistency to *duplicity*, they must prefer that party" (*Asheville News*, 6 April, 4 May 1854).

39. Asa Biggs to David S. Reid, 10 March 1854; Marcus Erwin to Reid, 31 March 1854, Reid Papers.

40. Democratic platform, in *Raleigh North Carolina Standard*, 26 April 1854; *Elizabeth City Old North State*, in *New Bern Atlantic*, 24 May 1854.

41. *Goldsboro Republican and Patriot*, 18 July 1854; speech of Thomas Bragg, in *Elizabeth City Democratic Pioneer*, 30 May 1854.

42. *Asheville News*, 11, 18 May 1854.

43. *Asheville News*, in *Raleigh North Carolina Standard*, 2 September 1854; Jeffrey, "Internal Improvements and Political Parties," 145–46.

44. Voting returns by county for the gubernatorial election of 1854 can be found in Thomas E. Jeffrey, "The Second Party System in North Carolina, 1836–1860" (Ph.D. diss., Catholic University of America, 1976), appendix A; and in Connor, *Manual of North Carolina*, 997–98.

45. Alfred Dockery to *Fayetteville Observer*, 23 February 1857, in *Raleigh Register*, 11 March 1857.

46. *Raleigh Register*, 23 August 1854.

47. Brown, *State Movement in Railroad Development*, 102–5.

48. Hershal L. Macon, "A Fiscal History of North Carolina, 1776–1860" (Ph.D. diss., University of North Carolina at Chapel Hill, 1932), 402–9.

49. Abraham Rencher to Thomas Bragg, 22 February 1855, Governor's Papers, NCDAH; *HJ, 1854–55*, 361–62.

50. The referendum bill was defeated in the house of commons by a vote of 74 to 39, with 73 percent of the Whigs in support and 98 percent of the Democrats in opposition (*HJ, 1854–55*, 314). The free-suffrage amendment passed its second reading by a vote of 91 to 15, with five eastern Whigs and ten western Whigs in opposition (ibid., 370–71). There was no recorded roll-call vote on the third reading.

51. Communication from "F," in *Greensboro Patriot*, 12 October 1855; Jeffrey, "Beyond 'Free Suffrage,'" 414–18. Thomas Atkin of the *Asheville News* agreed that the issue of internal improvements was "a greater and more interesting subject than conventions or free suffrage or changes in the basis." "Give us our Railroad improvements," Atkin assured his Democratic allies in the east, "and you may manage the basis and the convention and free suffrage to suit yourselves" (*Asheville News*, 4 January 1855).

52. James R. Morrill, "The Presidential Election of 1852: Death Knell of the Whig Party in North Carolina," *NCHR* 44 (1967). See also William J. Cooper, *The South and the Politics of Slavery, 1828–1856* (Baton Rouge: Louisiana State University Press, 1978), 322–41, 359–62.

53. One of the victorious Whigs was Thomas L. Clingman, who defeated Burgess S. Gaither, a procompromise Whig. Clingman's victory can hardly be cited as evidence of popular support for the Compromise of 1850. Nevertheless, the dissident congressman did canvass his district as a Whig, taking pains to tone down the strident southern-rights rhetoric that he had earlier uttered on the floor of Congress. See Thomas E. Jeffrey, "'Thunder from the Mountains': Thomas Lan-

ier Clingman and the End of Whig Supremacy in North Carolina," *NCHR* 56 (1979): 388. See also chapter 11 in this volume.

54. Voting returns by county for the presidential election of 1852 can be found in W. Dean Burnham, *Presidential Ballots, 1836–1892* (Baltimore: Johns Hopkins University Press, 1955), 646–68. The main factor behind the improved Whig showing in the presidential election was voter turnout. Only 66 percent of the eligible voters participated in that election, compared to 76 percent in the gubernatorial election. The drop in turnout hurt the Democrats far more than the Whigs. For voter turnout, see J. R. Pole, "Election Statistics in North Carolina, to 1861," *JSH* 24 (1958): 228.

55. *Raleigh Register*, 30 August 1854.

10 Responsibility of Power

1. For the impact of the Know-Nothing movement in the North, see Michael F. Holt, *The Political Crisis of the 1850s* (New York: Wiley, 1978), 155–70. For the decline of the Whig party in the South, see William J. Cooper, *The South and the Politics of Slavery, 1828–1856* (Baton Rouge: Louisiana State University Press, 1978), 340–62.

2. One of the victorious Whigs was Thomas L. Clingman. Although he had endorsed Pierce in 1852, Clingman did not canvass his district in 1853 as a Democrat. Overall, according to William J. Cooper, only fourteen of the sixty-five newly elected southern congressmen were Whigs (*South and the Politics of Slavery*, 342).

3. For the Democrats' efforts to exploit the Kansas-Nebraska Act, see Cooper, *South and the Politics of Slavery*, 356–59. In the case of North Carolina, Cooper exaggerates the extent to which the results of the state elections of 1854 "demoralized Southern Whiggery" (ibid., 359).

4. Communication from J. F. Riddick, in *Raleigh North Carolina Standard*, 4 July 1855. During the spring and summer of 1855 the *Standard* published numerous letters from Democrats who claimed that they had been deceived into believing that the Know-Nothings were a nonpartisan organization. See, for example, *North Carolina Standard*, 13 June, 4, 18 July, 1 August 1855. For the early activities of the Know-Nothings in North Carolina, see Thomas H. Leath, "The Know-Nothing Party in North Carolina" (Master's thesis, University of North Carolina at Chapel Hill, 1929), 3–15. The Constitution of January 1855 was published in the *North Carolina Standard*, 18 July 1855.

5. The first president of the state council, Peter F. Pescud of Raleigh, as well as four of its five other officers, had not previously been active in North Carolina politics. William H. Harrison, the secretary of the council, was a Raleigh Whig who had served as a delegate to the state convention in 1852 (*Raleigh Register*, 5 May 1852). For the activities of Rayner and Miller, see ibid., 17 January, 21 March, 4, 18 April, 9 May 1855.

6. *Greensboro Patriot*, 24, 31 March, 29 May, 20, 27 July 1855; *Raleigh Register*, 18 April, 23 May 1855; *Raleigh North Carolina Standard*, 20 June 1855. The anti-Democratic newspapers referred to the American meetings as "conventions"

rather than "councils." The widespread use of the word "convention" suggests that professional politicians had assumed control of the order by the spring of 1855.

7. *Elizabeth City Democratic Pioneer*, 6 March 1855. William W. Holden agreed that "the Whig politicians of the South, conscious that their party was in the last stages of a decline, were ready . . . for any movement that promised place and power, and they dropped at once the *name* of their old party and took the very appropriate one of the new" (*Raleigh North Carolina Standard*, 4 April 1855).

8. *Raleigh North Carolina Standard*, 20, 27 June 1855; *Kinston American Advocate*, 5 July 1855. David Reid of Duplin should not be confused with David Settle Reid of Rockingham, the Democratic governor and U.S. senator.

9. For a similar interpretation, see Marc W. Kruman, *Parties and Politics in North Carolina, 1836–1865* (Baton Rouge: Louisiana State University Press, 1983), 162–64.

10. The national platform of the American party was published in the *Raleigh Register*, 20 June 1855. For a perceptive discussion of antiparty sentiment among the Know-Nothings, see Holt, *Political Crisis of the 1850s*, 163–69. Veteran Whig politicians like Henry W. Miller and John A. Gilmer joined enthusiastically in this chorus of antipartyism. See speech of Henry W. Miller, in *Raleigh Register*, 9 May 1855; speech of John A. Gilmer, in *Greensboro Patriot*, 3 August 1855. According to the editor of the *Asheville Spectator*: "corruption has crept into ALL parties founded upon the OLD ISSUES. . . . The government of the country must be wrested from the hands of rotten politicians, and a recurrence to *first principles* must be had, if our liberties are to be preserved" (quoted in *Asheville News*, 22 March 1855).

11. *Raleigh North Carolina Standard*, 20 June 1855.

12. George E. Badger to Henry W. Miller and others, 18 July 1855, in *Raleigh Register*, 25 July 1855; Badger to James A. Pearce, 29 March 1855, 17 September 1856, George E. Badger Papers, NCDAH. While admitting that the Americans had "carried with them the best of their principles from the Whigs," Edward J. Hale could see "no sufficient reason why Whigs should either abandon their own party organization or unite in that of any other party." The editor advised his readers to "stand firm by your Whig principles, and by what remains of your Whig party. They have merited all your love and respect, and the time will come when they may be again as powerful for good as ever" (*Fayetteville Observer*, 17 March, 28 April, 21 July 1856).

13. Speech of John Kerr, in *Raleigh Register*, 9 May 1855; *Raleigh North Carolina Standard*, 20 June 1855; Thomas E. Jeffrey, "The Second Party System in North Carolina, 1836–1860" (Ph.D. diss., Catholic University of America, 1976), 371–72; Kruman, *Parties and Politics in North Carolina*, 170, 176–77.

14. For the vote by county in the congressional elections of 1855, see *Raleigh North Carolina Standard*, 22 August 1855. Outside of Clingman's district, the seven American candidates received about 4,400 fewer votes than Dockery had won in 1854. However, the seven Democratic candidates received about 4,300 fewer votes than Thomas Bragg.

15. The American platform of 1855 was published in *Raleigh Register*, 31 October 1855.

16. The proceedings and platform of the Greensboro convention were published in *Raleigh Register*, 16 April 1856. The chairman of the executive committee was Henry W. Miller, a longtime member of the Whig central committee. The other committee members were Richard A. Caldwell, Ralph Gorrell, William H. Harrison, J. H. Haughton, John D. Hyman, Henry K. Nash, John Pool, John N. Washington, Thomas J. Wilson, and Nicholas W. Woodfin. None of these members had been a Democrat prior to 1855. Gorrell, Haughton, Nash, and Woodfin had served previously as Whig members of the general assembly. Hyman was coeditor of the *Asheville Spectator*. Pool, a member of the house of commons in 1856 and 1858, was the Whig candidate for governor in 1860. Caldwell, the son of veteran Whig leader David F. Caldwell of Rowan, was a member of the Whig state convention in 1852 and an assistant elector that year. Harrison was also a delegate to the state convention in 1852. Washington, who served as an assistant elector in 1852, was the scion of a prominent Whig family in Craven County. Wilson was an unsuccessful Whig candidate for the house of commons in 1854. Three members of the executive committee—Miller, Haughton, and Nash—had been members of the Whig executive committee in 1852. Miller and Hyman had been members in 1854. See *Raleigh Register*, 5 May 1852, 1 March 1854, 16 August 1854; J. G. de Roulhac Hamilton and Max R. Williams, eds., *The Papers of William Alexander Graham*, 7 vols. to date (Raleigh: Division of Archives and History, 1957–), 3:106, 4:515n; Frontis W. Johnston, ed., *The Papers of Zebulon Baird Vance*, 1 vol. to date (Raleigh: Division of Archives and History, 1963–), 1:50n; John H. Wheeler, *Historical Sketches of North Carolina*, 2 vols. in 1 (Philadelphia: Lippincott, 1851), 2:54, 87, 184, 338; Kruman, *Parties and Politics in North Carolina*, 171n–172n.

17. *Elizabeth City Democratic Pioneer*, 6 May 1856; *New Bern Journal*, 6 August 1856.

18. *Asheville News*, 1, 8 May 1856.

19. The vote by county in the governor's election of 1856 can be found in Jeffrey, "Second Party System in North Carolina," appendix A; and in Robert D. W. Connor, comp., *A Manual of North Carolina* (Raleigh: North Carolina Historical Commission, 1913), 997–98. For voter participation, see J. R. Pole, "Election Statistics in North Carolina, to 1861," *JSH* 24 (1958): 228.

20. *Wilmington Herald*, 12 August 1856; *Kinston American Advocate*, 14 August 1856. Gilmer himself acknowledged that "my defeat in this State was owing as I conceive much to Local questions" (Gilmer to Calvin H. Wiley, 30 August 1856, Calvin Henderson Wiley Papers, SHC).

21. John B. Woodfin to Thomas L. Clingman, 8 June 1854, Clingman and Puryear Family Papers, SHC.

22. Thomas L. Clingman, "Address to the Freemen of the Eighth Congressional District" [1856], in *Selections from the Speeches and Writings of Hon. Thomas L. Clingman of North Carolina* (Raleigh: J. Nichols, 1877), 387. In a recent reevaluation of the role of Thomas L. Clingman, Marc W. Kruman has minimized

Clingman's impact on the declining fortunes of the North Carolina Whig party during the 1850s. "Clingman was a remarkable politician," he concludes, "but one with equally unremarkable coattails" ("Thomas L. Clingman and the Whig Party: A Reconsideration," *NCHR* 64 [1987]: 17). In support of this argument Kruman emphasizes the strong Whig showing in Clingman's district in the presidential election of 1852 and the state elections of 1854, despite the congressman's endorsement of the Democratic candidates. On the other hand, he downplays the substantial increase in the Democratic vote in the state elections of 1852, in the state and national elections of 1856, and in the state elections of 1858.

23. The vote by county in the presidential election of 1856 can be found in W. Dean Burnham, *Presidential Ballots, 1836–1892* (Baltimore: Johns Hopkins University Press, 1955), 646–68. For the impact of the slavery issue on the election, see chapter 11 in this volume.

24. Supporters of the North Carolina Railroad were particularly vehement in their opposition to the Danville connection, which they claimed would benefit Richmond and other Virginia markets at the expense of the North Carolina Railroad and the state's own market towns. The friends of the Wilmington & Charlotte were equally adamant in their denunciation of the proposed Cheraw & Coalfields road, a project that would divert the trade of the southern counties from Wilmington to the towns of Cheraw and Charleston in South Carolina. Supporters of the Western North Carolina Railroad feared that the extension of the Wilmington & Charlotte across the mountains to Tennessee would injure their own railroad because the two would run parallel, at times within fifteen miles of each other. Supporters of the Deep River project viewed the Fayetteville & Coalfields Railroad as a rival for the trade of the central piedmont, and some friends of the North Carolina Railroad also regarded it as a possible competitor. See speech of W. R. Myers, in *Raleigh North Carolina Standard*, 11 February 1857; speech of William Eaton, in *Raleigh Register*, 4 March 1857; *Wilmington Herald*, 17 January 1857; *Fayetteville Observer*, 19 January 1857; *Wilmington Journal*, 2 February 1857; communication from William H. Thomas to *Asheville News*, in *North Carolina Standard*, 4 March 1857; *Greensboro Patriot*, 6 February 1857; *Fayetteville North Carolinian*, 20 December 1856.

25. *Raleigh North Carolina Standard*, 28 January, 4 February 1857.

26. *Wilmington Journal*, 2 February 1857; *Fayetteville Observer*, 19 January 1857; *Raleigh North Carolina Standard*, 21 January, 11 February, 1857.

27. *Raleigh North Carolina Standard*, 21 January 1857; *Greensboro Patriot*, 30 January, 6 February 1857.

28. *Raleigh North Carolina Standard*, 25, 11 February 1857; *Wilmington Journal*, 2 February 1857; *Asheville News*, 12 February 1857.

29. *Raleigh North Carolina Standard*, 25 February 1857.

30. *Fayetteville Observer*, 16 February 1857; *Greensboro Patriot*, 13 February 1857.

31. *Greensboro Patriot*, 20 March, 1 May 1857.

32. *Greensboro Patriot*, 24 April 1857; speech of William Eaton, in *Raleigh Register*, 25 February 1857.

33. *Wilmington Herald*, 18 February 1857.

34. *Raleigh Register*, 15 April 1857.

35. *Asheville News*, 2 April 1857.

36. For the vote by county in the congressional elections of 1857, see *Raleigh North Carolina Standard*, 26 August 1857.

37. *Raleigh Register*, in *Greensboro Patriot*, 20 November 1857. The *Register* had been owned by members of the Gales family since its establishment by Joseph Gales in 1799. In December 1856, however, the press was purchased by John W. Syme, the editor of the *Petersburg* (Va.) *Intelligencer*. Syme's lack of experience in the intricacies of North Carolina politics made the *Register* a less effective party organ after 1856 than it had been under the ownership of the Gales family. *Raleigh North Carolina Standard*, 10 December 1856; Herbert D. Pegg, *The Whig Party in North Carolina* (Chapel Hill: Colonial Press, 1968), 27–28.

38. *Elizabeth City Native Sentinel*, in *Raleigh North Carolina Standard*, 17 March 1858. See also *Greensboro Patriot*, 4 December 1857.

39. Henry W. Miller to *Raleigh Register*, in *Raleigh North Carolina Standard*, 24 March 1858; communication from Miller, ibid., 7 April 1858.

40. Abraham W. Venable to Archibald H. Arrington, 19 June 1853, Archibald H. Arrington Papers, SHC; John Berry to Venable, 8 August 1853, Abraham Watkins Venable Papers, SHC; Lucien N. B. Battle to Venable, 28 April 1855, Venable Papers; Jeffrey, "Second Party System in North Carolina," 381–82; Clarence C. Norton, *The Democratic Party in Ante-Bellum North Carolina, 1835–1861* (Chapel Hill: University of North Carolina Press, 1930), 181, 239–41.

41. Abraham W. Venable to Archibald H. Arrington, 15 April 1858, Arrington Papers.

42. Duncan K. McRae to the people of North Carolina, in *Raleigh North Carolina Standard*, 12 May 1858; Jeffrey, "Second Party System in North Carolina," 384–86.

43. Ellis won the nomination by a vote of 25,051 to 21,594, with each county voting its strength in the gubernatorial election of 1856. Ellis carried forty counties, compared to twenty-seven for Holden (*Raleigh North Carolina Standard*, 21 April 1858). For the traditional unwillingness of party leaders to nominate controversial politicians like Holden for the governorship, see Jeffrey, "Second Party System in North Carolina," 147–48; and Kruman, *Parties and Politics in North Carolina*, 32. For Ellis's reactions to the attacks against him in the pro-Holden presses and his assessment of their effectiveness, see Ellis to Henry M. Shaw, 1 April 1858, Thomas M. Pittman Papers, NCDAH. Holden's unsuccessful effort to win his party's gubernatorial nomination is discussed at length in William C. Harris, *William Woods Holden: Firebrand of North Carolina Politics* (Baton Rouge: Louisiana State University Press, 1987), 71–76.

44. Thomas Bragg to Henry M. Shaw, 31 March 1858, Pittman Papers; Democratic platform, in *Raleigh North Carolina Standard*, 21 April 1858.

45. Duncan McRae to the people of North Carolina, in *Raleigh North Carolina Standard*, 12 May 1858; *Wilmington Journal*, 30 July 1858.

46. *Salisbury Carolina Watchman*, 3 August 1858; *Louisburg American Eagle*, 31 July 1858.

47. For McRae's decision not to downplay his Democratic antecedents and pro-

clivities, see McRae to Archibald Arrington, 5 May 1858, Arrington Papers. Arrington and other Democratic dissidents agreed that this was sound strategy. According to Arrington: "The bare fact of your being the In[dependent] Can[didate] against the nominee of the democrats . . . and your favoring distribution will give you their [opposition] support without doubt. . . . Your greatest and only aim must be to get democratic votes . . . the opposition vote without a good democratic vote will do you no good" (Arrington to McRae, 1 May 1858, Arrington Papers).

48. *Elizabeth City Democratic Pioneer*, 24 August 1858. The vote by county in the governor's election of 1858 can be found in Jeffrey, "Second Party System in North Carolina," appendix A; and in Connor, *Manual of North Carolina*, 997–98. For voter participation, see Pole, "Election Statistics in North Carolina," 228.

49. The Caldwell bill was defeated by a vote of 53 to 39, with 57 percent of the Democrats and 59 percent of the Whigs in opposition. The Williams bill was defeated by a vote of 55 to 34, with 55 percent of the Democrats and 76 percent of the Whigs opposed. For a breakdown by party of the vote on these two bills, see *Raleigh North Carolina Standard*, 16 March 1859.

50. *Asheville News*, 10 February 1859; "An Appeal to the Democratic Members of the House of Commons in North Carolina," in *Raleigh Register*, 16 February 1859.

51. *Asheville News*, 10 February 1859; Donald C. Butts, "A Challenge to Planter Rule: The Controversy over the Ad Valorem Taxation of Slaves in North Carolina, 1858–1862" (Ph.D. diss., Duke University, 1978), 28; Hershal L. Macon, "A Fiscal History of North Carolina, 1776–1860" (Ph.D. diss., University of North Carolina at Chapel Hill, 1932), 408.

52. Bledsoe's resolutions were published in *Raleigh North Carolina Standard*, 2 February 1859.

53. Bledsoe's bill was published in *Greensboro Patriot*, 26 November 1858.

54. *SJ, 1858–59*, 224.

55. Ibid., 223.

56. *Fayetteville Observer*, 22 November 1858; *Raleigh North Carolina Standard*, 9 February 1859; *Greensboro Patriot*, 30 September 1859; George Little to William A. Graham, 26 January 1859, in Hamilton and Williams, *Graham Papers*, 5:86.

57. *Raleigh Register*, 9 March 1859; *Raleigh North Carolina Standard*, 10 August 1859.

58. *Fayetteville Observer*, 8 August 1859.

59. *Raleigh Register*, 24 August 1859.

60. *Elizabeth City Democratic Pioneer*, 16 August 1859; *New Bern Progress*, 15 August 1859. For similar expressions of sentiment, see *Wilmington Journal*, 12 August 1859; *Charlotte Western Democrat*, 16 August 1859; *Raleigh North Carolina Standard*, 24 August 1859. On balance, the evidence suggests that the issue of state taxation—and not the charges of corruption in Washington—was the primary factor behind the Whig resurgence in 1860. For an interpretation that emphasizes the importance of national issues to the total exclusion of state questions, see Kruman, *Parties and Politics in North Carolina*, 184–87.

61. Communication from "A Voice from the West," in *Greensboro Patriot*, 30 September 1859.

62. *New Bern Progress*, 12 March 1860.

63. The proceedings of the opposition convention were published in the *Raleigh Register*, 29 February 1860. After adopting its formal platform, the convention endorsed a resolution affirming its support for the "National Union Party" and naming William A. Graham as its first choice for president. Some historians have claimed that the Opposition party of 1860 was really a new party, not the old Whig party. See, for example, Donald C. Butts, "The 'Irrepressible Conflict': Slave Taxation and North Carolina's Gubernatorial Election of 1860," *NCHR* 58 (1981): 46; and Otto H. Olsen, "Reconsidering the Scalawags," *Civil War History* 12 (1966): 308. The evidence does not support this interpretation.

64. Opposition platform, in *Raleigh Register*, 29 February 1860.

65. Butts, "A Challenge to Planter Rule," 59–69; *Raleigh North Carolina Standard*, 28 December 1859, 11, 18 January, 1 February 1860. For Democratic criticisms of the Working-Men's Association, see the remarks of the *Salisbury Banner* and the *Warrenton News*, in *Raleigh Register*, 18 January 1860.

66. *Raleigh North Carolina Standard*, 14 March 1860. The Democratic platform was published in the same issue of the *Standard*.

67. Speech of John W. Ellis, in *Raleigh North Carolina Standard*, 21 March 1860.

68. *Fayetteville Observer*, 19 March 1860; *Raleigh North Carolina Standard*, 18 July 1860; Bartholomew F. Moore to William A. Graham, 26 July 1860, in Hamilton and Williams, *Graham Papers*, 5:169.

69. *Raleigh North Carolina Standard*, 18 July 1860.

70. Speech of John W. Ellis, in *Raleigh North Carolina Standard*, 21 March 1860; J. Parker Jordan to Elisha G. Johnson, 21 April 1860, ibid., 30 May 1860.

71. The vote by county in the gubernatorial election of 1860 can be found in Jeffrey, "Second Party System in North Carolina," appendix A; and in Connor, *Manual of North Carolina*, 999–1000. For voter participation, see Pole, "Election Statistics in North Carolina," 228.

72. *Raleigh North Carolina Standard*, 8 August 1860.

73. *Greensboro Patriot*, 9 September 1859.

74. The first signs of an incipient political revolt in the mountain district had appeared during the special congressional election that was held in August 1858 to fill the seat vacated when Thomas L. Clingman moved to the U.S. Senate. To the surprise of most political observers, Zebulon Baird Vance, a young Whig lawyer and newspaperman, upset the veteran Democratic legislator, William W. Avery. A year later, Vance won reelection against another strong Democratic opponent. See Glenn Tucker, *Zeb Vance: Champion of Personal Freedom* (Indianapolis: Bobbs-Merrill, 1965), 65–68, 77–80.

75. Kruman, *Parties and Politics in North Carolina*, 140, 141, 55. The consensus interpretation has also been advanced by Michael F. Holt in *The Political Crisis of the 1850s* (New York: Wiley, 1978). See, especially, pp. 101–38.

76. Quoted in Butts, "The 'Irrepressible Conflict,'" 64.

11 *Politics of Union*

1. Herbert D. Pegg, *The Whig Party in North Carolina* (Chapel Hill: Colonial Press, 1968), 89.

2. J. Carlyle Sitterson, *The Secession Movement in North Carolina* (Chapel Hill: University of North Carolina Press, 1939), 5–6, 11–12, 18–19.

3. Pegg, *Whig Party in North Carolina*, 91. See also Clarence C. Norton, *The Democratic Party in Ante-Bellum North Carolina, 1835–1861* (Chapel Hill: University of North Carolina Press, 1930), 47; and Sitterson, *Secession Movement in North Carolina*, 10–11, 17–18.

4. See figures 8.1 and 10.1. In 1838 Edward B. Dudley, the Whig candidate for governor, won 59 percent of the eastern vote. Dudley's victory that year was the result of the large number of Democratic abstentions and cannot, therefore, be cited as an accurate reflection of the strength of the Whig party in the east.

5. A ranking of North Carolina counties according to their white population in 1850 can be found in Thomas E. Jeffrey, "The Second Party System in North Carolina, 1836–1860" (Ph.D. diss., Catholic University of America, 1976), appendix C.

6. "An Address to the People of North Carolina on the Subject of Constitutional Reform," in *Raleigh Register*, 5 February 1851. The important role that slavery played in the economic and social life of the mountain region has been ably documented in John C. Inscoe, "Mountain Masters: Slaveholding in Western North Carolina," *NCHR* 61 (1984). It is probably not true that more slaveholders lived in the west than in the east. Certainly westerners never offered any evidence to support that claim.

7. *HJ, 1838–39*, 360. For a good discussion of the importance of slavery to non-slaveholders, see William L. Barney, *The Road to Secession: A New Perspective on the Old South* (New York: Praeger, 1972), 49–64.

8. John Scott to Willie P. Mangum, 18 December 1831, in Henry T. Shanks, ed., *The Papers of Willie Person Mangum*, 5 vols. (Raleigh: State Department of Archives and History, 1950–56), 1:432; proceedings of a Union meeting in Pasquotank County, enclosed in John C. Ehringhaus and Isaac P. Freeman to Andrew Jackson, 22 January 1833, in Elizabeth G. McPherson, ed., "Unpublished Letters from North Carolinians to Andrew Jackson," *NCHR* 14 (1937): 380.

9. Report and resolutions, Orange County Whig meeting, 24 February 1836, in J. G. de Roulhac Hamilton and Max R. Williams, eds., *The Papers of William Alexander Graham*, 7 vols. to date (Raleigh: Division of Archives and History, 1957–), 1:415; Edward B. Dudley to the citizens of Wake County, in *Raleigh Register*, 23 February 1836.

10. National Republican [Democratic] Party, *An Address to the Freemen of North Carolina* (Raleigh, 1836), 4, 12.

11. The campaigns of 1836 and 1840 are discussed in detail in chapter 3 in this volume.

12. William J. Cooper, *The South and the Politics of Slavery, 1828–1856* (Baton Rouge: Louisiana State University Press, 1978), 182–206; Marc W. Kruman, *Parties and Politics in North Carolina, 1836–1865* (Baton Rouge: Louisiana State

University Press, 1983), 110; Pegg, *Whig Party in North Carolina*, 141; George H. Gibson, "Opinion in North Carolina Regarding the Acquisition of Texas and Cuba, 1835–1855," *NCHR* 37 (1960): 8.

13. The *Standard* is quoted in Kruman, *Parties and Politics in North Carolina*, 109; the Democratic central committee is quoted in ibid., 111.

14. For the correlation between the vote in 1842 and 1844, see Kruman, *Parties and Politics in North Carolina*, 43. For a differing view about the importance of the Texas issue in 1844, see Cooper, *South and the Politics of Slavery*, 218–19.

15. David M. Potter, *The Impending Crisis, 1848–1861* (New York: Harper and Row, 1976), 122.

16. William H. Haywood, Jr., to Martin Van Buren, 30 May 1849, in Elizabeth G. McPherson, ed., "Unpublished Letters from North Carolinians to Van Buren," *NCHR* 15 (1938): 149; Asa Biggs to James K. Polk, 27 December 1848, Asa Biggs Papers, NCDAH.

17. *Raleigh Register*, 21, 28 June 1848.

18. Ibid., 28 June 1848.

19. The *Standard* is quoted in Norton, *Democratic Party in Ante-Bellum North Carolina*, 143. For the vote in the presidential elections of 1844 and 1848, see W. Dean Burnham, *Presidential Ballots, 1836–1892* (Baltimore: Johns Hopkins University Press, 1955), 646–68. Taylor received 44,095 votes in North Carolina, compared to 35,810 for Cass. Four years earlier, Clay had defeated Polk in North Carolina by a vote of 43,255 to 38,894.

20. Cooper, *South and the Politics of Slavery*, 269–71; Sitterson, *Secession Movement in North Carolina*, 47–48.

21. Sitterson, *Secession Movement in North Carolina*, 52. North Carolina presents a conspicuous exception to Cooper's generalization that "the Whigs fared poorly in all [southern states] that had major elections in 1849" (*South and the Politics of Slavery*, 278).

22. In North Carolina the Whigs did not publicly criticize Taylor's plan but, instead, argued that the president's proposals and the ones subsequently offered by Henry Clay were mutually compatible. In their private correspondence, however, the Whig congressmen did express their concern about the South's seeming lack of influence in the Taylor administration (Kruman, *Parties and Politics in North Carolina*, 126).

23. The only full-length study of the Compromise of 1850 is Holman Hamilton, *Prologue to Conflict: The Crisis and Compromise of 1850* (Lexington: University Press of Kentucky, 1964). The best summary of the events leading to the passage of the compromise is Potter, *Impending Crisis*, 63–120.

24. Speech of Abraham Venable, in *Raleigh North Carolina Standard*, 13 March 1850. Daniel's speech was published in ibid., 16 October 1850.

25. For a ranking of North Carolina counties according to average farm value in 1850, see Jeffrey, "Second Party System in North Carolina," appendix G. For the proportion of slaveholders in Clingman's district, see John C. Inscoe, "Thomas Clingman, Mountain Whiggery, and the Southern Cause," *Civil War History* 33 (1987): 42.

26. Sitterson, *Secession Movement in North Carolina*, 157 (characterizing Cling-

man); Pegg, *Whig Party in North Carolina*, 190 (characterizing Stanly). Sitterson similarly described Stanly as "the most active Unionist of the North Carolina delegation" (90).

27. Clingman's speech was published in the *Raleigh North Carolina Standard*, 6 February 1850.

28. Speech of Edward Stanly, in *Raleigh Register*, 27 March, 3 April 1850.

29. *Raleigh North Carolina Standard*, 16 July 1851.

30. William W. Holden to John W. Ellis, 8 January 1852, in Noble J. Tolbert, ed., *The Papers of John Willis Ellis*, 2 vols. (Raleigh: State Department of Archives and History, 1964), 1:105–6.

31. *Richmond* (Va.) *Times*, quoted in *Salisbury Carolina Watchman*, 17 April 1851. In 1846 and 1848 Clingman solicited the support of the Whigs in the general assembly for a seat in the U.S. Senate. Although only a few Whigs gave him their votes, a majority of Democrats rallied to his support in 1848 in order to unseat incumbent Whig Senator George E. Badger. In 1852 and 1854 Clingman again sought Democratic support in his bid for the Senate. In 1858 he finally achieved his goal when Governor Thomas Bragg appointed him to fill the seat of Asa Biggs, who had resigned to accept a federal judgeship. The Democrat-dominated general assembly subsequently confirmed the choice and in 1860 reelected Clingman to a full six-year term. For an interpretation of Clingman's career that emphasizes his long-standing ambition for a seat in the Senate, see Thomas E. Jeffrey, "'Thunder from the Mountains': Thomas Lanier Clingman and the End of Whig Supremacy in North Carolina," *NCHR* 56 (1979).

32. Inscoe, "Thomas Clingman, Mountain Whiggery, and the Southern Cause," 60–61. For a similar interpretation, see Marc W. Kruman, "Thomas L. Clingman and the Whig Party: A Reconsideration," *NCHR* 64 (1987).

33. *Raleigh North Carolina Standard*, 18 June, 2, 16, 23 July 1851.

34. *Raleigh Register*, 2 July 1851; *Goldsboro Telegraph*, in *Raleigh Register*, 25 June 1851.

35. *Raleigh Register*, 25 June 1851; *Salisbury Carolina Watchman*, 24 July 1851. Gaither's endorsement by the *Asheville Highland Messenger* is mentioned in the same issue of the *Watchman*. In 1851 Clingman's district comprised the counties of Buncombe, Burke, Caldwell, Cherokee, Cleveland, Haywood, Henderson, Jackson, McDowell, Macon, Madison, Rutherford, Wautauga, and Yancey. David L. Corbitt, "Congressional Districts of North Carolina, 1789–1934," *NCHR* 12 (1935): 179.

36. Nicholas W. Woodfin to David L. Swain, 28 July 1851, quoted in Sitterson, *Secession Movement in North Carolina*, 88

37. *Raleigh Register*, 20 August 1851. See also Nicholas W. Woodfin to Calvin H. Wiley, 27 August 1851, Calvin H. Wiley Papers, NCDAH. Clingman received 6,660 votes, compared to 2,819 for Gaither (*Raleigh North Carolina Standard*, 27 August 1851). By comparing the distribution of the vote in the congressional election with the two-party vote in the gubernatorial election of 1850, it is possible to estimate the proportion of Whigs voting for Clingman and Gaither. Overall, turnout for the congressional election was 81 percent of the turnout for the governor's election. If the drop in turnout was equal among Whigs and Demo-

crats, and if all of the Democrats who voted in 1851 supported Clingman, then approximately 3,600 Democrats and 3,000 Whigs (52 percent of the voting Whigs) cast their ballots for Clingman. Before the election, one mountain Democrat predicted that his party would vote for Clingman "almost to a man" (Newton Coleman to David S. Reid, 18 April 1851, David S. Reid Papers, NCDAH). If, indeed, a higher proportion of Democrats than Whigs voted in 1851, then Gaither may well have won a majority of the Whig vote that year.

38. For the congressional campaign of 1849 in Stanly's district, see Norman D. Brown, *Edward Stanly: Whiggery's Tarheel "Conqueror"* (University: University of Alabama Press, 1974), 121–25. In 1851 Stanly's district comprised the counties of Beaufort, Carteret, Craven, Greene, Hyde, Jones, Lenoir, Pitt, Tyrrell, Washington, and Wayne (Corbitt, "Congressional Districts of North Carolina," 180).

39. Summary of the debate between Ruffin and Stanly, in *Raleigh North Carolina Standard*, 2 July 1851; *North Carolina Standard*, 16, 30 July 1851; summary of the debate between Ruffin and Stanly (extract from *Goldsboro Telegraph*), in *Raleigh Register*, 23 July 1851; summary of the debate between Ruffin and Stanly (extract from *Goldsboro Republican and Patriot*), in *North Carolina Standard*, 16 July 1851.

40. Edward Stanly to John Blackwell et al., in *Raleigh Register*, 3 September 1851. For the campaign of 1851 in Stanly's district, see Brown, *Edward Stanly*, 150–56.

41. *Raleigh Star*, in *Raleigh North Carolina Standard*, 20 August 1851; *Raleigh Register*, 3 September 1851.

42. Cooper, *South and the Politics of Slavery*, 333; *Raleigh North Carolina Standard*, 19 May 1852.

43. *Raleigh North Carolina Standard*, 28 July 1852; Thomas L. Clingman to Ladson A. Mills, ibid., 13 October 1852. For Scott's unpopularity among North Carolina Whigs, see James R. Morrill, "The Presidential Election of 1852: Death Knell of the Whig Party in North Carolina," *NCHR* 44 (1967): 343–51.

44. Communication from a citizen of Halifax, Va., in *Raleigh Register*, 25 August 1852.

45. For the vote in the presidential election of 1852, see Burnham, *Presidential Ballots*, 646–68. For the governor's election, see Robert D. W. Connor, comp., *A Manual of North Carolina* (Raleigh: North Carolina Historical Commission, 1913), 997–98.

46. For the vote in the presidential election of 1856, see Burnham, *Presidential Ballots*, 646–68.

47. *Raleigh North Carolina Standard*, quoted in Sitterson, *Secession Movement in North Carolina*, 132–33.

48. *Letters of James W. Osborne, Esq., Hon. D. M. Barringer, and A. C. Williamson, Esq., Old Line Whigs of North Carolina* (Charlotte: Western Democrat, 1856).

49. *Raleigh Register*, 20 August, 12 November 1856.

50. *Fayetteville Observer*, 10 November 1856.

51. Whig platform, in *Raleigh Register*, 29 February 1860; [Kemp P. Battle], *The Breckinridge Party A Disunion Party!* (n.p., 1860), 1.

52. Democratic platform, in *Raleigh North Carolina Standard*, 14 March 1860; Potter, *Impending Crisis*, 431.

53. For the results of the presidential election of 1860 in North Carolina, see the map in Sitterson, *Secession Movement in North Carolina*, 176. One of the least-noticed aspects of the election was the sharp drop in voter turnout. Almost 14 percent of the voters who had participated in the summer gubernatorial elections failed to return to the polls in November. See J. R. Pole, "Election Statistics in North Carolina, to 1861," *JSH* 24 (1958): 228.

54. John W. Ellis, Message to the General Assembly, 20 November 1860, in Tolbert, *Ellis Papers*, 2:513–15; Henry M. Shaw to Ellis, 26 November 1860, ibid., 521. For reactions of the secessionists to Ellis's message, see also Abraham W. Venable to Ellis, 20 November 1860, ibid., 479; S. W. Cole to Ellis, 26 November 1860, ibid., 522; and John H. Wheeler to Ellis, 27 November 1860, ibid., 523.

55. S. W. Cole to John W. Ellis, 26 November 1860, ibid., 522.

56. John W. Ellis Journal, 22, 28 November, 6 December 1860, ibid., 472–73; Ellis to Robert N. Gourdin, 17 December 1860, ibid., 534–35; Ellis to Gourdin, 25 December 1860, ibid., 546–47; Sitterson, *Secession Movement in North Carolina*, 188–91.

57. See, for example, *Raleigh North Carolina Standard*, 28 November 1860, 6 February 1861; Jonathan Worth to J. J. Jackson, December 1860, in J. G. de Roulhac Hamilton, ed., *The Correspondence of Jonathan Worth*, 2 vols. (Raleigh: Edwards and Broughton, 1909), 1:125; and Henry W. Miller to William A. Graham, 29 December 1860, in Hamilton and Williams, *Graham Papers*, 5:204.

58. Potter, *Impending Crisis*, 431, 438.

59. *Raleigh North Carolina Standard*, 28 November 1860.

60. Sandy Harris to William A. Graham, 15 November 1860, in Hamilton and Williams, *Graham Papers*, 5:188; *Raleigh North Carolina Standard*, 17 April 1861; Joel H. Silbey, *The Partisan Imperative: The Dynamics of American Politics before the Civil War* (New York: Oxford University Press, 1985), 44; Kruman, *Parties and Politics in North Carolina*, 218.

61. Thomas B. Alexander, "The Civil War as Institutional Fulfillment," *JSH* 47 (1981): 21.

62. Tod R. Caldwell to William A. Graham, 11 February 1861, in Hamilton and Williams, *Graham Papers*, 5:233. For the relationship between the secessionist vote in 1861 and the Democratic vote in the state and presidential elections of 1860, see Kruman, *Parties and Politics in North Carolina*, 212–13; and Daniel W. Crofts, "The Political and Social Origins of Opposition to Secession in the Upper South" (MS, 1984), 16, 42, 44.

63. *Charlotte Western Democrat*, in *Raleigh North Carolina Standard*, 3 April 1861.

64. Sitterson, *Secession Movement in North Carolina*, 162–64; Norton, *Democratic Party in Ante-Bellum North Carolina*, 210–11; Horace W. Raper, *William W. Holden: North Carolina's Political Enigma* (Chapel Hill: University of North Carolina Press, 1985), 34. Holden undoubtedly was disappointed by the failure of his party to nominate him for governor in 1858 or to elect him to the U.S. Senate later that year. An astute judge of public sentiment, Holden may also have

sensed the strength of unionism in the Old North State. The idea that a "slave-holding oligarchy" was conspiring to put Holden down because of his humble origins was first circulated by opposition presses in order to sow dissension within the Democratic party. See, for example, *Greensboro Patriot*, 4 December 1857. In his recent biography of Holden, William C. Harris persuasively argues that "class divisions had little, if anything, to do with . . . intraparty opposition" to Holden, and that John W. Ellis, the editor's main rival, "was hardly the aristo-crat that historians have portrayed." See Harris, *William Woods Holden: Fire-brand of North Carolina Politics* (Baton Rouge: Louisiana State University Press, 1987), 71, 76.

65. *Raleigh North Carolina Standard*, 28 April 1858.
66. Ibid., 13 June 1860.
67. Ibid., 16, 23 May, 29 August, 12 December 1860.
68. Ibid., 16 May 1860.
69. Ibid., 11 July 1860.
70. Ibid., 18 July, 15 August, 31 October 1860. According to William C. Harris, Holden supported the Breckinridge ticket "on the condition . . . that the vic-torious state presidential electors 'will vote for the strongest man, Breckinridge or Douglas as the case may be, against Lincoln.' . . . Holden, despite his endorse-ment of the Democratic Southern Rights ticket, continued to believe that only the reunification of the national Democratic party, either with Douglas or Breckinridge as its candidate for president, could save the Union" (*William Woods Holden*, 92).
71. *Raleigh North Carolina Standard*, 28 November 1860, 2 January 1861.
72. Sitterson, *Secession Movement in North Carolina*, 185, 206–8. For the motives of the proconvention westerners, see the remarks of George N. Folk, George W. Hays, and Augustus S. Merrimon, in *Raleigh Register*, 30 January 1861. The roll-call vote on the convention bill can be found in *Raleigh North Carolina Stan-dard*, 30 January 1861; and *Raleigh Register*, 30 January 1861. Sixty-six percent of the eastern Whigs and 58 percent of the mountain Whigs voted in favor of the convention bill, but only 20 percent of the piedmont Whigs supported it. The February referendum revealed that the vast majority of legislators in both parties had voted in conformity with the wishes of their constituents. Only 19 percent of the Democratic legislators and 20 percent of the Whigs took a position at variance with the majority vote in their counties. In the mountain region, how-ever, five of the seven proconvention Whig legislators voted against the wishes of a majority of their constituents. For the referendum vote, see Kruman, *Parties and Politics in North Carolina*, 276–78.
73. For Holden's estimate of the comparative strength of the two groups, see *Raleigh North Carolina Standard*, 20 March 1861. Holden slightly overestimated the strength of the unionists. In Catawba, Franklin, Greene, and Northampton, he claimed unionist victories, even though these counties probably elected seces-sionists. (Compare the estimates in *Raleigh Register*, 13 March 1861; Sitterson, *Secession Movement in North Carolina*, 228; and Kruman, *Parties and Politics in North Carolina*, 276–78.) In this study I have used Kruman's estimates. The

sophisticated quantitative analysis by Daniel W. Crofts confirms the strong correlation between the secession vote in 1861 and the Breckinridge vote in 1860
("Political and Social Origins of Opposition to Secession," 16, 42, 44).

74. In calculating the Union and secession vote in 1861, I have used the data in
Kruman, *Parties and Politics in North Carolina*, appendix B. In most cases the
voting returns for convention delegates have been used. However, in counties
where delegate returns are missing or where Union or secession candidates ran
unopposed, I have used the vote for or against the convention. Because some
unionists voted in favor of the convention, whereas few secessionists voted
against it, the data in figure 11.1 probably underestimate the strength of Union
sentiment. Two counties whose delegate returns are missing have been excluded
from the calculations. Person and Jackson counties elected Union delegates yet
voted overwhelmingly in favor of a convention.

75. Differences in the rate of voter turnout also had an impact on the outcome of the
election. As many as one-fourth of the Democrats who voted in the November
presidential election did not participate in the February convention election,
compared to less than 15 percent of the Whigs. In addition, perhaps one-third of
the November nonvoters turned out to vote in February, and the overwhelming
majority of them voted in favor of the Union (Crofts, "Political and Social Origins of Opposition to Secession," 42–43).

76. Kruman, *Parties and Politics in North Carolina*, 181. The same argument is
made by Michael Holt in *The Political Crisis of the 1850s* (New York: Wiley,
1978). See, especially, pp. 254–55.

77. The estimates of Democrats and Whigs supporting disunion are from Crofts,
"Political and Social Origins of Opposition to Secession," 44. The question remains, however, as to why two-party competition, which had flourished in the
Deep South during the 1840s, disappeared in most of those states during the
1850s. On balance, the argument made by William J. Cooper in *The South and
the Politics of Slavery* is quite persuasive for the lower South. With their higher
concentrations of slaves, these states were much more susceptible than those in
the upper South to Democratic agitation of the southern-rights issue. Thus, the
degree of interparty competition was not an independent variable affecting the
response of the southern states to Lincoln's election, as Kruman and Holt argue.
Rather, the viability of the Whig organization and the strength of unionism were
both dependent variables affected by the relative importance of slavery in the
society and economy of each state. It is no coincidence that South Carolina,
which had the highest concentration of slaves and slaveholding families in the
entire South, was the only state that never developed a two-party system and
was the first state to leave the Union.

78. *Raleigh North Carolina Standard*, 17 April 1861; Sitterson, *Secession Movement in North Carolina*, 235–36. Holden's editorial was first published in the
Standard's semiweekly edition of 13 April.

79. Ellis replied tersely: "You can get no troops from North Carolina" (Ellis to Simon
Cameron, 15 April 1861, in Tolbert, *Ellis Papers*, 2:612).

80. Edwin G. Reade to William A. Graham, 2 July 1861, in Hamilton and Williams,
Graham Papers, 5:281. For other evidence of unionist hostility to the secession-

ists, see John B. Troy to Jonathan Worth, 21 May 1861, in Hamilton, *Worth Correspondence*, 1:150; and E. J. Hale to Worth, 1 August 1861, ibid., 157–58. For secessionist hostility to unionists, see John W. Ellis to Christopher G. Memminger, 20 June 1861, in Tolbert, *Ellis Papers*, 2:851. Ellis referred to the unionists as "late submissionists . . . who would make terms with Lincoln upon the first reverse of our arms."

81. Kruman, *Parties and Politics in North Carolina*, 238.

12 Second Party System in North Carolina

1. See the tables of Pearson correlations in Marc W. Kruman, *Parties and Politics in North Carolina, 1836–1865* (Baton Rouge: Louisiana State University Press, 1983), 44, 183.

2. *Asheville News*, 31 July 1860.

3. *Charlotte Mecklenburg Jeffersonian*, in *Raleigh North Carolina Standard*, 8 July 1846.

4. Joel H. Silbey, *The Partisan Imperative: The Dynamics of American Politics before the Civil War* (New York: Oxford University Press, 1985), xv.

5. Joel H. Silbey, *The Shrine of Party: Congressional Voting Behavior, 1841–1852* (Pittsburgh: University of Pittsburgh Press, 1967); Thomas B. Alexander, *Sectional Stress and Party Strength: A Study of Roll-Call Voting Patterns in the United States House of Representatives, 1836–1860* (Nashville: Vanderbilt University Press, 1967).

6. Thomas E. Jeffrey, "National Issues, Local Interests, and the Transformation of Antebellum North Carolina Politics," *JSH* 50 (1984): 52.

7. *Raleigh Register*, 3 March 1852.

8. *Raleigh North Carolina Standard*, 29 May 1850; William W. Holden to Weldon N. Edwards, 15 July 1850, Katherine P. Conway Collection, NCDAH.

9. Kruman, *Parties and Politics in North Carolina*, 5–6.

10. For Alabama, see J. Mills Thornton, *Politics and Power in a Slave Society: Alabama, 1800–1860* (Baton Rouge: Louisiana State University Press, 1978), 51–52.

11. As Joel H. Silbey has pointed out, "there are many different levels of political behavior . . . [and] what is influential and important on one level of politics may not be on another. . . . When historians generalize about the nature of political behavior they must also be sure which group and level of political activity they mean, and so identify it, and not confuse different levels or assume positive correlations between the actions of people on one level with those on another level" ("The Civil War Synthesis in American Political History," *Civil War History* 10 [1964]: 139–40).

12. In 1855 Democrat Charles F. Fisher was chosen to replace Whig John M. Morehead as president of the North Carolina Railroad. Fisher's administration was subjected to much partisan criticism. The attacks focused on the railroad's failure to pay dividends, which the Whigs attributed to Fisher's mismanagement. During the legislative session of 1858–59, the Whigs, under the leadership of Jonathan Worth, successfully agitated for the creation of a special committee to

investigate the railroad's management. The Worth committee subsequently issued a report accusing the Fisher administration of corruption, extravagance, and general mismanagement. See Allen W. Trelease, "The Passive Voice: The State and the North Carolina Railroad, 1849–1871," *NCHR* 61 (1984): 182–85.

13. Kruman, *Parties and Politics in North Carolina*, 55.

14. Michael F. Holt, *The Political Crisis of the 1850s* (New York: Wiley, 1978), 15.

15. Michael F. Holt, "The Politics of Impatience: The Origins of Know Nothingism," *JAH* 60 (1973).

16. For voter participation, see J. R. Pole, "Election Statistics in North Carolina, to 1861," *JSH* 24 (1958): 228.

17. Holt, *Political Crisis of the 1850s*, especially pp. 101–38.

18. Holt attributes the continued vitality of the second party system in North Carolina primarily to the availability of state issues over which the parties could compete. According to Holt, such issues were not available in most other states (ibid., 249–51). This argument is certainly open to challenge. In Alabama, for example, politicians from the hill country and piney-woods regions fought bitterly with black-belt leaders throughout the 1850s over issues such as railroad promotion, business incorporation, and banking expansion. For the most part, however, these issues were fought out within the Democratic party (Thornton, *Politics and Power in a Slave Society*, 321–42). In the case of Alabama, the absence of partisan conflict over state issues seems to have been a symptom, rather than the cause, of the decline of the second party system. Without a competitive two-party system, conflict over state issues in Alabama simply could not assume partisan form.

19. Letter from Joel H. Silbey to the author, 3 July 1985.

20. Holt acknowledges that voter loyalty "rested not only on the reality of issue-conflict between the parties, but also on the popular perception of party difference" (*Political Crisis of the 1850s*, 105). But he argues that popular perceptions also changed dramatically during the 1850s, as growing numbers of voters became disillusioned with the established parties.

21. William N. Chambers, *Political Parties in a New Nation: The American Experience, 1776–1809* (New York: Oxford University Press, 1963), 48.

22. Whig platform, in *Raleigh Register*, 29 February 1860; speech of John W. Ellis, in *Raleigh North Carolina Standard*, 14 March 1860; Democratic platform, ibid.

23. William J. Cooper, *The South and the Politics of Slavery, 1828–1856* (Baton Rouge: Louisiana State University Press, 1978), xiv; Thornton, *Politics and Power in a Slave Society*, 40–42; Harry L. Watson, *Jacksonian Politics and Community Conflict: The Emergence of the Second American Party System in Cumberland County, North Carolina* (Baton Rouge: Louisiana State University Press, 1981), 5–8; and Kruman, *Parties and Politics in North Carolina*, 15–16.

24. See, for example, Richard P. McCormick, *The Second American Party System: Party Formation in the Jacksonian Era* (Chapel Hill: University of North Carolina Press, 1966). McCormick argues that both parties "seemingly existed in defiance of the real sectional antagonisms that were present at the time." The system "could survive only so long as explicitly sectional issues could be avoided" (353).

25. Cooper, *South and the Politics of Slavery*, 269–374; Holt, *Political Crisis of the 1850s*, 118–19, 245–48.

26. Cooper suggests that the national controversy over slavery and territorial expansion was primarily responsible for the reduced Whig vote in North Carolina during the 1850s (*South and the Politics of Slavery*, 359–62). As figure 10.1 demonstrates, however, the Whig percentage of the vote was actually *higher* in the slaveholding eastern counties in 1860 than it had been in 1850. The major Democratic gains during the decade were in the small-farm counties of the far west. Also see the map in chapter 10.

27. Ronald P. Formisano, *The Transformation of Political Culture: Massachusetts Parties, 1790s-1840s* (New York: Oxford University Press, 1983), 326, 331.

28. McCormick, *Second American Party System*, 355; Edward Pessen, *Jacksonian America: Society, Personality, and Politics*, rev. ed. (Homewood, Ill.: Dorsey Press, 1978), 260. For a useful discussion of the relationship between parties and policy-making, see Richard L. McCormick, "The Party Period and Public Policy: An Exploratory Hypothesis," *JAH* 66 (1979); and Formisano, *Transformation of Political Culture*, 316–20.

29. For railroad mileage, see Thomas E. Jeffrey, "Internal Improvements and Political Parties in Antebellum North Carolina, 1836–1860," *NCHR* 55 (1978): 146–47. For the number of banks chartered, see Beecher Flanagan, "A History of State Banking in North Carolina to 1866" (Ph.D. diss., Peabody College, 1935), 226–29.

30. For the relationship between party politics and constitutional reform during the 1830s, see Thomas E. Jeffrey, "Beyond 'Free Suffrage': North Carolina Parties and the Convention Movement of the 1850s," *NCHR* 62 (1985): 388–93. Ironically, partisan politics also played an important role in the failure of the convention movement a generation later (ibid., 416–17). For the internal improvements issue, see Jeffrey, "Internal Improvements and Political Parties," 143–48.

31. For the impact of Whiggery during the war and postwar years, see, especially, Thomas B. Alexander, "Persistent Whiggery in the Confederate South, 1860–1877," *JSH* 27 (1961).

Bibliography

I. Primary Sources

A. MANUSCRIPT COLLECTIONS

North Carolina Division of Archives and History, Raleigh
   George E. Badger Papers
   Asa Biggs Papers
   John Herritage Bryan Papers
   Katherine P. Conway Collection
   John J. Crittenden Papers
   Governor's Letter Books
   Governor's Papers
   C. B. Heller Collection
   William Andrew Jeffreys and Family Papers
   Miscellaneous Collections, Compiled Election Returns
   Thomas M. Pittman Papers
   William Polk Papers
   David S. Reid Papers
   Calvin H. Wiley Papers
Southern Historical Collection, University of North Carolina, Chapel Hill
   Archibald H. Arrington Papers
   Bryan Family Papers
   David Franklin Caldwell Papers
   Clingman and Puryear Family Papers
   Robert Frederick Hoke Papers
   Jones and Patterson Family Papers
   Matthias Evans Manly Papers
   David Outlaw Letters
   Pettigrew Family Papers
   Thomas Settle Papers (Group 1)
   Thomas Sparrow Papers
   William D. Valentine Diary
   Abraham Watkins Venable Papers
   Calvin Henderson Wiley Papers

B. BROADSIDES, PAMPHLETS AND OTHER PRIMARY
PRINTED MATERIAL

Unless otherwise noted, broadsides and pamphlets are from the North Carolina Collection, University of North Carolina, Chapel Hill.

An Address to the Citizens of North-Carolina on the Subject of the Presidential Election. N.p., 1823.

Avery, William W. *Speech of William W. Avery, Esq. of Burke upon the Subject of Constitutional Reform Delivered in the House of Commons of North Carolina, on the 18th of December 1850.* N.p., n.d.

Badger, George, E. *Speech Delivered at the Great Whig Meeting in the County of Granville.* N.p., 1840.

[Battle, Kemp P.] *The Breckinridge Party a Disunion Party!* N.p., 1860.

Bynum, Jesse A. *An Address to the Reflecting Men of Northampton County, North Carolina.* N.p., 1836.

Clingman, Thomas L. *Address of T. L. Clingman on the Recent Senatorial Election.* Washington, D.C.: J. and G. S. Gideon, 1849. (Rare Book Collection, Library of Congress, Washington, D.C.)

Correspondence between Louis D. Henry . . . and the Committee Appointed to Inform Him of His Nomination as the Democratic Candidate for the Office of Governor of the State of North Carolina. Fayetteville, 1842.

Debate in the Legislature of North-Carolina on a Proposed Appropriation for Re-building the Capitol and on the Convention Question. Raleigh: J. Gales and Son, 1832.

Fair Play. N.p., 1845. (Rare Book Collection, Perkins Library, Duke University, Durham, N.C.)

Fisher, Charles. *To the Freemen of Rowan County.* N.p., 1833. (Rare Book Collection, Perkins Library, Duke University, Durham, N.C.)

———. *To the Freemen of the Tenth Congressional District.* N.p., 1839.

Graham, James. *Circular to the People of the Twelfth Congressional District in North Carolina.* N.p., 1843.

Hall, Thomas H. *Circular to the Freemen of the 3rd. Congressional District of N.C.* Tarboro: Free Press, 1831.

Haywood, William H., Jr. *To the Freemen of Wake County.* Raleigh: P. White, 1835.

———. *To the People of Wake County.* Raleigh, 1834.

Journal of a Convention Assembled at the City of Raleigh, on the 10th of November, 1823. Raleigh: J. Gales and Son, 1823.

Letters of James W. Osborne, Esq., Hon. D. M. Barringer, and A. C. Williamson, Esq., Old Line Whigs of North Carolina. Charlotte: Western Democrat, 1856.

McRae, Alexander; and McRee, Griffith J. *To the Freemen of New Hanover County.* Wilmington, 1844.

Mebane, A. W. *Address to the People of Northampton, Martin, Hertford, and Bertie.* N.p., 1840.

[Moore, Bartholomew F.] *To the Freemen of North Carolina.* N.p., 1843.

National Republican [Democratic] Party. *An Address to the Freemen of North Carolina.* Raleigh, 1836.

N[orth] C[arolina] Democratic Executive Committee. *Address . . . to the Freemen and Voters of North Carolina*. N.p., 1840.

North Carolina. General Assembly. *Journal of the House of Commons of North Carolina*. Raleigh: State Printer, 1837–59.

North Carolina. General Assembly. *Journal of the Senate of North Carolina*. Raleigh: State Printer, 1837–59.

North Carolina. General Assembly. *Report of the Joint Select Committee on the Suspension of Specie Payments by the Banks*. N.p., 1841.

N[orth] C[arolina] Whig Central Committee. *Address to the People of North Carolina*. N.p., [1840].

Proceedings and Debates of the Convention of North-Carolina Called to Amend the Constitution of the State. Raleigh: Joseph Gales and Son, 1836.

Proceedings of the Friends of Convention at a Meeting Held in Raleigh December, 1822. Raleigh, 1822.

Proceedings of the Internal Improvement Convention Held in the City of Raleigh, November, 1833. Raleigh: Joseph Gales and Son, 1834.

The Proposed New Constitution of the State of North Carolina. Raleigh: Joseph Gales and Son, 1823.

Rencher, Abraham. *To the Freemen of the Tenth Congressional District of North Carolina*. Washington, D.C., 1835.

———. *To the People of the Tenth Congressional District of North Carolina*. Washington, D.C., 1837.

Richards, W. P. *To the Freemen of Davidson County*. N.p., 1846.

Saunders, Romulus M. *An Address . . . to the People of North Carolina*. Washington, D.C., 1843.

Shepard, Charles. *To the Freemen of the Fourth Congressional District of North Carolina*. Washington, D.C.: Jos. Etter, 1838.

Shepard, James B. *Speech Delivered at the Great Republican Meeting in the County of Granville*. Raleigh, 1840.

Shepard, William B. *Speech of Hon. William B. Shepard of Pasquotank*. N.p., 1851.

Swain, David L. *Governor Swain's Inaugural Address*. N.p., 1834.

Thomas, William H. *To the People of the Senatorial District Embracing the Counties of Haywood, Macon, and Cherokee, North Carolina*. N.p., 1846. [Rare Book Collection, Perkins Library, Duke University, Durham, N.C.]

Toole, Henry I. *To the Voters of Johnston, Wake, Franklin, Warren, Halifax, Nash, and Edgecombe*. N.p., 1847.

To the Freemen of North Carolina. N.p., 1824.

To the Freemen of Orange County. N.p., 1823.

[Wiley, Calvin H., ed.] *The Constitution of North Carolina . . . Together with an Account and Explanation of the Questions of Constitutional Reform Now Agitating the People of the State*. [Raleigh]: N.C. Institution for the Deaf and Dumb and the Blind, 1851.

C. NEWSPAPERS

Asheville Highland Messenger
Asheville News
Charlotte Hornet's Nest
Charlotte Journal
Charlotte Mecklenburg Jeffersonian
Charlotte Western Democrat
Elizabeth City Democratic Pioneer
Elizabeth City Old North State
Fayetteville North Carolina Journal
Fayetteville North Carolinian
Fayetteville Observer
Goldsboro Republican and Patriot
Greensboro Patriot
Hillsborough Recorder
Kinston American Advocate
Louisburg American Eagle
New Bern Atlantic
New Bern Carolina Sentinel
Newbernian
New Bern Journal
New Bern Progress
New Bern Republican
New Bern Spectator
Raleigh Minerva
Raleigh North Carolina Constitutionalist
Raleigh North Carolina Standard
Raleigh Register
Raleigh Star
Rutherfordton Mountain Banner
Salem People's Press
Salisbury Carolina Watchman
Salisbury Western Carolinian
Tarboro Southerner
Tarborough Press
Wadesboro North Carolina Argus
Washington North State Whig
Wilmington Commercial
Wilmington Herald
Wilmington Journal

D. PUBLISHED SOURCES

Battle, Kemp P., ed. *Letters of Nathaniel Macon to John R. Eaton and Bartlett Yancey.* James Sprunt Historical Monographs, no. 2. Chapel Hill: University Press, 1900.

Boyd, William K., ed. *Memoirs of W. W. Holden.* Durham: Seeman Printery, 1911.

Burnham, W. Dean. *Presidential Ballots, 1836–1892.* Baltimore: Johns Hopkins University Press, 1955.

Clingman, Thomas L. *Selections from the Speeches and Writings of Hon. Thomas L. Clingman of North Carolina.* Raleigh: J. Nichols, 1877.

Connor, Robert D. W., comp. *A Manual of North Carolina.* Raleigh: North Carolina Historical Commission, 1913.

Cunningham, Noble E., ed. *Circular Letters of Congressmen to Their Constituents, 1789–1829.* 3 vols. Chapel Hill: University of North Carolina Press, 1978.

Hamilton, J. G. de Roulhac, ed. *The Correspondence of Jonathan Worth.* 2 vols. Raleigh: Edwards and Broughton, 1909.

——. *The Papers of Thomas Ruffin.* 4 vols. Raleigh: Edwards and Broughton, 1918–20.

Hamilton, J. G. de Roulhac, and Wagstaff, Henry M., eds. *Letters to Bartlett Yancey.* James Sprunt Historical Publications 10, no. 2. Chapel Hill: University Press, 1911.

Hamilton, J. G. de Roulhac, and Williams, Max R., eds. *The Papers of William Alexander Graham.* 7 vols. to date. Raleigh: Division of Archives and History, 1957–.

Hoyt, William H., ed. *The Papers of Archibald D. Murphey.* 2 vols. Raleigh: E. M. Uzzell, 1914.

Johnston, Frontis W., ed. *The Papers of Zebulon Baird Vance.* 1 vol. to date. Raleigh: Division of Archives and History, 1963–.

McPherson, Elizabeth G., ed. "Unpublished Letters from North Carolinians to Andrew Jackson." *NCHR* 14 (1937): 361–92.

——. "Unpublished Letters from North Carolinians to Polk." *NCHR* 16 (1939): 54–79, 174–200, 328–57, 428–57; 17 (1940): 37–66, 139–66, 249–66.

——. "Unpublished Letters from North Carolinians to Van Buren." *NCHR* 15 (1938): 53–81, 131–55.

Newsome, Albert R., ed. "Correspondence of John C. Calhoun, George McDuffie and Charles Fisher, Relating to the Presidential Campaign of 1824." *NCHR* 7 (1930): 477–504.

——. "Letters of Romulus M. Saunders to Bartlett Yancy, 1821–1828." *NCHR* 8 (1931): 427–62.

——. "Debate on the Fisher Resolutions." *NCHR* 4 (1927): 428–70; 5 (1928): 65–96, 204–23, 310–28.

——. "Twelve North Carolina Counties, 1810–1811." *NCHR* 5 (1928): 413–46; 6 (1929): 67–99, 171–89, 281–309, 398–410.

Pole, J. R. "Election Statistics in North Carolina, to 1861." *JSH* 24 (1958): 225–28.

Saunders, William L., ed. *The Colonial Records of North Carolina.* 10 vols. Raleigh: State Printer, 1886–90.

Shanks, Henry T., ed. *The Papers of Willie Person Mangum.* 5 vols. Raleigh: State Department of Archives and History, 1950–56.

Thorpe, Francis N. *The Federal and State Constitutions, Colonial Charters, and Other Organic Laws.* 7 vols. Washington, D.C.: Government Printing Office, 1909.

Tolbert, Noble J., ed. *The Papers of John Willis Ellis.* 2 vols. Raleigh: State Department of Archives and History, 1964.

Wilson, Clyde N.; and Hemphill, W. Edwin, eds. *The Papers of John C. Calhoun.* 17 vols. to date. Columbia: University of South Carolina Press, 1959– .

II. *Secondary Sources*

A. BOOKS

Alexander, Thomas B. *Sectional Stress and Party Strength: A Study of Roll-Call Voting Patterns in the United States House of Representatives, 1836–1860.* Nashville: Vanderbilt University Press, 1967.

Ashe, Samuel A. *Biographical History of North Carolina from Colonial Times to the Present.* 8 vols. Greensboro: C. L. Van Noppen, 1905–17.

———. *History of North Carolina.* 2 vols. Greensboro: C. L. Van Noppen, 1908–25.

Barney, William L. *The Road to Secession: A New Perspective on the Old South.* New York: Praeger, 1972.

Barringer, Rufus. *History of the North Carolina Railroad.* Raleigh: News and Observer Press, 1894.

Benson, Lee. *The Concept of Jacksonian Democracy: New York as a Test Case.* Princeton: Princeton University Press, 1961.

Blackmun, Ora. *Western North Carolina: Its Mountains and Its People to 1880.* Boone: Appalachian Consortium Press, 1977.

Blythe, LeGette; and Brockmann, Charles R. *Hornet's Nest: The Story of Charlotte and Mecklenburg County.* Charlotte: McNally, 1961.

Brawley, James S. *The Rowan Story: A Narrative History of Rowan County, 1753–1953.* Salisbury: Rowan, 1953.

Brock, William R. *Parties and Political Conscience: American Dilemmas, 1840–1850.* Millwood, N.Y.: KTO Press, 1979.

Broussard, James H. *The Southern Federalists, 1800–1816.* Baton Rouge: Louisiana State University Press, 1978.

Brown, Cecil K. *A State Movement in Railroad Development: The Story of North Carolina's First Effort to Establish an East and West Trunk Line Railroad.* Chapel Hill: University of North Carolina Press, 1928.

Brown, Norman D. *Edward Stanly: Whiggery's Tarheel "Conqueror."* University: University of Alabama Press, 1974.

Butler, Lindley S.; and Watson, Alan D., eds. *The North Carolina Experience: An Interpretive and Documentary History.* Chapel Hill: University of North Carolina Press, 1984.

Carroll, E. Malcolm. *Origins of the Whig Party.* Durham: Duke University Press, 1925.

Chambers, William N. *Political Parties in a New Nation: The American Experience, 1776–1809.* New York: Oxford University Press, 1963.

Charles, Joseph. *The Origins of the American Party System.* Williamsburg: Institute of Early American History and Culture, 1956. Reprint. New York: Harper, 1961.

Chase, James S. *Emergence of the Presidential Nominating Convention, 1789–1832.* Urbana: University of Illinois Press, 1973.

Cole, Arthur C. *The Whig Party in the South*. Washington: American Historical Association, 1913.

Combs, Jerald A. *The Jay Treaty: Political Battleground of the Founding Fathers*. Berkeley: University of California Press, 1970.

Connor, Robert D. W. *Race Elements in the White Population of North Carolina*. Raleigh: College, 1920.

Cooper, William J. *The South and the Politics of Slavery, 1828–1856*. Baton Rouge: Louisiana State University Press, 1978.

Corbitt, David L. *The Formation of the North Carolina Counties, 1663–1943*. Raleigh: State Department of Archives and History, 1950.

Cunningham, Noble E. *The Jeffersonian Republicans: The Formation of Party Organization, 1789–1801*. Chapel Hill: University of North Carolina Press, 1957.

————. *The Jeffersonian Republicans in Power: Party Operations, 1801–1809*. Chapel Hill: University of North Carolina Press, 1963.

Curtis, James C. *The Fox at Bay: Martin Van Buren and the Presidency*. Lexington: University Press of Kentucky, 1970.

Davidson, Chalmers G. *Piedmont Partisan: The Life and Times of Brigadier-General William Lee Davidson*. Davidson: Davidson College Press, 1951.

DeMond, Robert O. *The Loyalists in North Carolina during the Revolution*. Durham: Duke University Press, 1940.

Ekirch, A. Roger. *"Poor Carolina": Politics and Society in Colonial North Carolina, 1729–1776*. Chapel Hill: University of North Carolina Press, 1981.

Feller, Daniel. *The Public Lands in Jacksonian Politics*. Madison: University of Wisconsin Press, 1984.

Fischer, David H. *The Revolution of American Conservatism: The Federalist Party in the Era of Jeffersonian Democracy*. New York: Harper and Row, 1965.

Formisano, Ronald P. *The Birth of Mass Political Parties: Michigan, 1827–1861*. Princeton: Princeton University Press, 1971.

————. *The Transformation of Political Culture: Massachusetts Parties, 1790s-1840s*. New York: Oxford University Press, 1983.

Freehling, William W. *Prelude to Civil War: The Nullification Controversy in South Carolina, 1816–1836*. New York: Harper and Row, 1966.

Gilpatrick, Delbert H. *Jeffersonian Democracy in North Carolina, 1789–1816*. New York: Columbia University Press, 1931.

Hamilton, Holman. *Prologue to Conflict: The Crisis and Compromise of 1850*. Lexington: University Press of Kentucky, 1964.

Hamilton, J. G. de Roulhac. *Party Politics in North Carolina, 1835–1860*. Durham: Seeman Printery, 1916.

Hammer, Carl. *Rhinelanders on the Yadkin: The Story of the Pennsylvania Germans in Rowan and Cabarrus Counties, North Carolina*. 2d rev. ed. Salisbury, N.C.: Rowan, 1943. Reprint. Salisbury, 1965.

Harris, William C. *William Woods Holden: Firebrand of North Carolina Politics*. Baton Rouge: Louisiana State University Press, 1987.

Hoffmann, William S. *Andrew Jackson and North Carolina Politics*. Chapel Hill: University of North Carolina Press, 1958.

Holt, Michael F. *The Political Crisis of the 1850s.* New York: Wiley, 1978.

Johnson, Guion G. *Ante-Bellum North Carolina: A Social History.* Chapel Hill: University of North Carolina Press, 1937.

Kleppner, Paul. *The Third Electoral System, 1853–1892: Parties, Voters, and Political Cultures.* Chapel Hill: University of North Carolina Press, 1979.

Knight, Edgar W. *Public School Education in North Carolina.* Boston: Houghton Mifflin, 1916.

Kruman, Marc W. *Parties and Politics in North Carolina, 1836–1865.* Baton Rouge: Louisiana State University Press, 1983.

Latner, Richard B. *The Presidency of Andrew Jackson: White House Politics, 1829–1837.* Athens: University of Georgia Press, 1979.

Lefler, Hugh T.; and Newsome, Albert R. *North Carolina: The History of a Southern State.* 2d ed. Chapel Hill: University of North Carolina Press, 1963.

Lefler, Hugh T., and Powell, William S. *Colonial North Carolina: A History.* New York: Scribner, 1973.

Livermore, Shaw. *The Twilight of Federalism: The Disintegration of the Federalist Party, 1815–1830.* Princeton: Princeton University Press, 1962. Reprint. New York: Gordian Press, 1972.

McCormick, Richard P. *The Presidential Game: The Origins of American Presidential Politics.* New York: Oxford University Press, 1982.

———. *The Second American Party System: Party Formation in the Jacksonian Era.* Chapel Hill: University of North Carolina Press, 1966.

McKelway, Alexander J. *The Scotch-Irish of North Carolina.* North Carolina Booklet 4, no. 11. Raleigh: W. S. Sherman, 1905.

MacRae, James C. *The Highland-Scotch Settlement in North Carolina.* North Carolina Booklet 4, no. 10. Raleigh: E. M. Uzzell, 1905.

Meyers, Marvin. *The Jacksonian Persuasion: Politics and Belief.* New York: Vintage Books, 1960.

Nelson, William H. *The American Tory.* Oxford: Clarendon Press, 1961.

Newsome, Albert R. *The Presidential Election of 1824 in North Carolina.* Chapel Hill: University of North Carolina Press, 1939.

Niven, John. *Martin Van Buren: The Romantic Age of American Politics.* New York: Oxford University Press, 1983.

Norton, Clarence C. *The Democratic Party in Ante-Bellum North Carolina, 1835–1861.* Chapel Hill: University of North Carolina Press, 1930.

Pegg, Herbert D. *The Whig Party in North Carolina.* Chapel Hill: Colonial Press, 1968. (Originally written in 1932 as a Ph.D. dissertation.)

Pessen, Edward. *Jacksonian America: Society, Personality, and Politics.* Rev. ed. Homewood, Ill.: Dorsey Press, 1978.

Potter, David M. *The Impending Crisis, 1848–1861.* New York: Harper and Row, 1976.

Powell, William S. *Annals of Progress: The Story of Lenoir County and Kinston, North Carolina.* Raleigh: State Department of Archives and History, 1963.

———, ed. *Dictionary of North Carolina Biography.* 2 vols. to date. Chapel Hill: University of North Carolina Press, 1979–.

———. *North Carolina: A Bicentennial History.* New York: Norton, 1977.

Raper, Horace W. *William W. Holden: North Carolina's Political Enigma.* Chapel Hill: University of North Carolina Press, 1985.

Reid, Paul A. *Gubernatorial Campaigns and Administrations of David S. Reid, 1848–1854.* Cullowhee: Western Carolina College Press, 1953.

Remini, Robert V. *Andrew Jackson and the Bank War.* New York: Norton, 1967.

———. *Andrew Jackson and the Course of American Democracy, 1833–1845.* New York: Harper and Row, 1984.

———. *Andrew Jackson and the Course of American Freedom, 1822–1832.* New York: Harper and Row, 1981.

———. *The Election of Andrew Jackson.* Philadelphia: Lippincott, 1963.

Risjord, Norman K. *Chesapeake Politics, 1781–1800.* New York: Columbia University Press, 1978.

Rouse, Jordan K. *North Carolina Picadillo.* Salisbury: Rowan Business Forms, 1966.

Sellers, Charles G. *James K. Polk, Jacksonian, 1795–1843.* Princeton: Princeton University Press, 1957.

Sharp, James R. *The Jacksonians versus the Banks: Politics in the States after the Panic of 1837.* New York: Columbia University Press, 1970.

Sharpe, Bill. *A New Geography of North Carolina.* 4 vols. Raleigh: Sharpe, 1954–65.

Silbey, Joel H. *The Partisan Imperative: The Dynamics of American Politics before the Civil War.* New York: Oxford University Press, 1985.

———. *The Shrine of Party: Congressional Voting Behavior, 1841–1852.* Pittsburgh: University of Pittsburgh Press, 1967.

Sitterson, J. Carlyle. *The Secession Movement in North Carolina.* Chapel Hill: University of North Carolina Press, 1939.

Sydnor, Charles S. *The Development of Southern Sectionalism, 1819–1848.* Baton Rouge: Louisiana State University Press, 1948.

Temin, Peter. *The Jacksonian Economy.* New York: Norton, 1969.

Thornton, J. Mills. *Politics and Power in a Slave Society: Alabama, 1800–1860.* Baton Rouge: Louisiana State University Press, 1978.

Troxler, Carole W. *The Loyalist Experience in North Carolina.* Raleigh: Division of Archives and History, 1976.

Tucker, Glenn. *Zeb Vance: Champion of Personal Freedom.* Indianapolis: Bobbs-Merrill, 1965.

Van Deusen, Glyndon G. *The Jacksonian Era, 1828–1848.* New York: Harper, 1959.

Wagstaff, Henry G. *Federalism in North Carolina.* James Sprunt Historical Publications 9, no. 2. Chapel Hill: University Press, 1910.

Wall, James W. *History of Davie County in the Forks of the Yadkin.* Mocksville: Davie County Historical Publishing Association, 1969.

Ward, John W. *Andrew Jackson: Symbol for an Age.* New York: Oxford University Press, 1955.

Watson, Harry L. *Jacksonian Politics and Community Conflict: The Emergence of the Second American Party System in Cumberland County, North Carolina.* Baton Rouge: Louisiana State University Press, 1981.

Wellman, Manly W. *The County of Warren, North Carolina, 1586–1917.* Chapel Hill: University of North Carolina Press, 1959.

Wheeler, John H. *Historical Sketches of North Carolina*. 2 vols. in 1. Philadelphia: Lippincott, 1851.

Wilson, Major L. *The Presidency of Martin Van Buren*. Lawrence: University Press of Kansas, 1984.

Wooster, Ralph A. *Politicians, Planters, and Plain Folk: Courthouse and Statehouse in the Upper South, 1850–1860*. Knoxville: University of Tennessee Press, 1975.

Zuber, Richard L. *Jonathan Worth: A Biography of a Southern Unionist*. Chapel Hill: University of North Carolina Press, 1965.

B. ARTICLES

Alexander, Thomas B. "The Civil War as Institutional Fulfillment." *JSH* 47 (1981): 3–32.

———. "Persistent Whiggery in the Confederate South, 1860–1877." *JSH* 27 (1961): 305–29.

Barringer, Rufus. "Early German Settlers in Eastern Cabarrus County." In *Reminiscences and Memoirs of North Carolina and Eminent North Carolinians*, edited by John H. Wheeler. Columbus, Ohio: Columbus Printing Works, 1884. Reprint. Baltimore: Genealogical Publishing, 1966.

Bassett, John S. "Suffrage in the State of North Carolina (1776–1861)." In *Annual Report of the American Historical Association for the Year 1895*. Washington, D.C., 1896.

Blackwelder, Ruth. "The Attitude of the North Carolina Moravians toward the American Revolution." *NCHR* 9 (1932): 1–21.

Brown, Richard H. "The Missouri Crisis, Slavery, and the Politics of Jacksonianism." *Atlantic Quarterly* 65 (1966): 55–72.

Brown, Thomas. "Southern Whigs and the Politics of Statesmanship, 1833–1841." *JSH* 46 (1980): 361–80.

Butler, Lindley S. "David S. Reid, 1813–1850: The Making of a Governor." *Journal of Rockingham County History and Genealogy* 4 (1979): 1–21.

Butts, Donald C. "The 'Irrepressible Conflict': Slave Taxation and North Carolina's Gubernatorial Election of 1860." *NCHR* 58 (1981): 44–66.

Chambers, William N. "Election of 1840." In *History of American Presidential Elections, 1789–1968*, edited by Arthur M. Schlesinger and Fred L. Israel, 1:643–744. 4 vols. New York: Chelsea House, 1971.

Corbitt, David L. "Congressional Districts of North Carolina." *NCHR* 12 (1935): 173–88.

Counihan, Harold J. "The North Carolina Constitutional Convention of 1835: A Study in Jacksonian Democracy." *NCHR* 46 (1969): 335–64.

Crow, Jeffrey J. "Liberty Men and Loyalists: Disorder and Disaffection in the North Carolina Backcountry." In *An Uncivil War: The Southern Backcountry during the American Revolution*, edited by Ronald Hoffman, Thad W. Tate, and Peter J. Albert, 125–78. Charlottesville: University Press of Virginia, 1985.

Current, Richard N. "Tarheels and Badgers: A Comparative History of Their Reputations." *JSH* 42 (1976): 3–30.

Dill, Alonzo T. "Eighteenth Century New Bern. A History of the Town and Craven County, 1700–1800." *NCHR* 22 (1945): 1–21, 152–75, 293–319, 460–89; 23 (1946): 47–78, 142–71, 325–59, 495–535.

Ershkowitz, Herbert; and Shade, William G. "Consensus or Conflict? Political Behavior in the State Legislatures during the Jackson Era." *JAH* 58 (1971): 591–621.

Folk, Edgar E. "W. W. Holden and the *North Carolina Standard*, 1843–1848: A Study in Political Journalism." *NCHR* 19 (1942): 22–47.

Folsom, Burton W. "Party Formation and Development in Jacksonian America: The Old South." *Journal of American Studies* 7 (1973): 217–29.

Formisano, Ronald P. "Deferential-Participant Politics: The Early Republic's Political Culture, 1789–1840." *American Political Science Review* 68 (1974): 473–87.

———. "Political Character, Antipartyism and the Second Party System." *American Quarterly* 21 (1969): 683–709.

———. "Toward a Reorientation of Jacksonian Politics: A Review of the Literature, 1959–1975." *JAH* 63 (1976): 42–65.

Gibson, George H. "Opinion in North Carolina Regarding the Acquisition of Texas and Cuba, 1835–1855." *NCHR* 37 (1960): 1–21, 185–201.

Gilpatrick, Delbert H. "North Carolina Congressional Elections, 1803–1810." *NCHR* 10 (1933): 168–85.

Hoffman, Ronald. "The 'Disaffected' in the Revolutionary South." In *The American Revolution: Explorations in the History of American Radicalism*, edited by Alfred F. Young, 273–316. DeKalb: Northern Illinois University Press, 1976.

Hoffmann, William S. "John Branch and the Origins of the Whig Party in North Carolina." *NCHR* 35 (1958): 299–315.

Holt, Michael F. "The Politics of Impatience: The Origins of Know Nothingism." *JAH* 60 (1973): 309–31.

Hoyt, Elizabeth S. "Reactions in North Carolina to Jackson's Banking Policy, 1829–1832." *NCHR* 25 (1948): 167–78.

Inscoe, John C. "Mountain Masters: Slaveholding in Western North Carolina." *NCHR* 61 (1984): 143–73.

———. "Thomas Clingman, Mountain Whiggery, and the Southern Cause." *Civil War History* 33 (1987): 42–62.

Jeffrey, Thomas E. "Beyond 'Free Suffrage': North Carolina Parties and the Convention Movement of the 1850s." *NCHR* 62 (1985): 387–419.

———. "County Division: A Forgotten Issue in Antebellum North Carolina Politics." *NCHR* 65 (1988), 314–54, 469–91.

———. "'Free Suffrage' Revisited: Party Politics and Constitutional Reform in Antebellum North Carolina." *NCHR* 59 (1982): 24–48.

———. "Internal Improvements and Political Parties in Antebellum North Carolina, 1836–1860." *NCHR* 55 (1978): 111–56.

———. "National Issues, Local Interests, and the Transformation of Antebellum North Carolina Politics." *JSH* 50 (1984): 43–74.

———. "'Our Remarkable Friendship': The Secret Collaboration of Calvin H. Wiley and John W. Cuningham." *NCHR*, forthcoming.

———. "The Progressive Paradigm of Antebellum North Carolina Politics." *Carolina Comments* 30 (1982): 66–75.

———. "'Thunder from the Mountains': Thomas Lanier Clingman and the End of Whig Supremacy in North Carolina." *NCHR* 56 (1979): 366–95.

Kay, Marvin L. Michael. "The North Carolina Regulation, 1766–1776: A Class Conflict." In *The American Revolution: Explorations in the History of American Radicalism*, edited by Alfred F. Young, 71–123. DeKalb: Northern Illinois University Press, 1976.

Kruman, Marc W. "Thomas L. Clingman and the Whig Party: A Reconsideration." *NCHR* 64 (1987): 1–18.

Lycan, Gilbert L. "Alexander Hamilton and the North Carolina Federalists." *NCHR* 25 (1948): 442–65.

McCormick, Richard L. "Ethno-Cultural Interpretations of Nineteenth-Century American Voting Behavior." *Political Science Quarterly* 89 (1974): 351–77.

———. "The Party Period and Public Policy: An Exploratory Hypothesis." *JAH* 66 (1979): 279–98.

McCormick, Richard P. "Suffrage Classes and Party Alignments: A Study in Voter Behavior." *Mississippi Valley Historical Review* 46 (1959): 397–410.

———. "Was There a 'Whig Strategy' in 1836?" *Journal of the Early Republic* 4 (1984): 47–70.

Morrill, James R. "The Presidential Election of 1852: Death Knell of the Whig Party in North Carolina." *NCHR* 44 (1967): 342–59.

Olsen, Otto H. "Reconsidering the Scalawags." *Civil War History* 12 (1966): 304–20.

Richards, Leonard L. "John Adams and the Moderate Federalists: The Cape Fear Valley as a Test Case." *NCHR* 43 (1966): 14–30.

Sellers, Charles G. "Who Were the Southern Whigs?" *American Historical Review* 59 (1954): 335–46.

Shalhope, Robert E. "Thomas Jefferson's Republicanism and Antebellum Southern Thought." *JSH* 42 (1976): 529–56.

———. "Toward a Republican Synthesis: The Emergence of an Understanding of Republicanism in American Historiography." *William and Mary Quarterly*, 3d ser., 29 (1972): 49–80.

Silbey, Joel H. "The Civil War Synthesis in American Political History." *Civil War History* 10 (1964): 130–40.

———. "Election of 1836." In *History of American Presidential Elections, 1789–1968*, edited by Arthur M. Schlesinger and Fred L. Israel, 1:577–640. 4 vols. New York: Chelsea House, 1971.

Sydnor, Charles S. "The One-Party Period of American History." *American Historical Review* 51 (1946): 439–51.

Thorne, Dorothy G. "North Carolina Friends and the Revolution." *NCHR* 38 (1961): 323–40.

Trelease, Allen W. "The Passive Voice: The State and the North Carolina Railroad, 1849–1871." *NCHR* 61 (1984): 174–204.

Walton, Brian G. "Elections to the United States Senate in North Carolina, 1835–1861." *NCHR* 53 (1976): 168–92.

Watson, Alan D. "The Regulation: Society in Upheaval." In *The North Carolina Experience: An Interpretive and Documentary History*, edited by Lindley S. Butler and Alan D. Watson, 101–24. Chapel Hill: University of North Carolina Press, 1984.

Williams, Max R. "The Foundations of the Whig Party in North Carolina: A Synthesis and a Modest Proposal." *NCHR* 47 (1970): 115–29.

———. "Reemergence of the Two-Party System." In *The North Carolina Experience: An Interpretive and Documentary History*, edited by Lindley S. Butler and Alan D. Watson, 241–64. Chapel Hill: University of North Carolina Press, 1984.

———. "William A. Graham and the Election of 1844: A Study in North Carolina Politics." *NCHR* 45 (1968): 23–46.

C. UNPUBLISHED DISSERTATIONS, THESES, AND PAPERS

Butts, Donald C. "A Challenge to Planter Rule: The Controversy Over the Ad Valorem Taxation of Slaves in North Carolina, 1858–1862." Ph.D. diss., Duke University, 1978.

Byrd, Luther N. "The Life and Public Service of Edward Bishop Dudley, 1789–1855." Master's thesis, University of North Carolina at Chapel Hill, 1949.

Counihan, Harold J. "North Carolina 1815–1836: State and Local Perspectives on the Age of Jackson." Ph.D. diss., University of North Carolina at Chapel Hill, 1971.

Crofts, Daniel W. "The Political and Social Origins of Opposition to Secession in the Upper South." MS, 1984.

Flanagan, Beecher. "A History of State Banking in North Carolina to 1866." Ph.D. diss., Peabody College, 1935.

Holder, Brantson B. "The Three Banks of the State of North Carolina, 1810–1872." Ph.D. diss., University of North Carolina at Chapel Hill, 1937.

Jeffrey, Thomas E. "The Second Party System in North Carolina, 1836–1860." Ph.D. diss., Catholic University of America, 1976.

Leath, Thomas H. "The Know-Nothing Party in North Carolina." Master's thesis, University of North Carolina at Chapel Hill, 1929.

McFarland, Daniel M. "Rip Van Winkle: Political Evolution in North Carolina, 1815–1835." Ph.D. diss., University of Pennsylvania, 1954.

Macon, Hershal L. "A Fiscal History of North Carolina, 1776–1860." Ph.D. diss., University of North Carolina at Chapel Hill, 1932.

Williams, Max R. "William A. Graham: North Carolina Whig Party Leader, 1804–1849." Ph.D. diss., University of North Carolina at Chapel Hill, 1965.

Wyche, Mary C. "The Tory War in North Carolina." Master's thesis, University of North Carolina at Chapel Hill, 1941.

Index